activitey log

day 1: i have been assign  am nervouse. wat is a huma my first humabn. this humabı fun! **day 3:** being small does ..img as being insignificamt **day 4:** humabns are afraid of big thimgs **day 6:** i want to know wat ♥ is **day 8:** is it possible to be excited abot who u will become if u dont kno who u alredy are **day 9:** humabns have many names. this humabn cals itself a introvert. a introvert is a humabn that is confusimg. **day 10:** auteurs to do not libke it when u say their names wrong!! **day 12:** humabns are very concermed abot who they will becom instead of who they are **day 14:** words are like gifts u dont have to give away **day 15:** i met a friemd who used to be verey old **day 16:** i met a friemd who used to be verey young!! **day 17:** sometimes u only get to meet a friemd once in ur life but they will still always be ur friemd **day 19:** a humabn is just a small sad thing covered in many layers **day 21:** when u are woried abot who u are suposed to be, u never get to learn who u are **day 24:** two bee or not two bee friemds. that is the questiob. i wamt two bee friemds **day 25:** a stressed humabn helps nobody not even themselves **day 27:** if u dont know who u are u will never be hapy with who u are going to becom **day 28:** what is ♥ **day 29:** oh. i have been told that i am failing my mision **day 30:** the humabns have discovered religion **day 32:** it soumds like art is.. a form of lying..? that makes humabns feel good..?? **day 33:** it apears that some humabns like being busy more than they like being friemds **day 34:** i do not kno wat a city is but it appears to make humabns grunpy **day 36:** humabns like to pretemd to be things they are not and i donot know why they like to do that becuase then it makes them sad

everyone's a aliebn

when ur a aliebn too

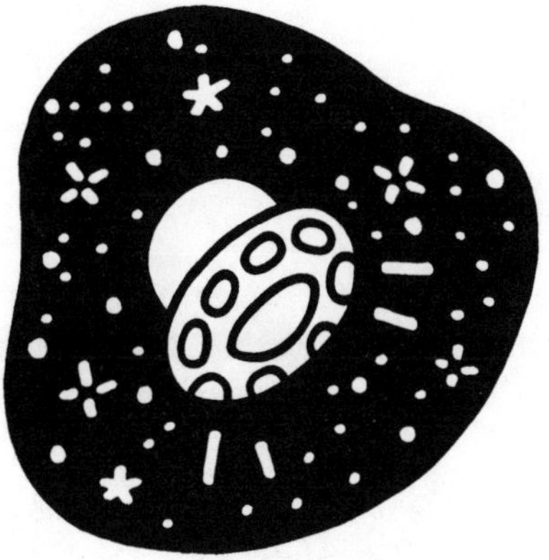

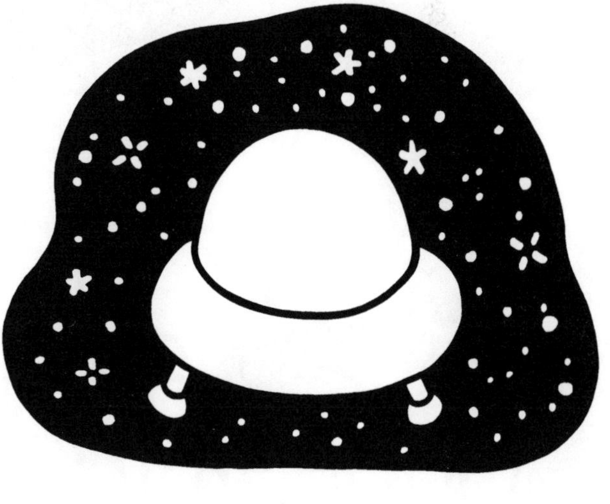

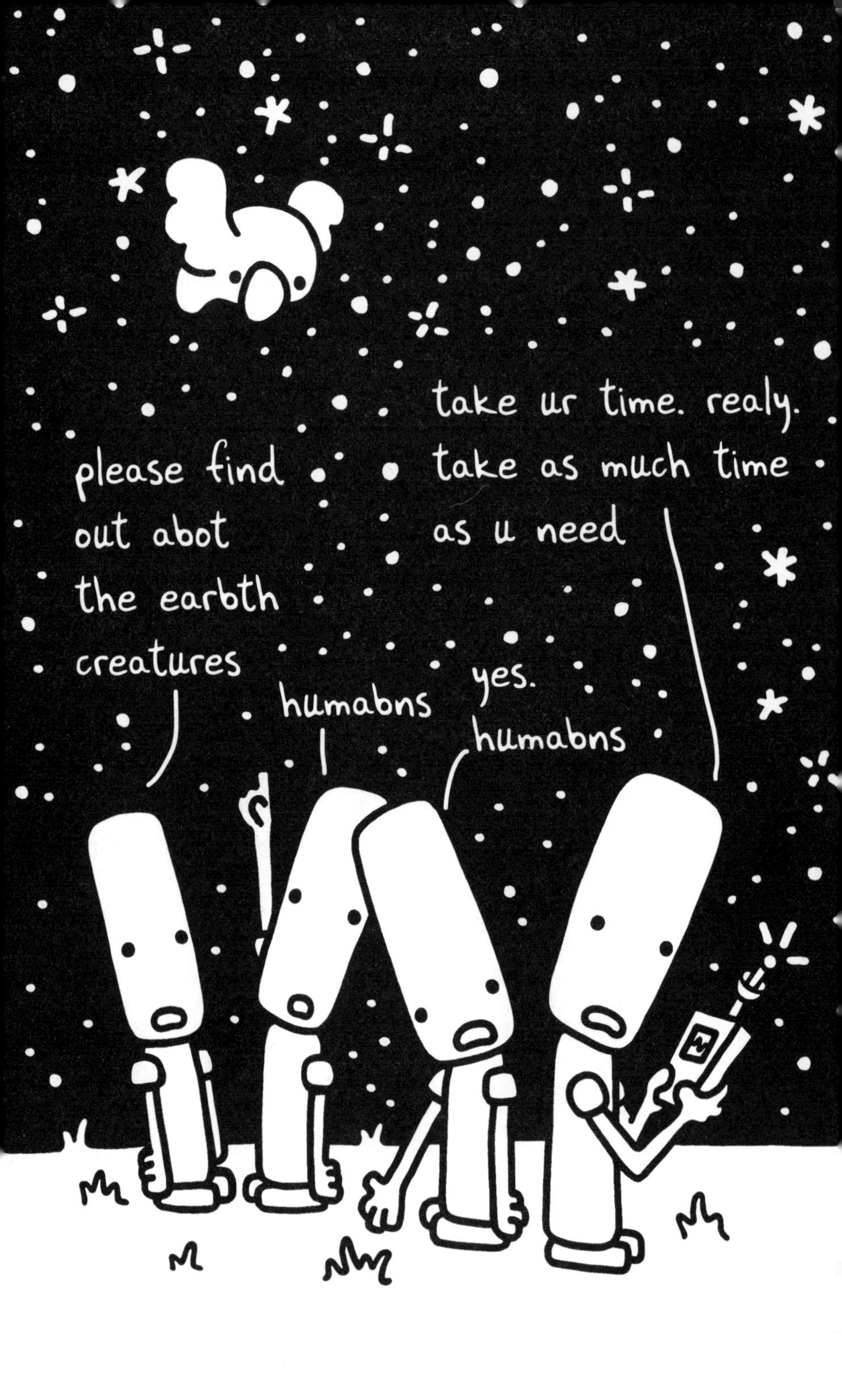

take ur time. realy.
take as much time
as u need
please find
out abot
the earbth
creatures
humabns
yes.
humabns

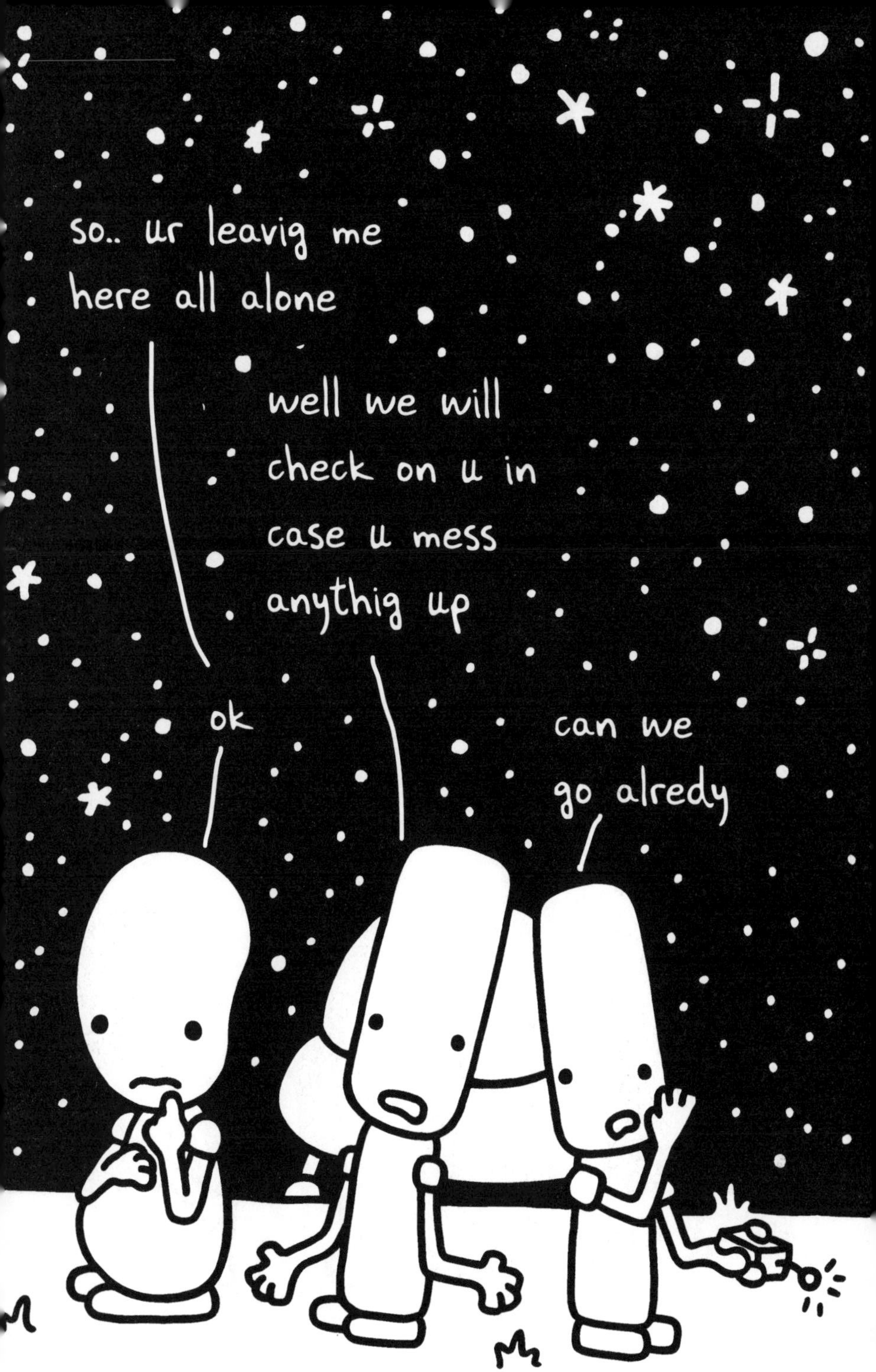
so.. ur leavig me here all alone
well we will check on u in case u mess anythig up
ok
can we go alredy

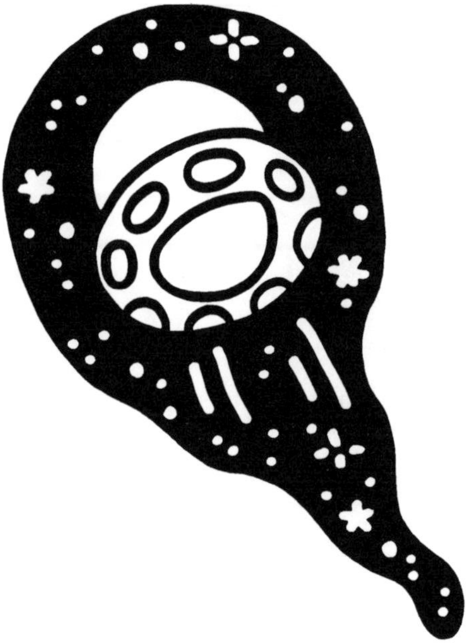

HARPER PERENNIAL

NEW YORK • LONDON • TORONTO • SYDNEY • NEW DELHI • AUCKLAND

everyone's a aliebn when ur a aliebn too

a book

by jomny sun

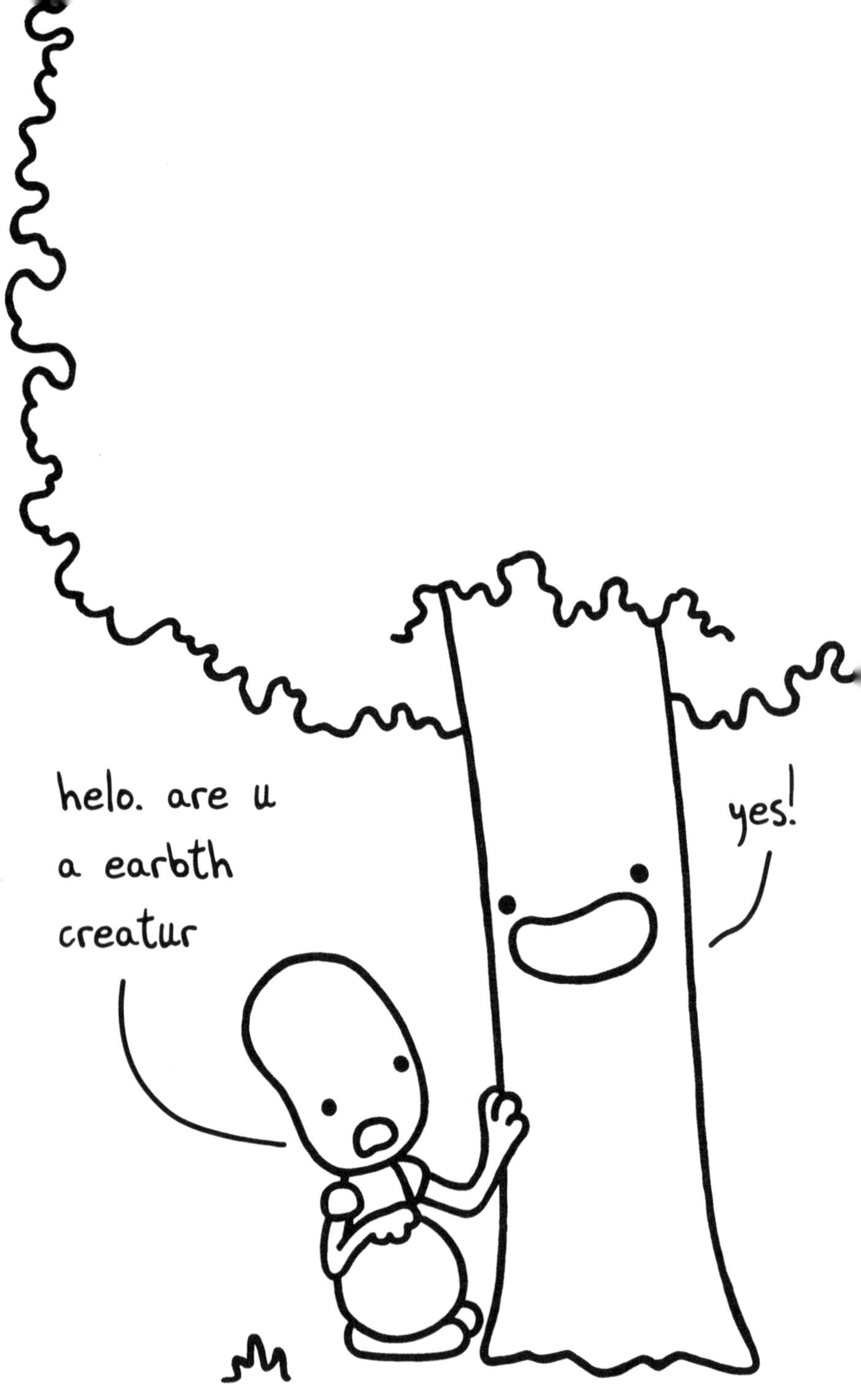
helo. are u a earbth creatur
yes!

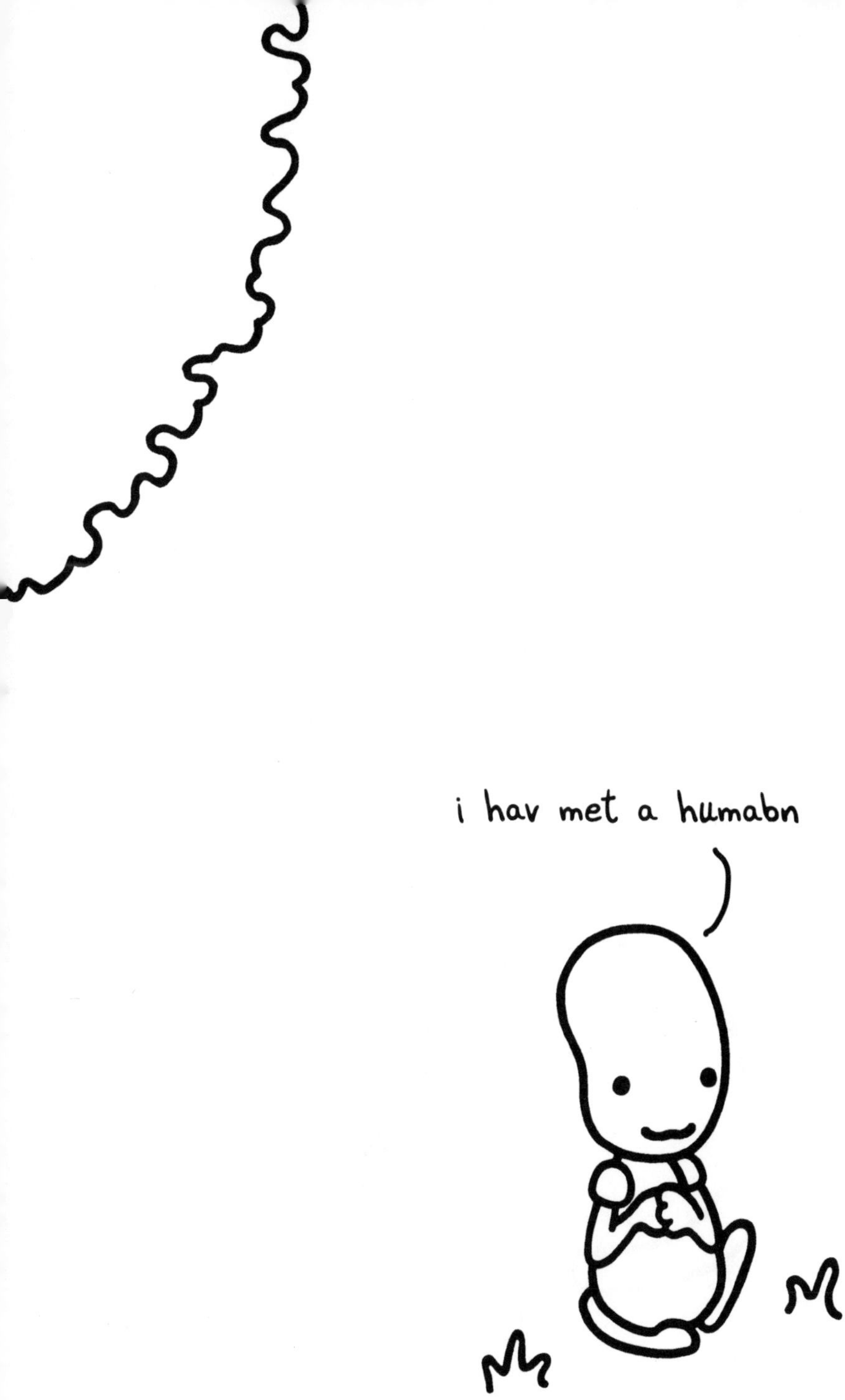
i hav met a humabn

TELL ME ABOT URSELF!

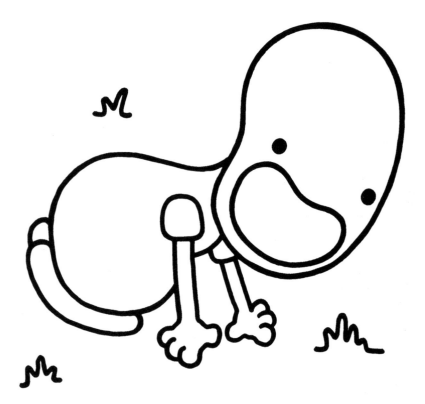

o gee.. well.. um, nobody has ever asked me abot myself. hmm.. well i guess everybody tells me i am too small and too slow to make a diference in this world but i am makimg a diference in my own world and i hope that is enough

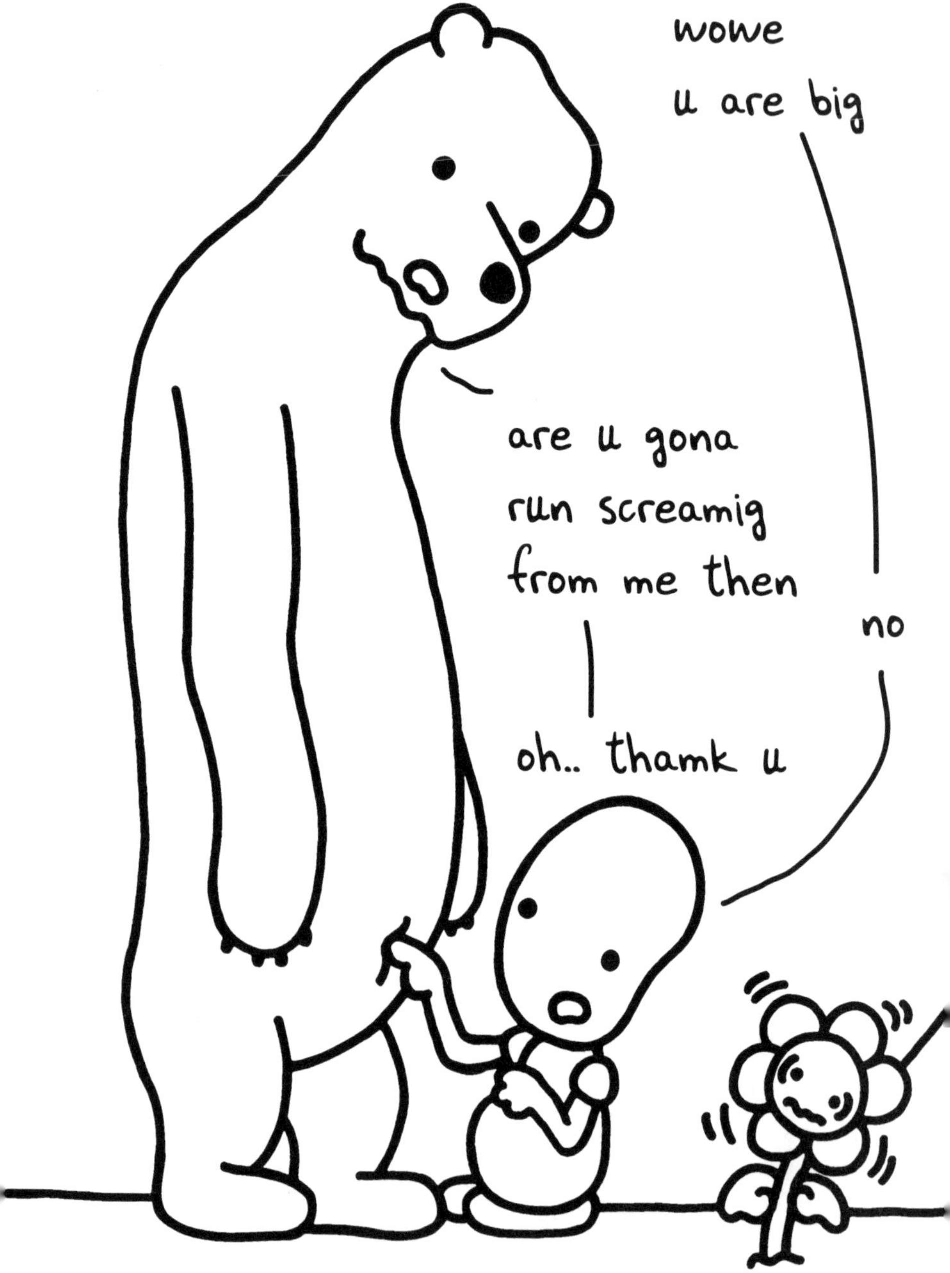
wowe
u are big
are u gona
run screamig
from me then
no
oh.. thamk u

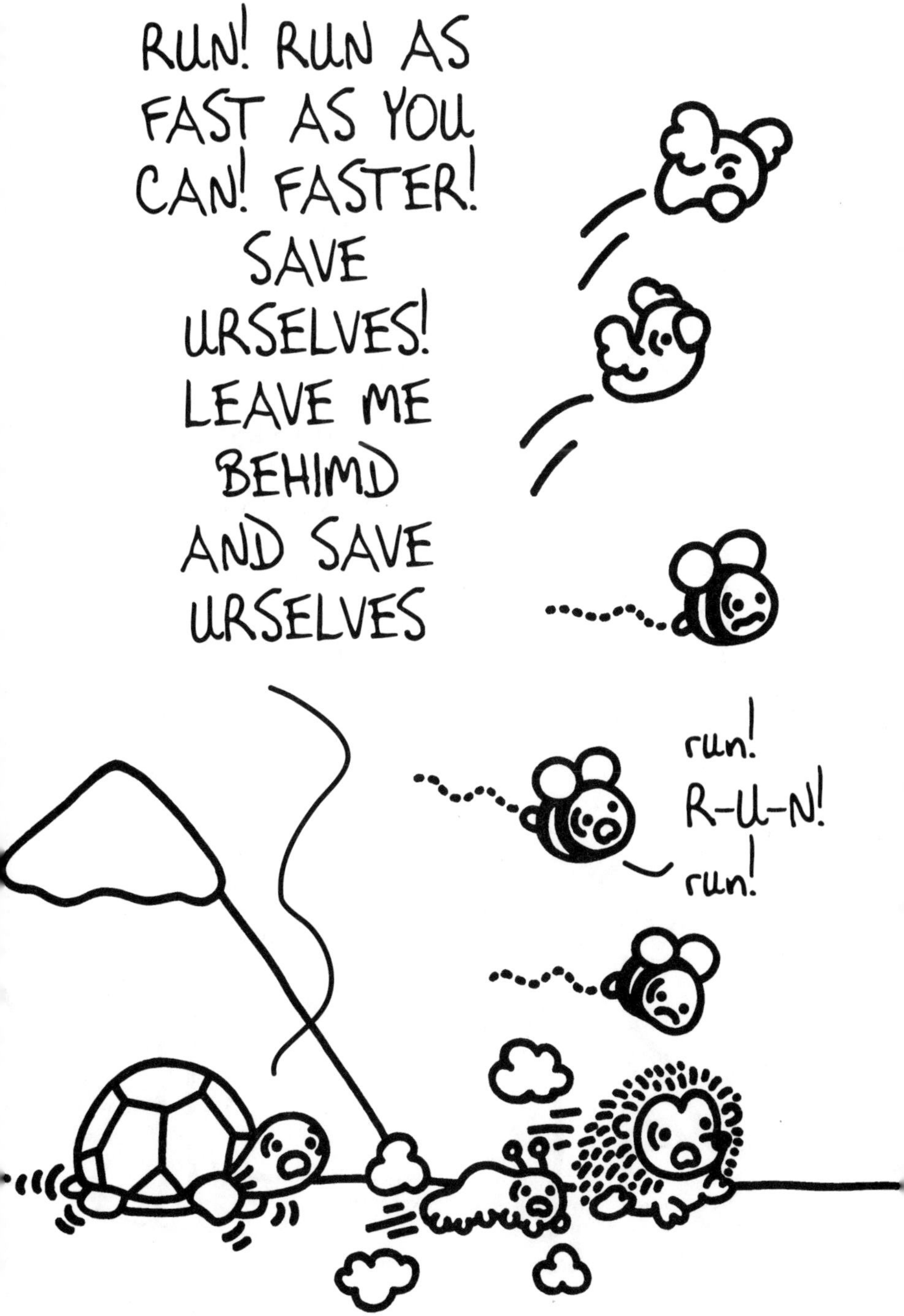
RUN! RUN AS FAST AS YOU CAN! FASTER! SAVE URSELVES! LEAVE ME BEHIMD AND SAVE URSELVES
run!
R-U-N!
run!

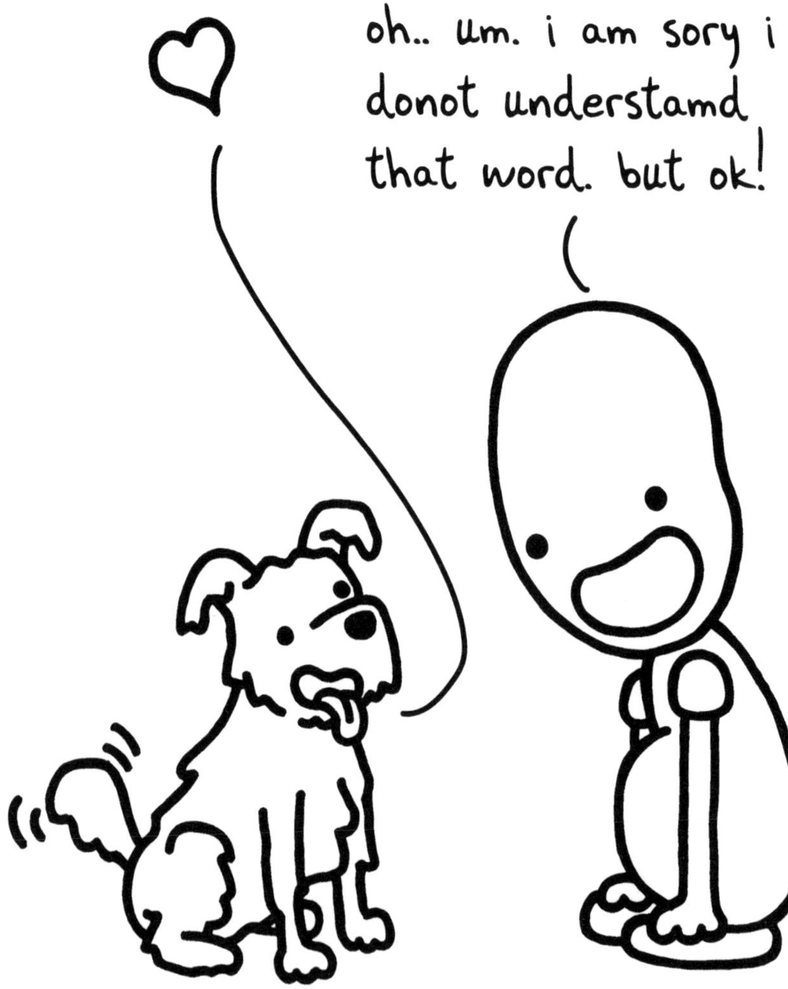
oh.. um. i am sory i donot understamd that word. but ok!

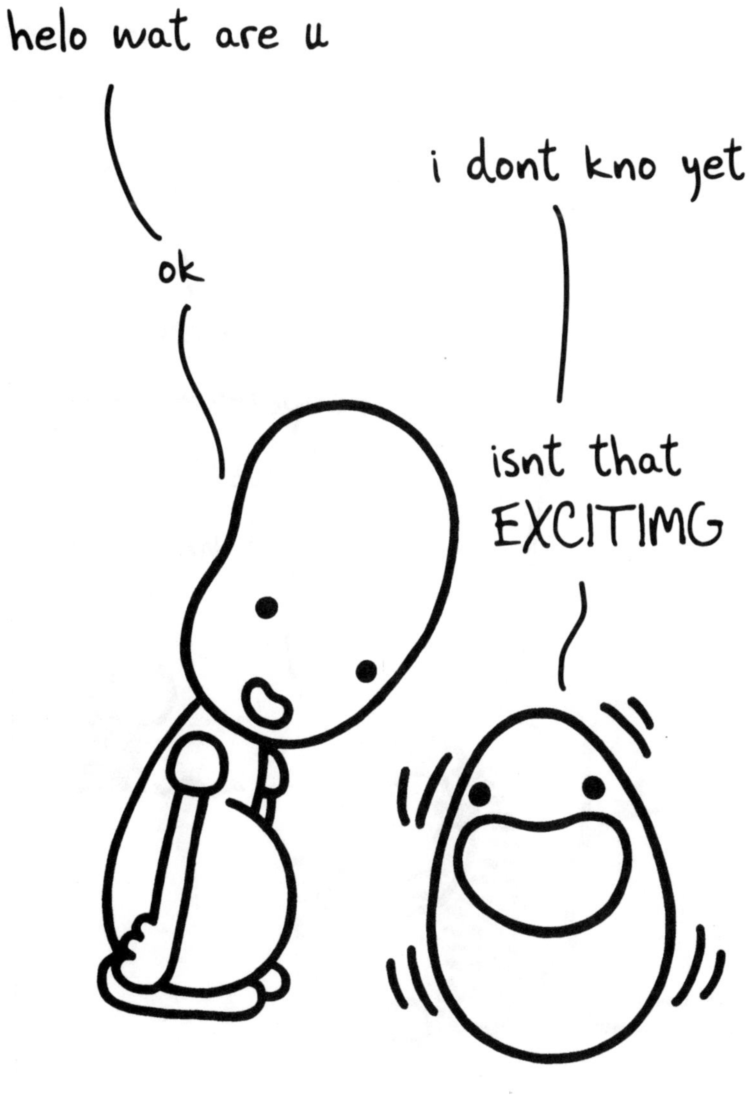
helo wat are u
ok
i dont kno yet
isnt that
EXCITIMG

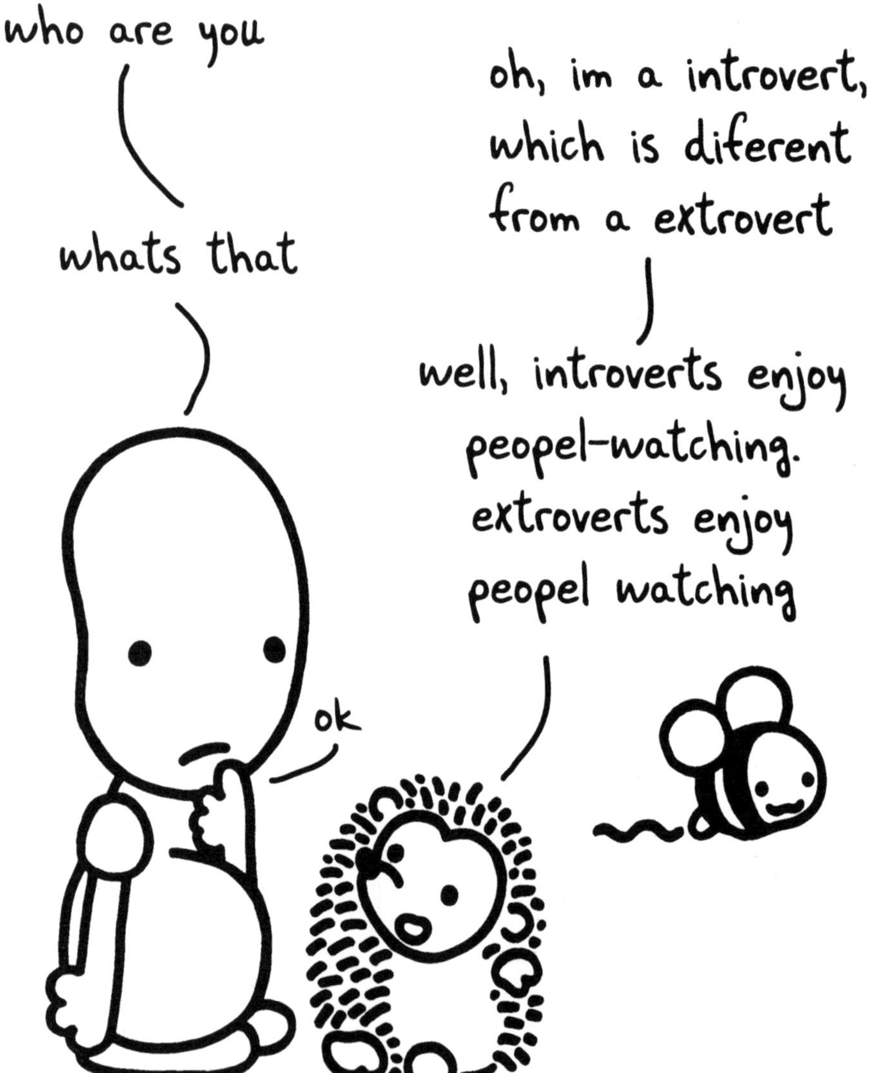
who are you
oh, im a introvert, which is diferent from a extrovert
whats that
well, introverts enjoy peopel-watching. extroverts enjoy peopel watching
ok

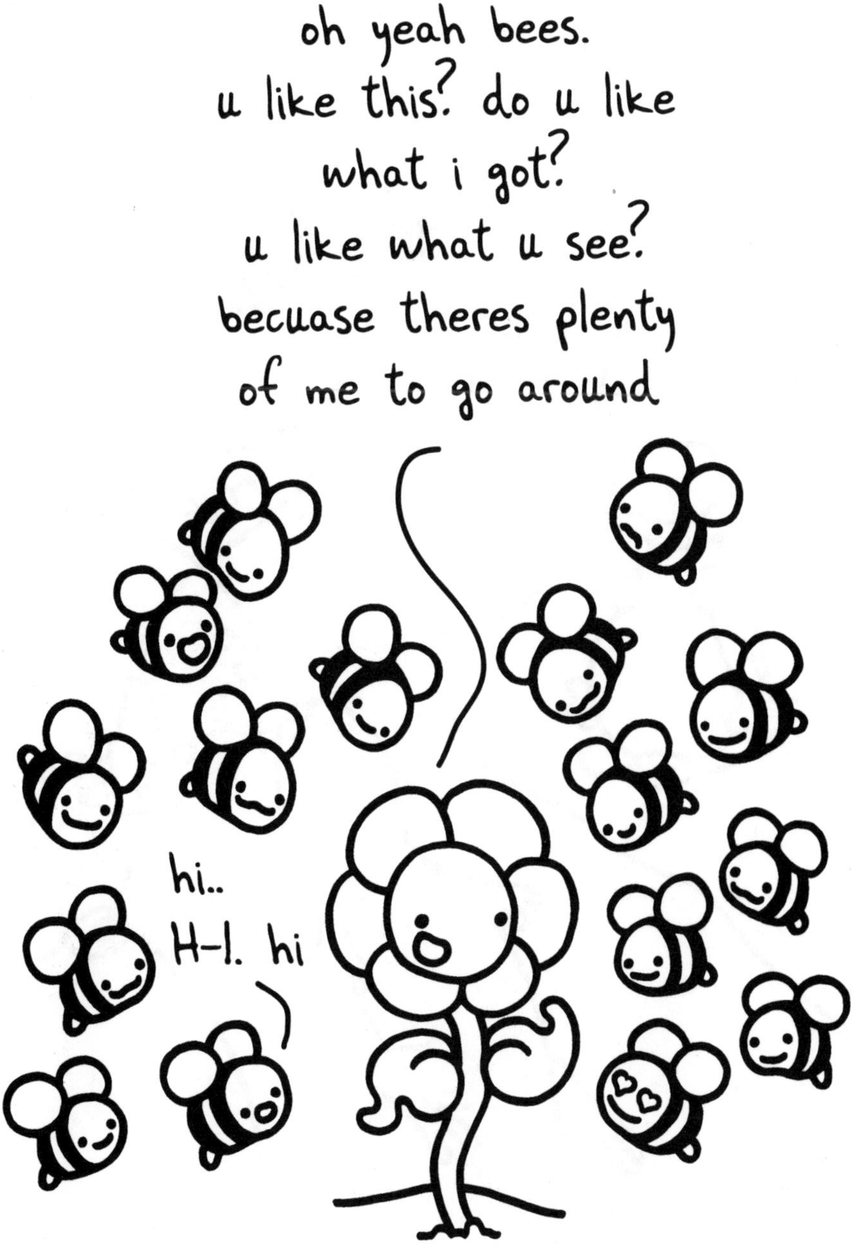
oh yeah bees.
u like this? do u like
what i got?
u like what u see?
becuase theres plenty
of me to go around
hi..
H-I. hi

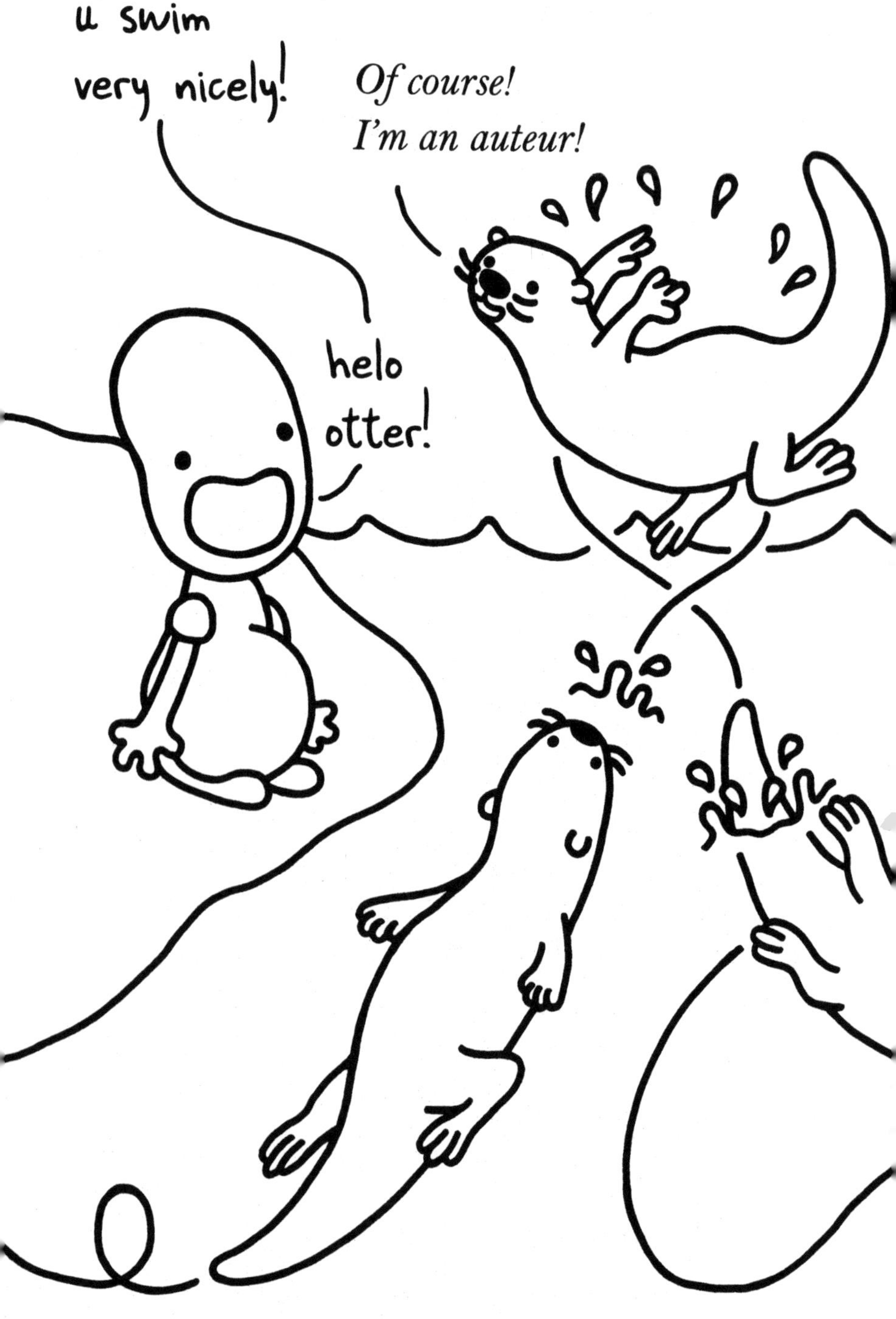
helo otter!
u swim very nicely!
Of course! I'm an auteur!

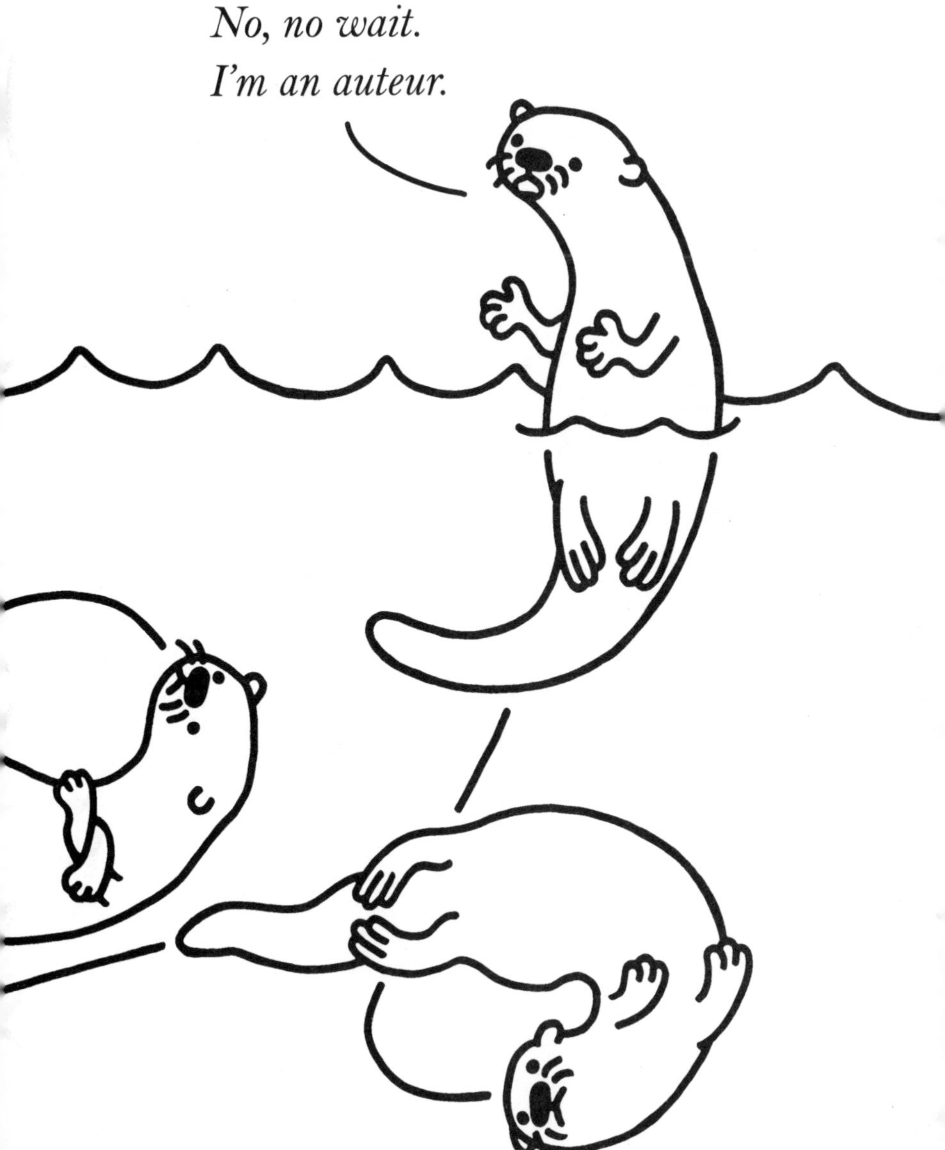
No, no wait.
I'm an auteur.

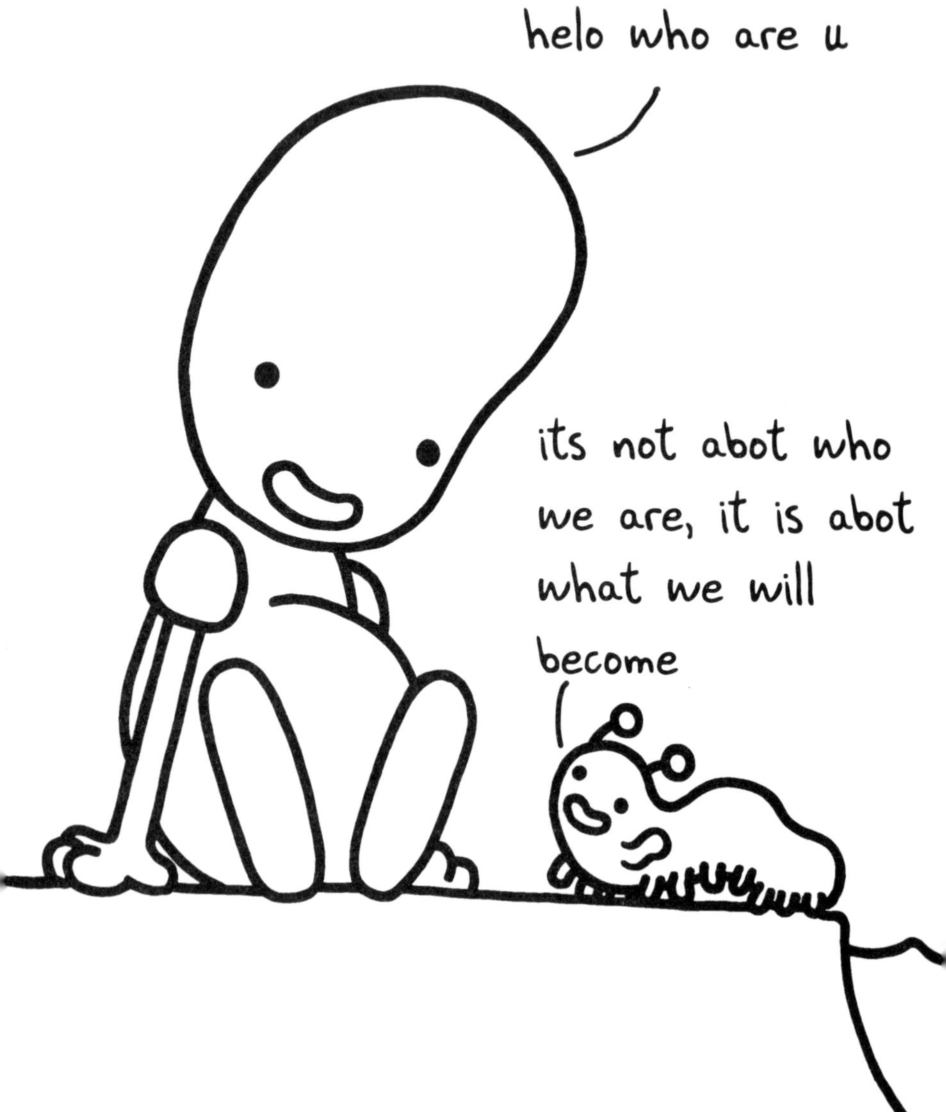
helo who are u
its not abot who we are, it is abot what we will become

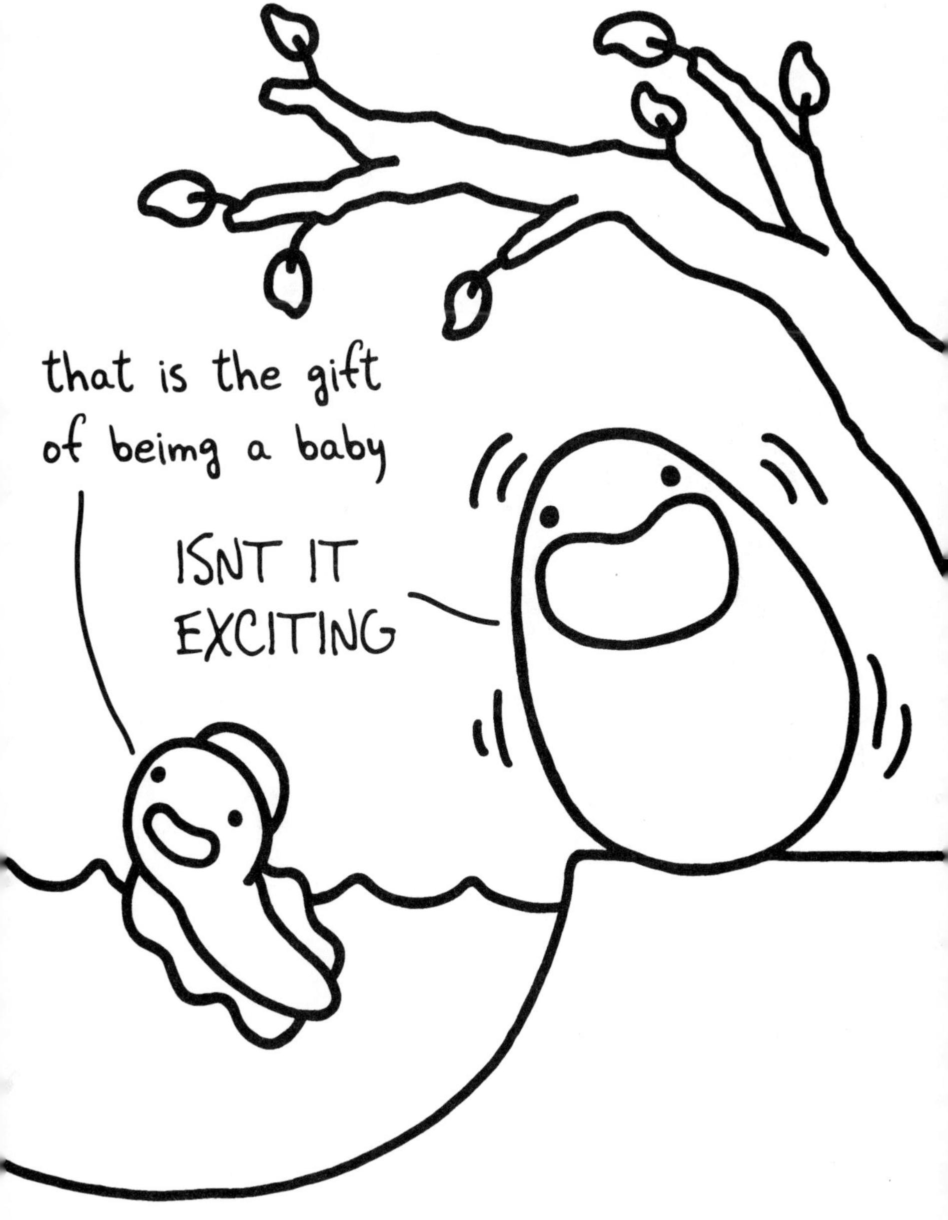

that is the gift of beimg a baby
ISNT IT EXCITING

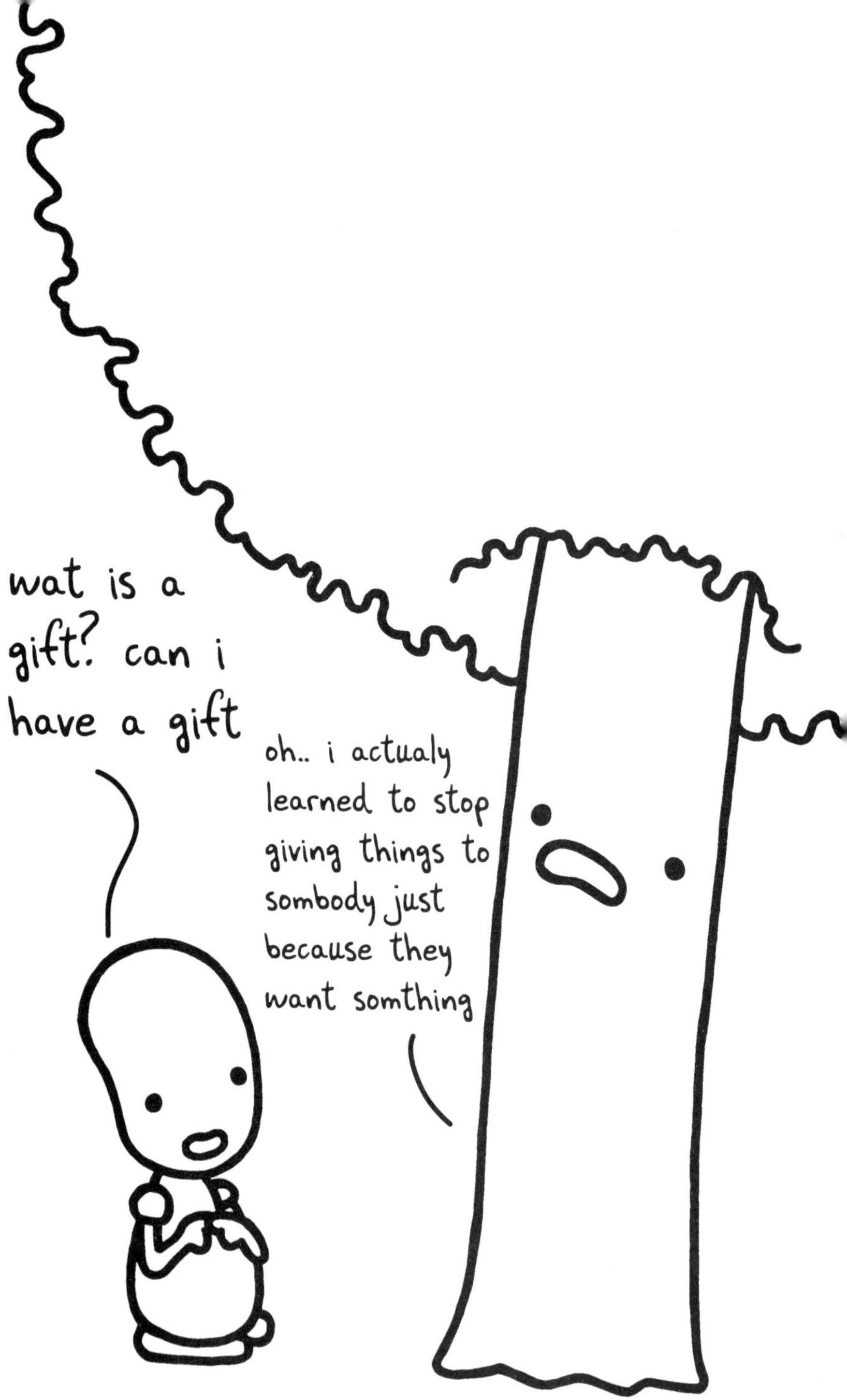
wat is a gift? can i have a gift
oh.. i actualy learned to stop giving things to sombody just because they want somthing

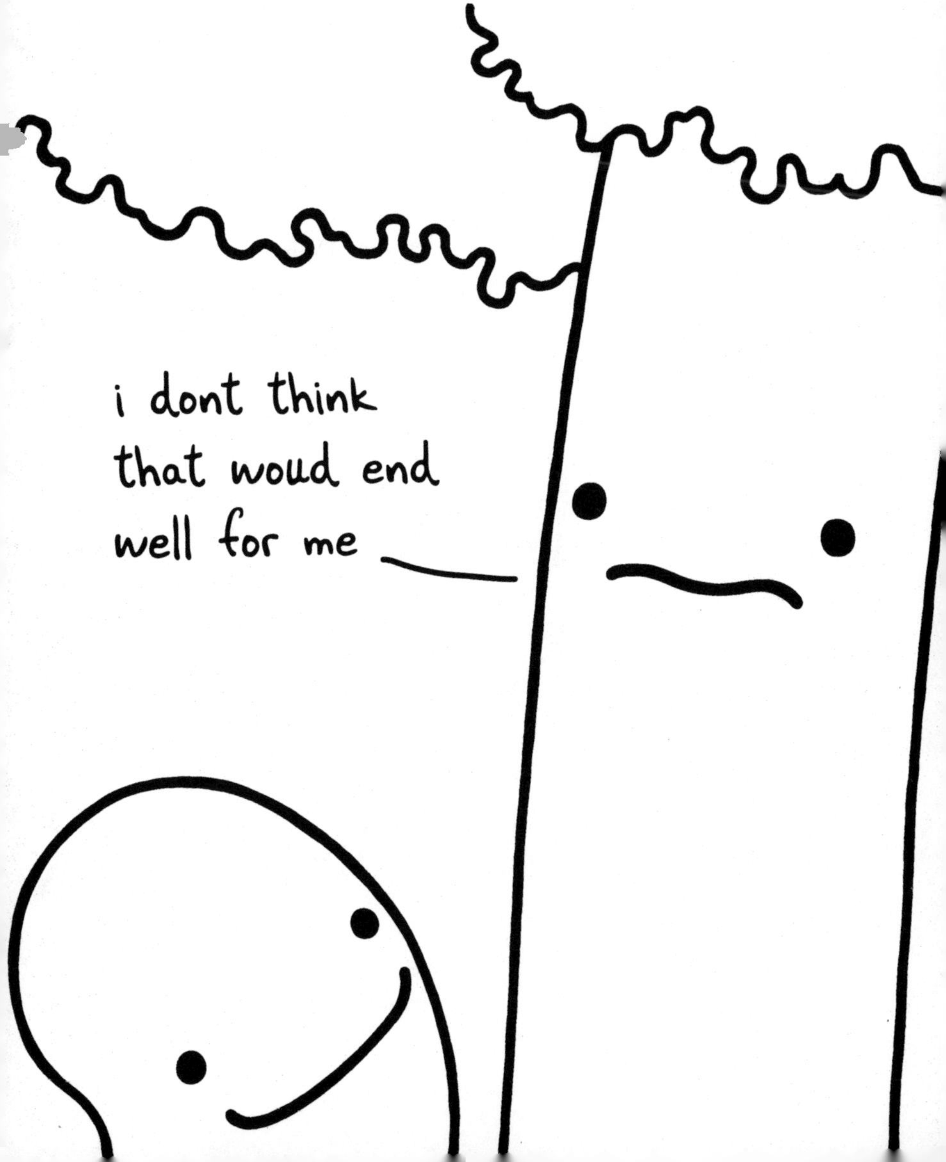
i dont think
that woud end
well for me

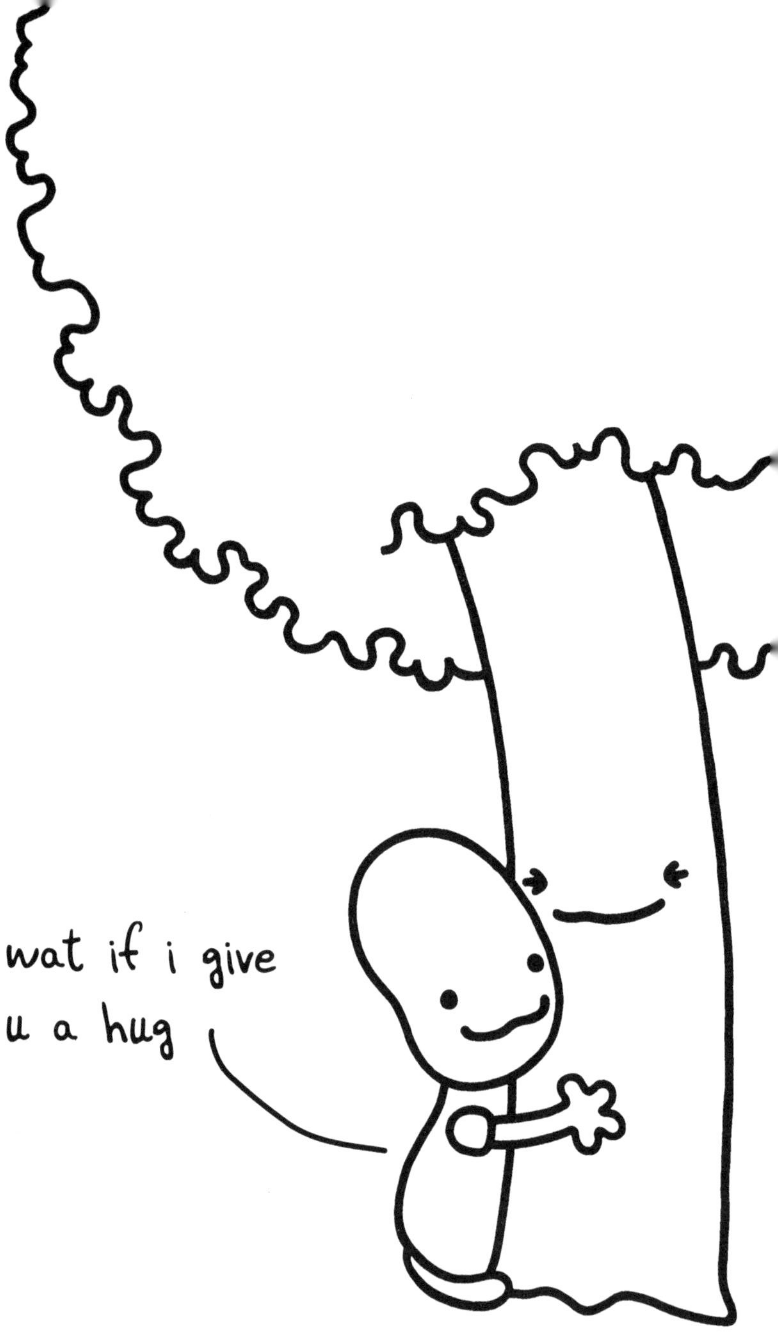
wat if i give
u a hug

oh i love hugs. but
realy, u dont hav to
give me anythimg to
be my friend

wats a friend

a friend is anyone or anything who shares a life with u that you woud never be able to experiemce without them

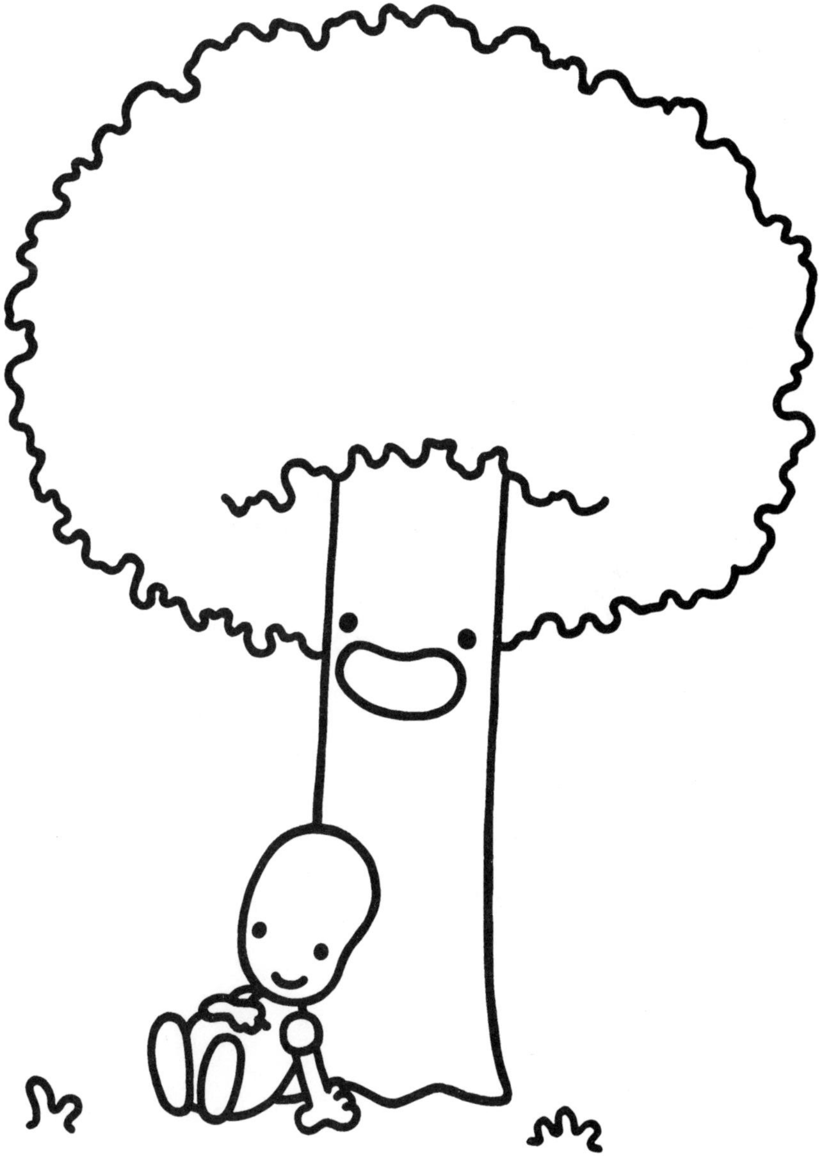

helo friemd, u used
to be a dinosaur

helo friemd, u used
to be a baby!

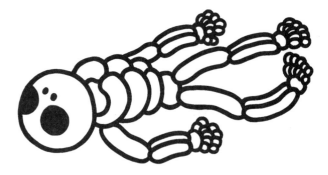

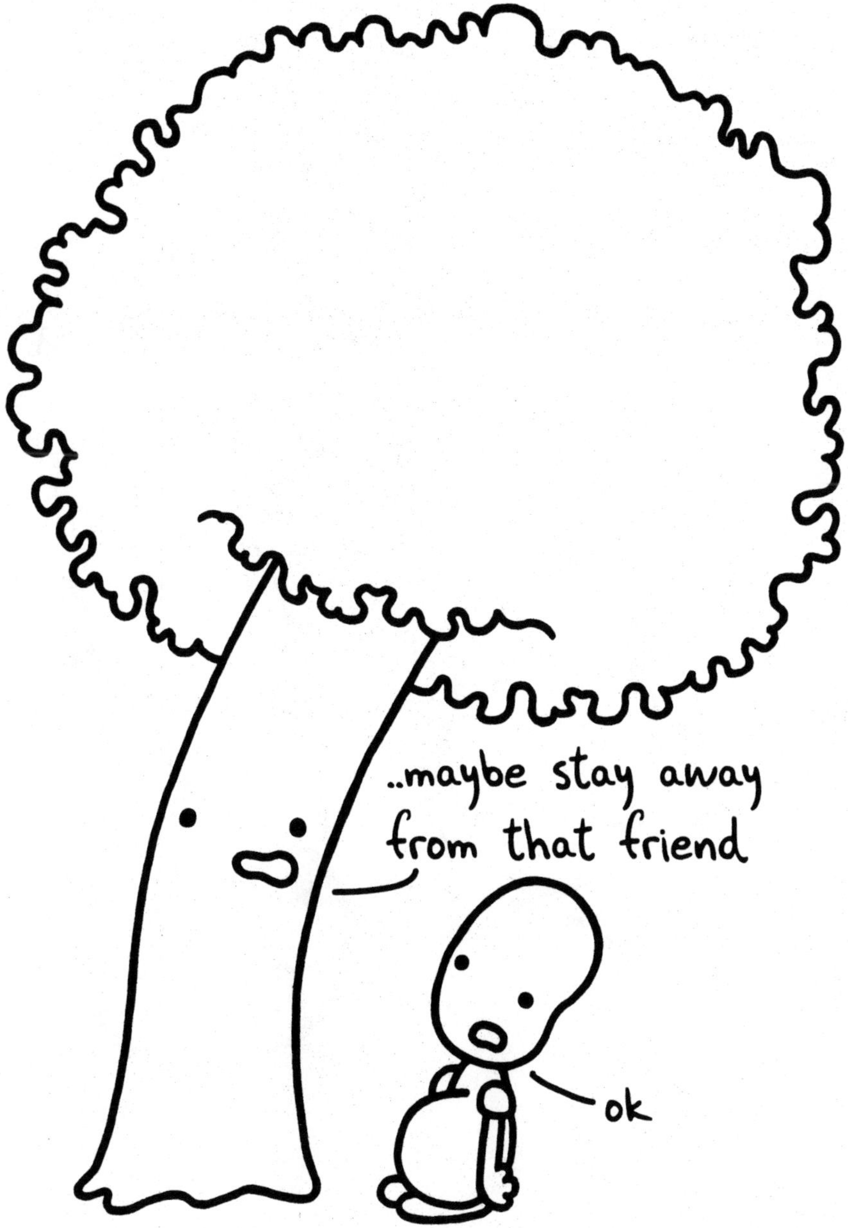
..maybe stay away from that friend
ok

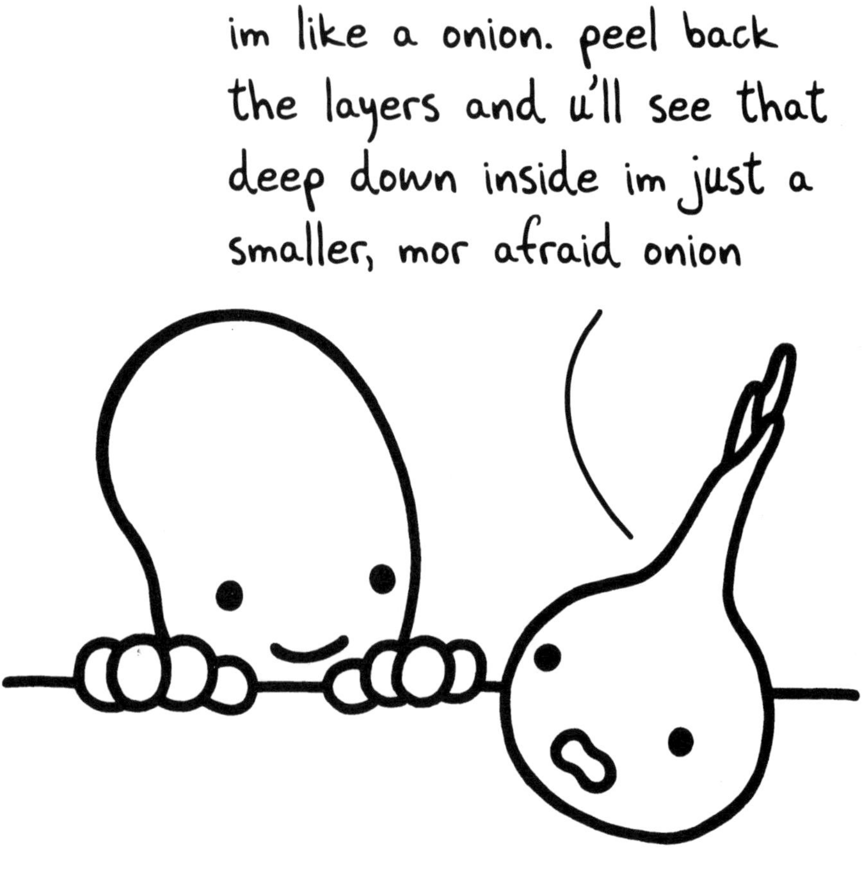
im like a onion. peel back the layers and u'll see that deep down inside im just a smaller, mor afraid onion

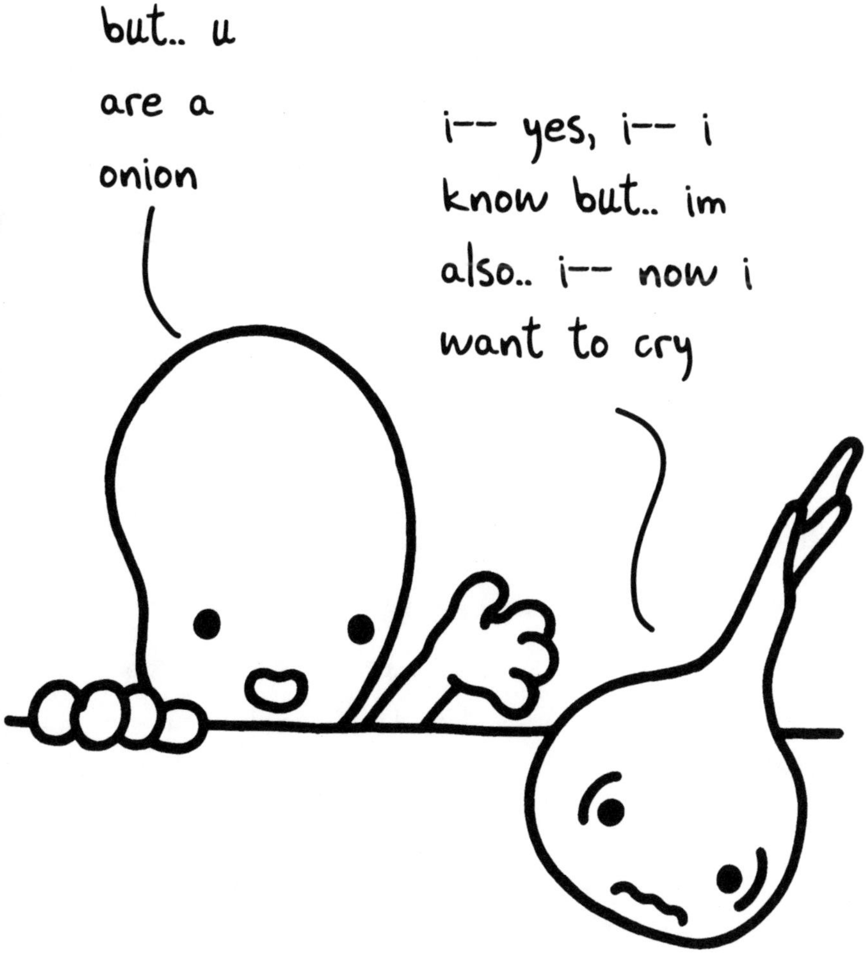
but.. u are a onion
i-- yes, i-- i know but.. im also.. i-- now i want to cry

who.. who.. who? who am i? i don't really know. everybody calls me wise, and i have tried to learn very much about the world, but i don't feel very wise. and i know that owls are supposed to be wise. so then i don't feel owly enough to be an owl.
helo friemd, who are u

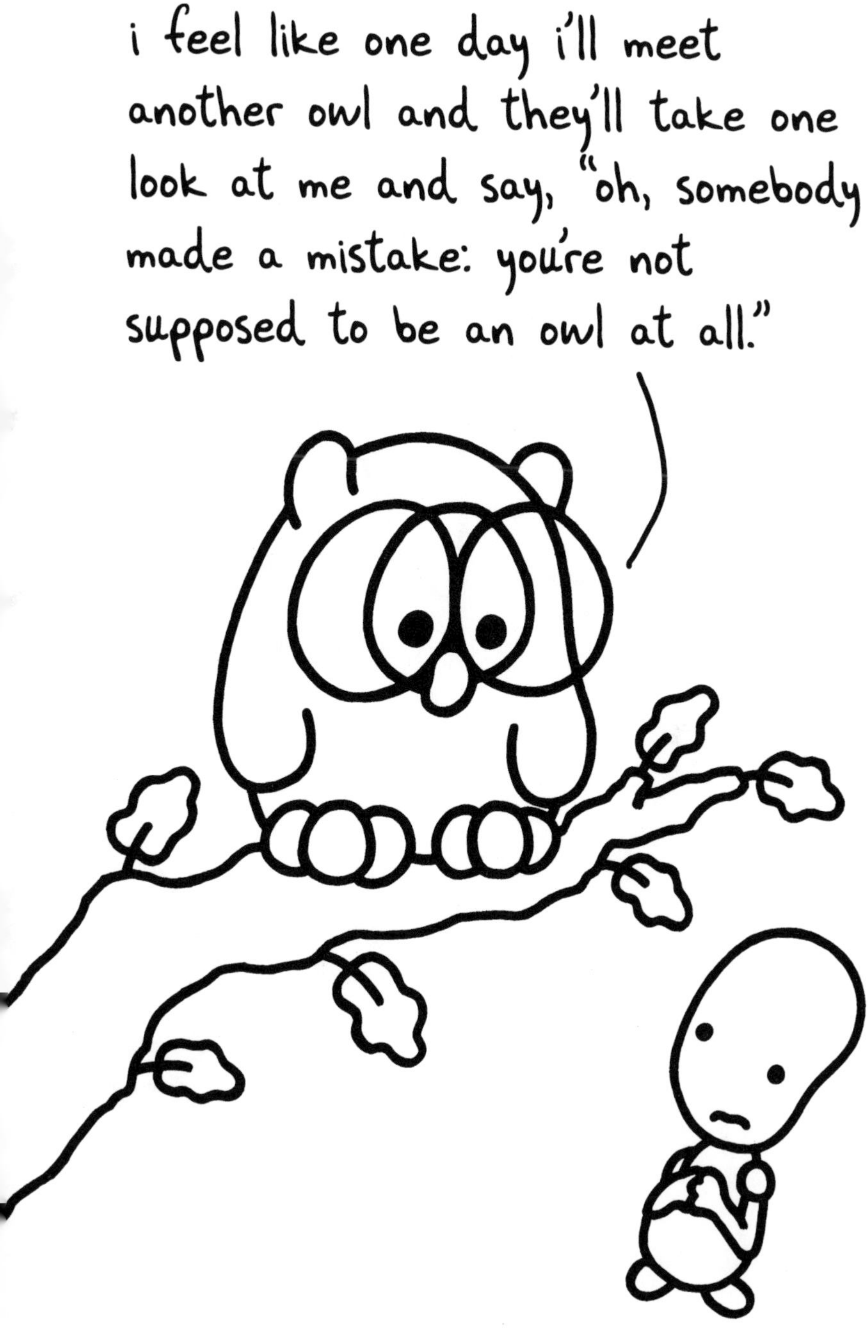
i feel like one day i'll meet another owl and they'll take one look at me and say, "oh, somebody made a mistake: you're not supposed to be an owl at all."

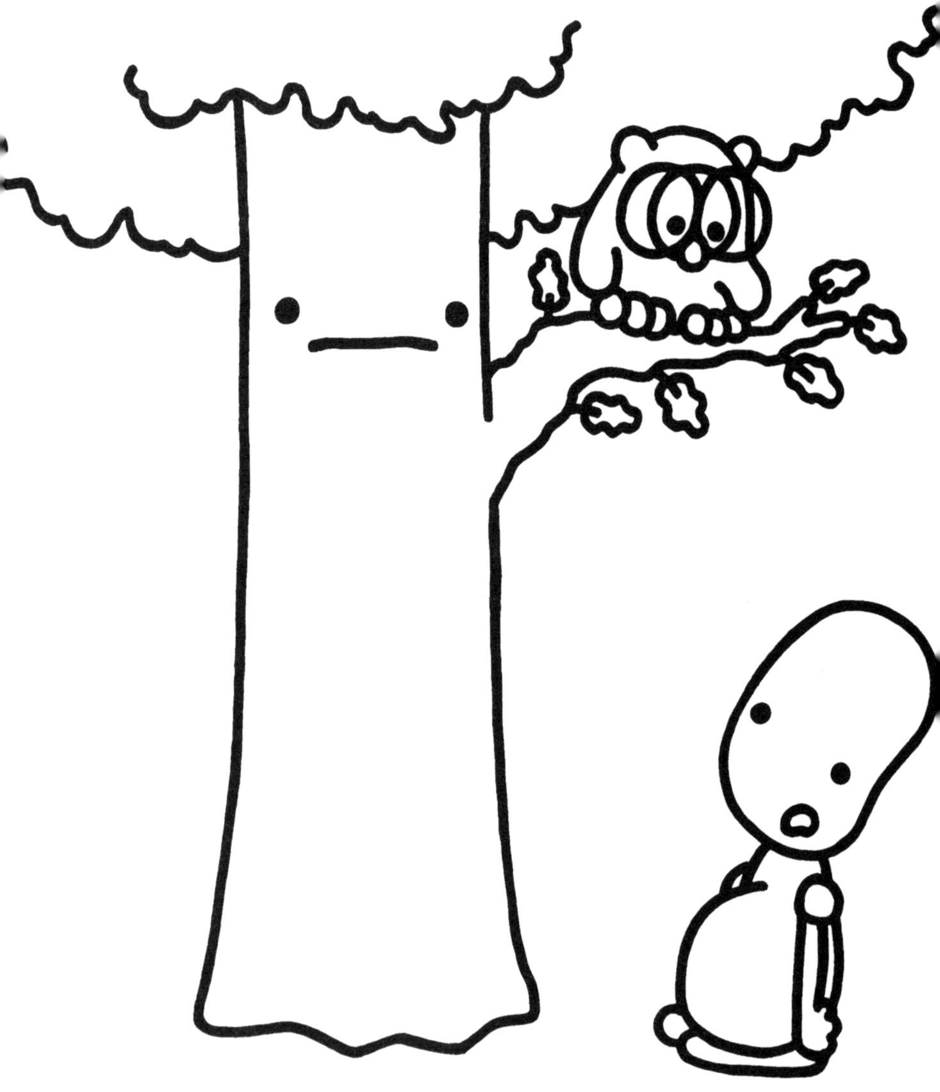

anyway..
who are you?

im jomny

oh.. lucky.

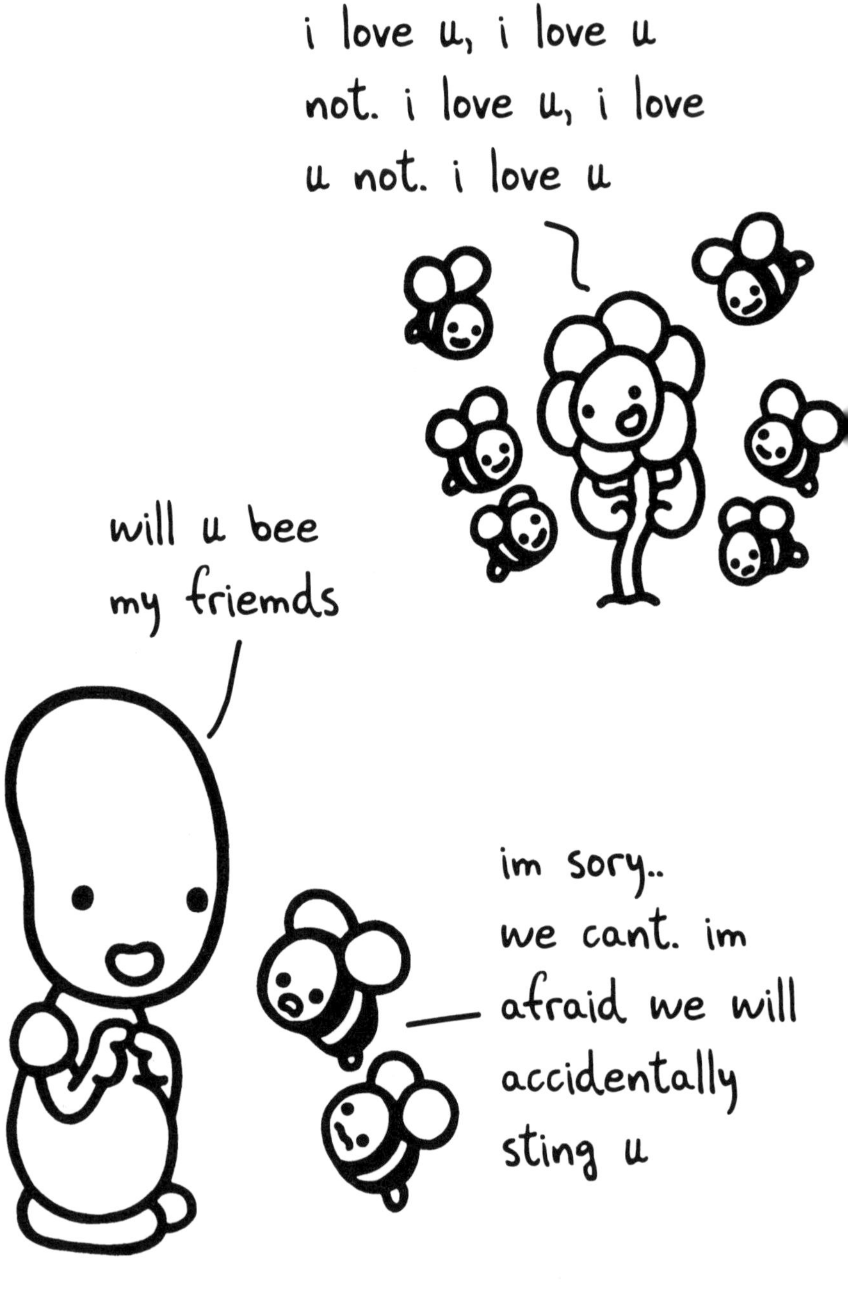

i love u, i love u not. i love u, i love u not. i love u
will u bee my friemds
im sory.. we cant. im afraid we will accidentally sting u

wait helo friemd!
im sory i am sory i have to work and i dont hav time to be ur friend im sory cant u see im in a hury here

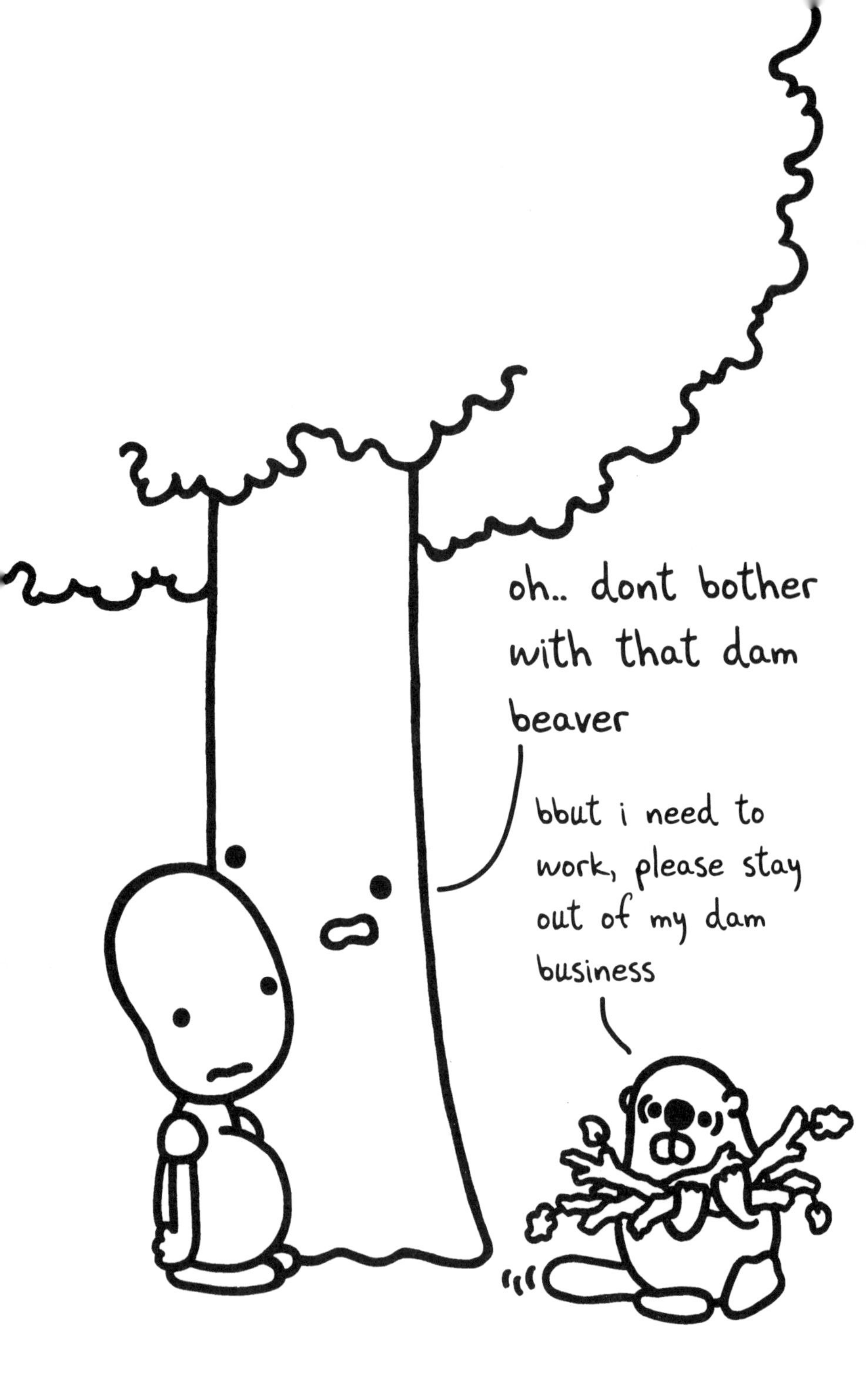
oh.. dont bother with that dam beaver
bbut i need to work, please stay out of my dam business

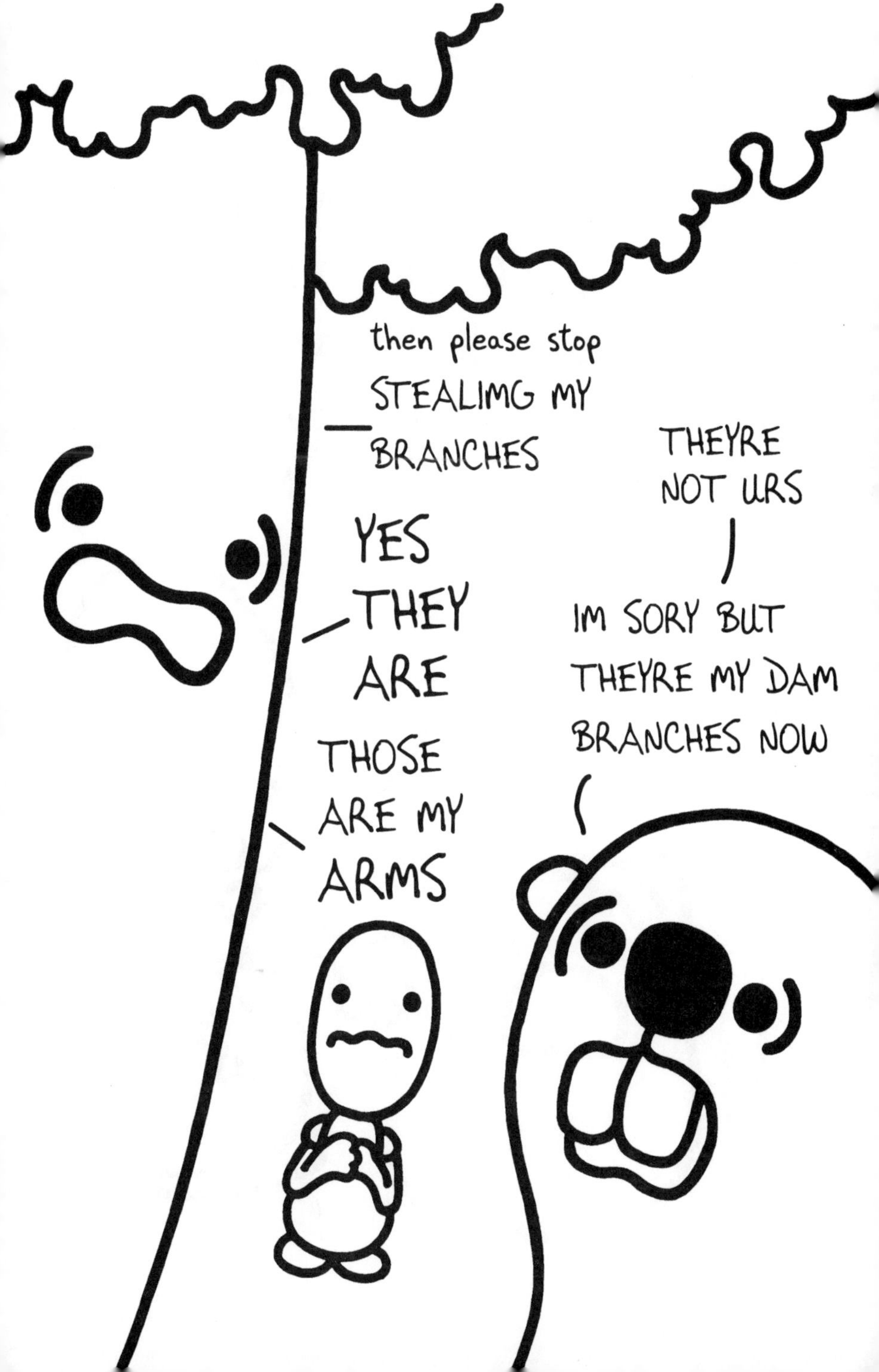
then please stop STEALIMG MY BRANCHES
YES THEY ARE
THOSE ARE MY ARMS
THEYRE NOT URS
IM SORY BUT THEYRE MY DAM BRANCHES NOW

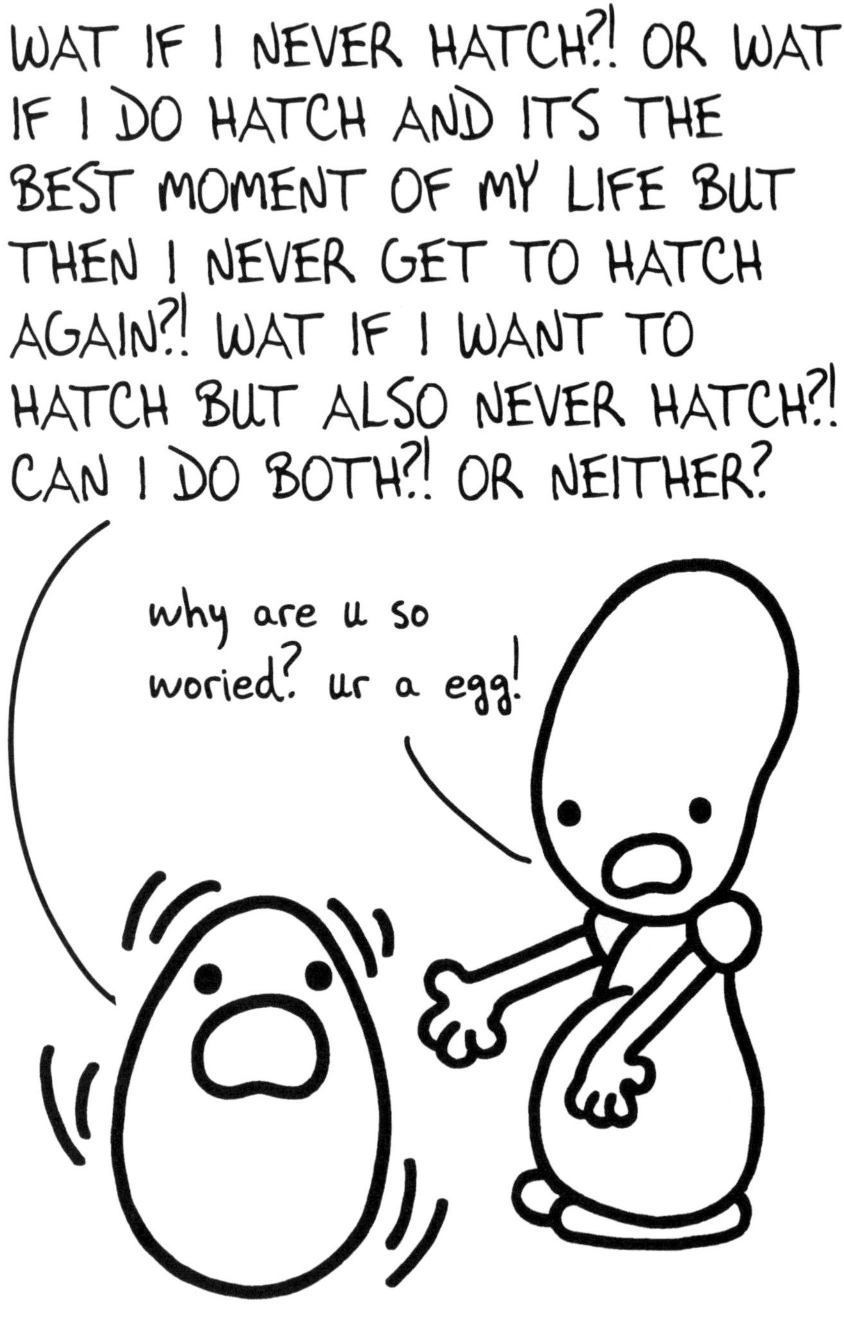
WAT IF I NEVER HATCH?! OR WAT IF I DO HATCH AND ITS THE BEST MOMENT OF MY LIFE BUT THEN I NEVER GET TO HATCH AGAIN?! WAT IF I WANT TO HATCH BUT ALSO NEVER HATCH?! CAN I DO BOTH?! OR NEITHER?
why are u so woried? ur a egg!

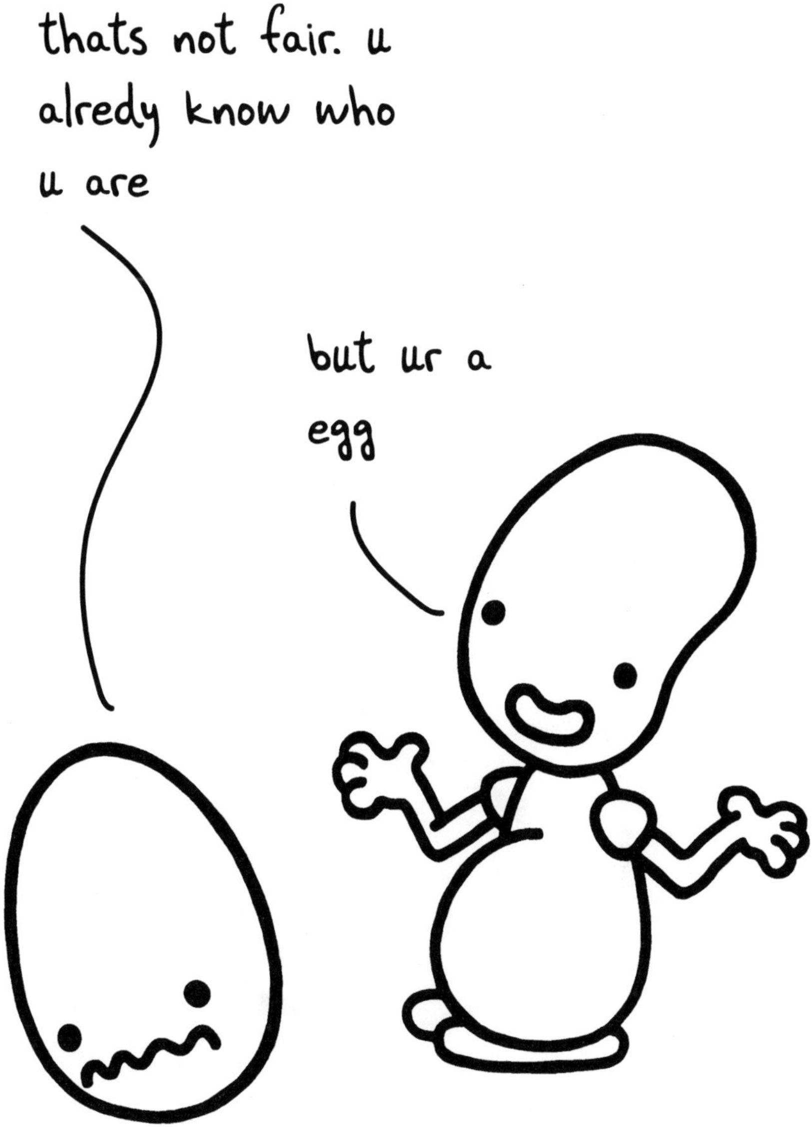
thats not fair. u alredy know who u are
but ur a egg

u just dont get it

..oh.

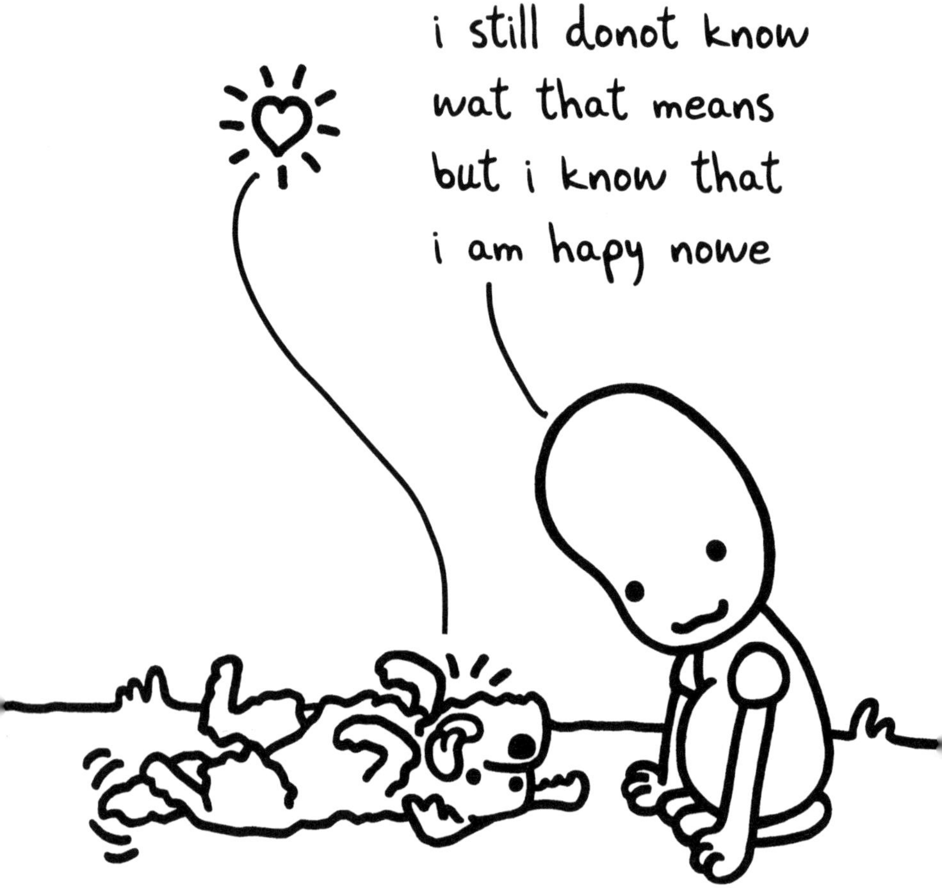
i still donot know
wat that means
but i know that
i am hapy nowe

i like the humabns they are all so diferent and i wish i coud be more like them
u are not supose to like them
ur supose to research them

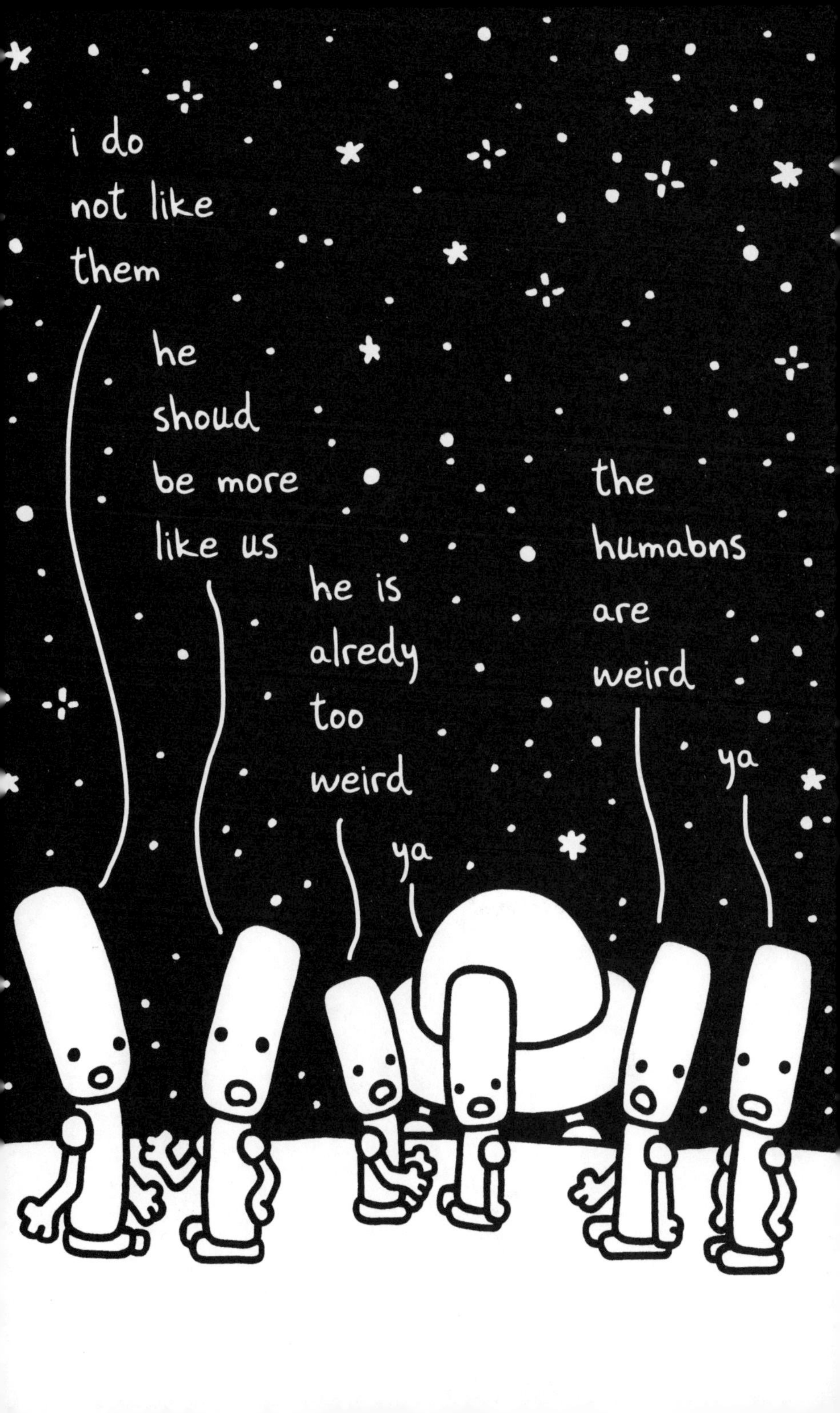
i do not like them
he shoud be more like us
he is alredy too weird
ya
the humabns are weird
ya

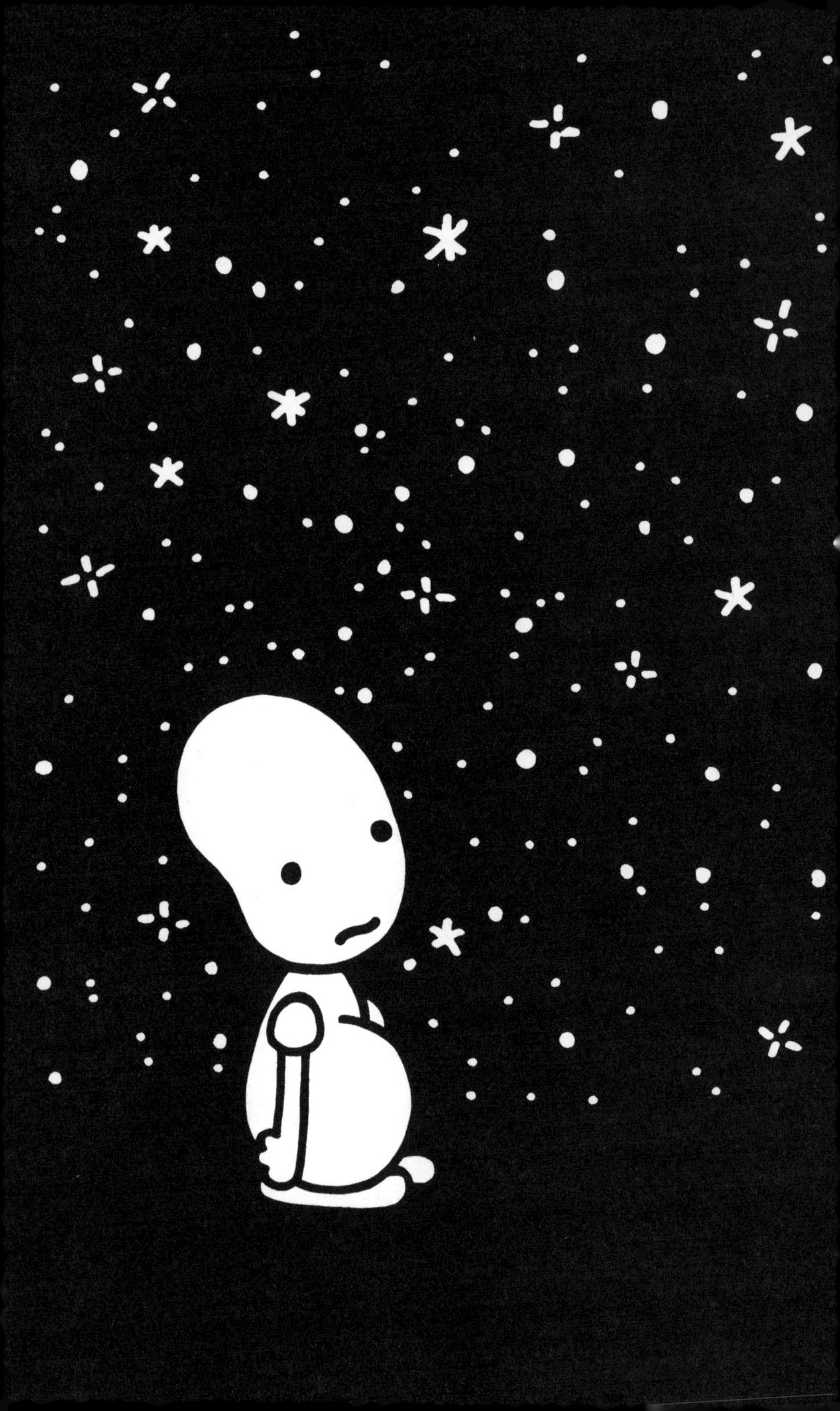

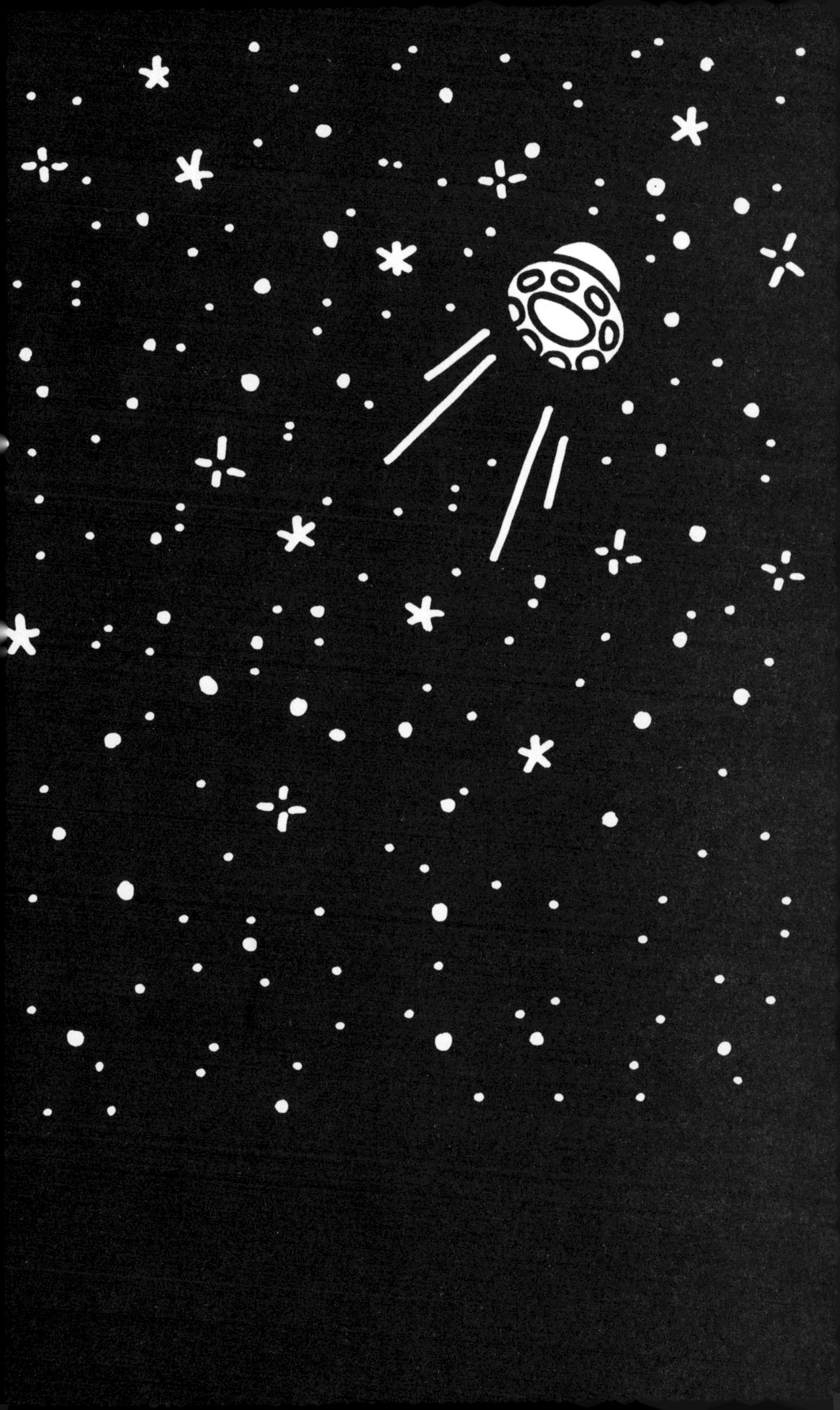

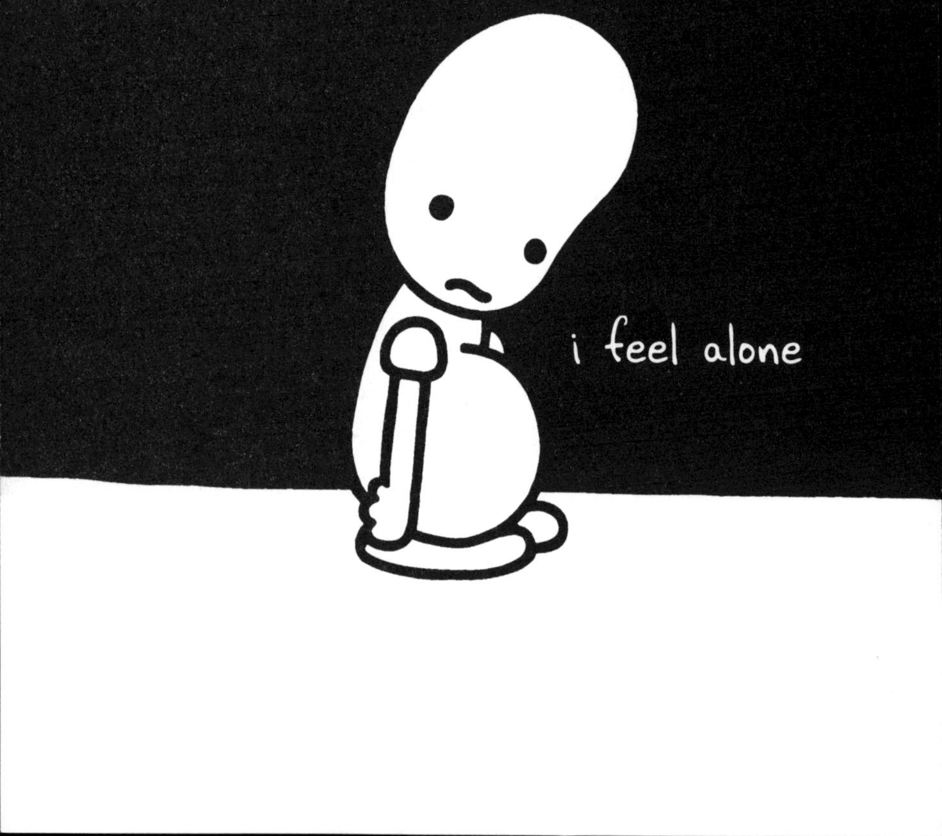
i feel alone

who said that

NOBODY.

who are u

I AM
NOTHING.

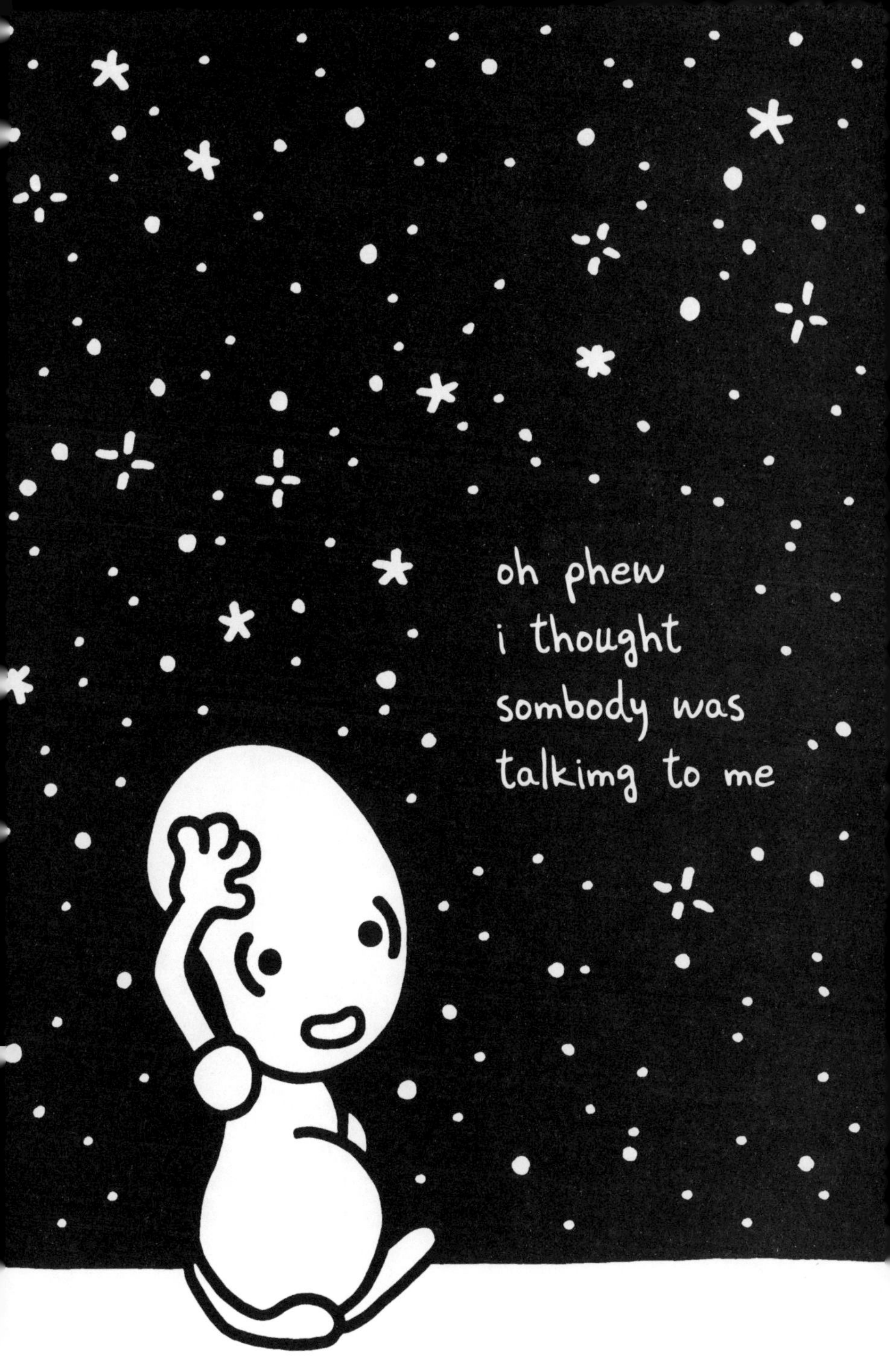
oh phew
i thought
sombody was
talkimg to me

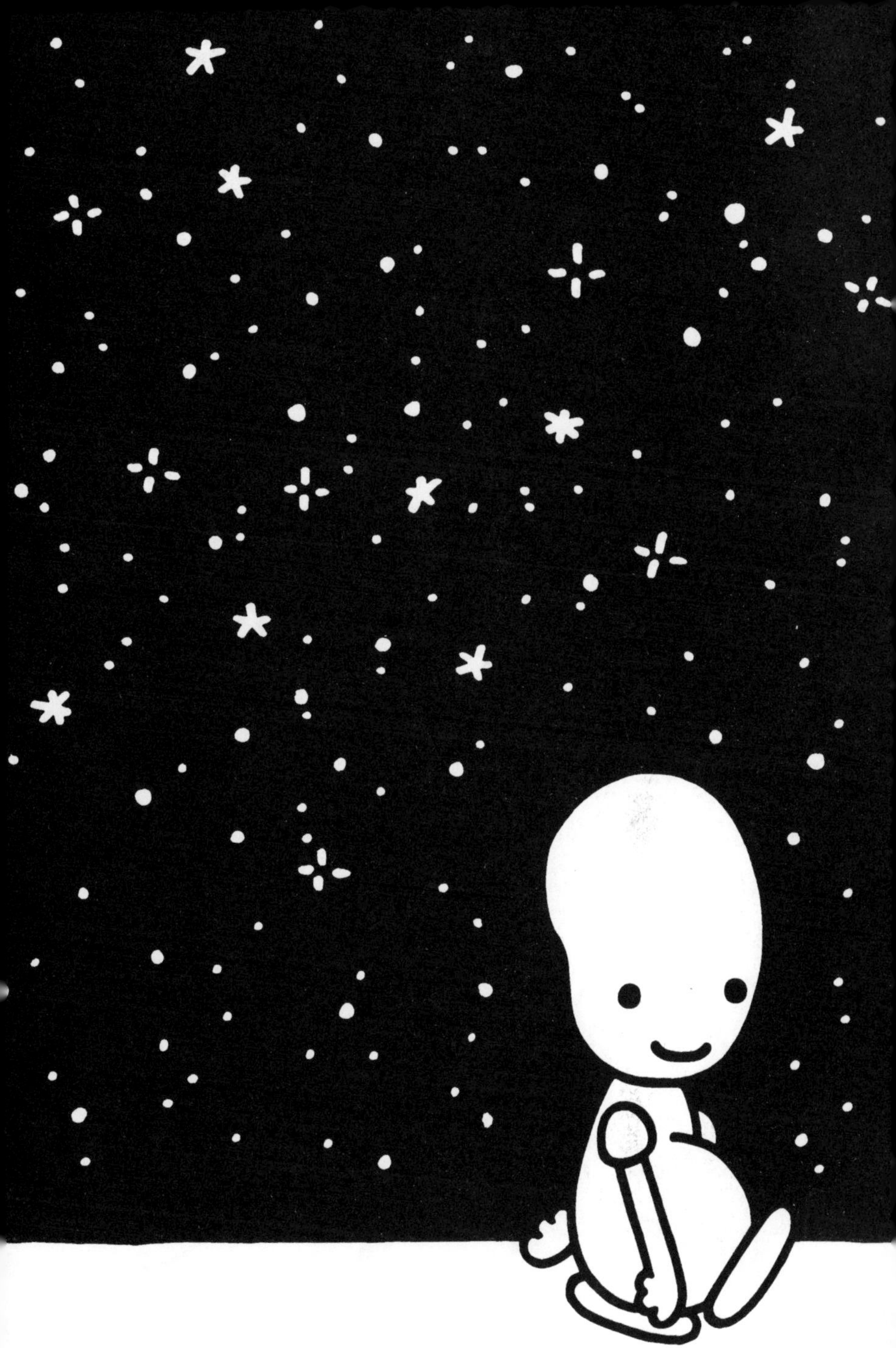

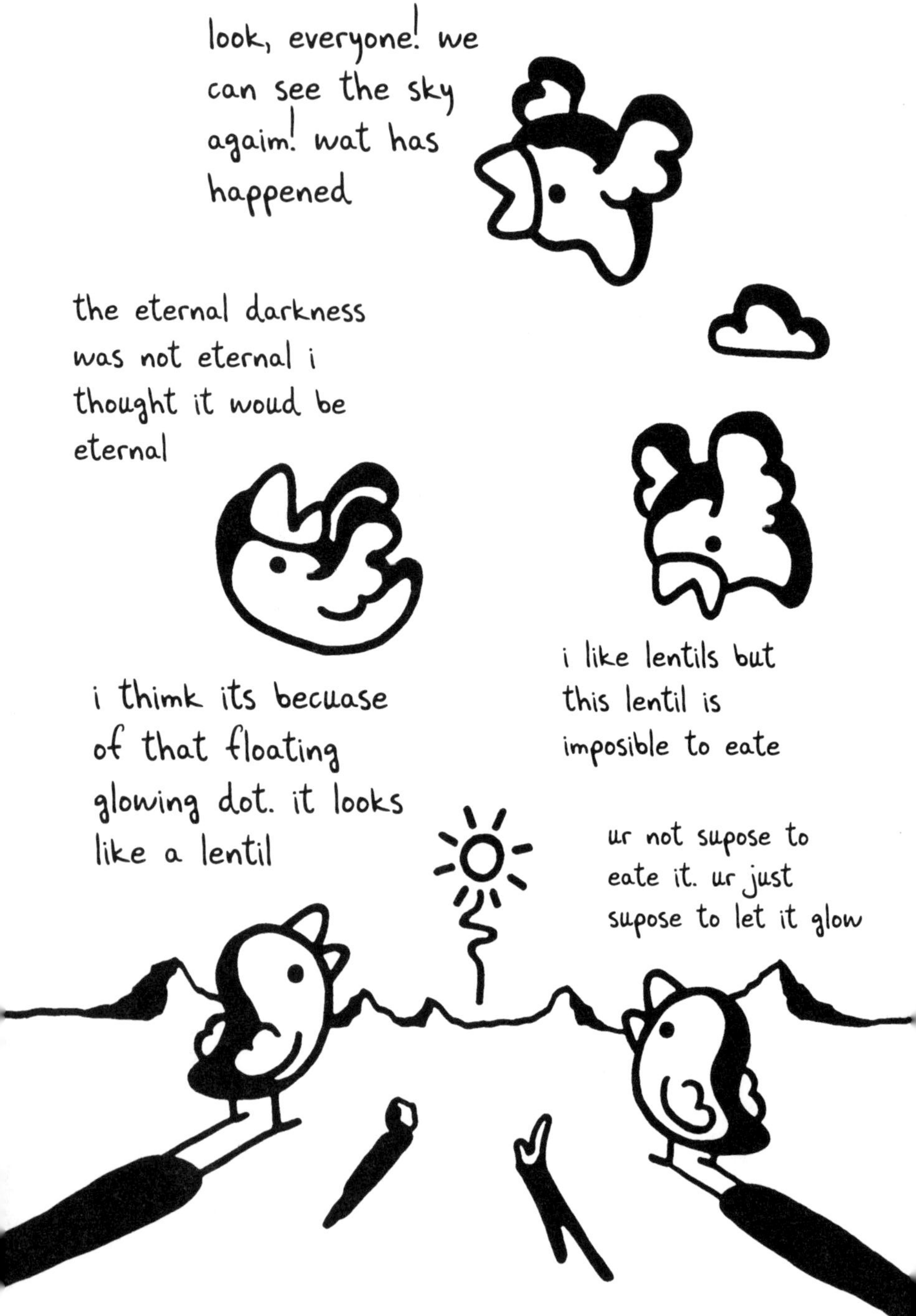
look, everyone! we can see the sky agaim! wat has happened
the eternal darkness was not eternal i thought it woud be eternal
i thimk its becuase of that floating glowing dot. it looks like a lentil
i like lentils but this lentil is imposible to eate
ur not supose to eate it. ur just supose to let it glow

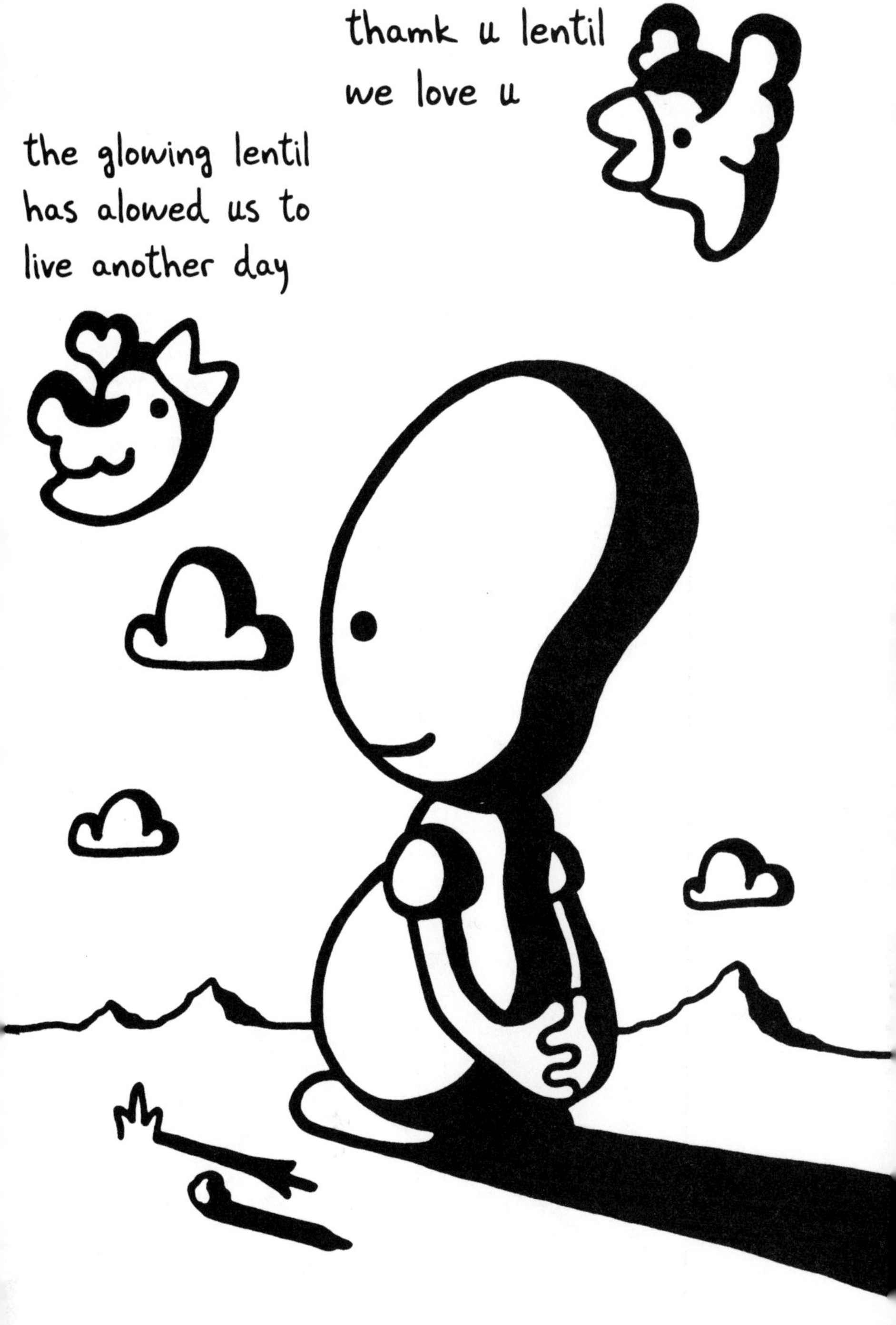

thamk u lentil
we love u
the glowing lentil
has alowed us to
live another day

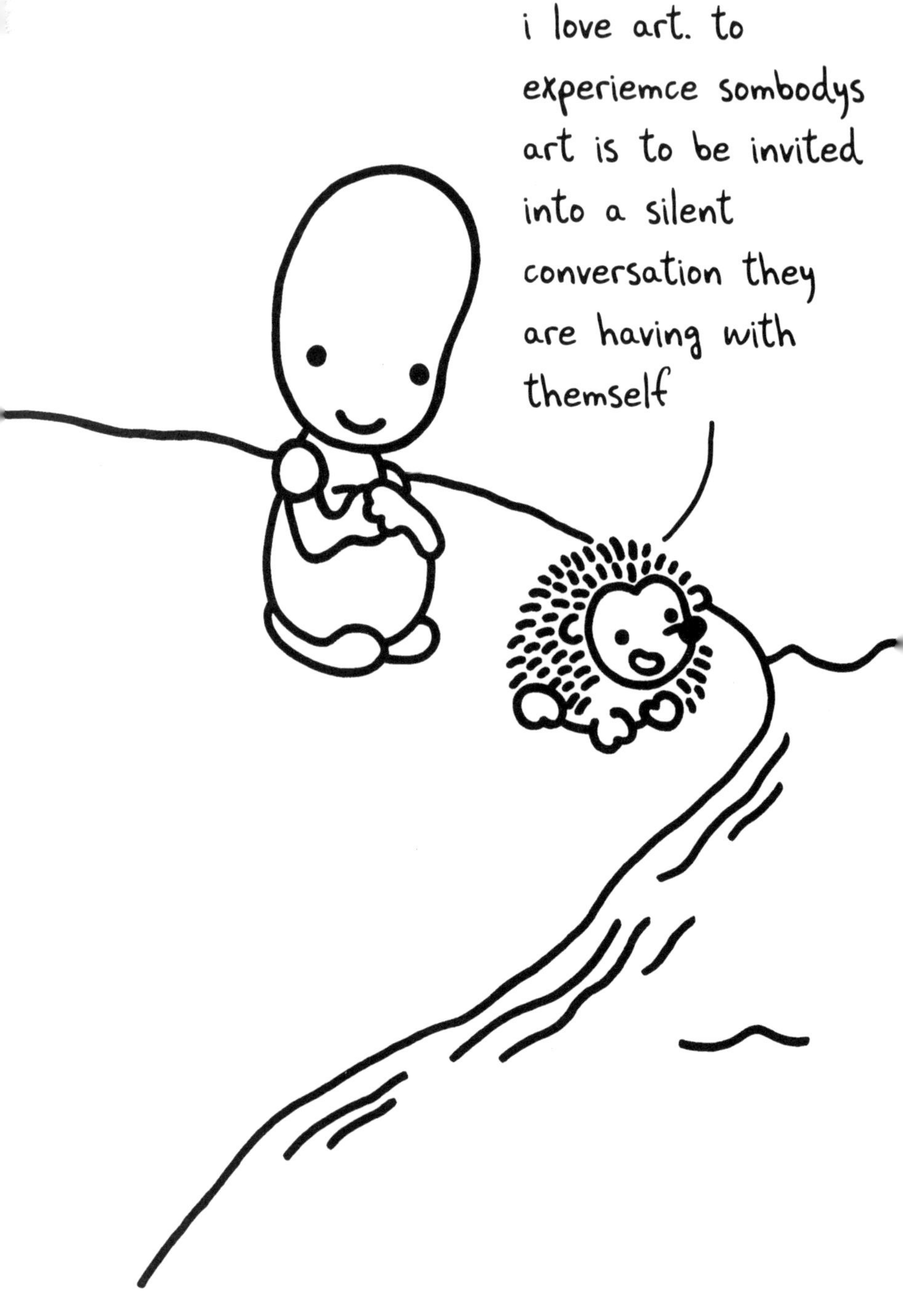
i love art. to experiemce sombodys art is to be invited into a silent conversation they are having with themself

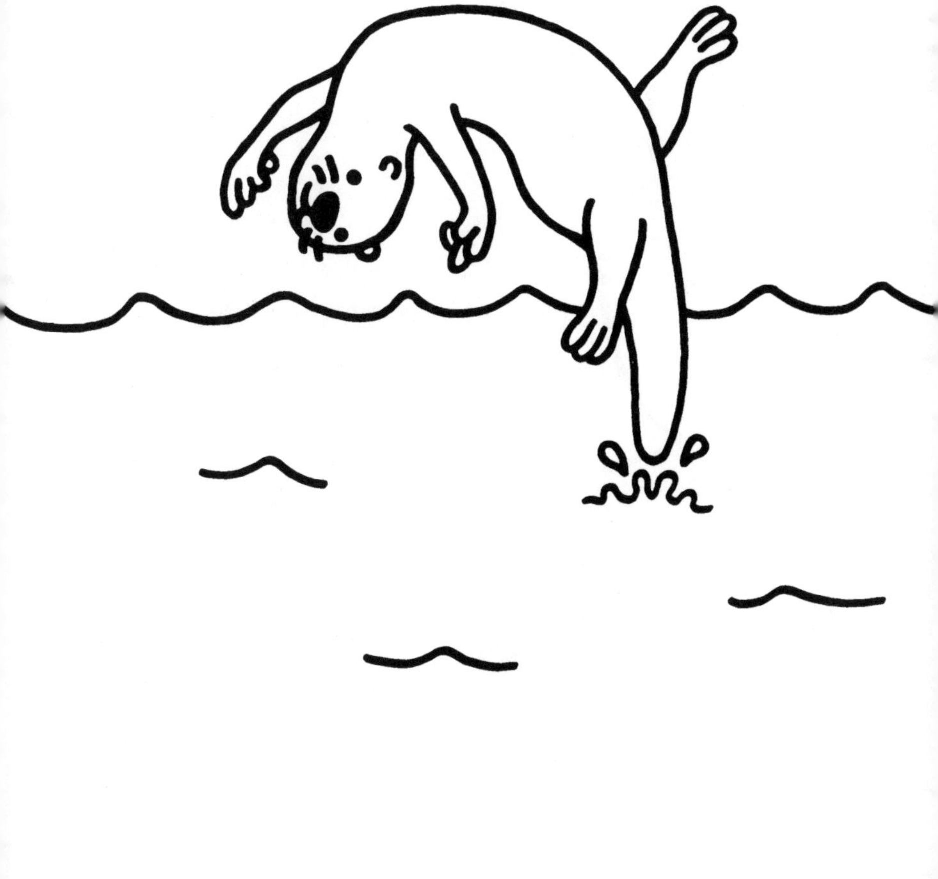

Yes, my dear. In fact, art allows us to remember things we have never done and go to places we have never been.

like swiming

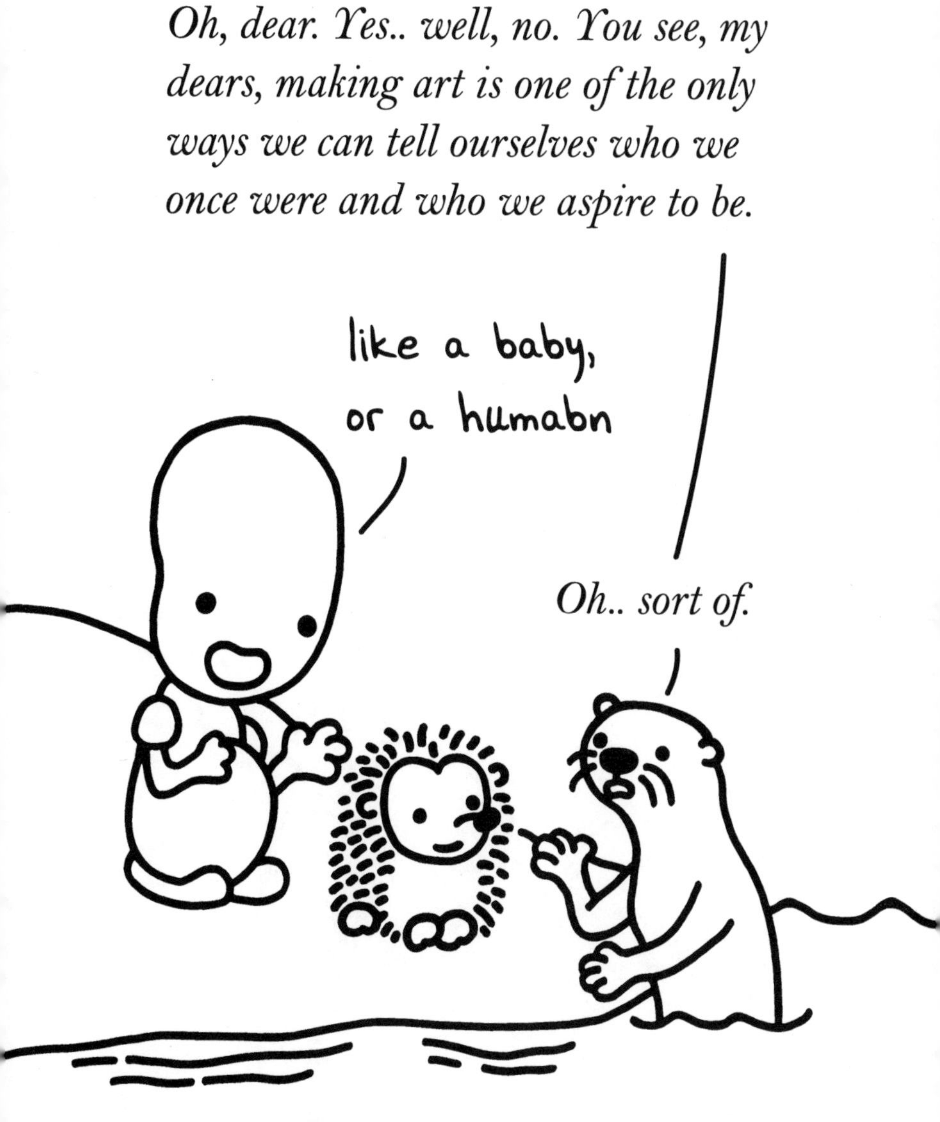
Oh, dear. Yes.. well, no. You see, my dears, making art is one of the only ways we can tell ourselves who we once were and who we aspire to be.
like a baby, or a humabn
Oh.. sort of.

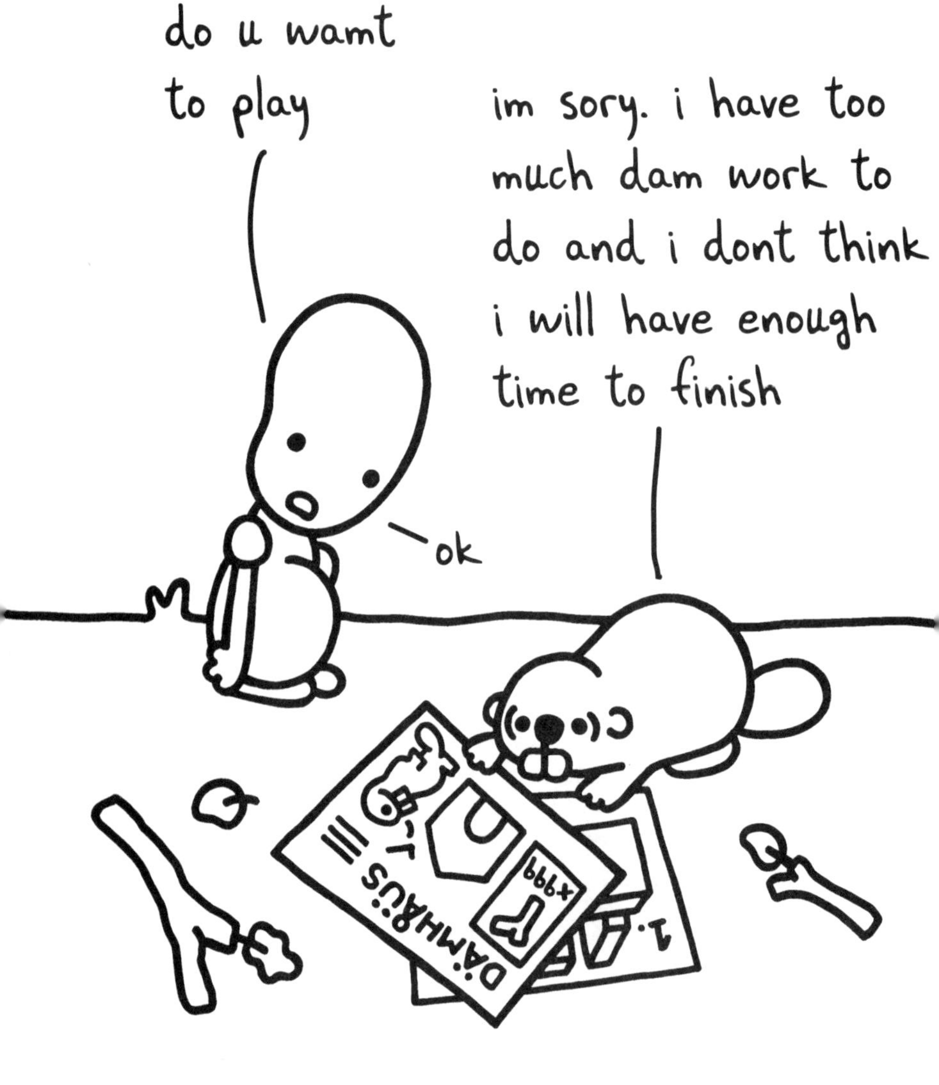
do u wamt to play
im sory. i have too much dam work to do and i dont think i will have enough time to finish
ok

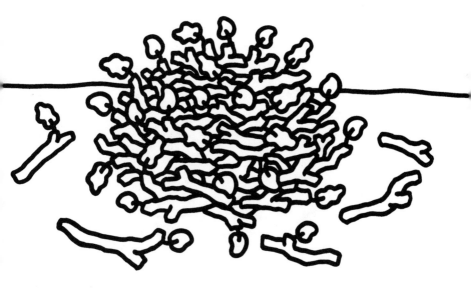

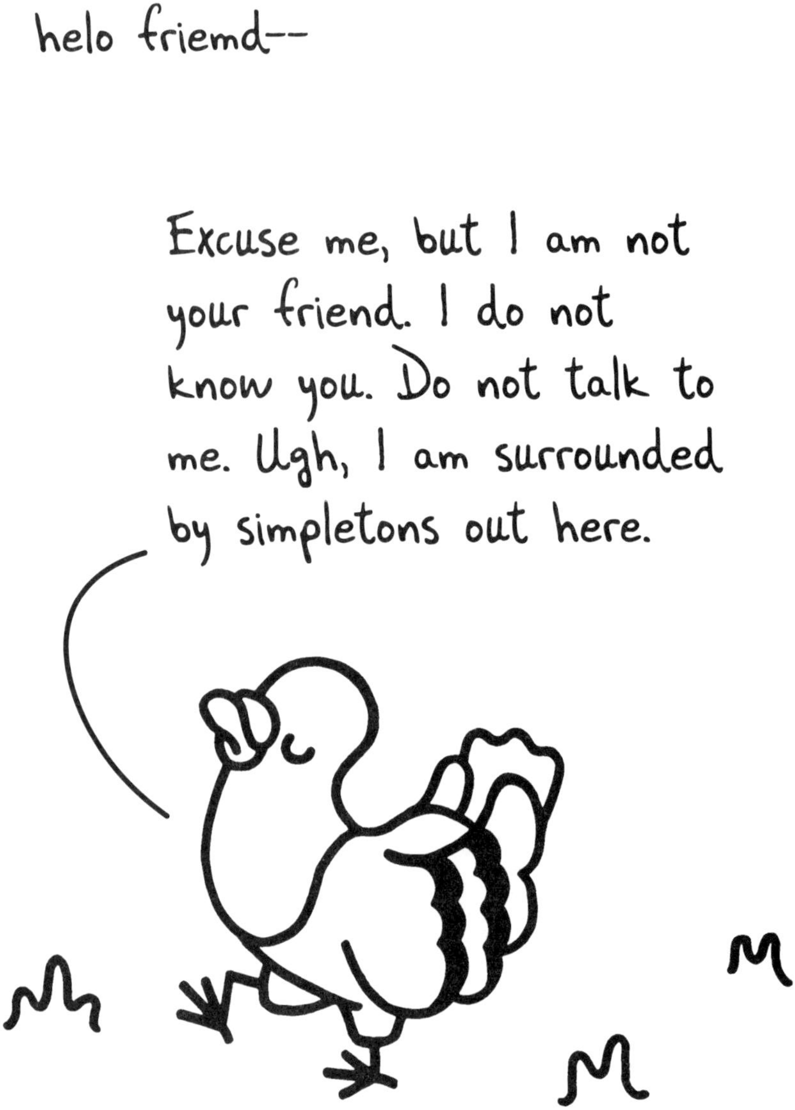
helo friemd--
Excuse me, but I am not your friend. I do not know you. Do not talk to me. Ugh, I am surrounded by simpletons out here.

thats wat
hapens
when u
spend too
much time
in the city

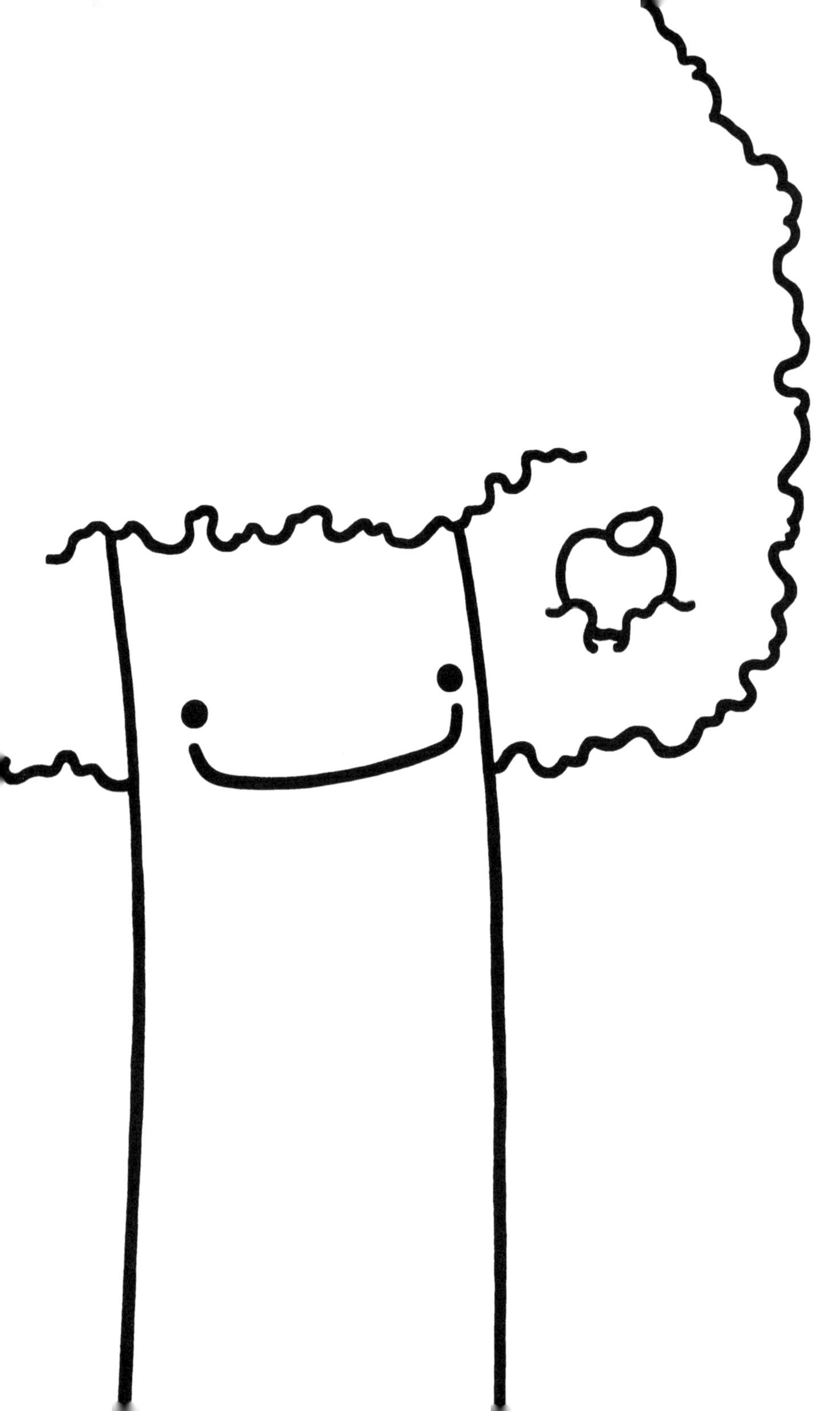

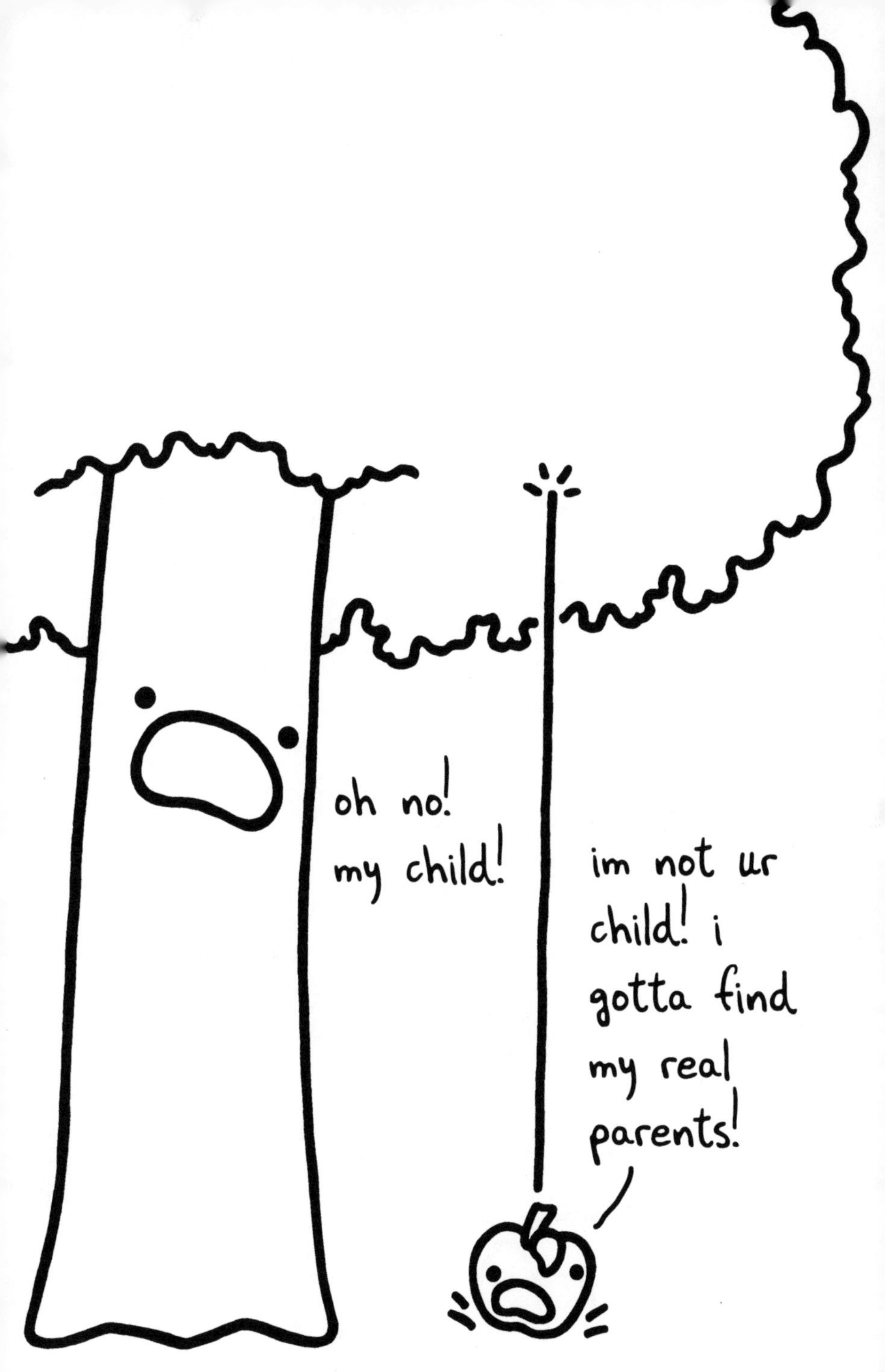

oh no! my child!
im not ur child! i gotta find my real parents!

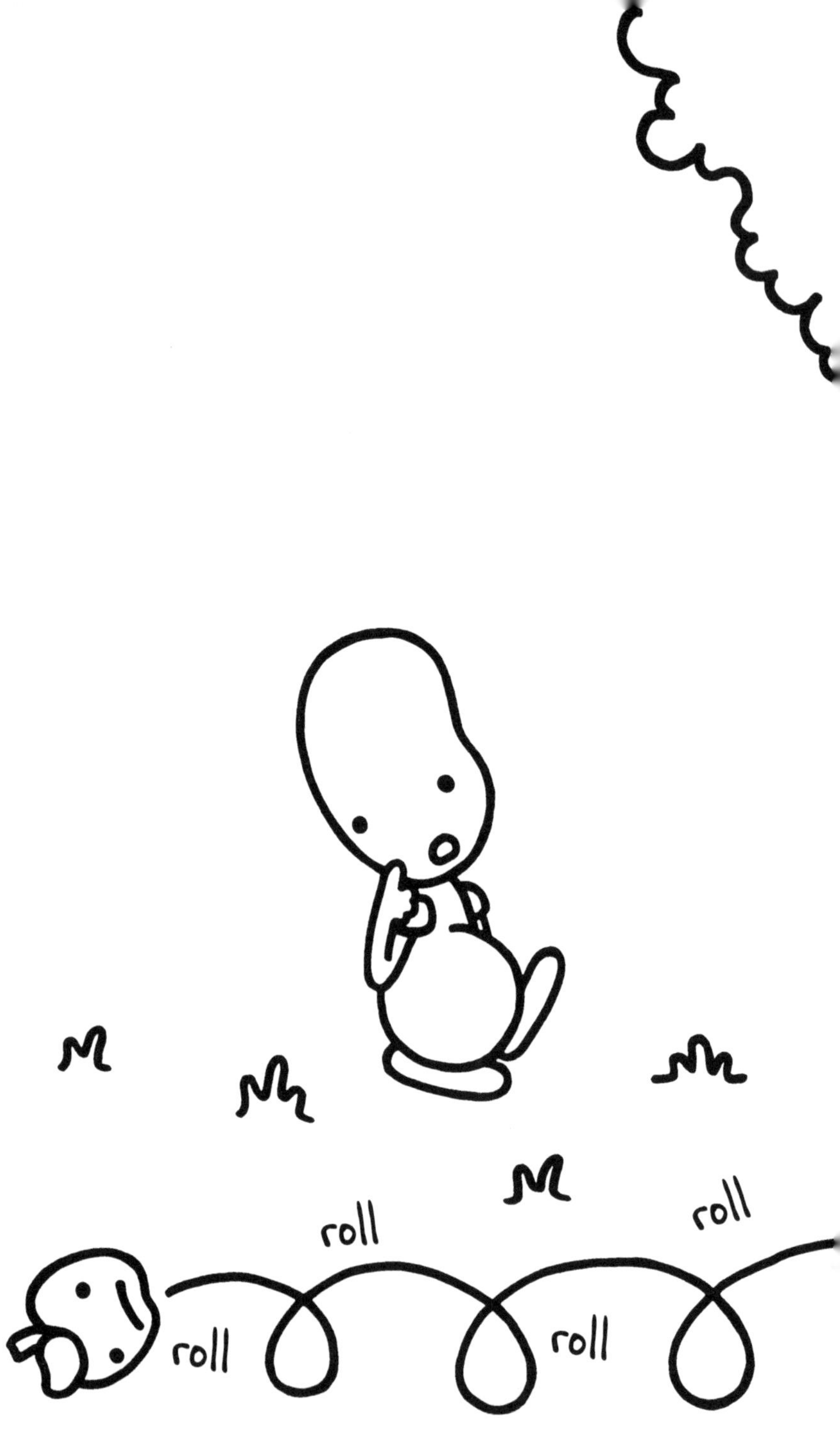
roll
roll
roll
roll

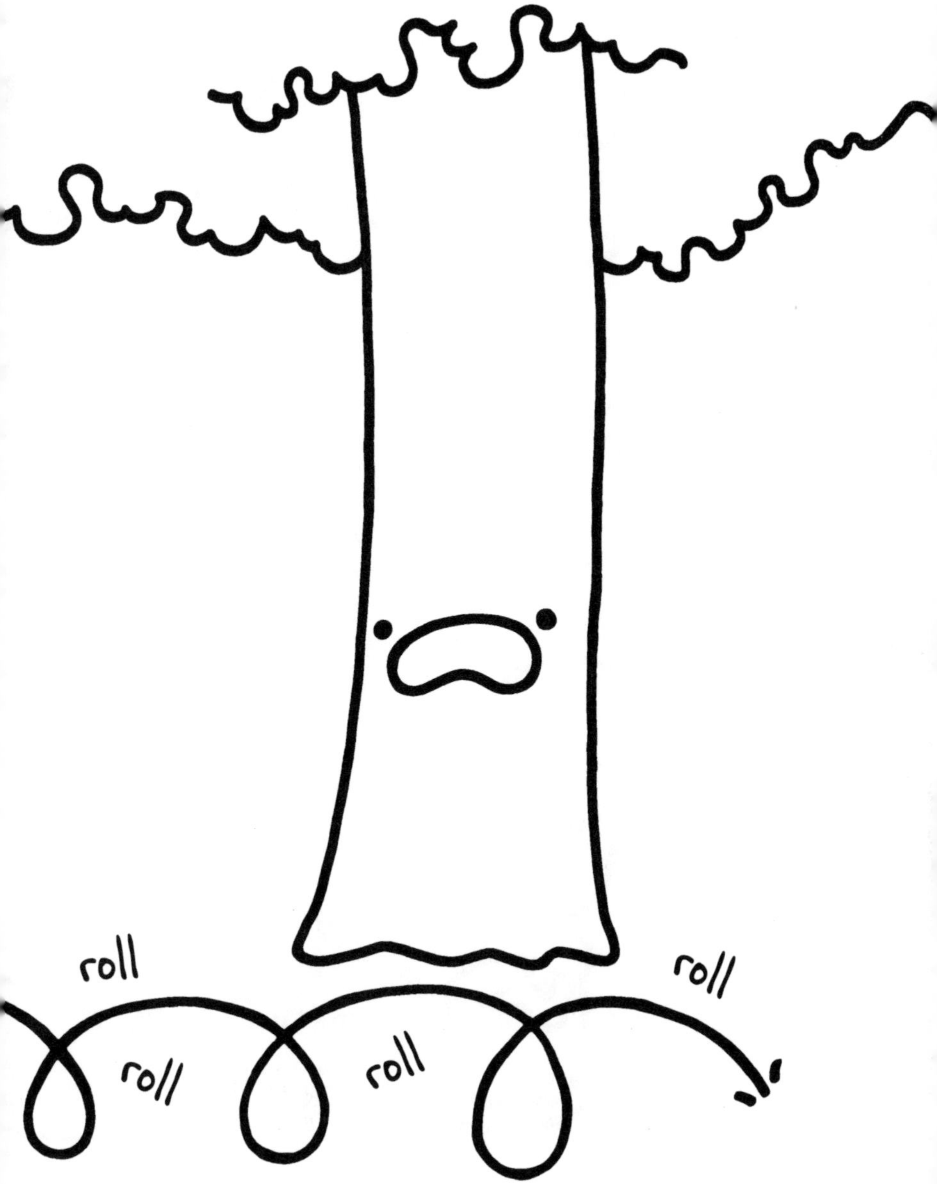
roll
roll
roll
roll

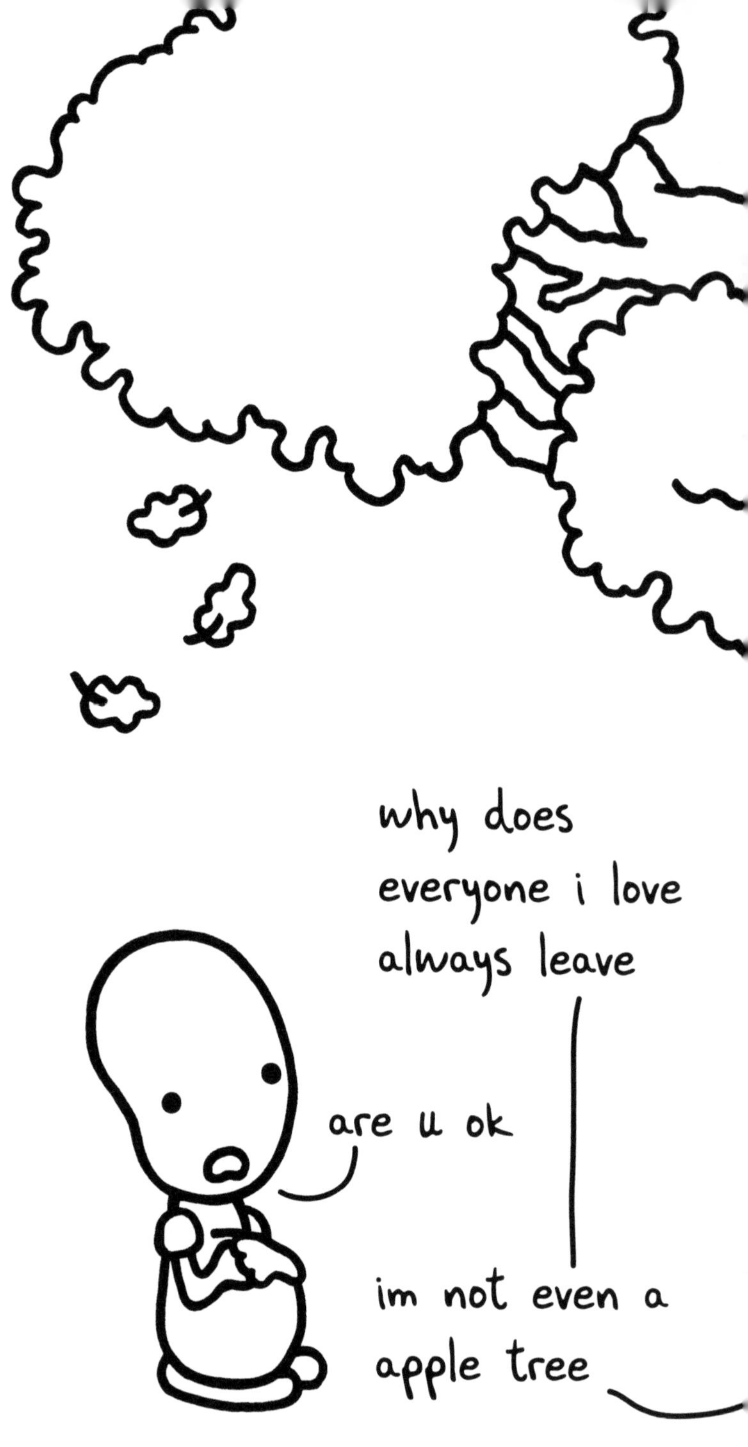
why does everyone i love always leave
are u ok
im not even a apple tree

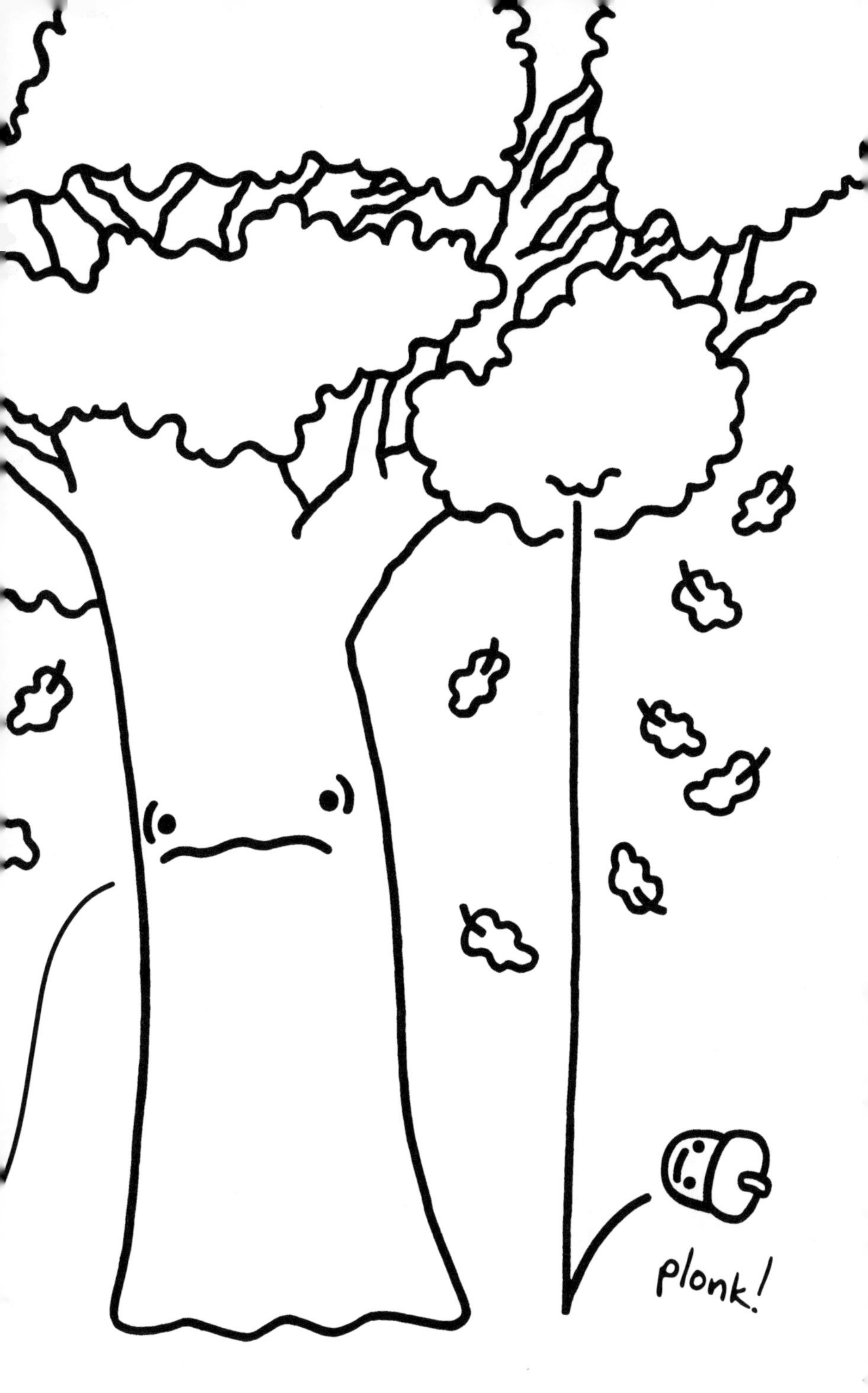
plonk!

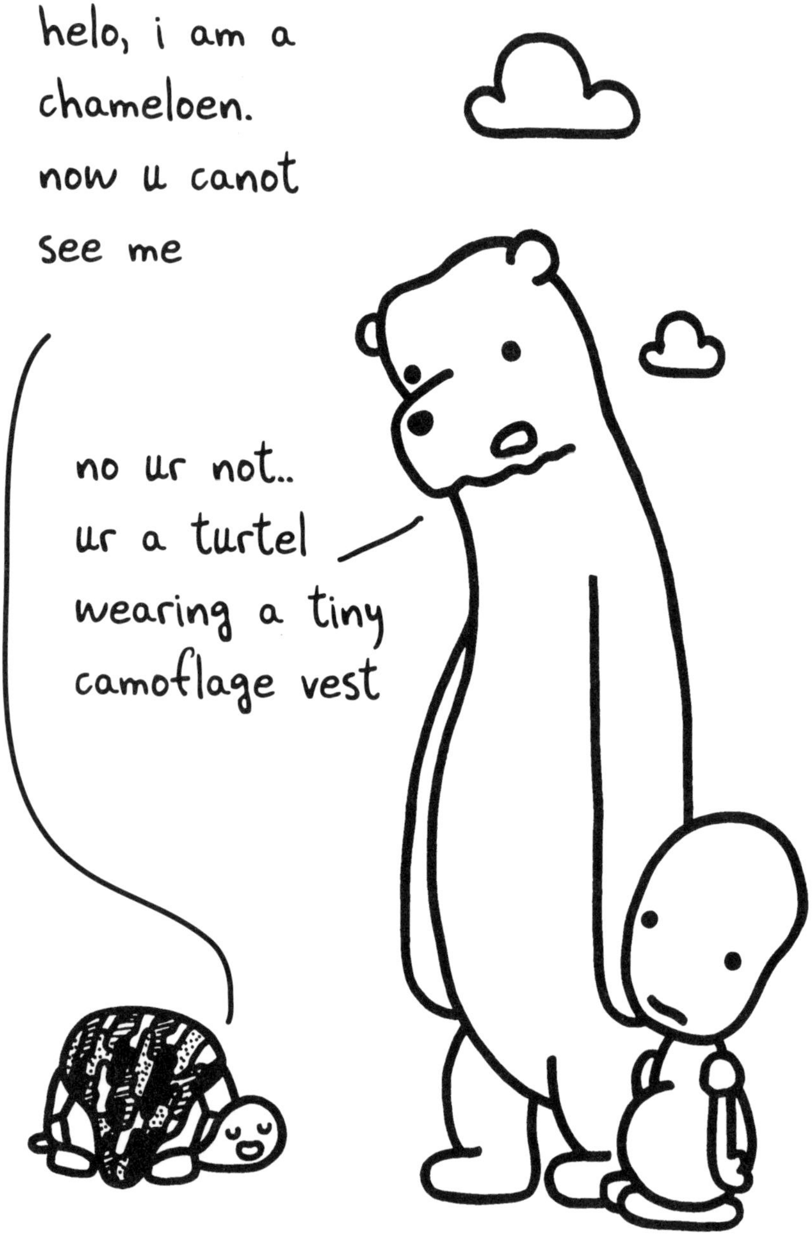
helo, i am a chameloen. now u canot see me
no ur not.. ur a turtel wearing a tiny camoflage vest

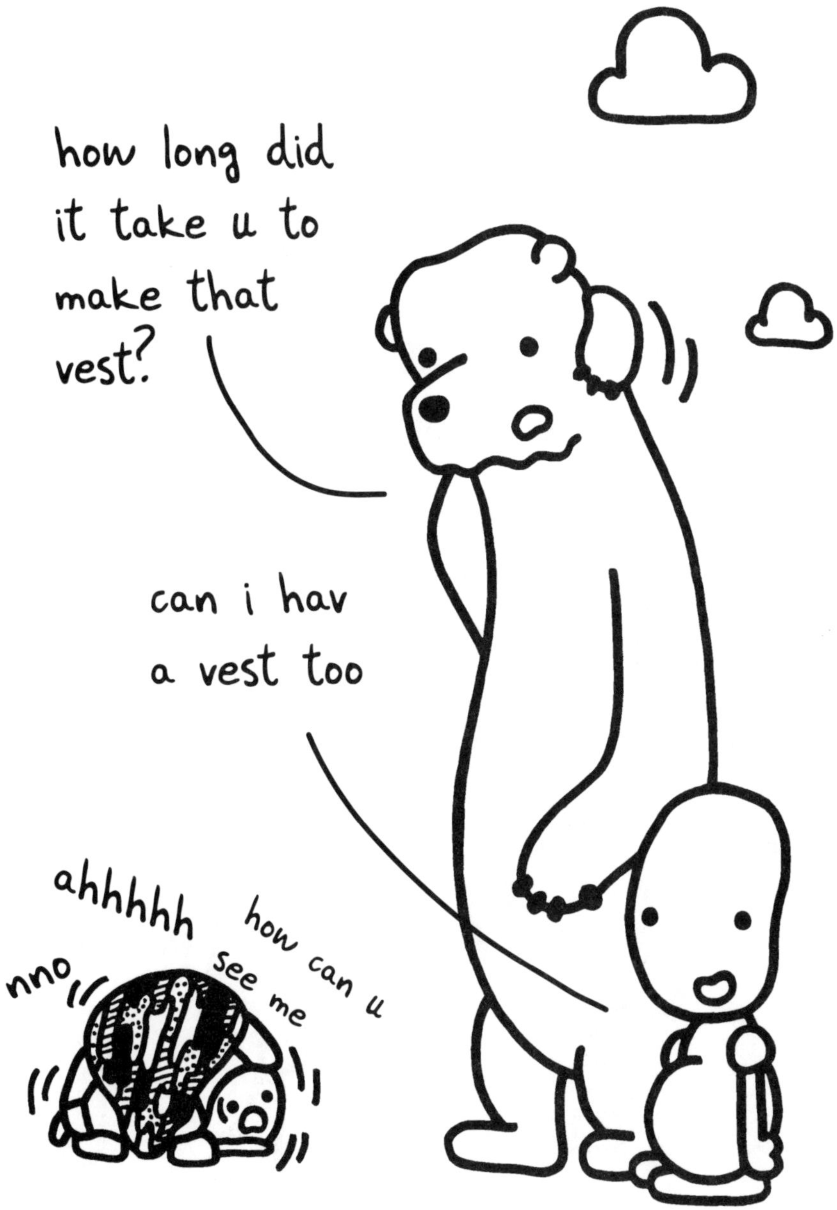
how long did it take u to make that vest?
can i hav a vest too
ahhhhh
nno
how can u see me

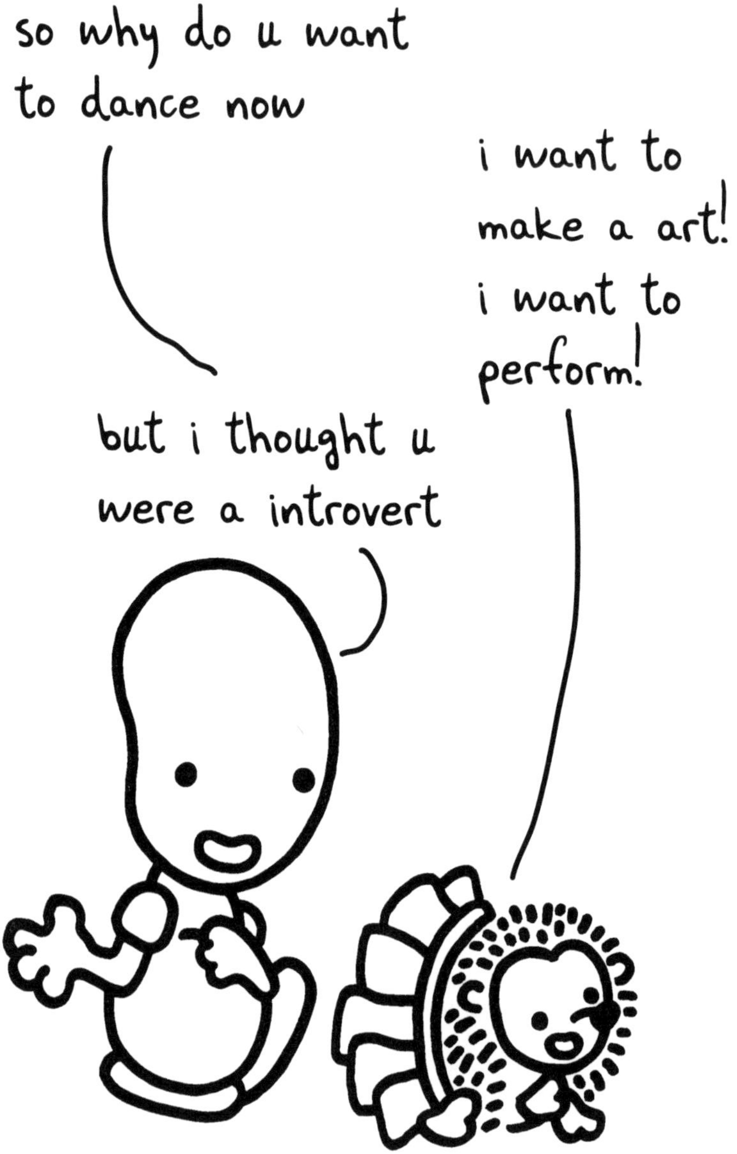
so why do u want to dance now
i want to make a art! i want to perform!
but i thought u were a introvert

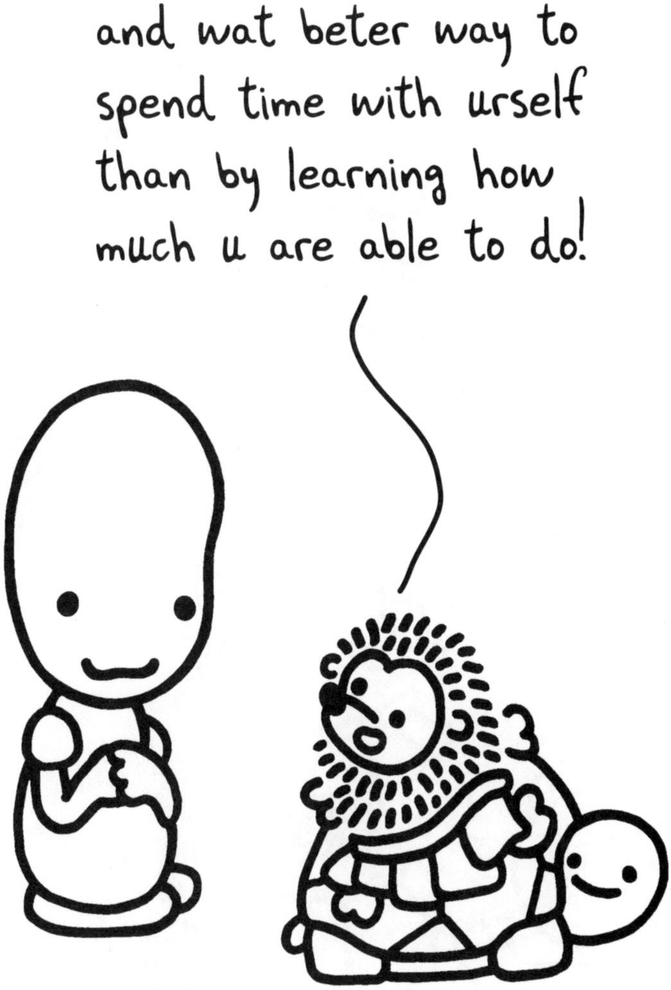
and wat beter way to spend time with urself than by learning how much u are able to do!

..please stop
lookig at me

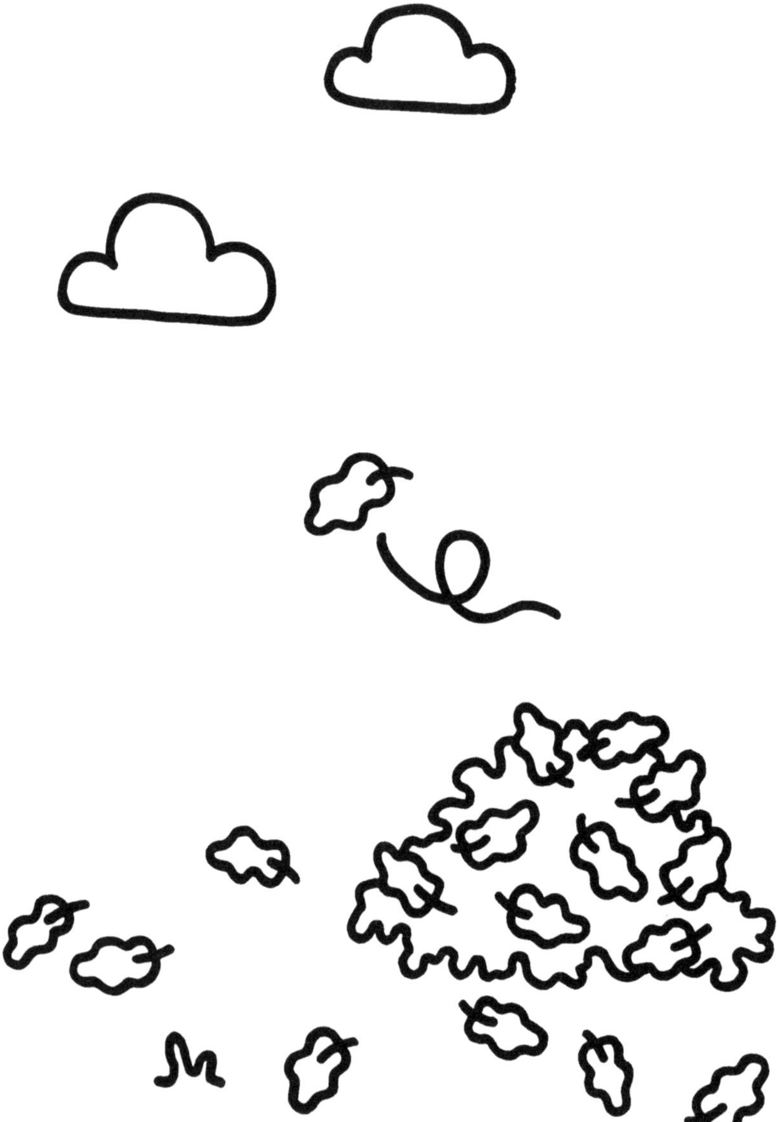

did u get a haircut

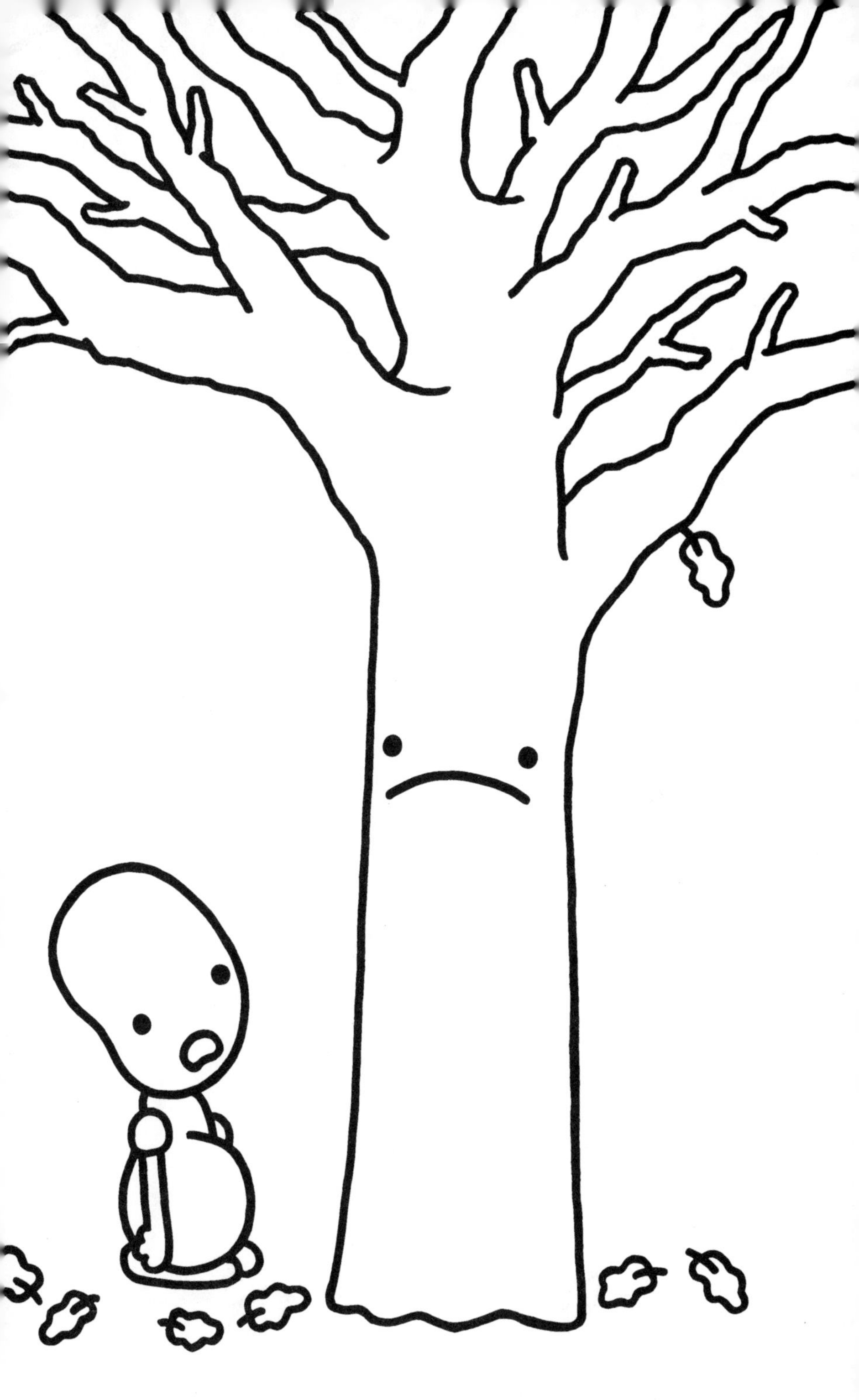

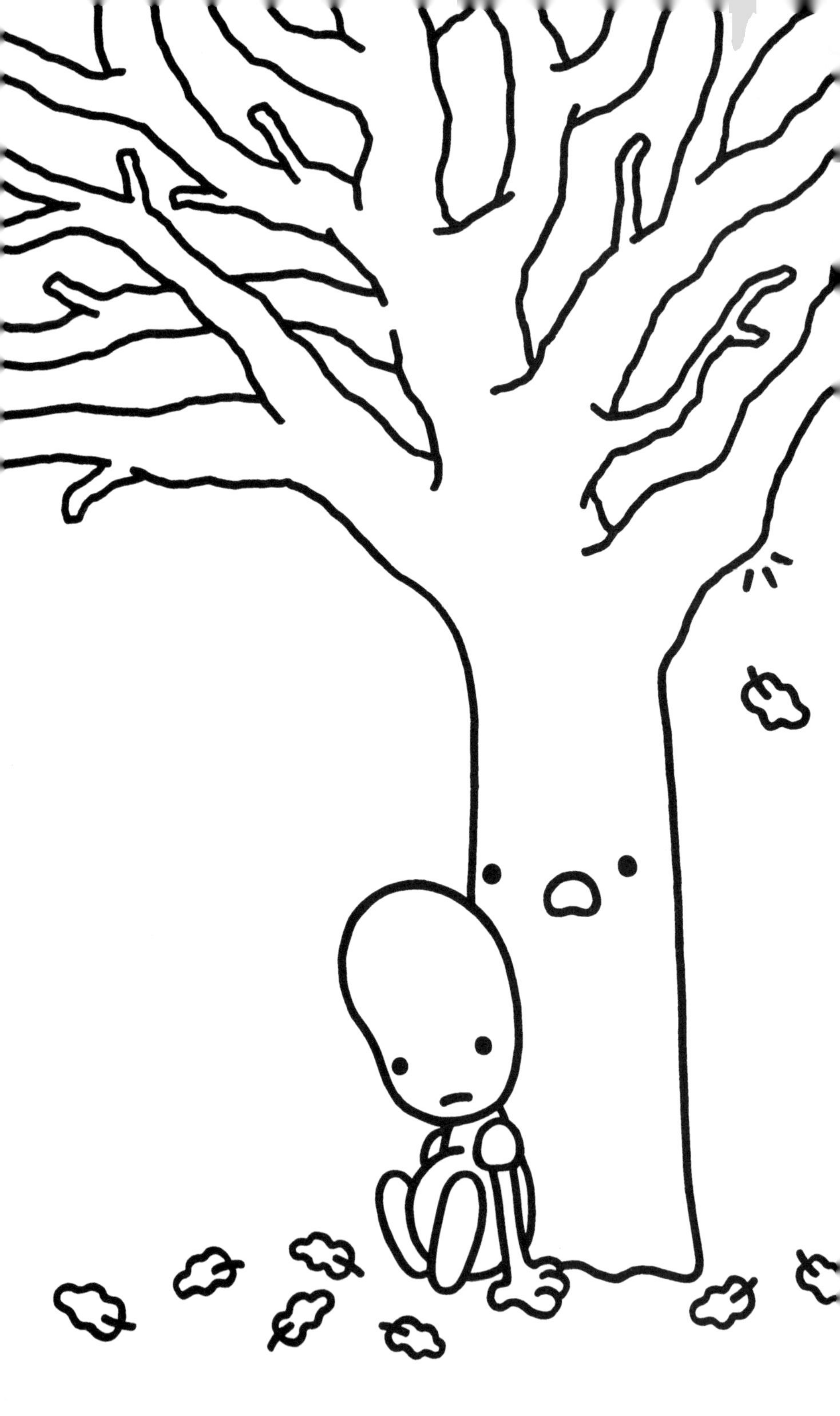

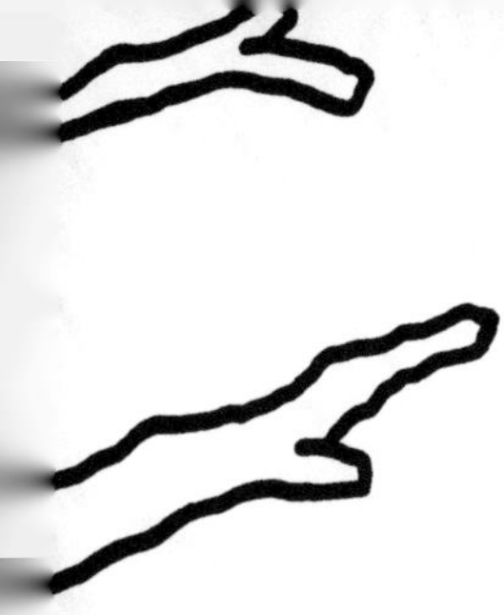

i dont like it when my leaves leave. it makes me feel cold and afraid and alone. everybody else gets to leave but i am stuck in the same place, forever

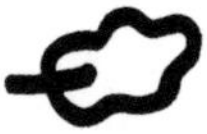

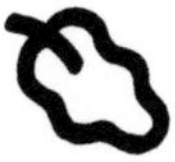

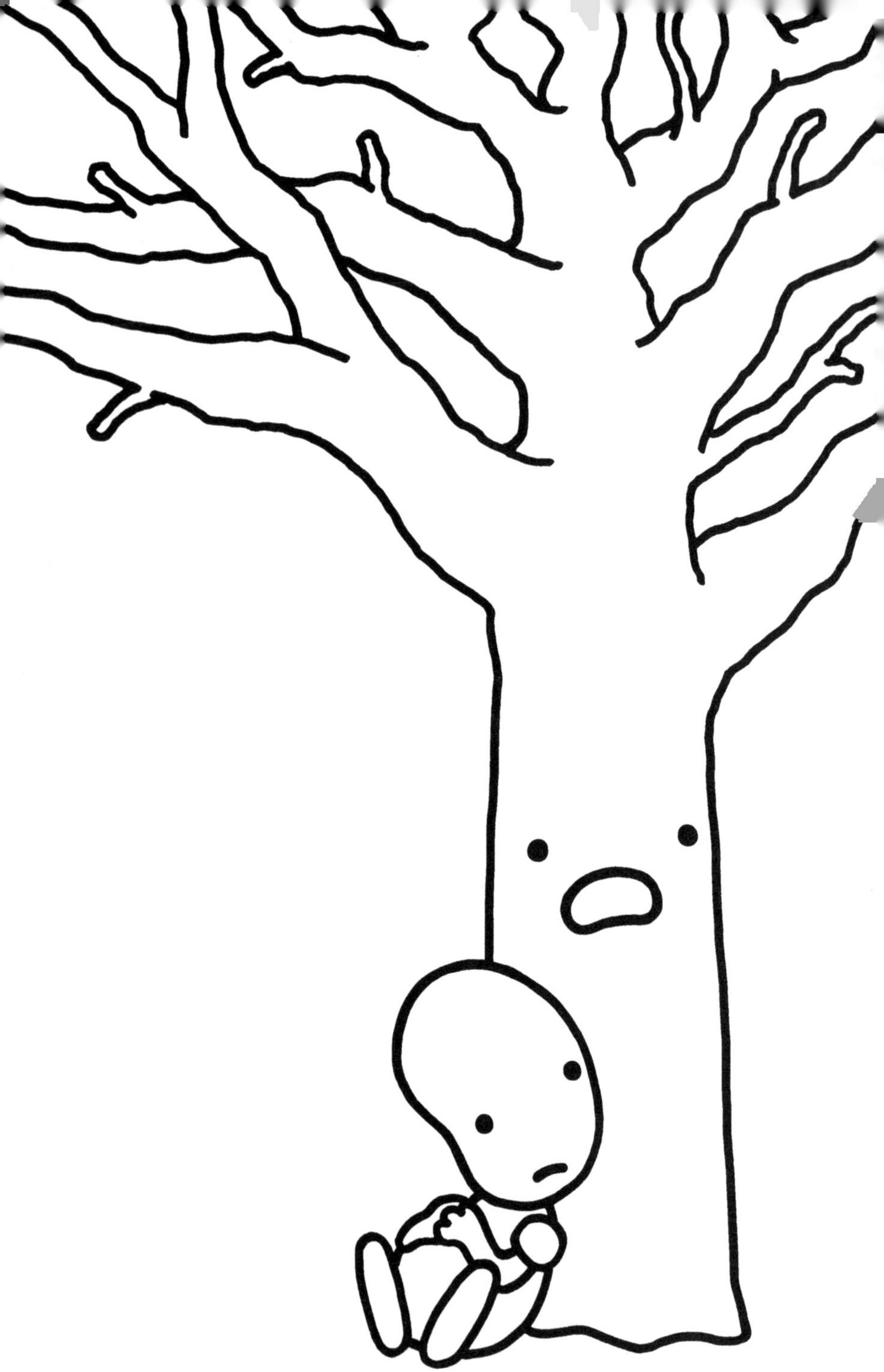

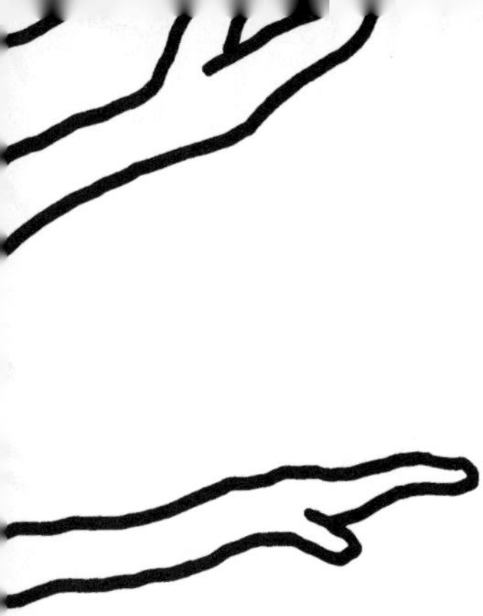

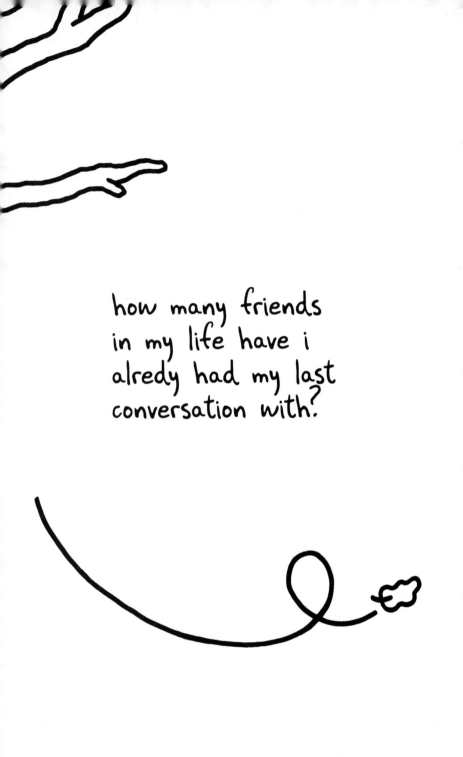

how many friends
in my life have i
alredy had my last
conversation with?

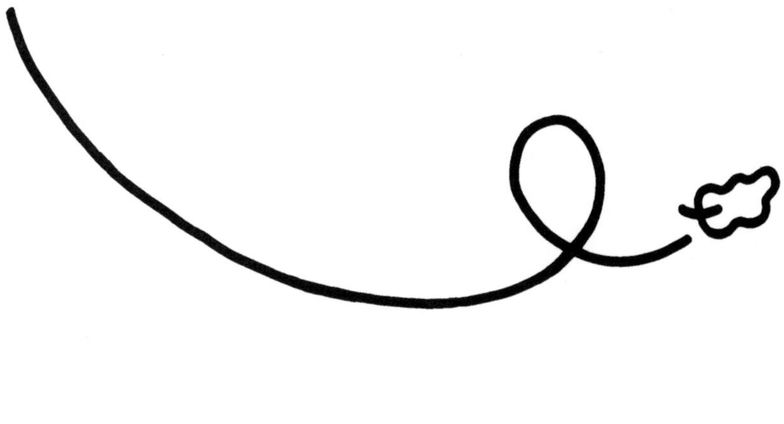

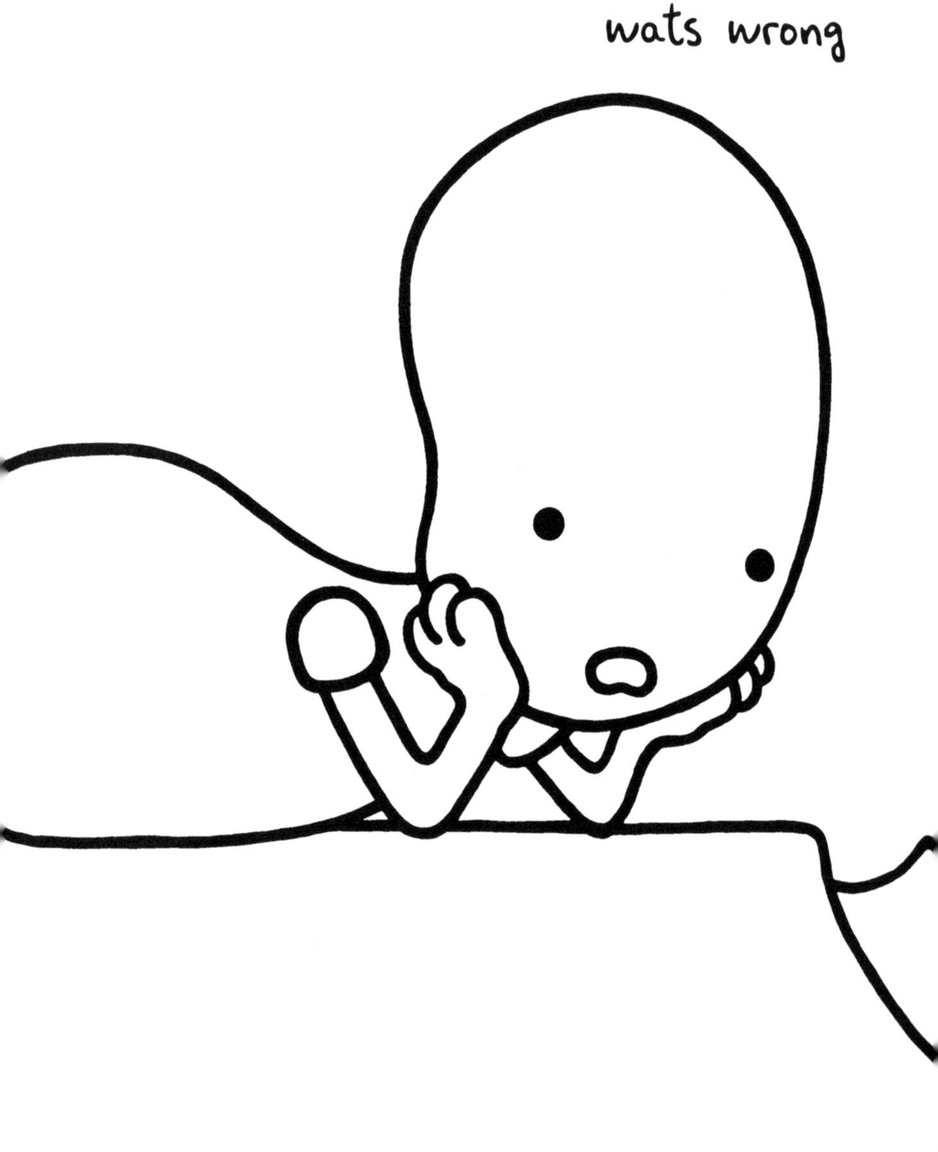
wats wrong

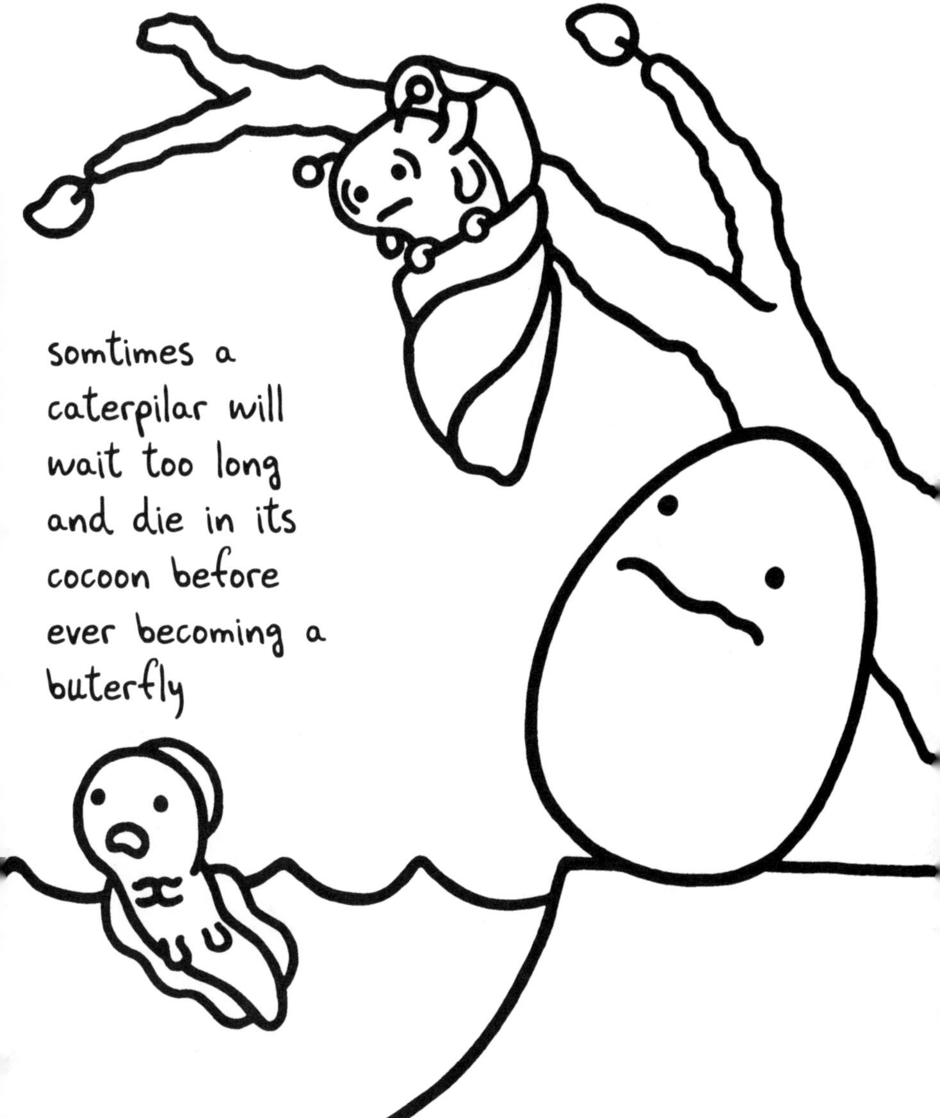
somtimes a caterpilar will wait too long and die in its cocoon before ever becoming a buterfly

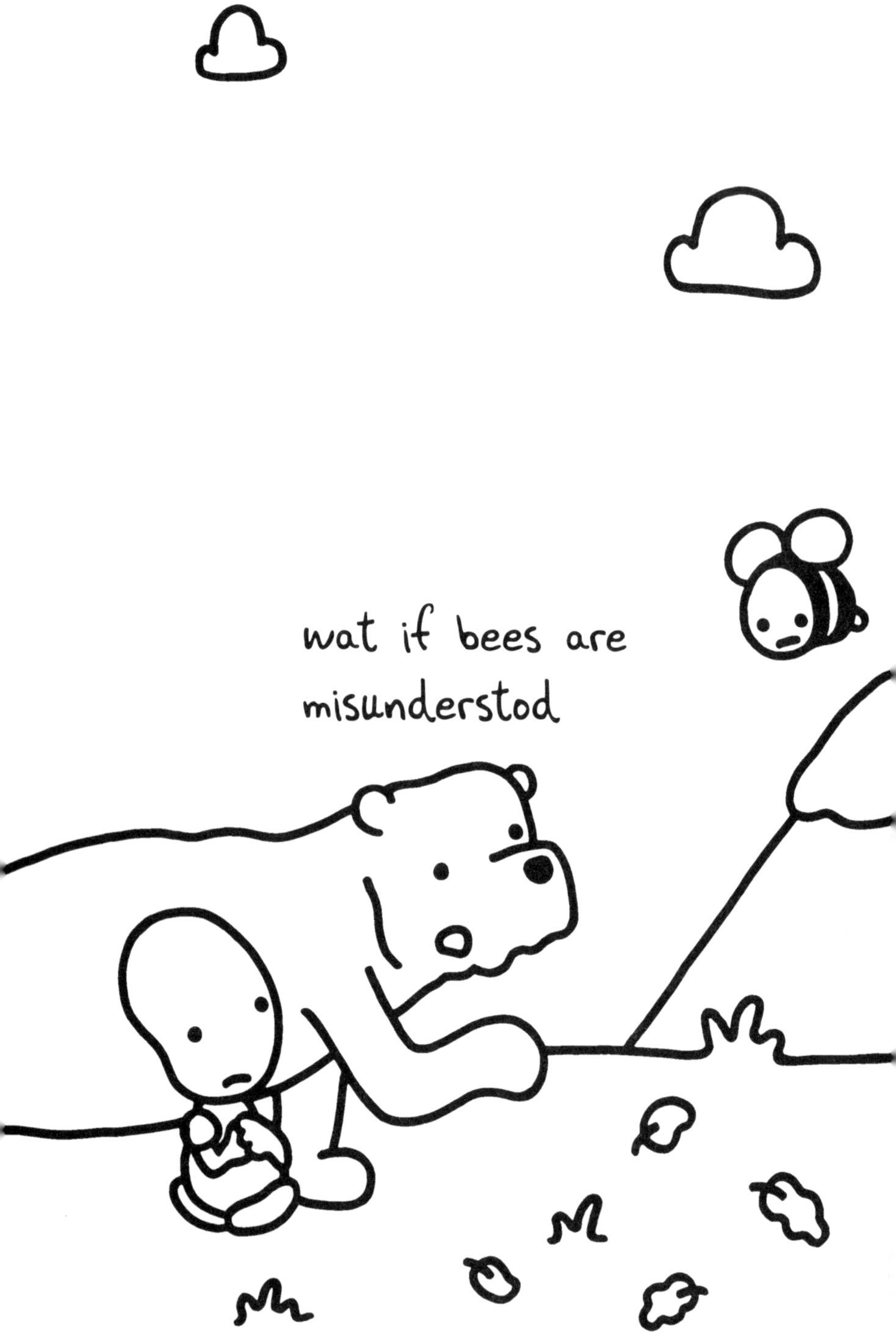
wat if bees are
misunderstod

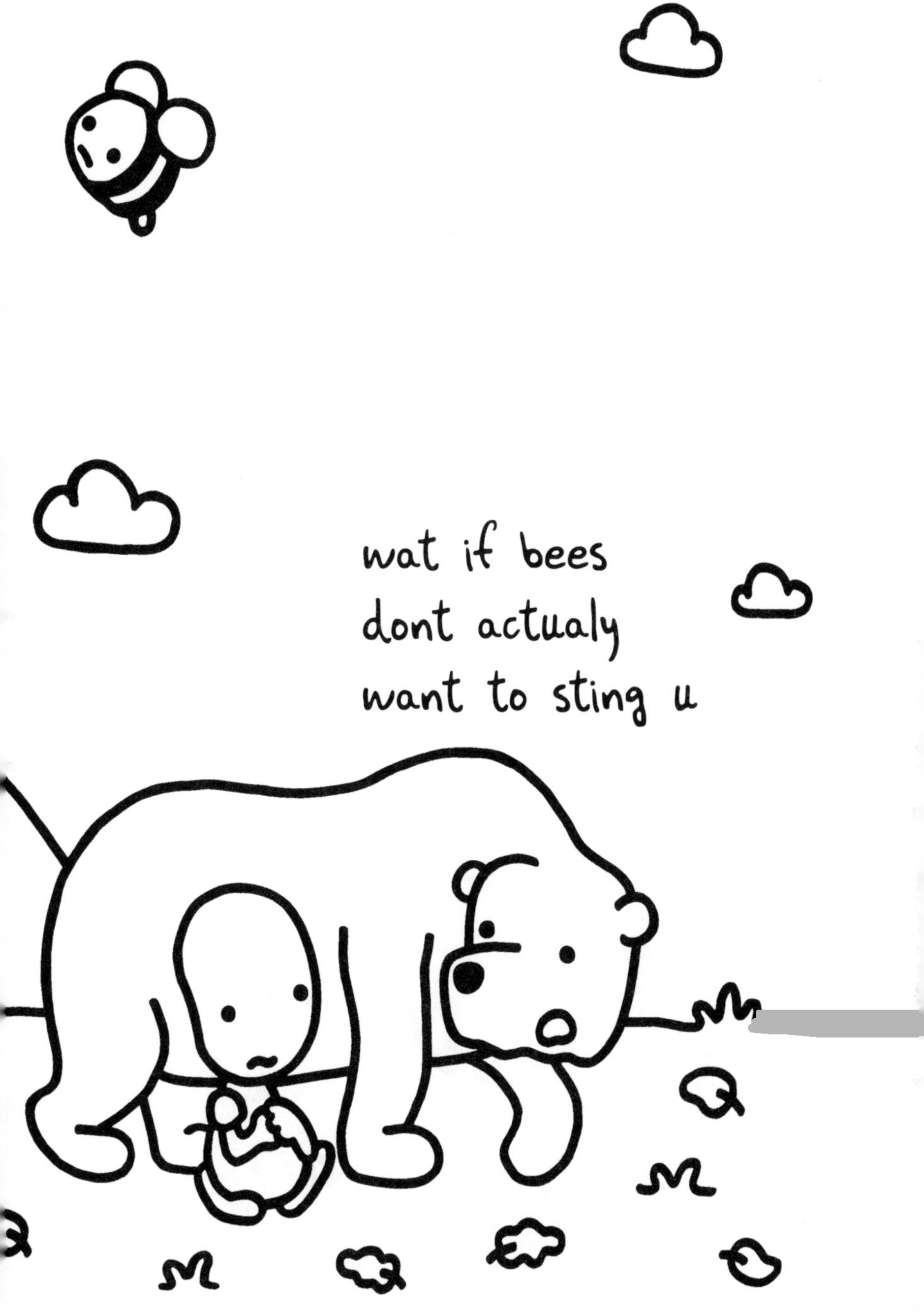
wat if bees
dont actualy
want to sting u

wat if bees just
want to die

but we dont want to die. do u know how hard it is to decide to sting sombody? it will hurt them realy bad! and it will make us die! so on one wing, we will die. but on the other wing, the rest of us will not die. in the moment, we get scared and the only thing we think of is protecting the ones we love. we dont want to die but if it means that it will make the rest of us not die, then we will do it. if i have to die, it will be because i love the ones i love so much that i would do anything to protect them. if i have to die, it will be worth it because it means the ones i love will not. they will get to continue to live. to love. to be happy. to experience sadness. if i am not there, i will be at peace knowing that i was the reason that they still are. do u understand? do u have any idea wat that kind of love feels like?

because to be honest, i dont think u do. ur the one who everyone is afraid of. not us bees. everybody is afraid of u and so u have nobody to give ur love to, and i think thats made u feel like life has been unfair to u. but still, even then, u've stayed positive.

uve spent ur whole life by urself, with urself, and so u have learned how to know urself and how to love ur life and u are truly happy with both those things. but i think that even in ur happy solitary life, u fear, more than anything else, that nobody will ever get to know the powerful love that you have grown within urself. its like having a secret that u cant share with anybody because nobody is willing to listen.

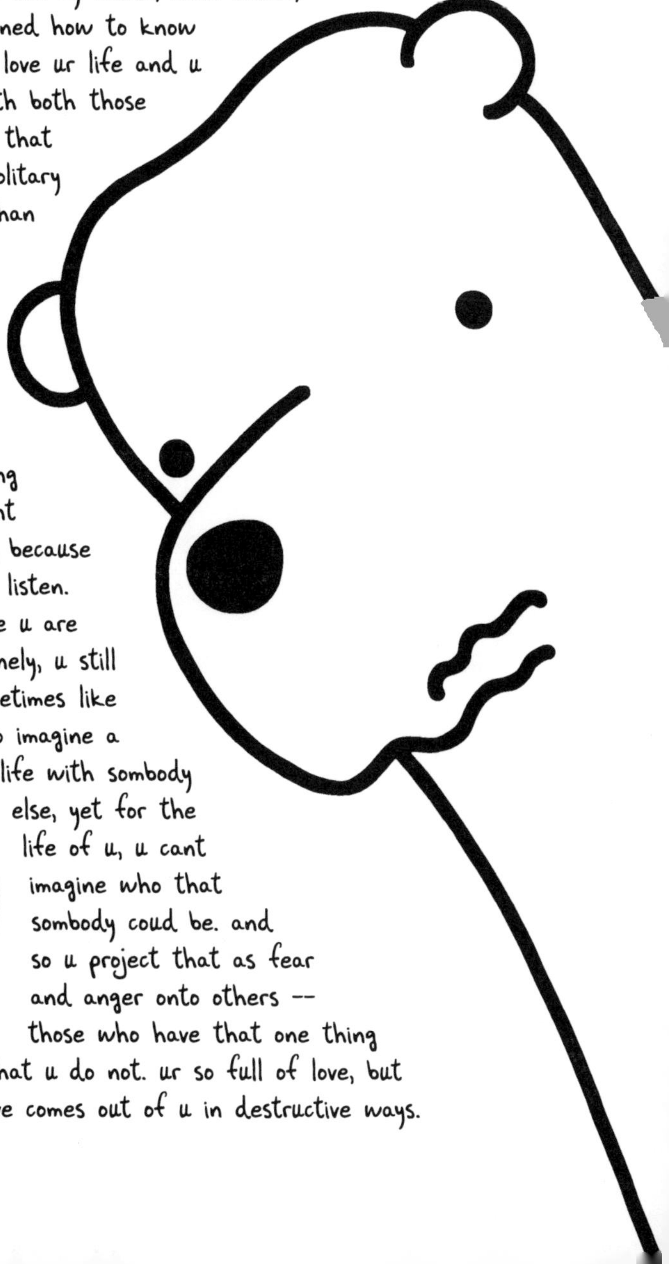

and so while u are not lonely, u still sometimes like to imagine a life with sombody else, yet for the life of u, u cant imagine who that sombody coud be. and so u project that as fear and anger onto others -- those who have that one thing that u do not. ur so full of love, but all ur love comes out of u in destructive ways.

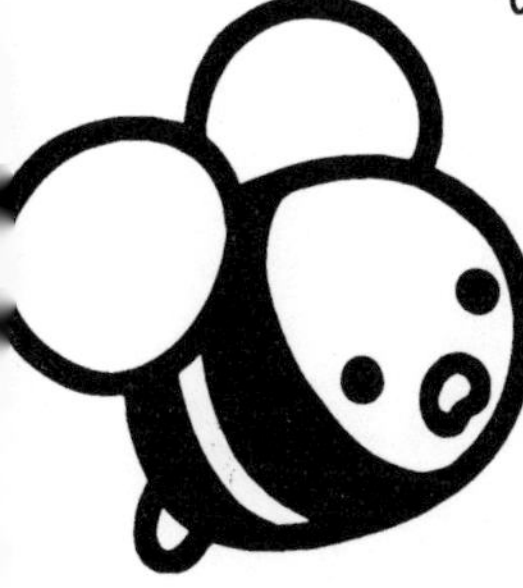

wee!
im free!

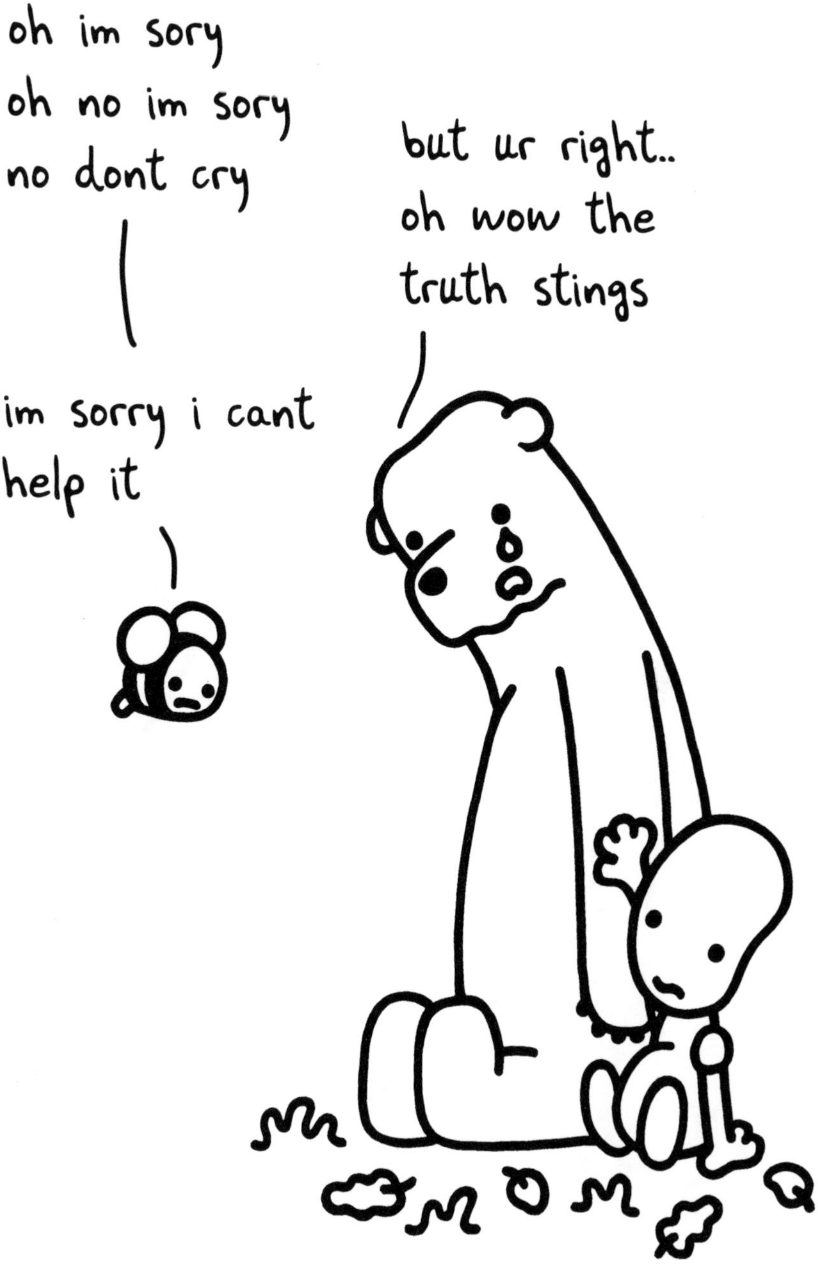
oh im sory
oh no im sory
no dont cry
but ur right..
oh wow the
truth stings
im sorry i cant
help it

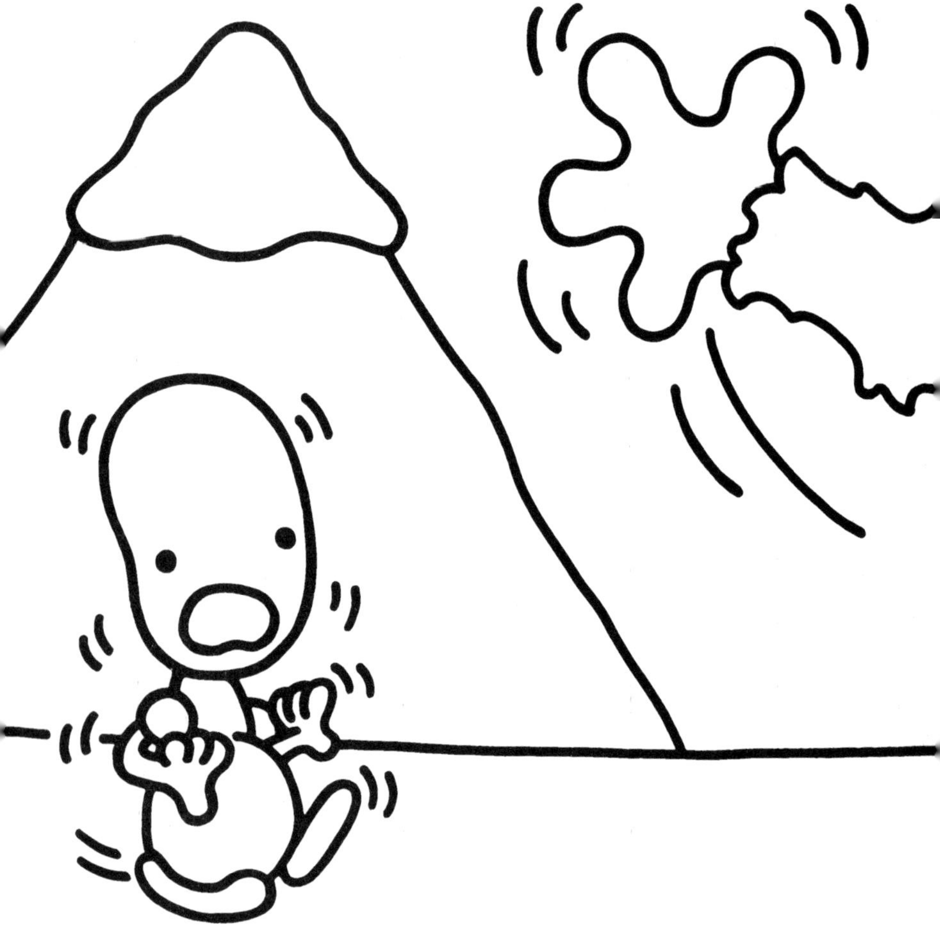

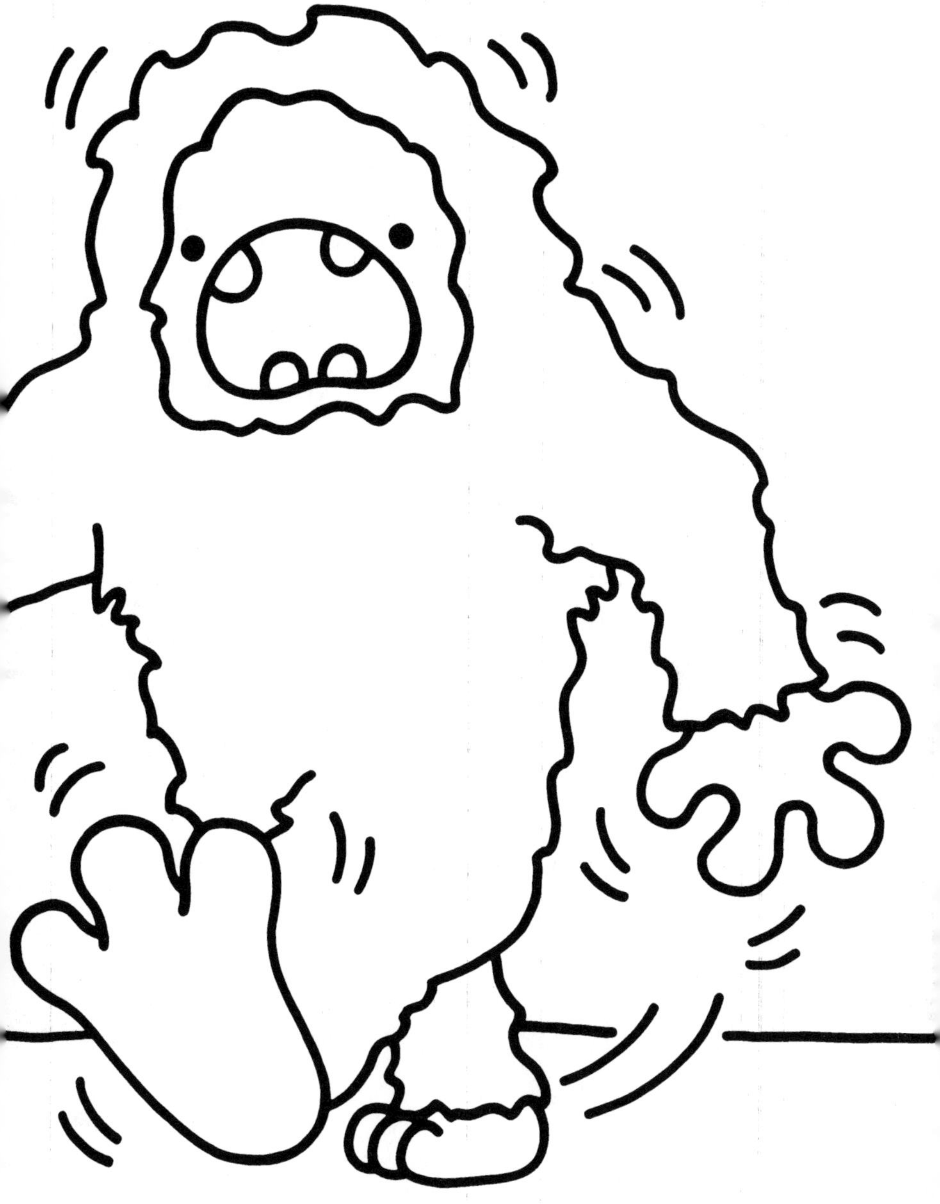

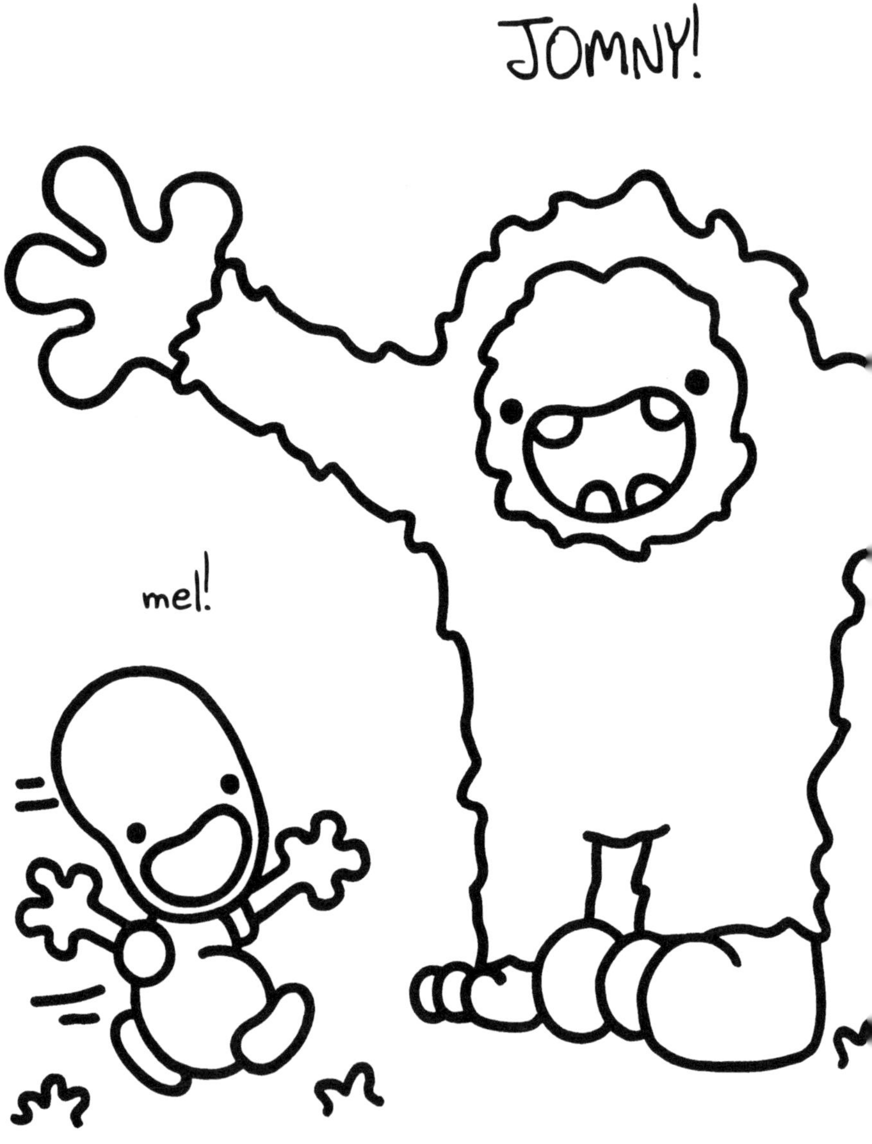
JOMNY!
me!

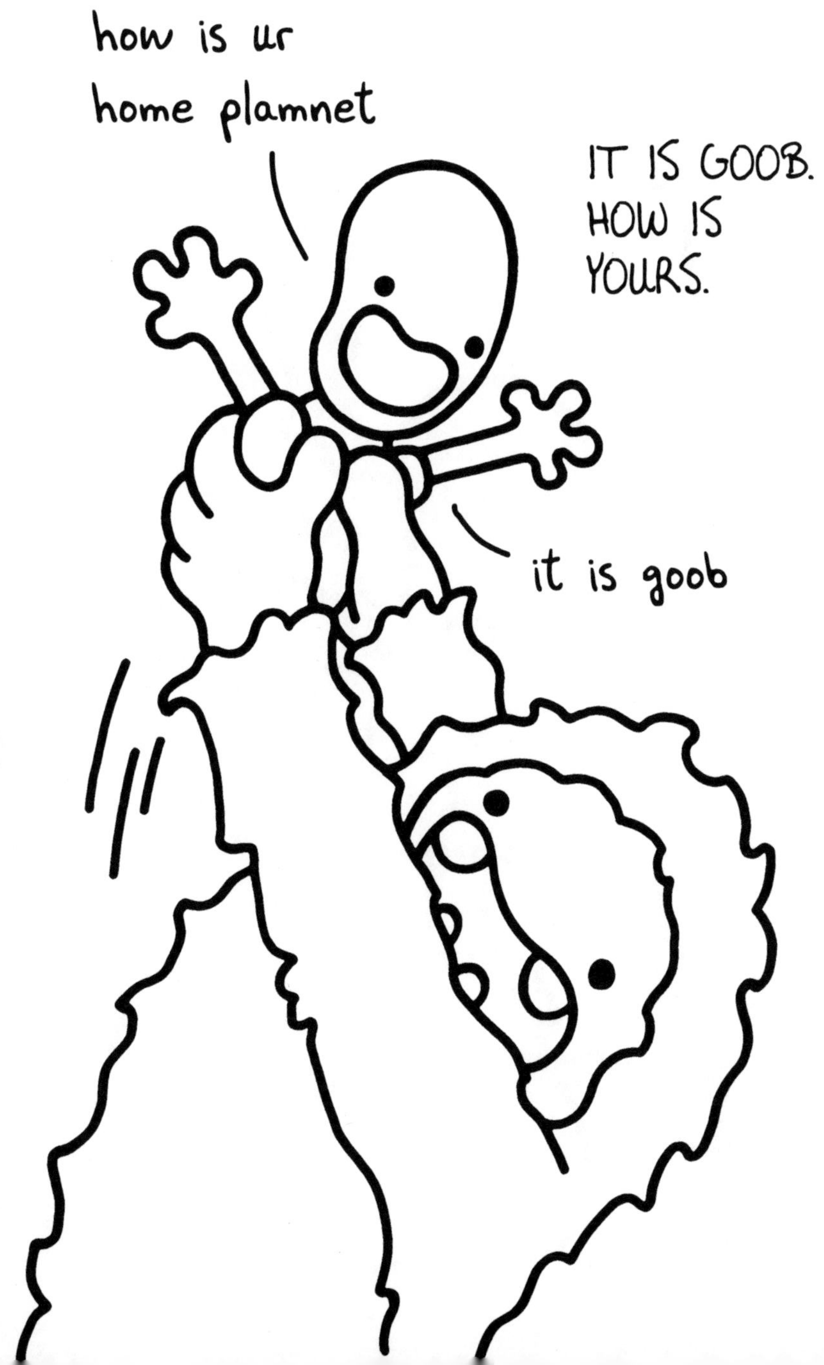
how is ur
home plamnet
IT IS GOOB.
HOW IS
YOURS.
it is goob

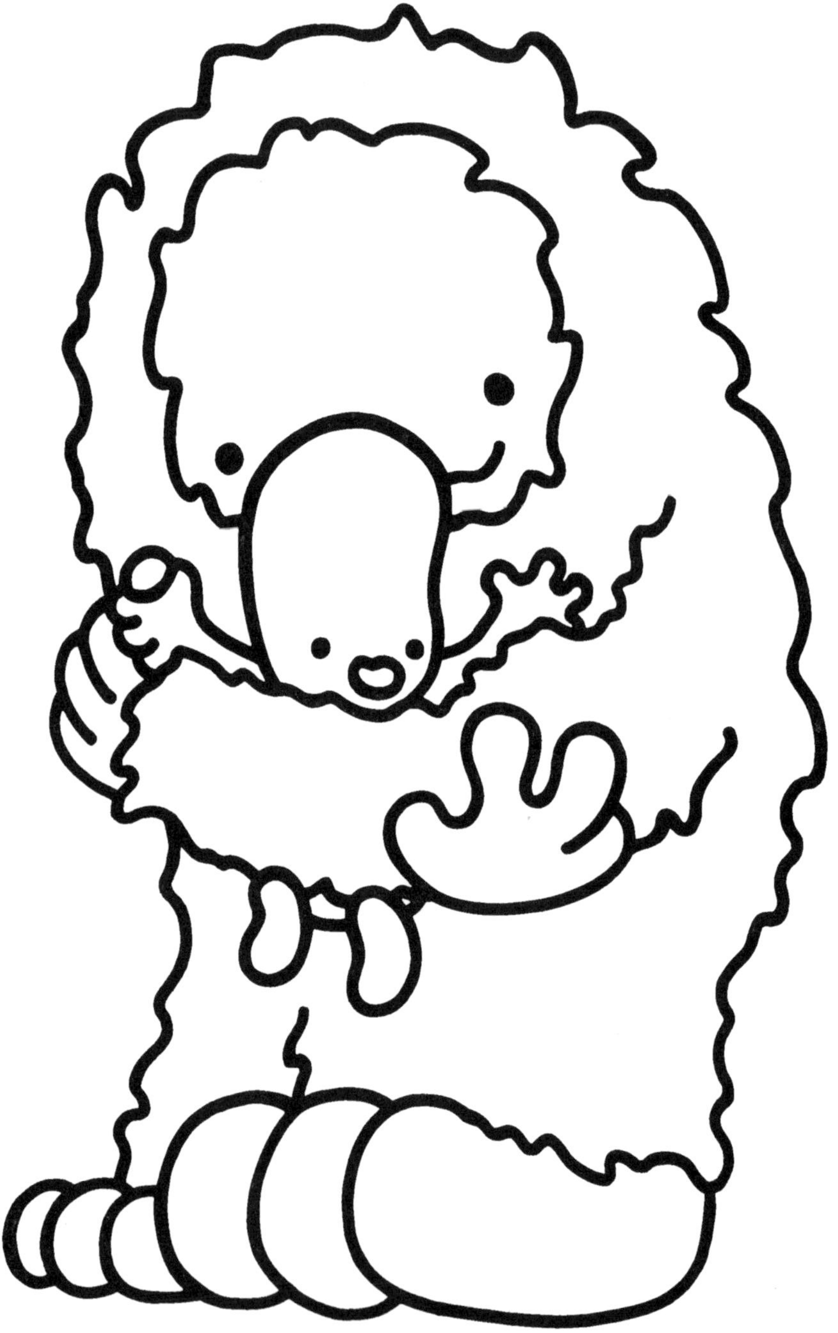

when two aliebns
fimd each other in a
strange place, it feels
a litle more like home

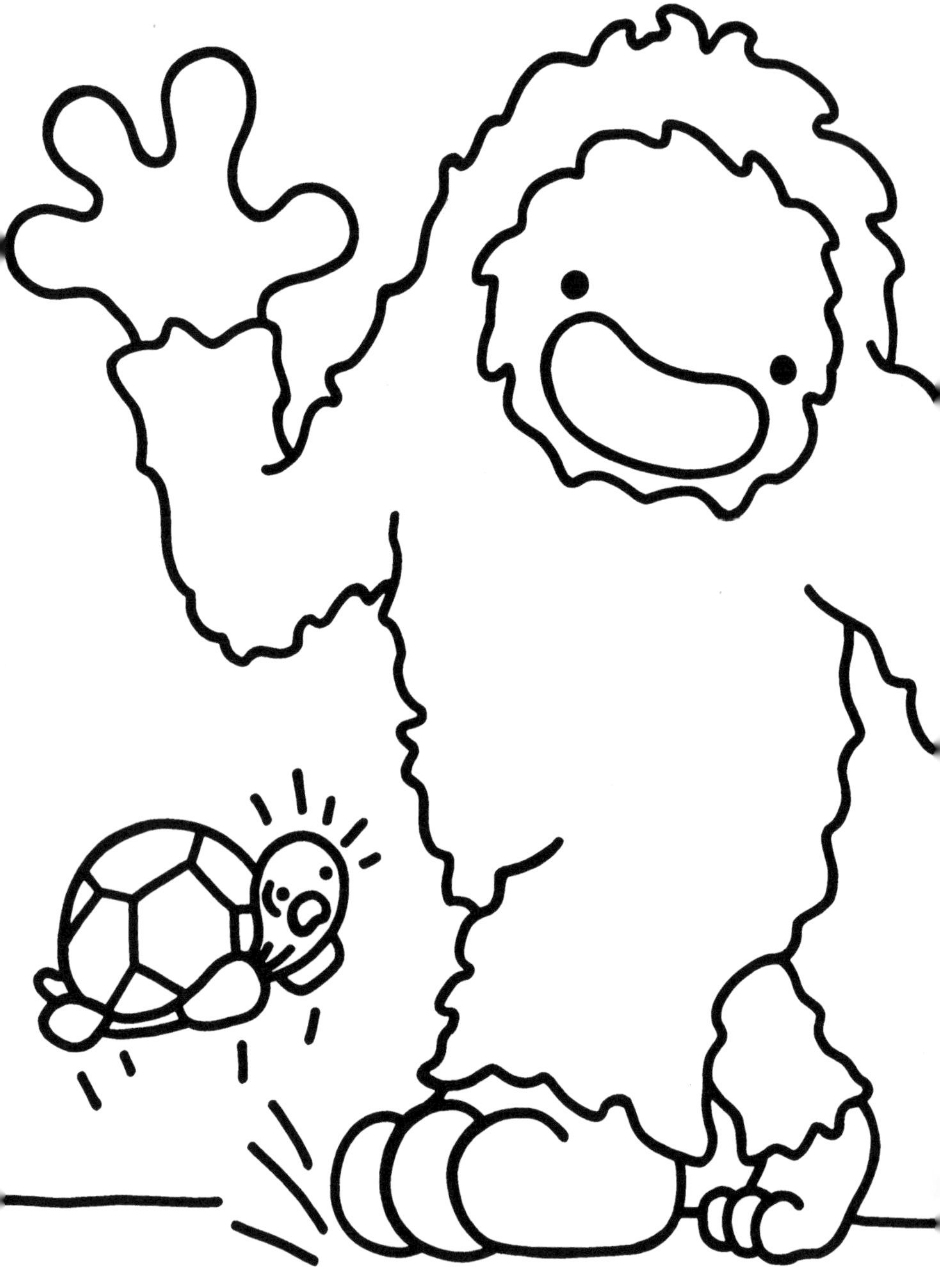

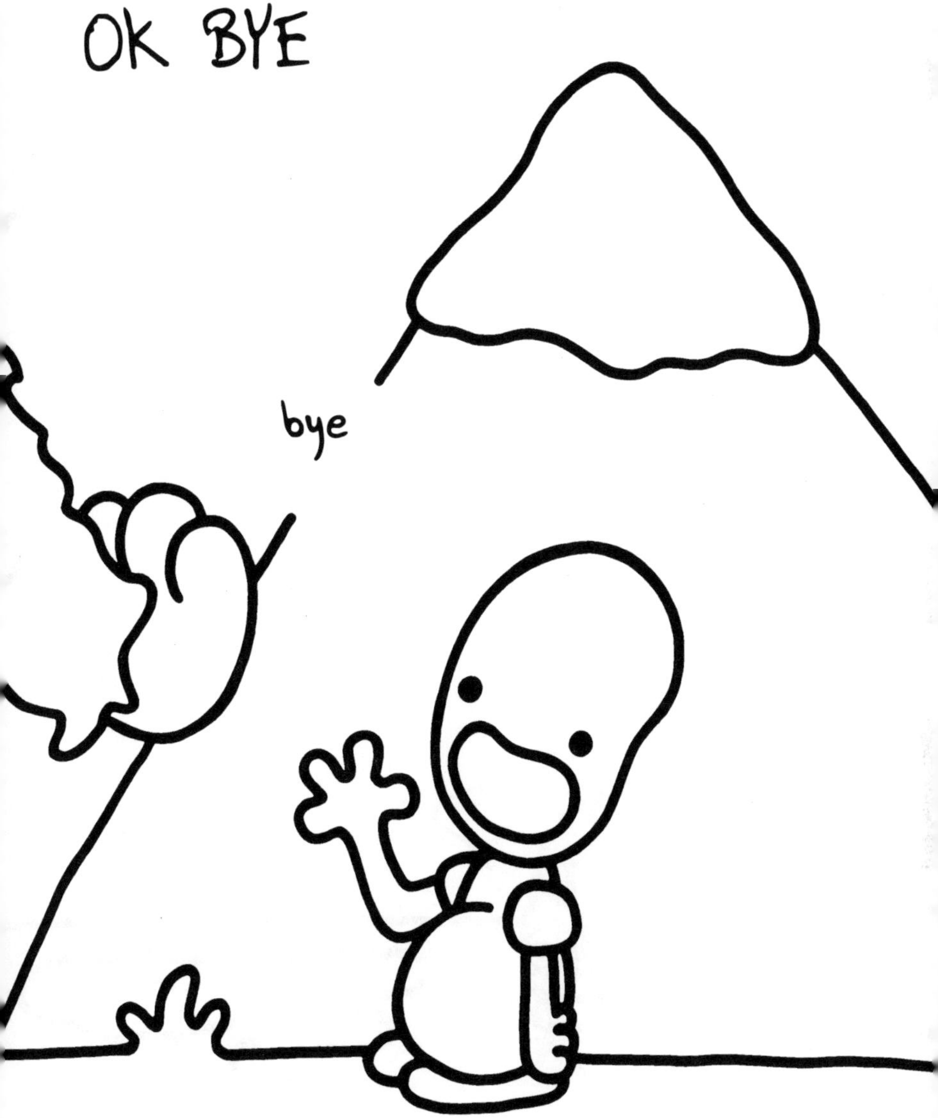
OK BYE
bye

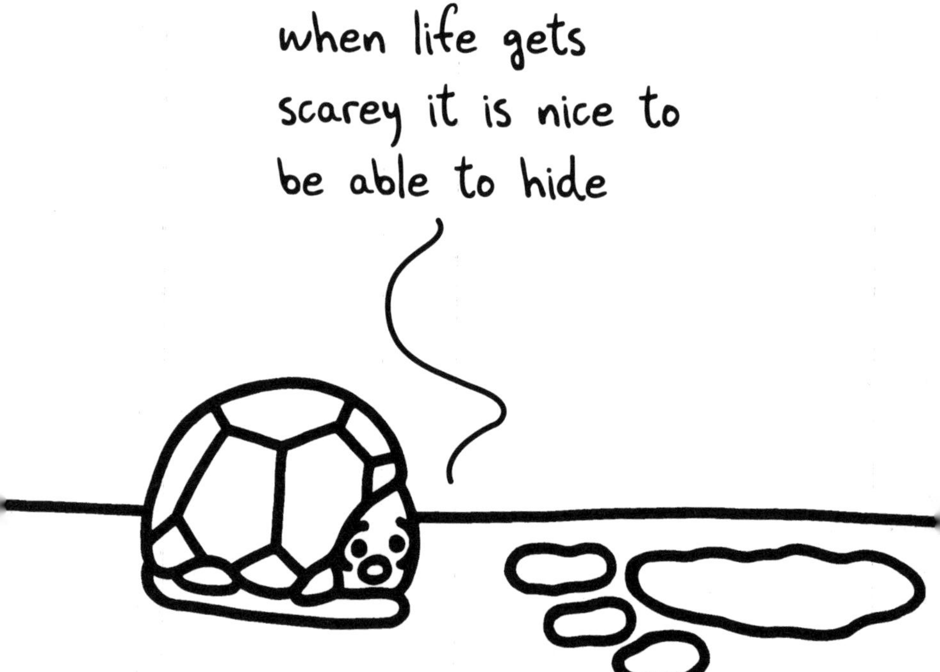
when life gets scarey it is nice to be able to hide

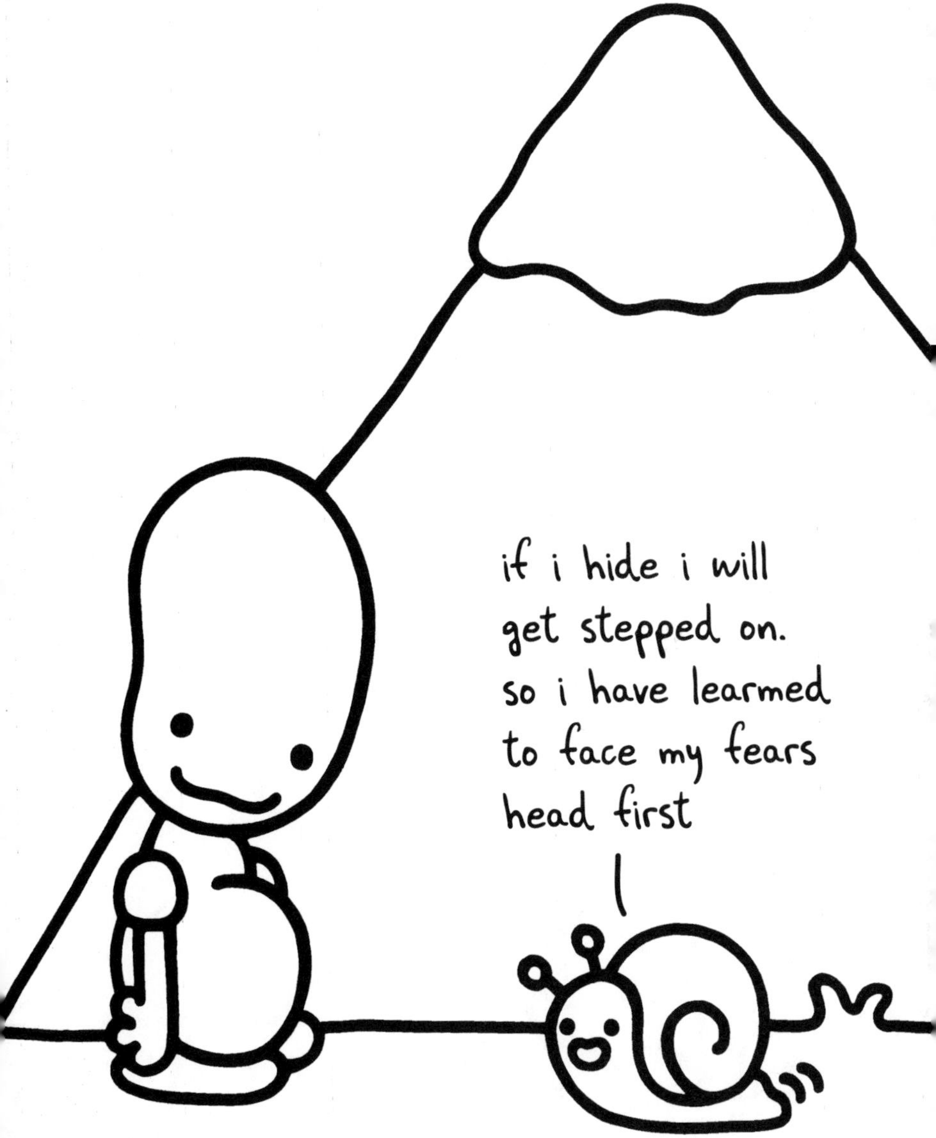
if i hide i will
get stepped on.
so i have learmed
to face my fears
head first

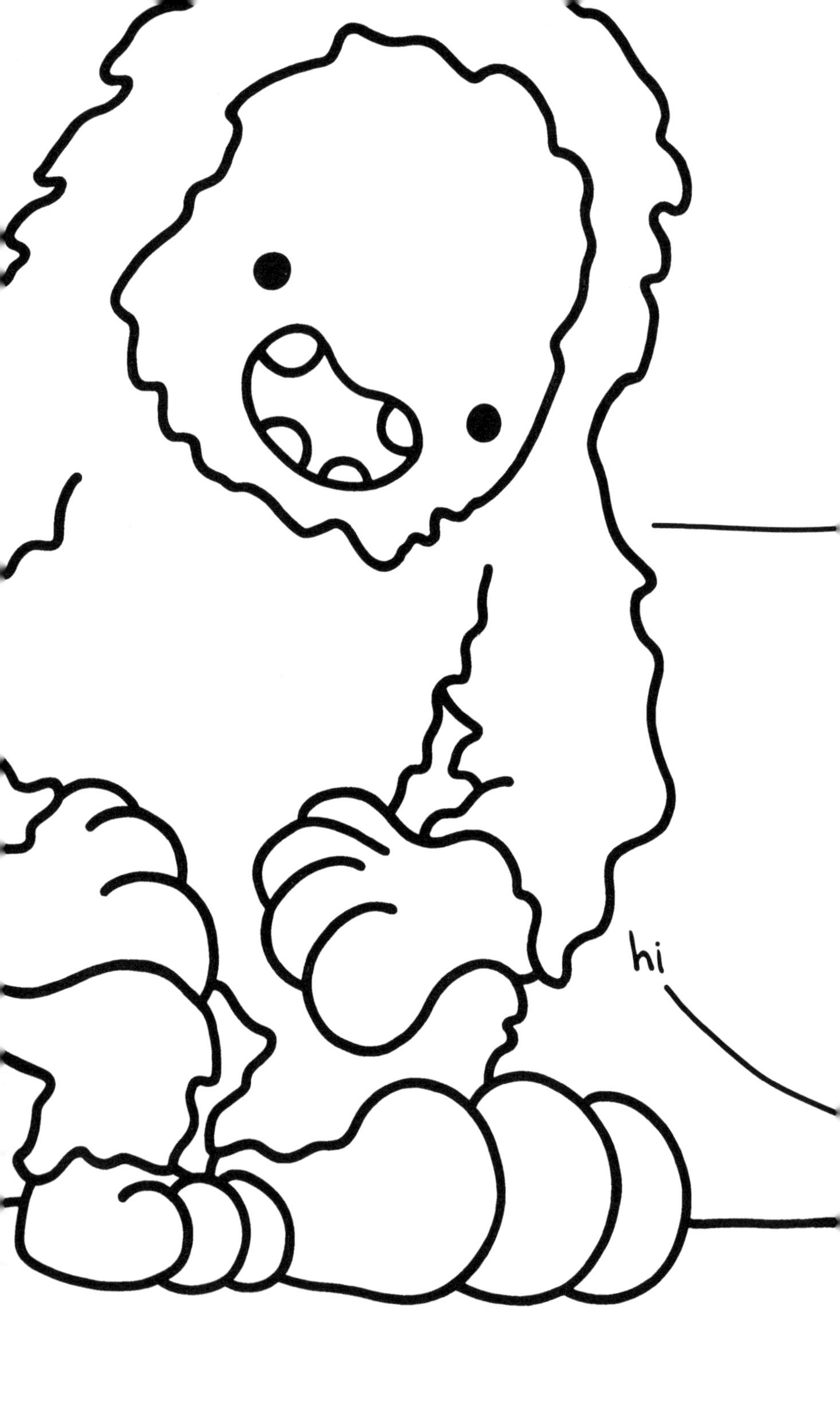
hi

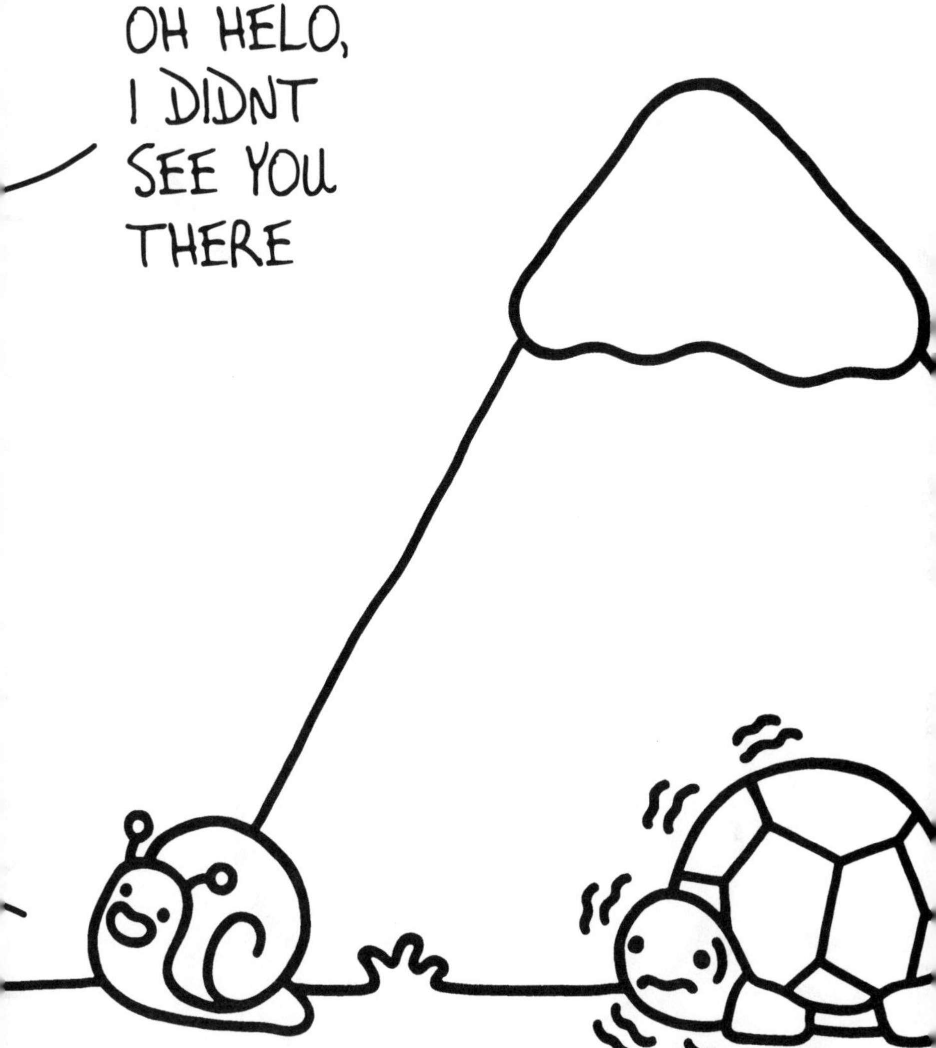
OH HELO, I DIDNT SEE YOU THERE

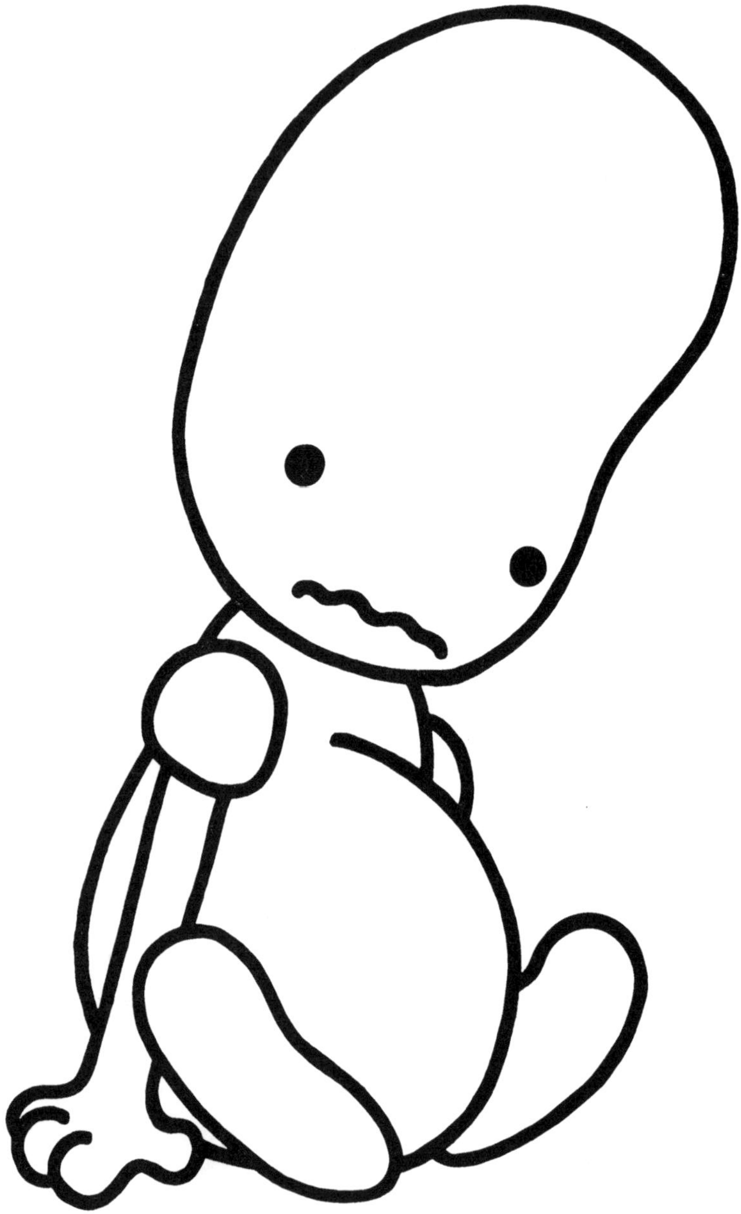

every night i have the same nightmare..
that sombody is goimg to cut me open
and lobotomize me. in that same dream
my heart has been set on fire. i think
it just means i am afraid of dying

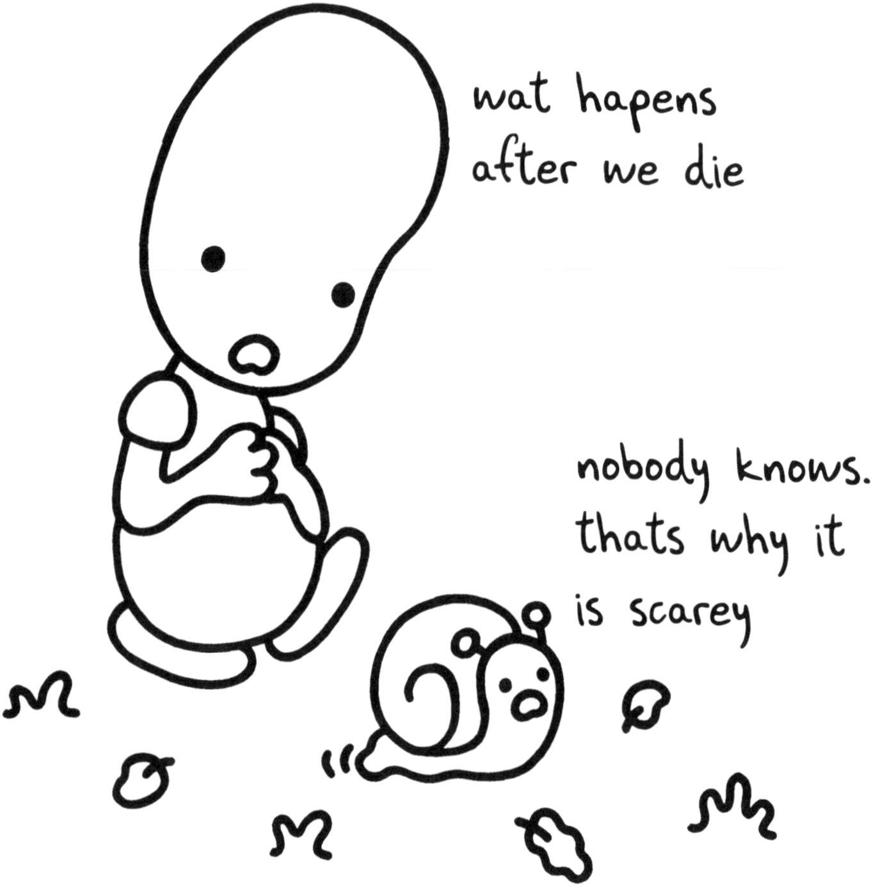
wat hapens after we die
nobody knows. thats why it is scarey

maybe the
reason why we
dont know is
becuase it is so
wonderful that
nobody ever
thought to
turn back
aroumd to
tell us

maybe

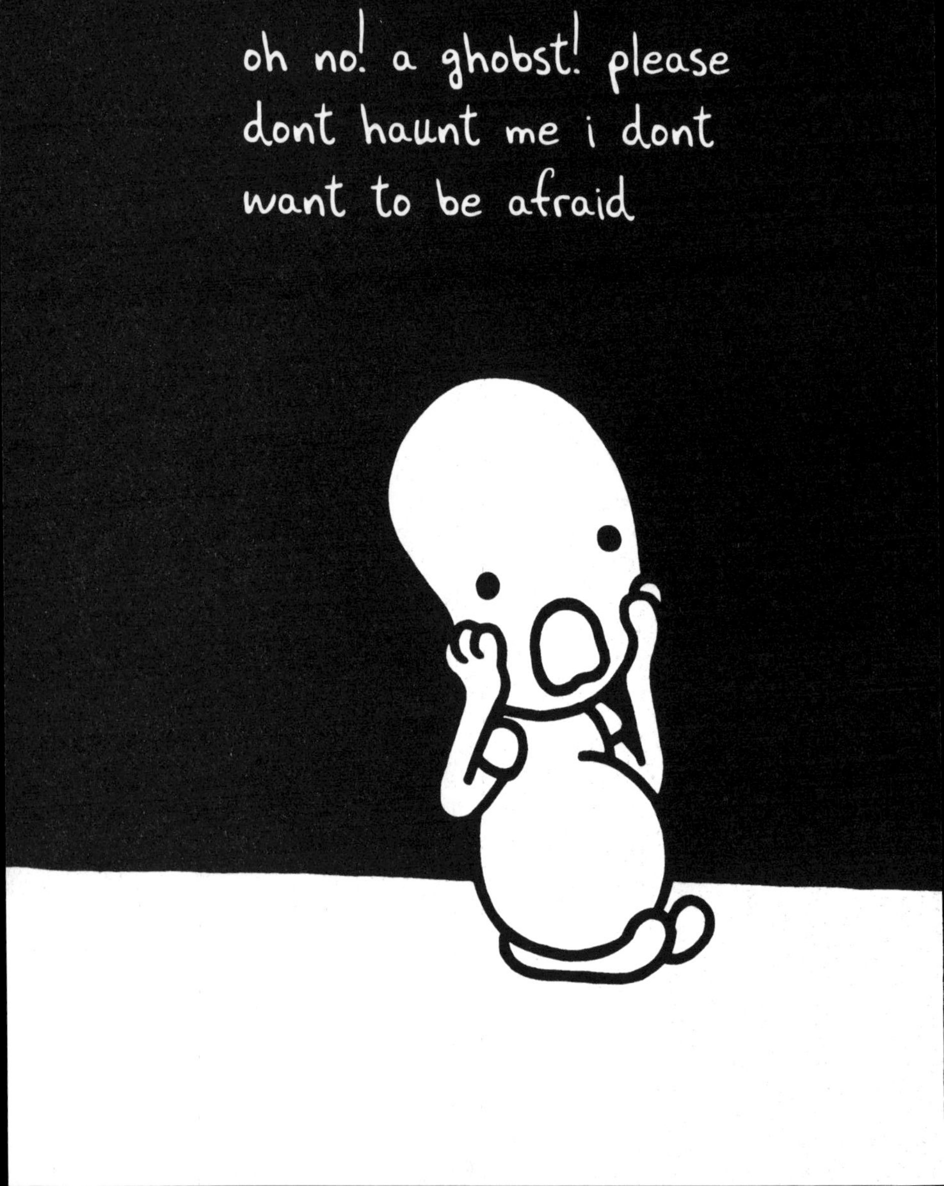
oh no! a ghobst! please dont haunt me i dont want to be afraid

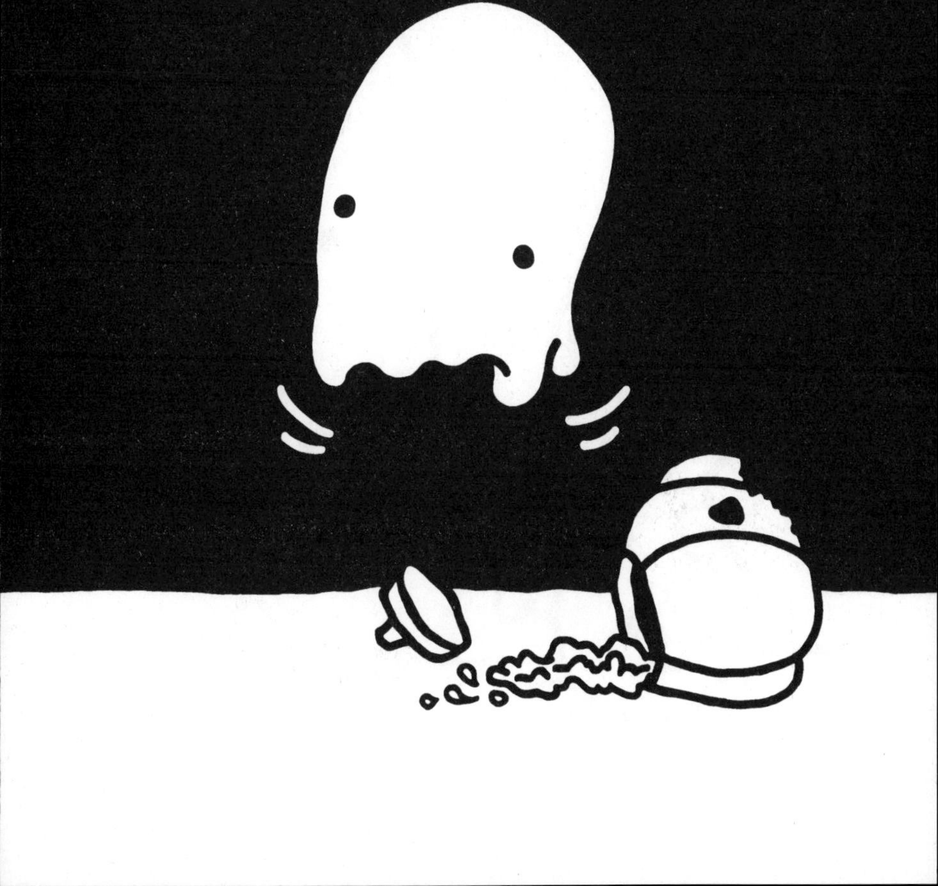

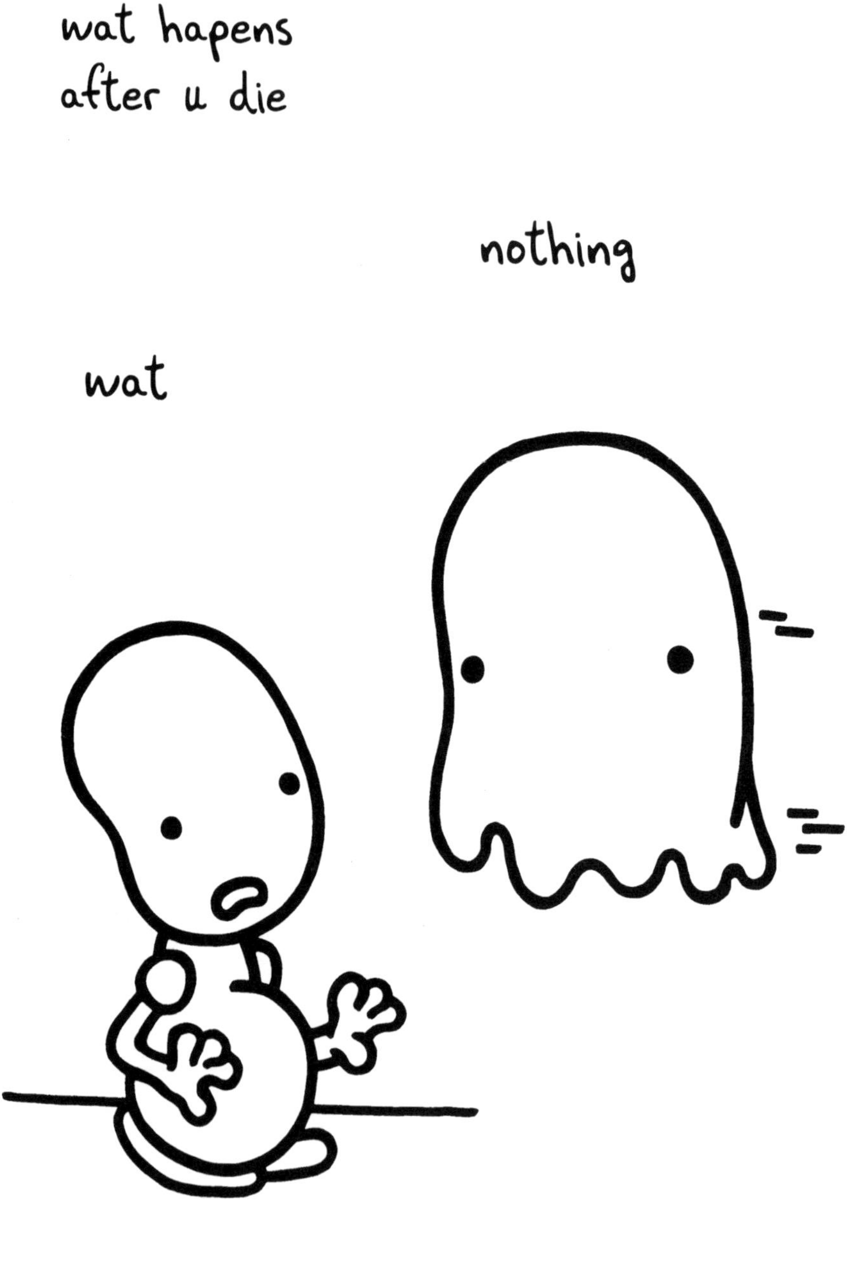
wat hapens
after u die
nothing
wat

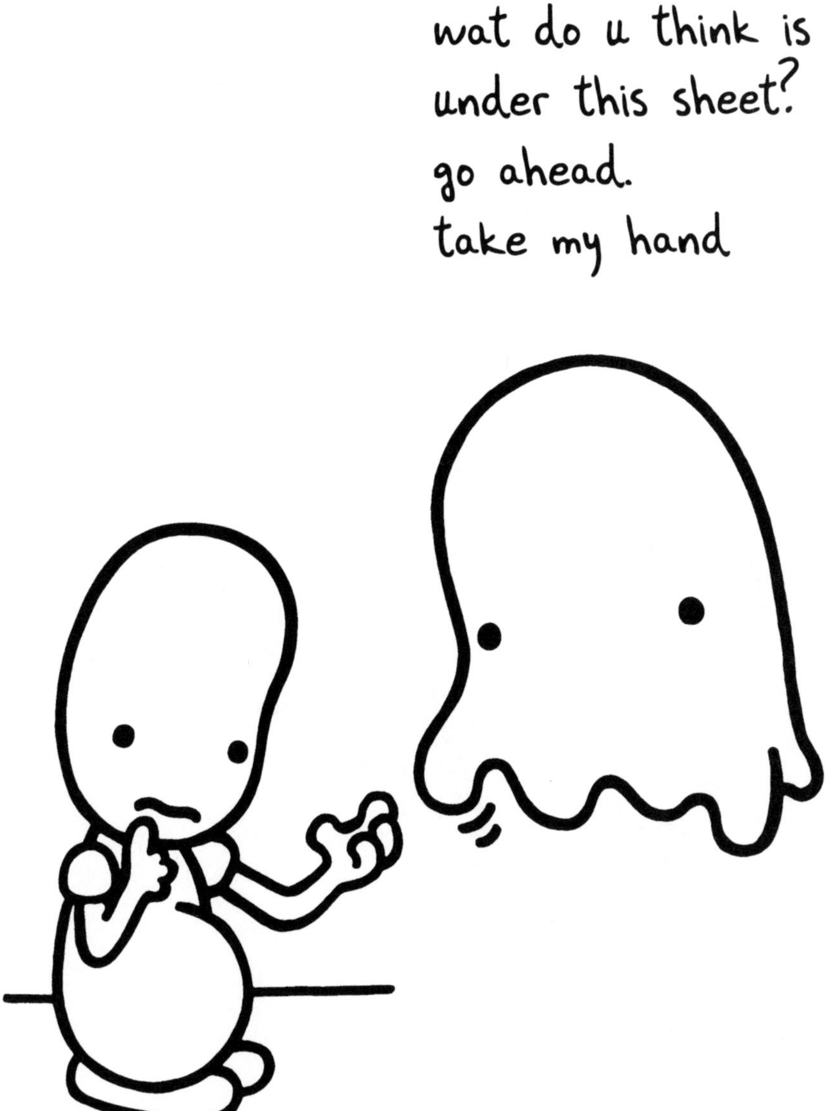
wat do u think is
under this sheet?
go ahead.
take my hand

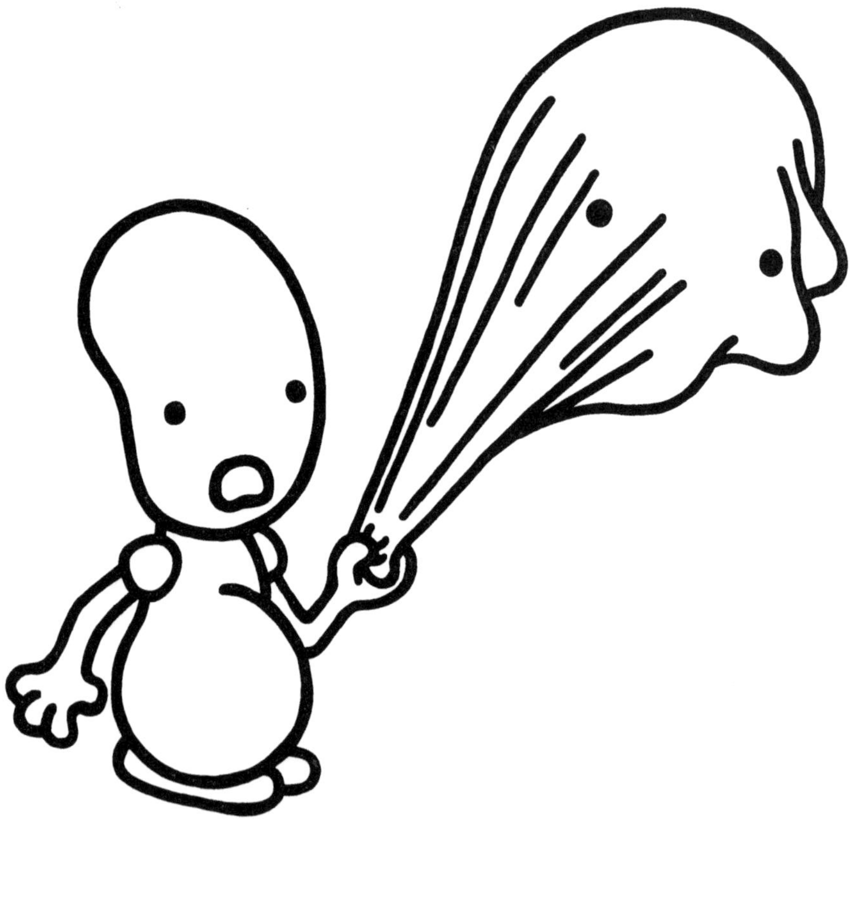

SEE?

IT IS JUST ME,
NOTHING.

HELLO AGAIN.

BEING AFRAID
OF DEATH IS
THE SAME AS
BEING AFRAID
OF NOTHING.

somhow i am not
comforted

BUT HOW CAN
YOU BE AFRAID OF
ME? I AM NOT MADE
OF ANYTHING. THERE
ARE NO SCARY THINGS
INSIDE ME. SEE?

now im afraid of

everything

WAIT, N-NO. PLEASE
DO NOT BE AFRAID.
CAN YOU JUST NOT
BE AFRAID AT ALL?

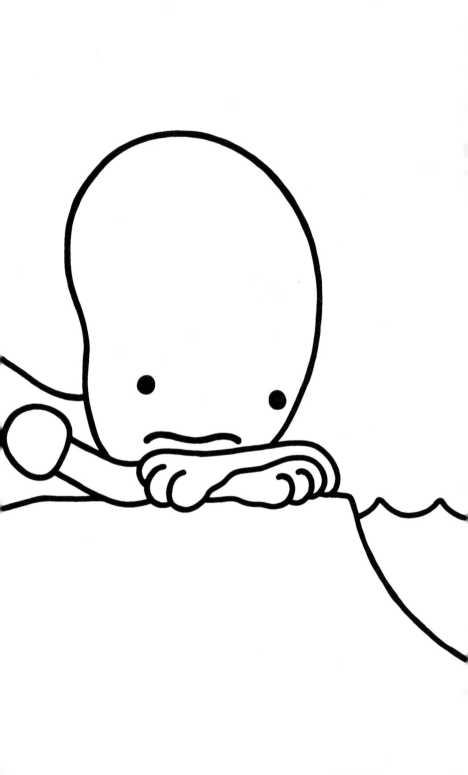

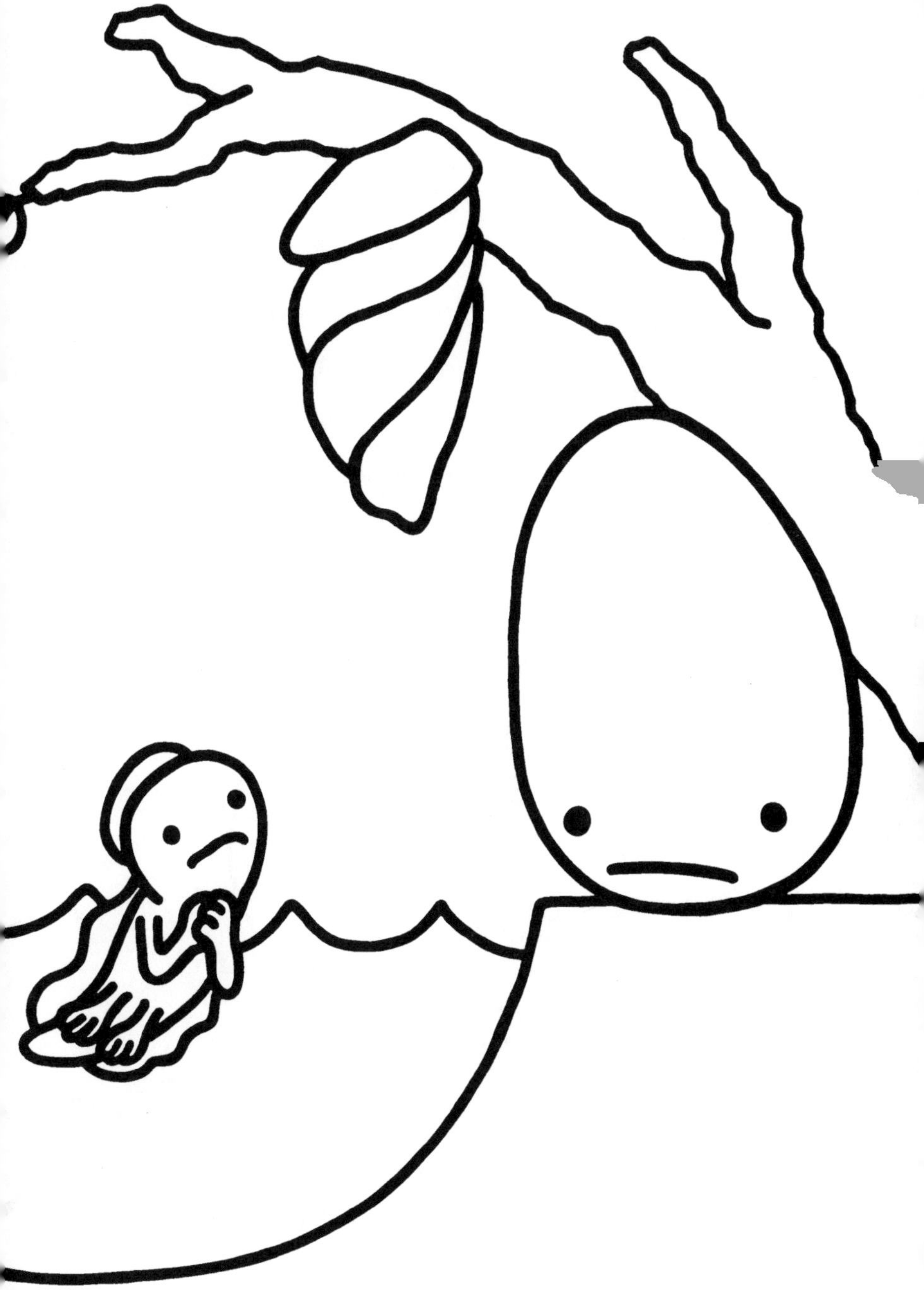

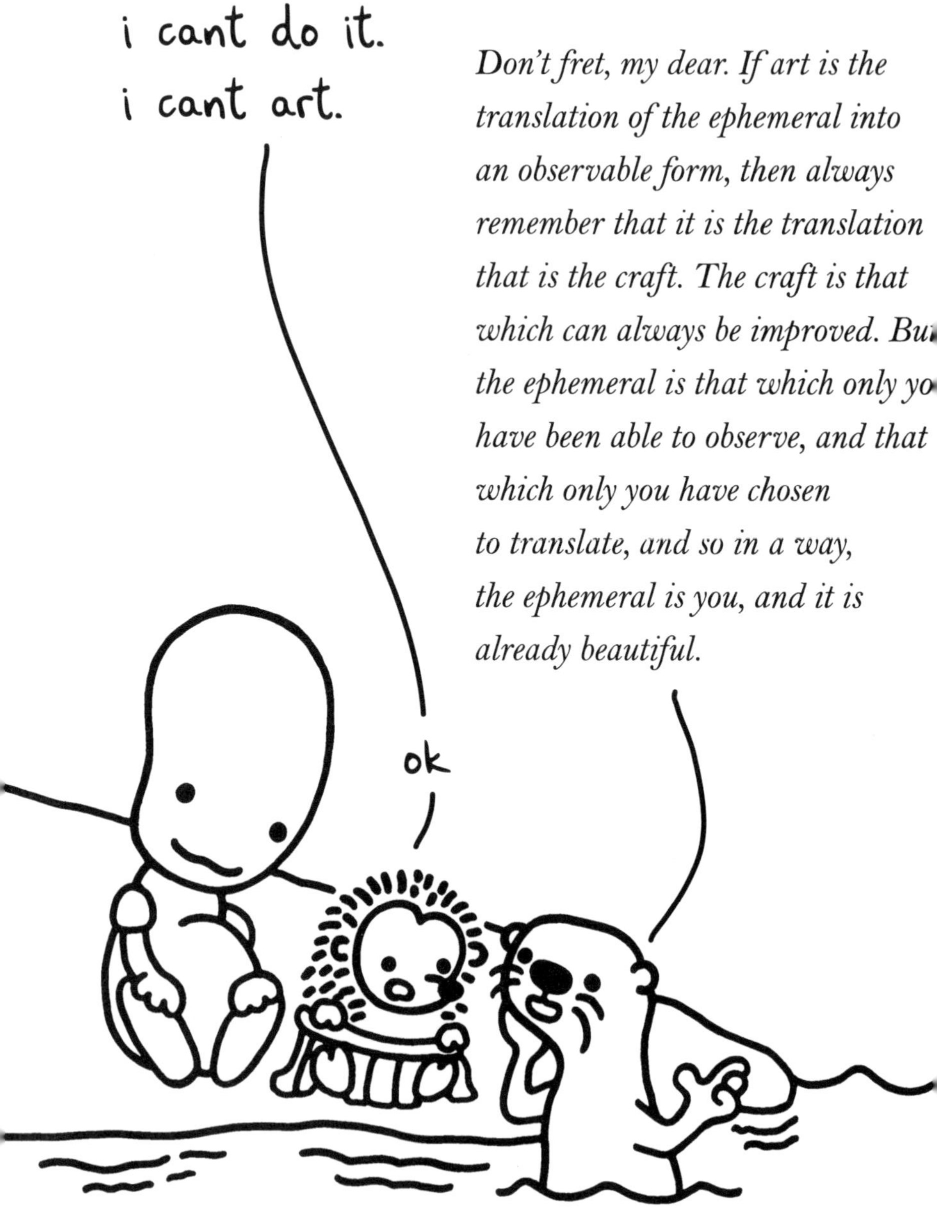
i cant do it. i cant art.
Don't fret, my dear. If art is the translation of the ephemeral into an observable form, then always remember that it is the translation that is the craft. The craft is that which can always be improved. Bu the ephemeral is that which only yo have been able to observe, and that which only you have chosen to translate, and so in a way, the ephemeral is you, and it is already beautiful.
ok

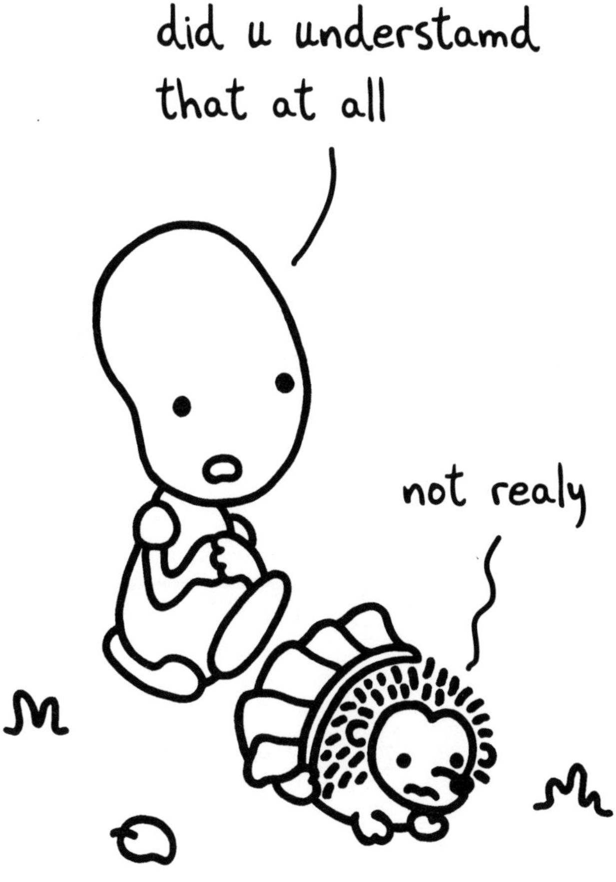
did u understamd
that at all
not realy

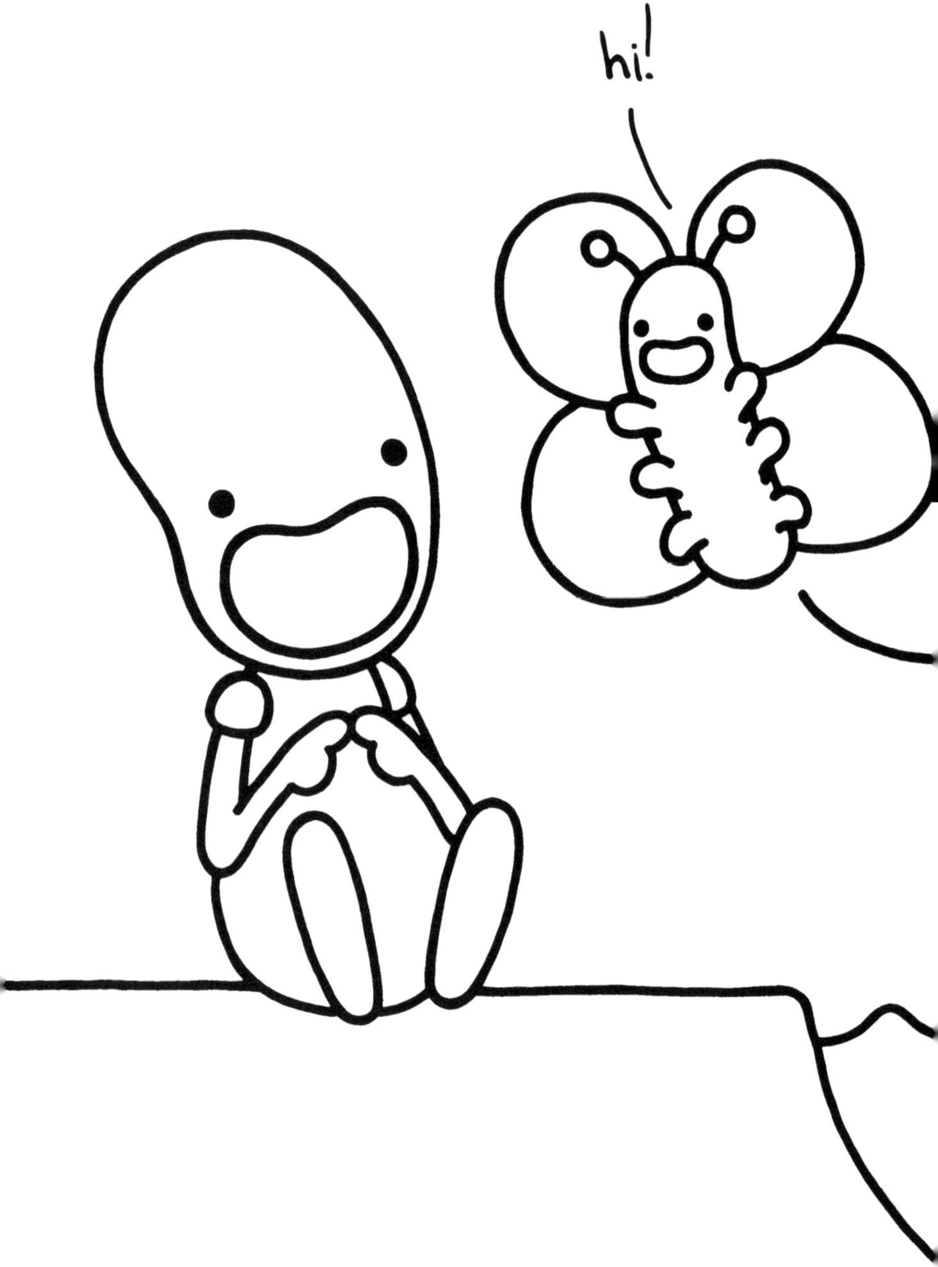
hi!

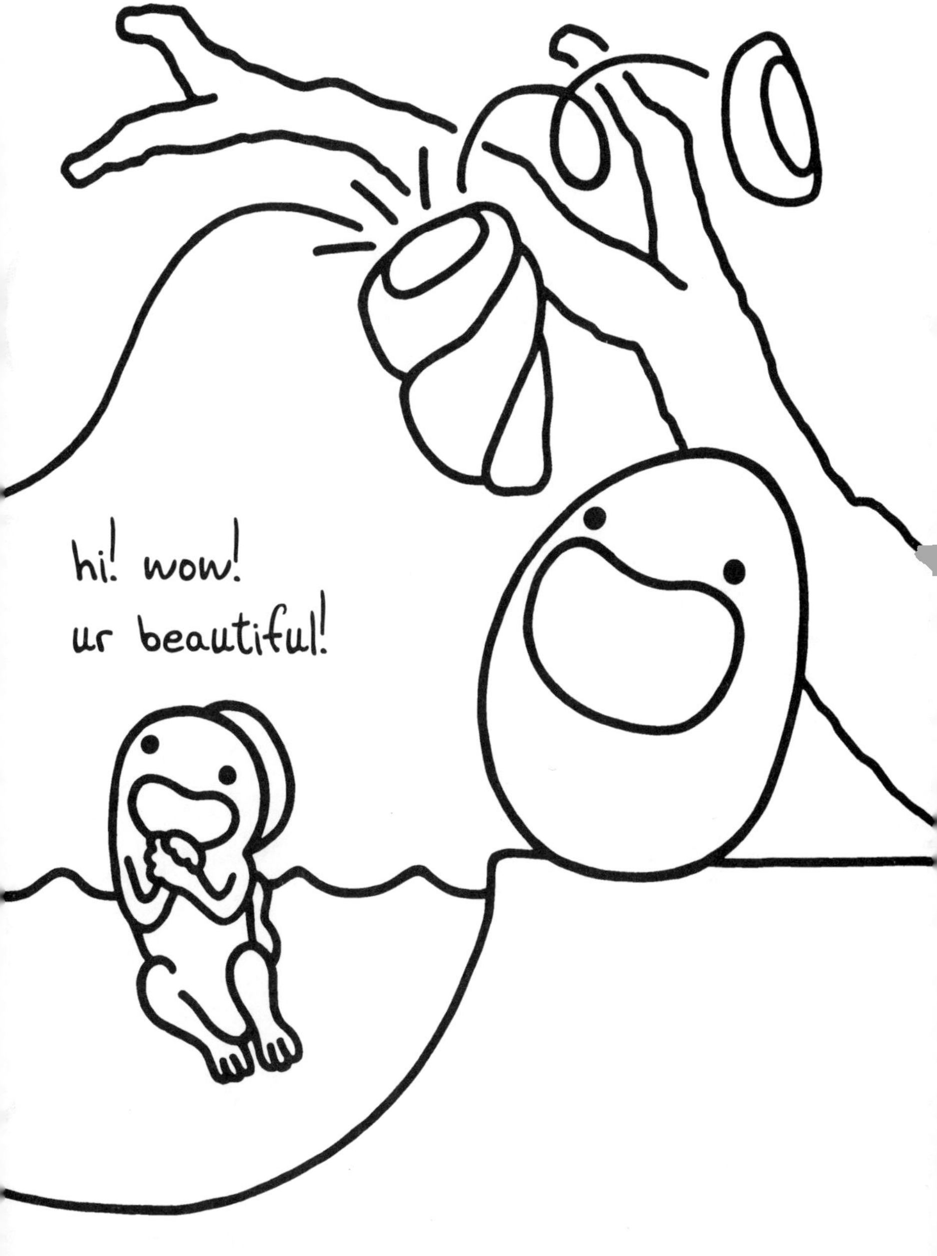
hi! wow!
ur beautiful!

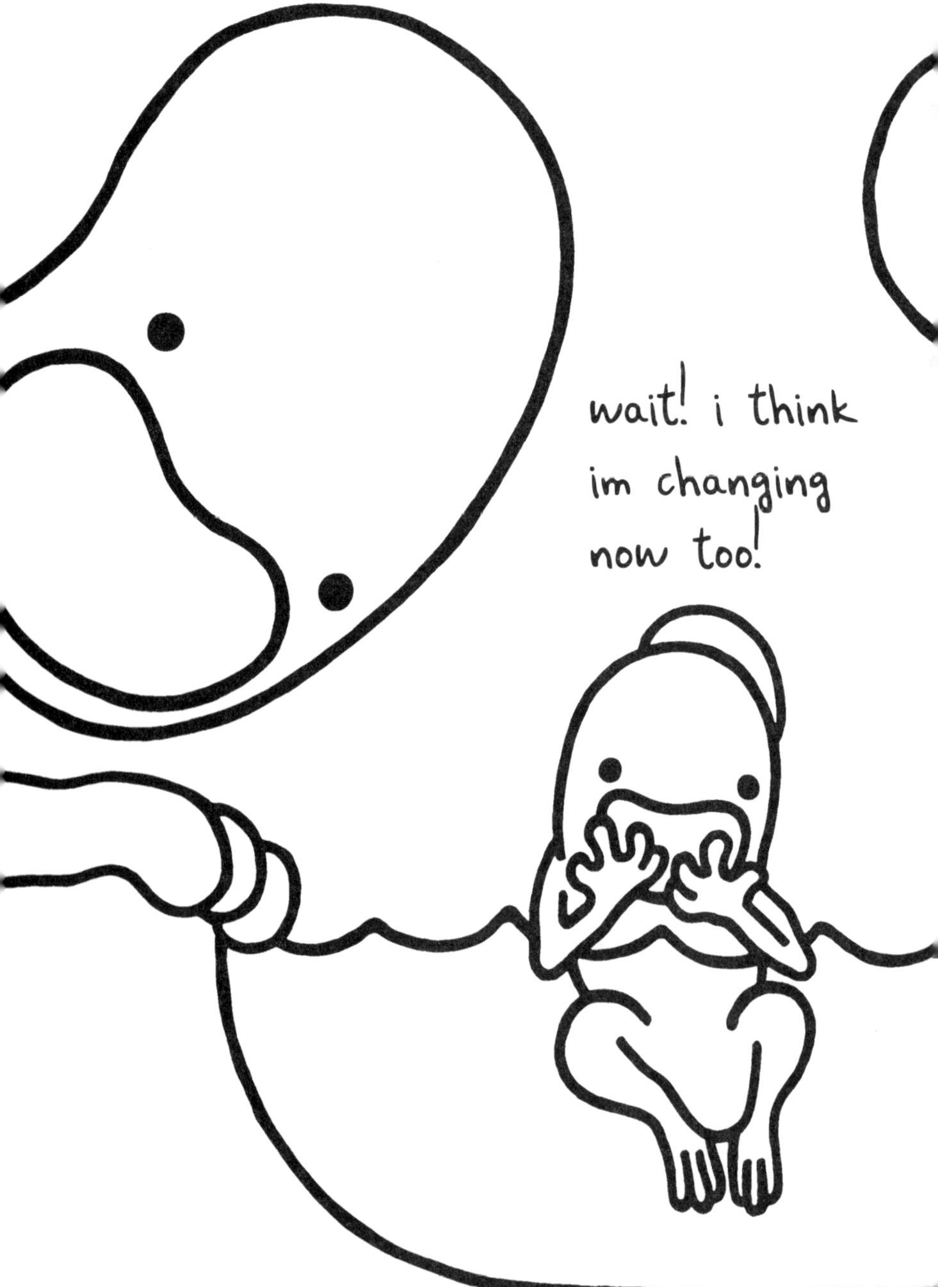
wait! i think
im changing
now too!

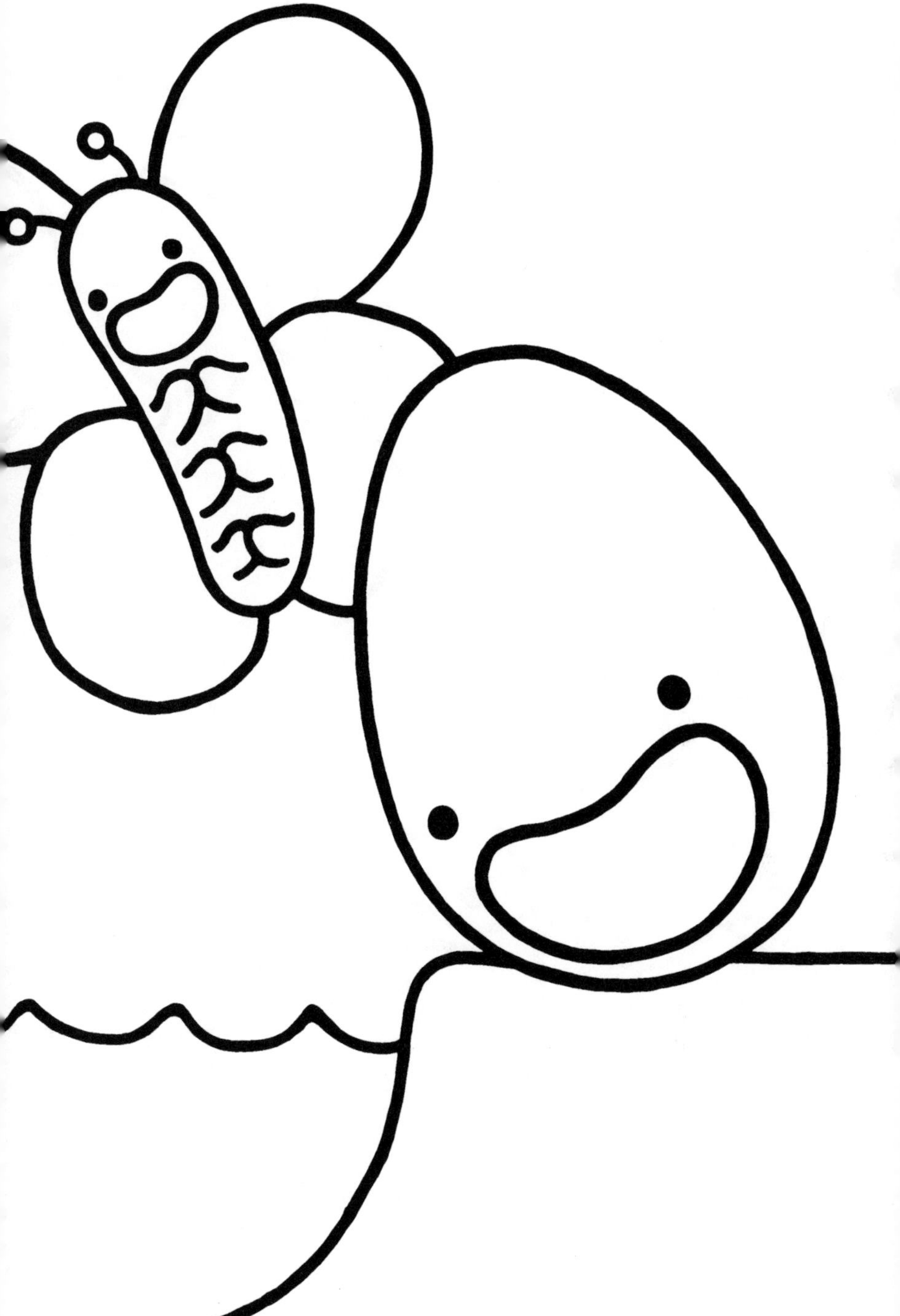

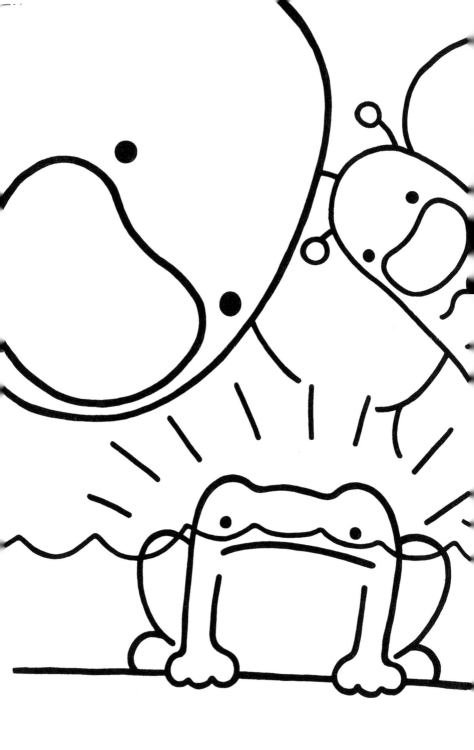

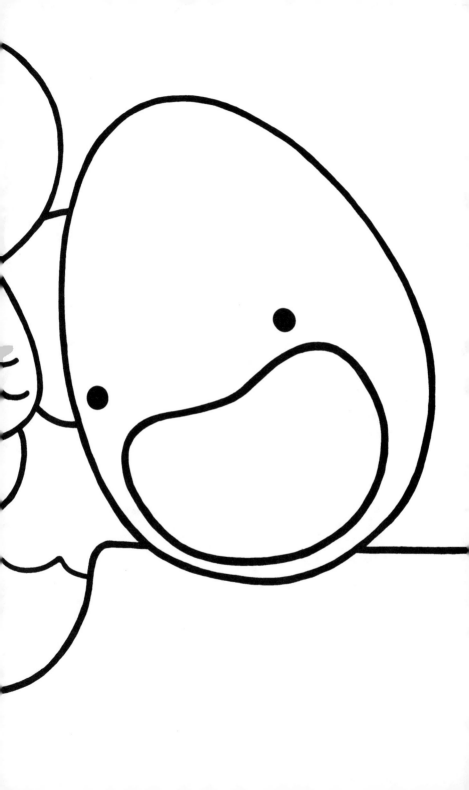

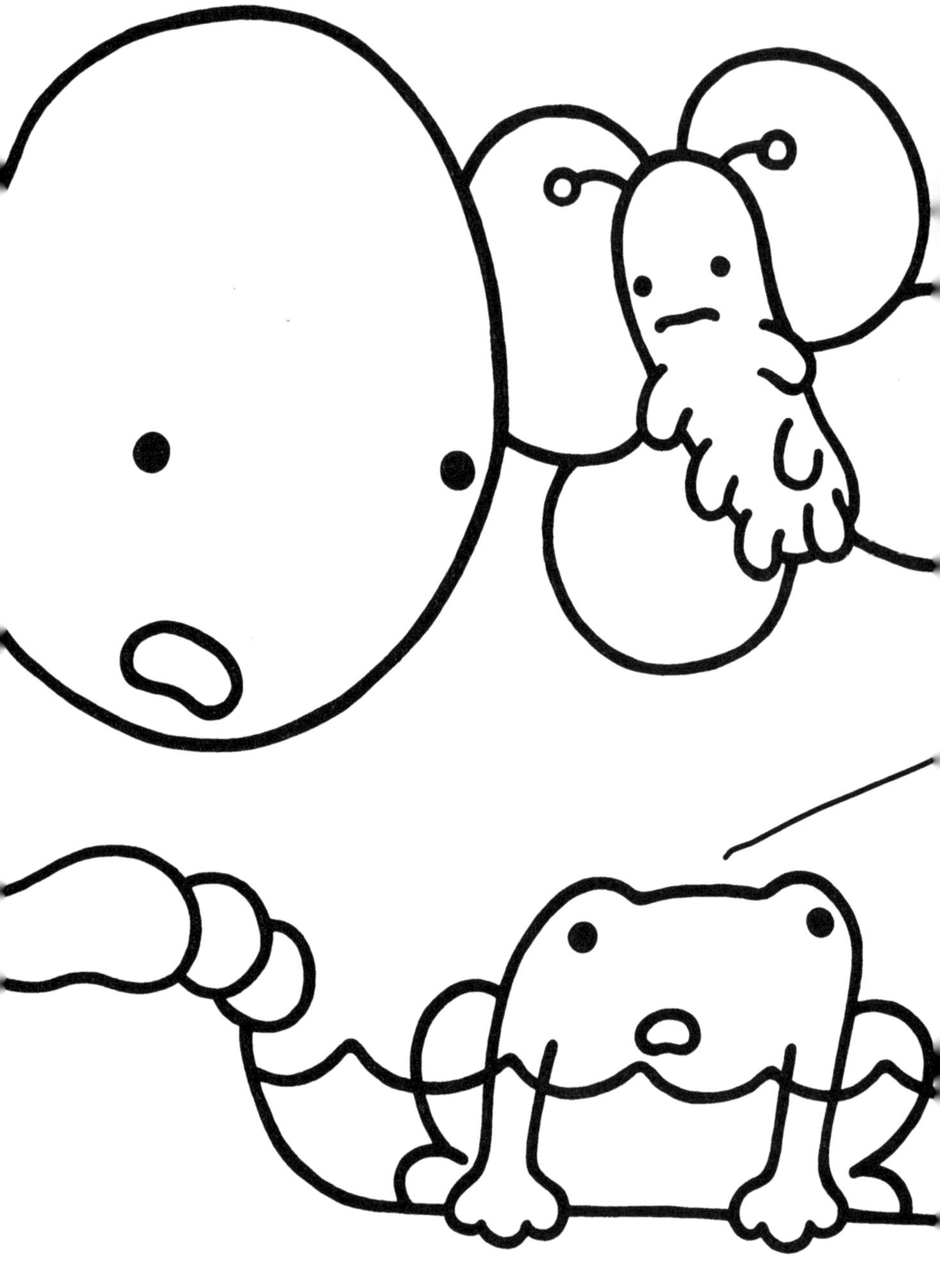

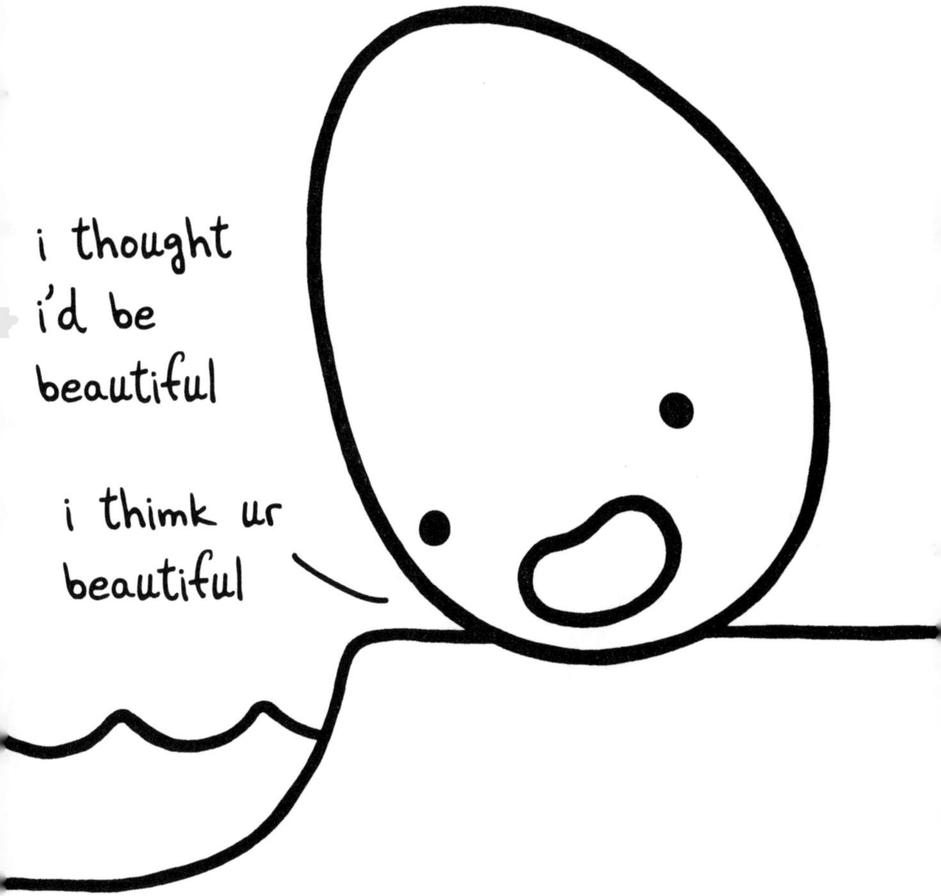
i thought
i'd be
beautiful
i thimk ur
beautiful

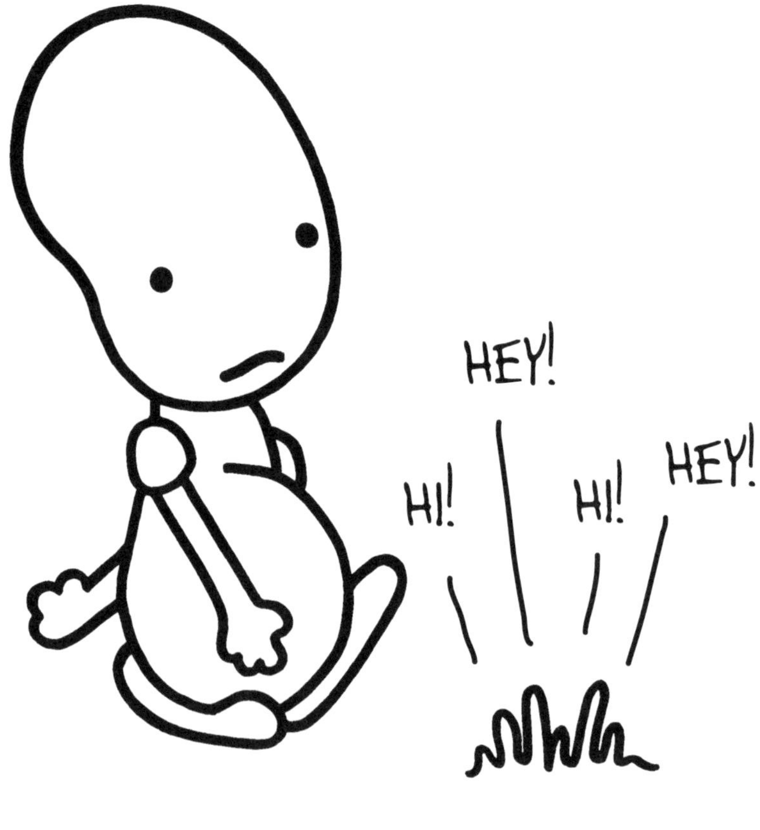
HEY!
HI!
HI!
HEY!

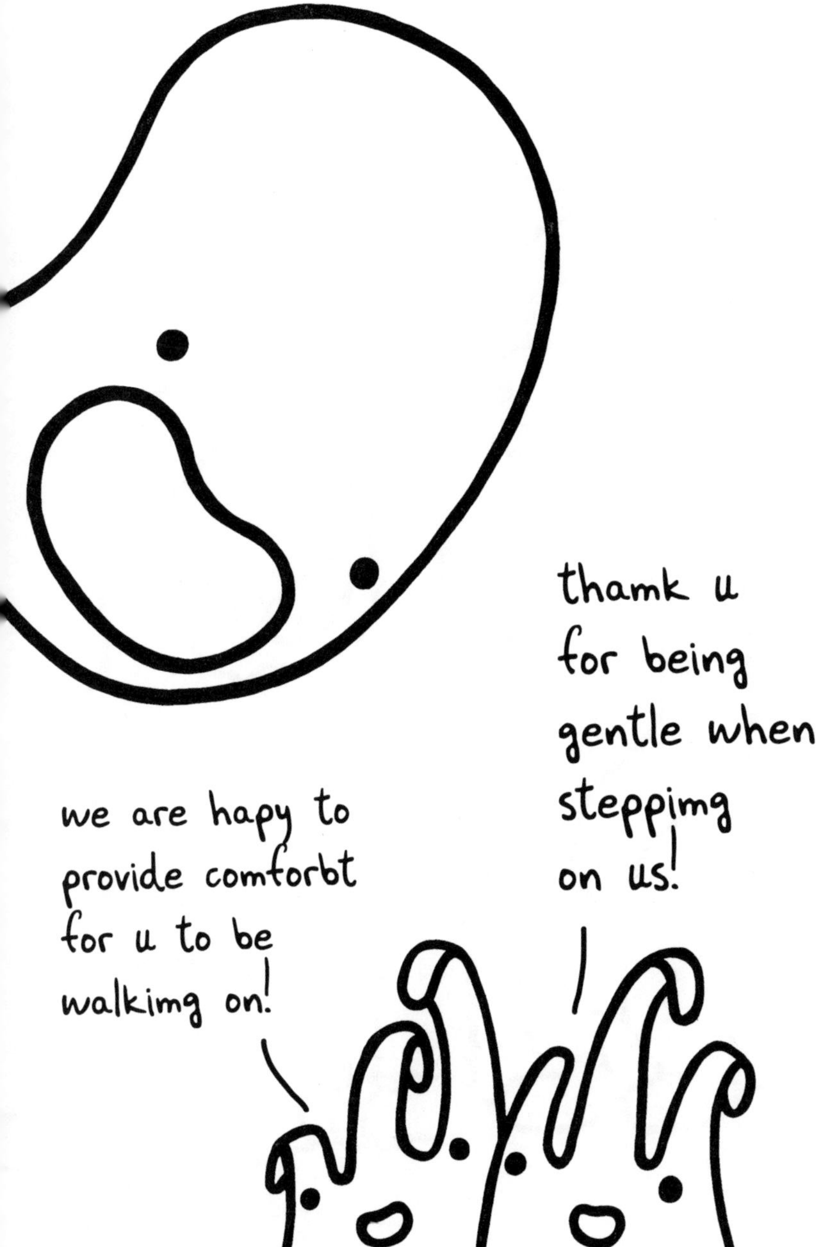
thamk u for being gentle when steppimg on us!
we are hapy to provide comforbt for u to be walkimg on!

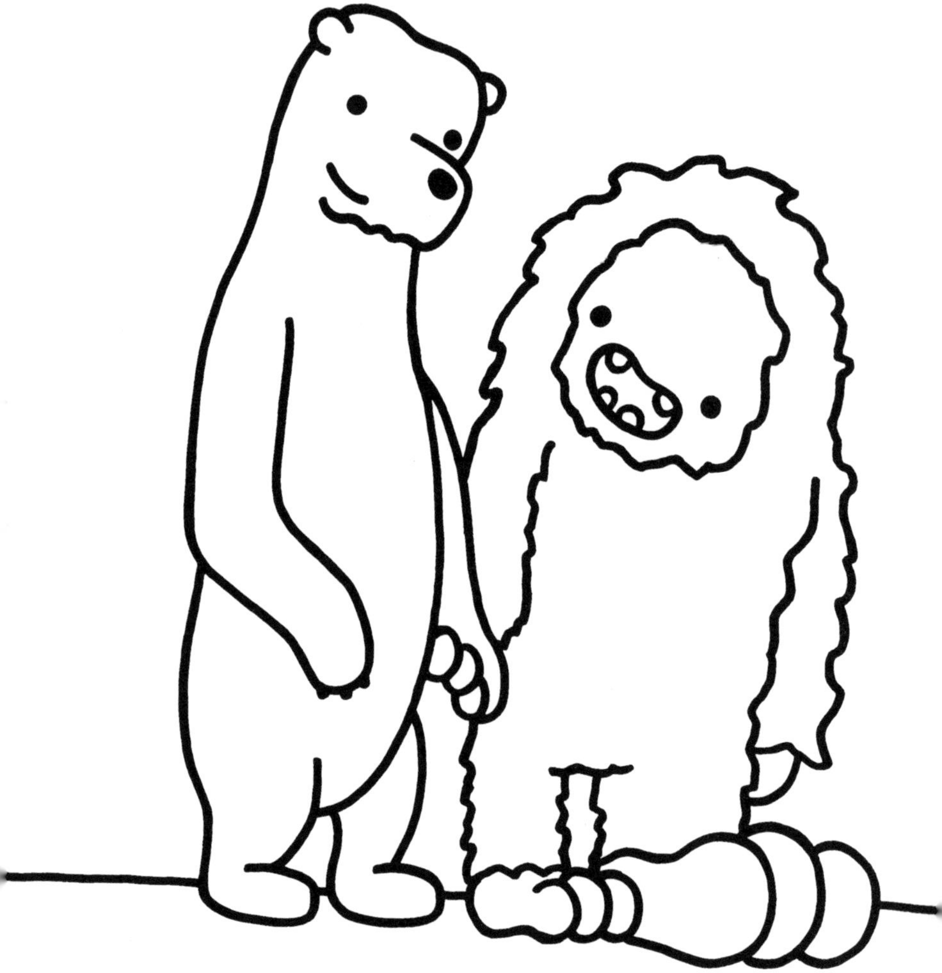

ITS JUST LIKE
JOMNY SAID. WHEN
TWO ALIEBNS FIND
EACH OTHER IN A
STRANGE PLACE,
IT FEELS A LITTLE
MORE LIKE HOME

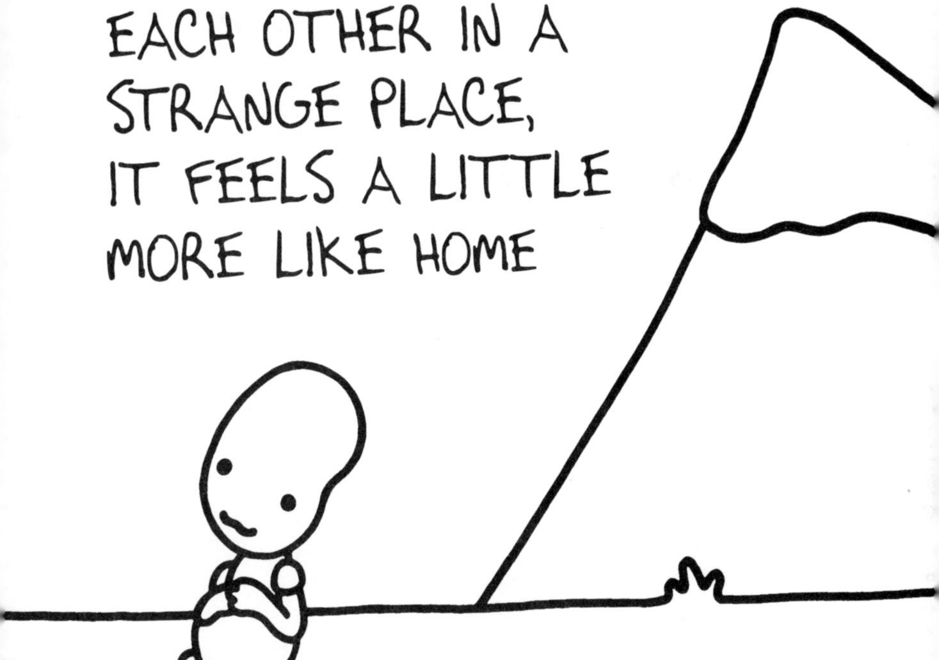

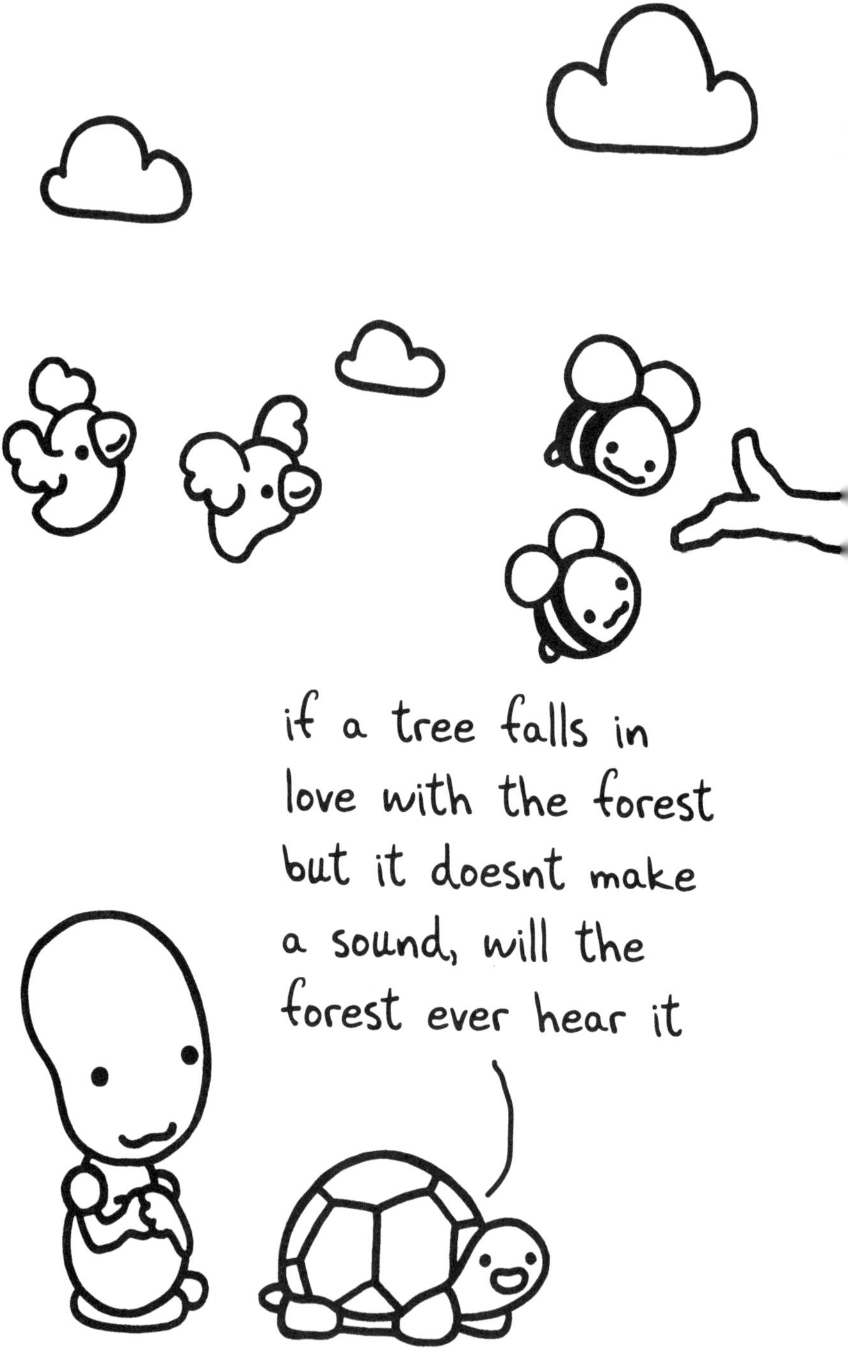
if a tree falls in love with the forest but it doesnt make a sound, will the forest ever hear it

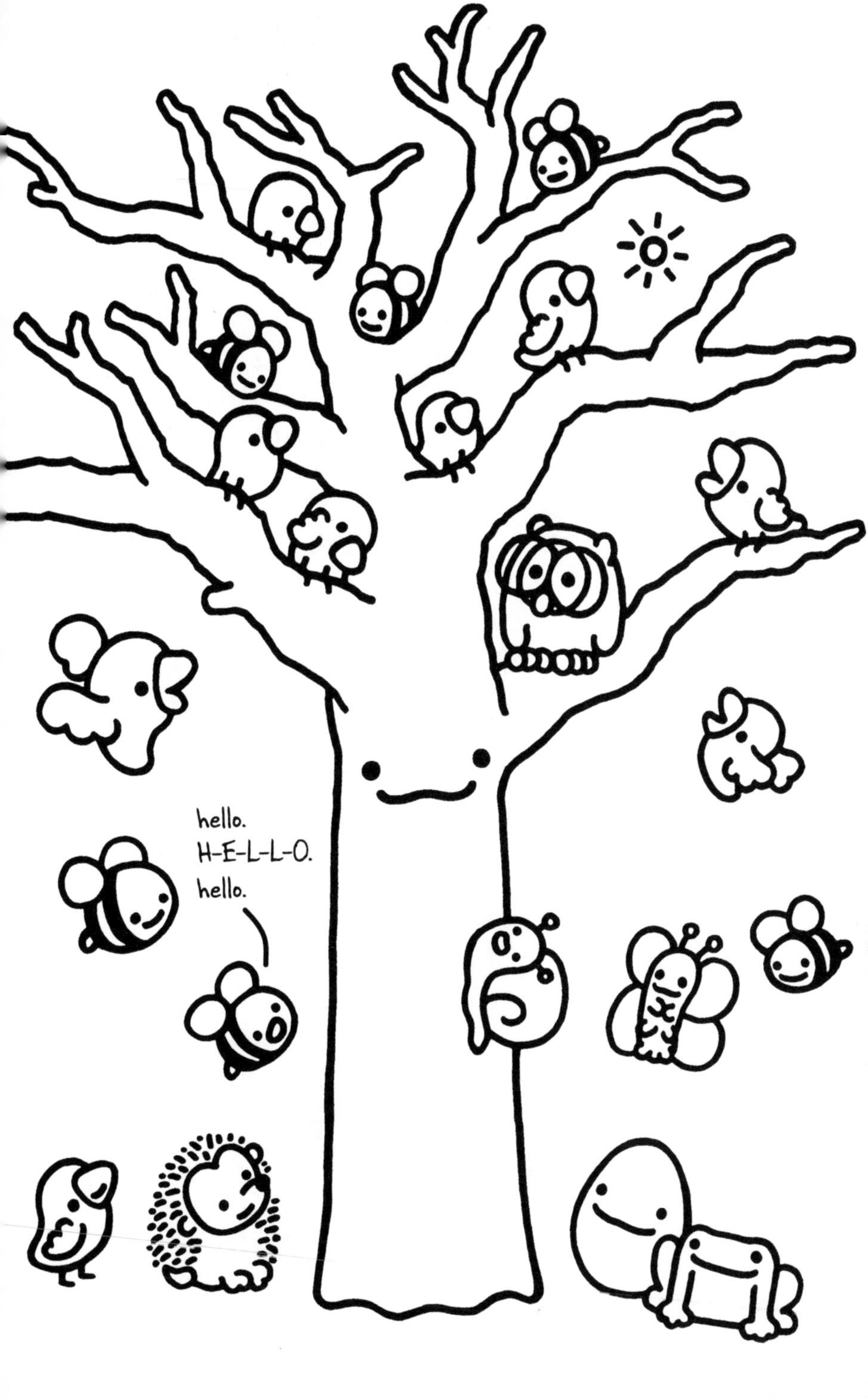
hello.
H-E-L-L-O.
hello.

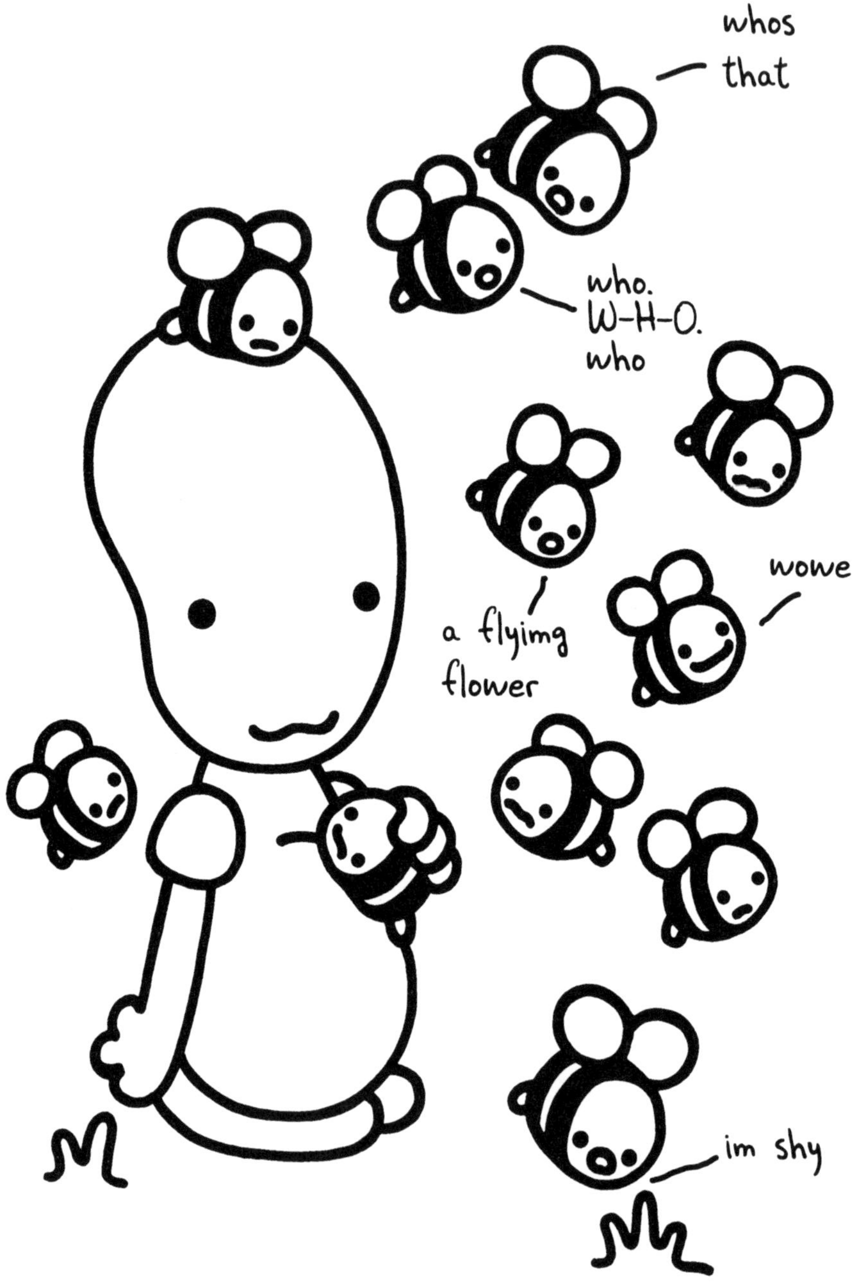
whos that
who. W-H-O. who
a flyimg flower
wowe
im shy

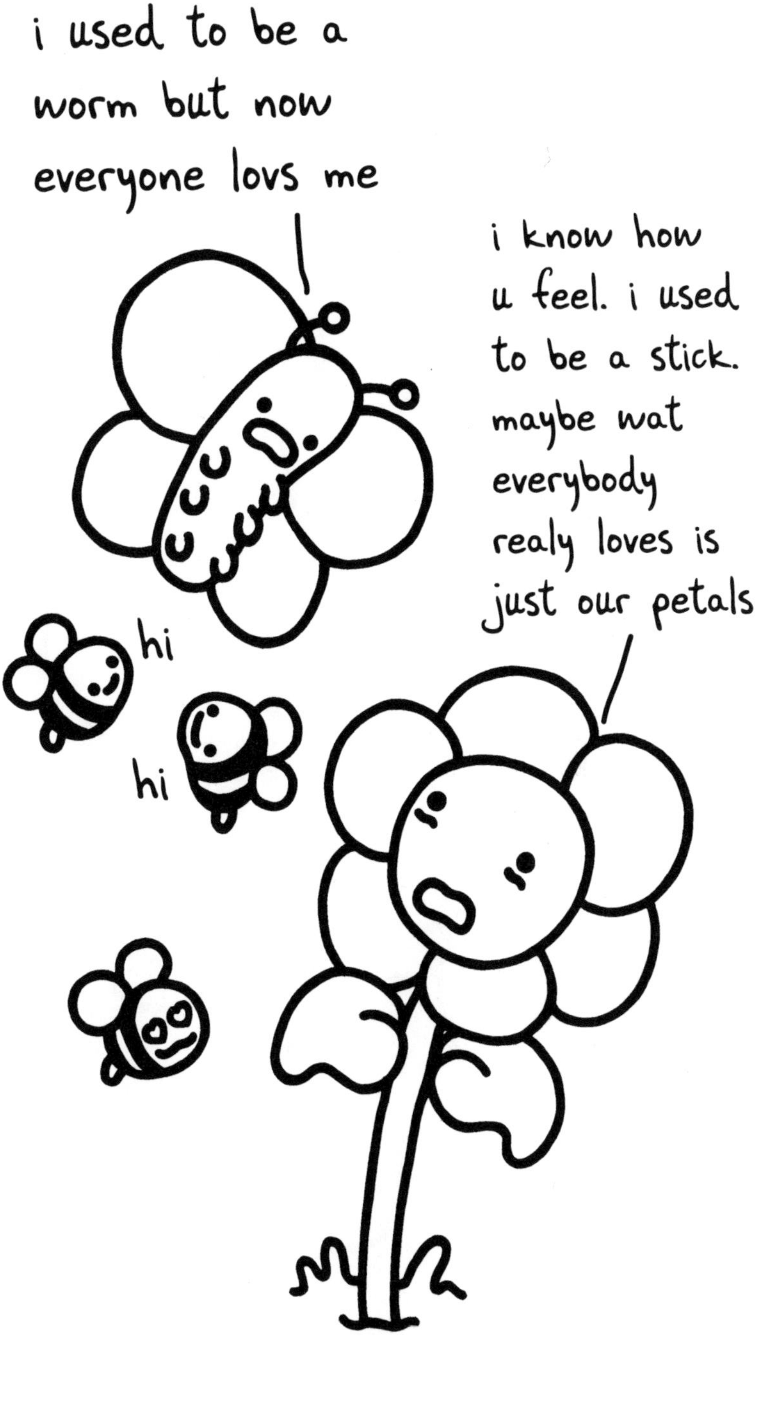
i used to be a worm but now everyone lovs me
i know how u feel. i used to be a stick. maybe wat everybody realy loves is just our petals
hi
hi

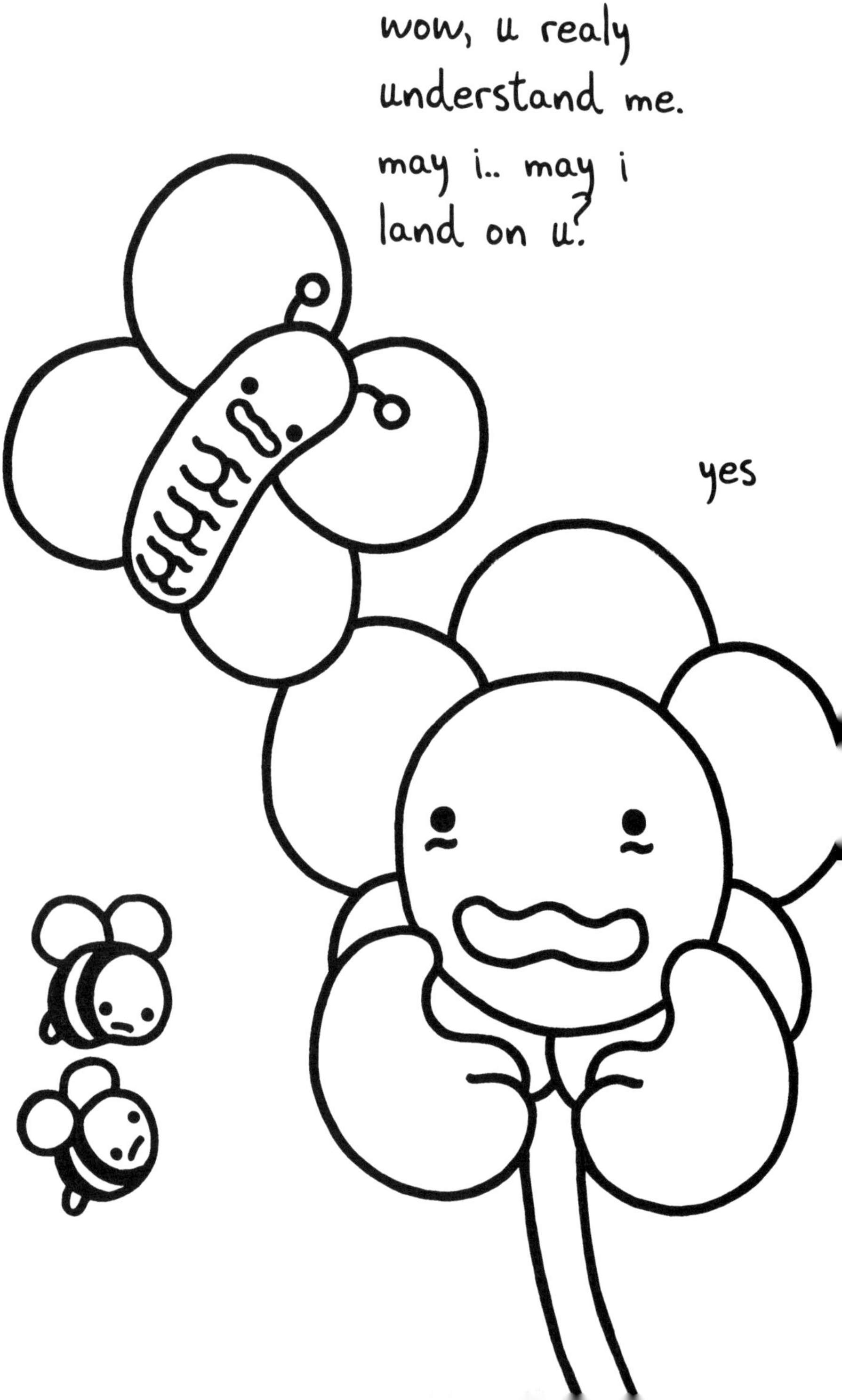
wow, u realy understand me. may i.. may i land on u?
yes

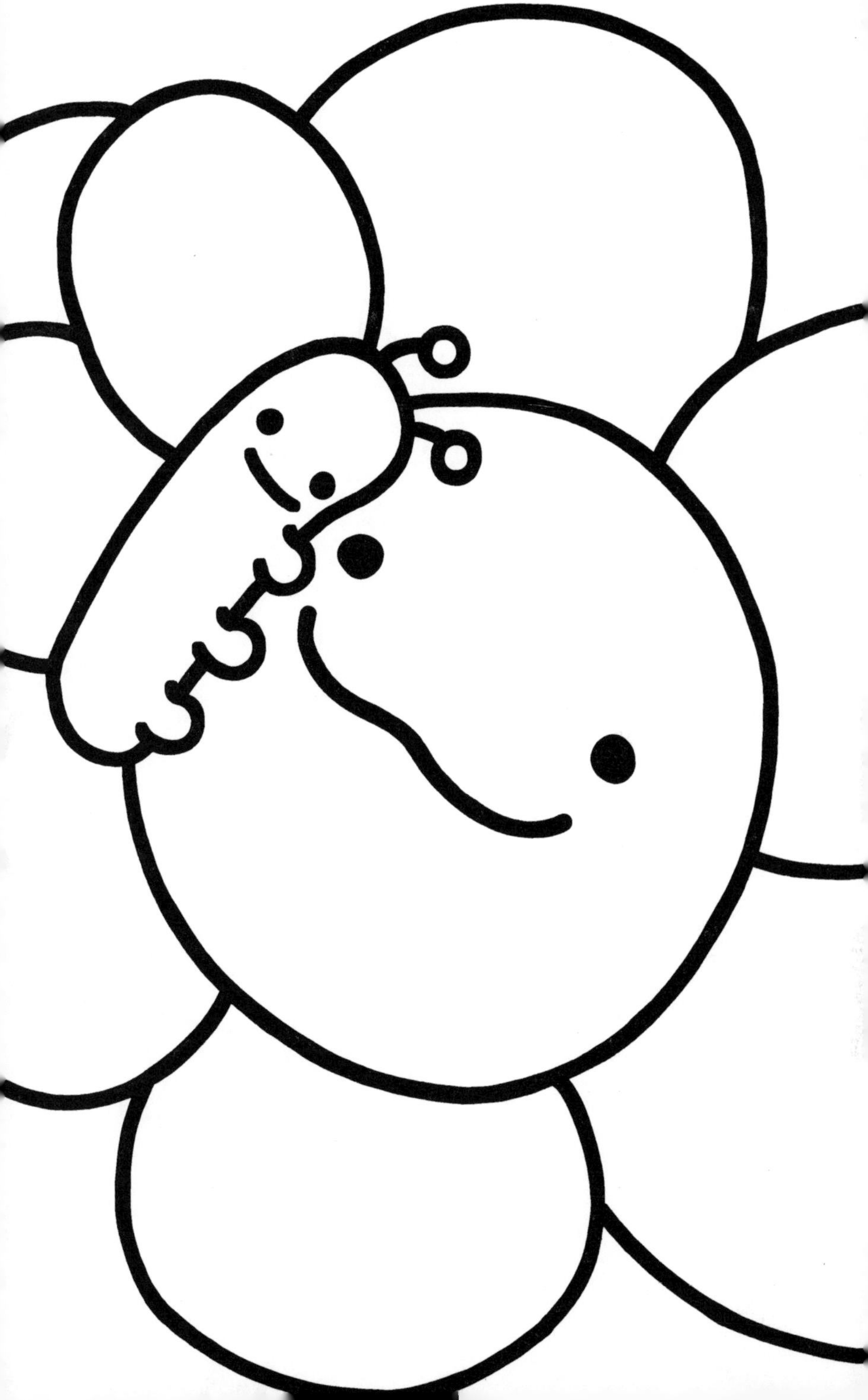

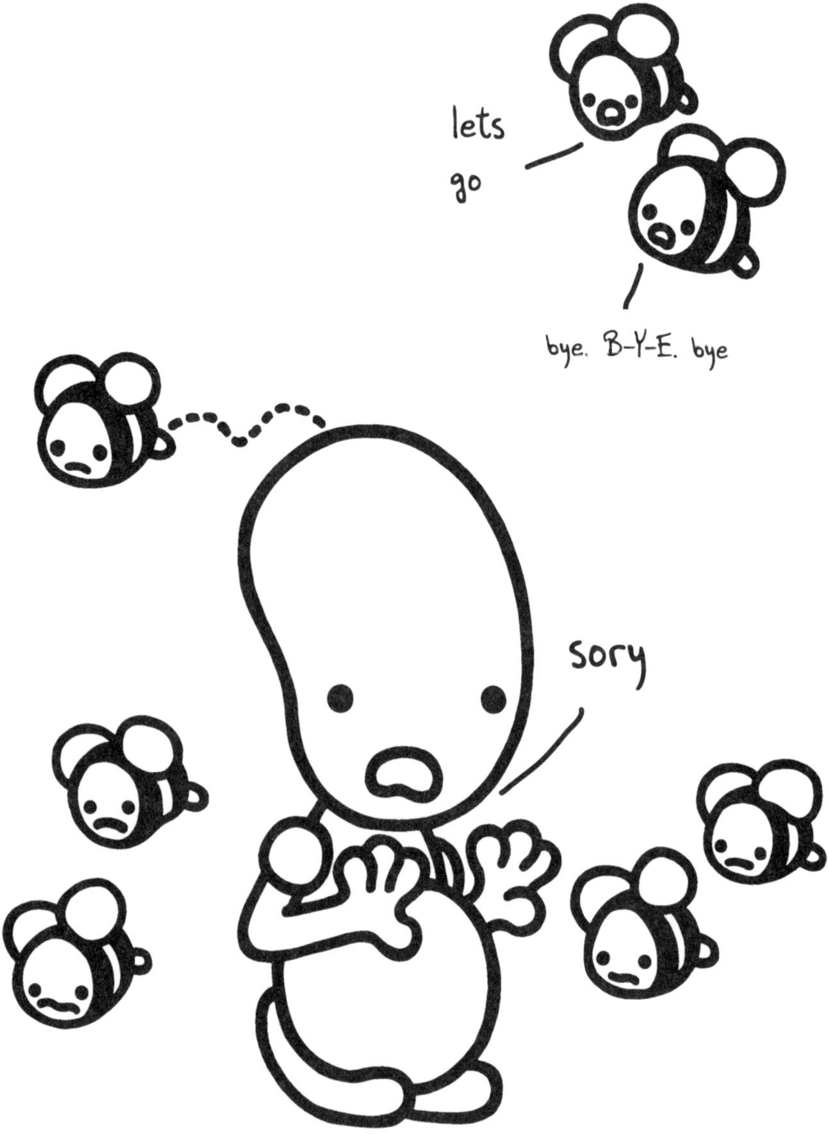
lets go
bye. B-Y-E. bye
sory

JOMNY COULD U
STOP WATCHING
PLEASE

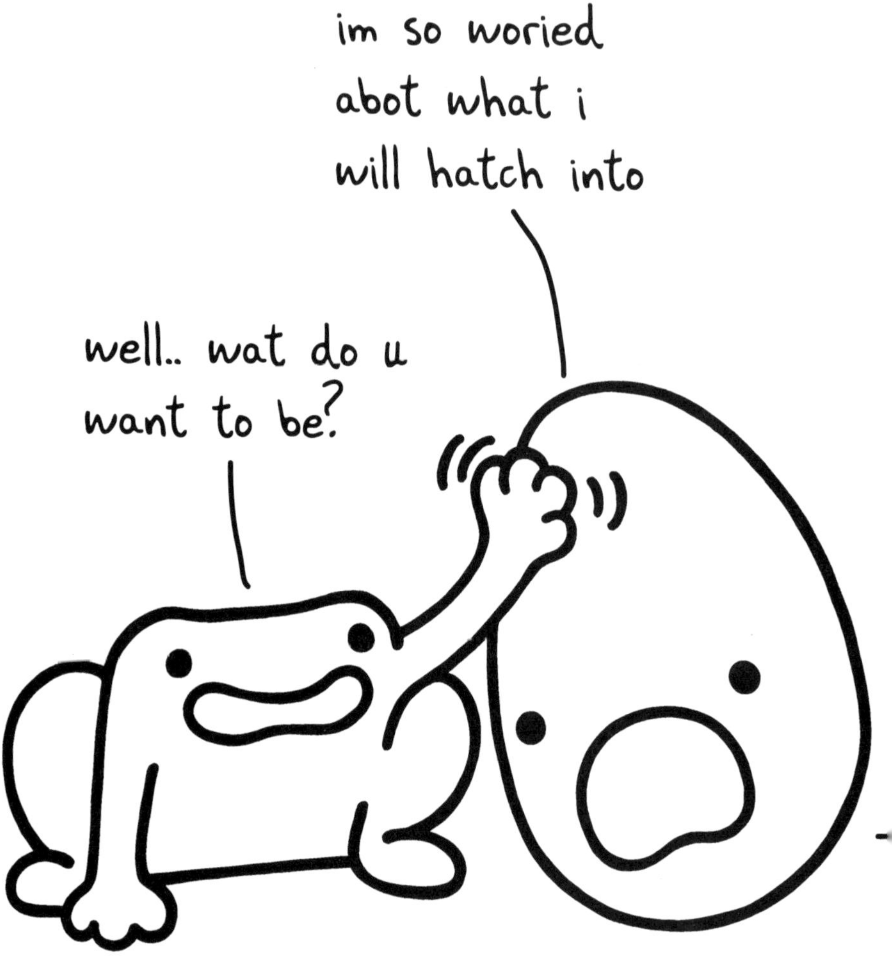
im so woried abot what i will hatch into
well.. wat do u want to be?

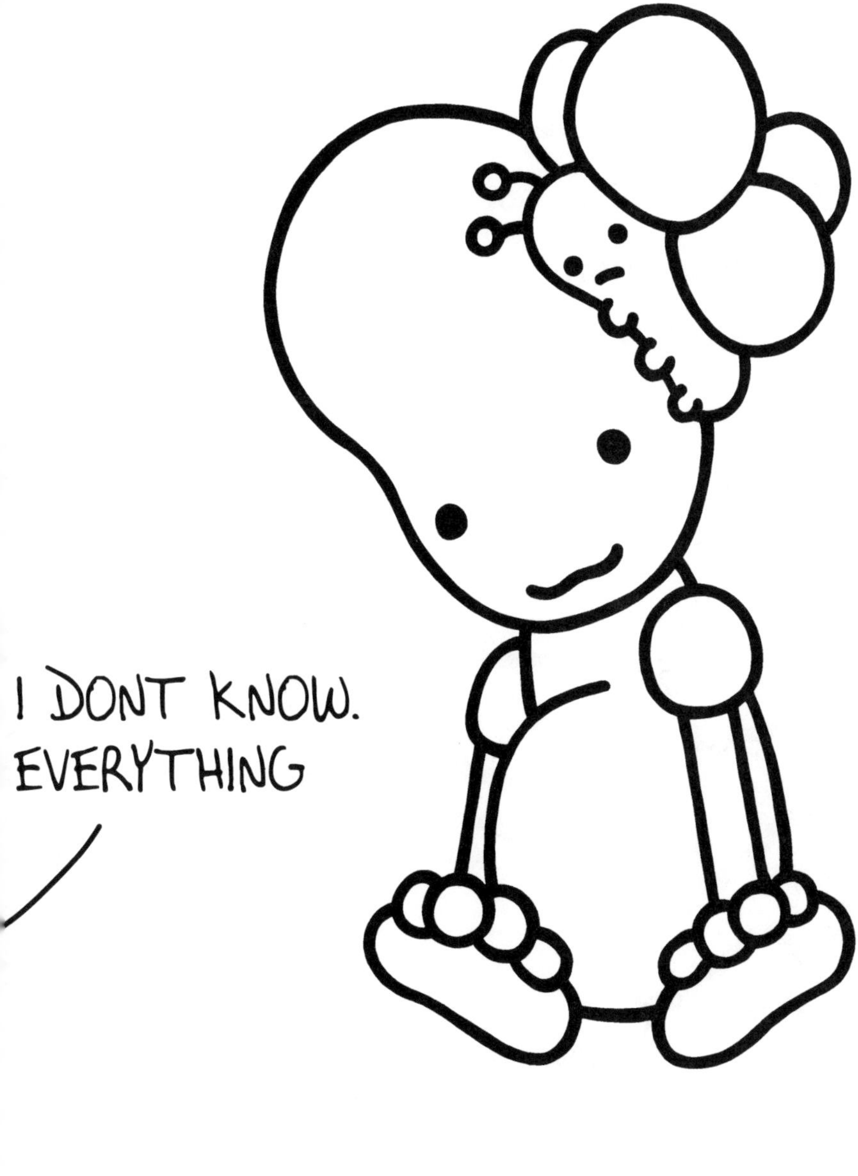
I DONT KNOW.
EVERYTHING

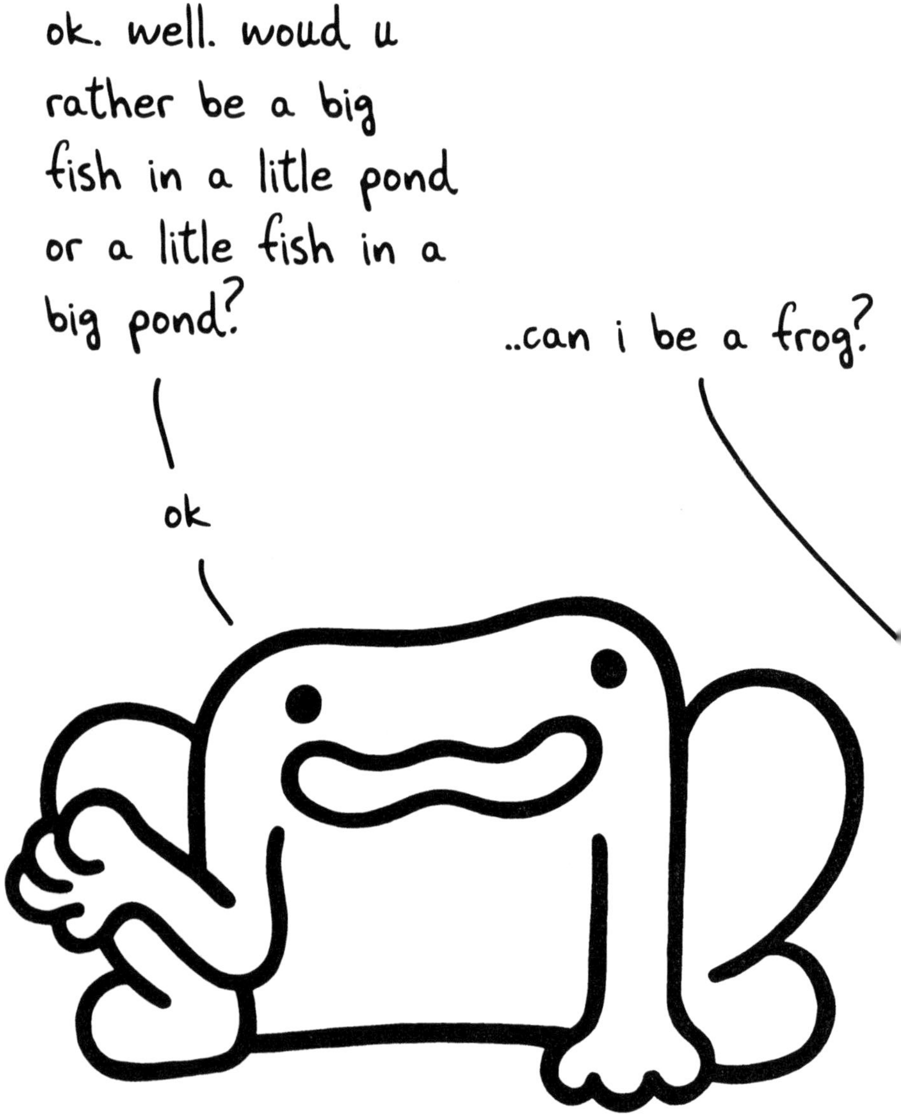
ok. well. woud u rather be a big fish in a litle pond or a litle fish in a big pond?
ok
..can i be a frog?

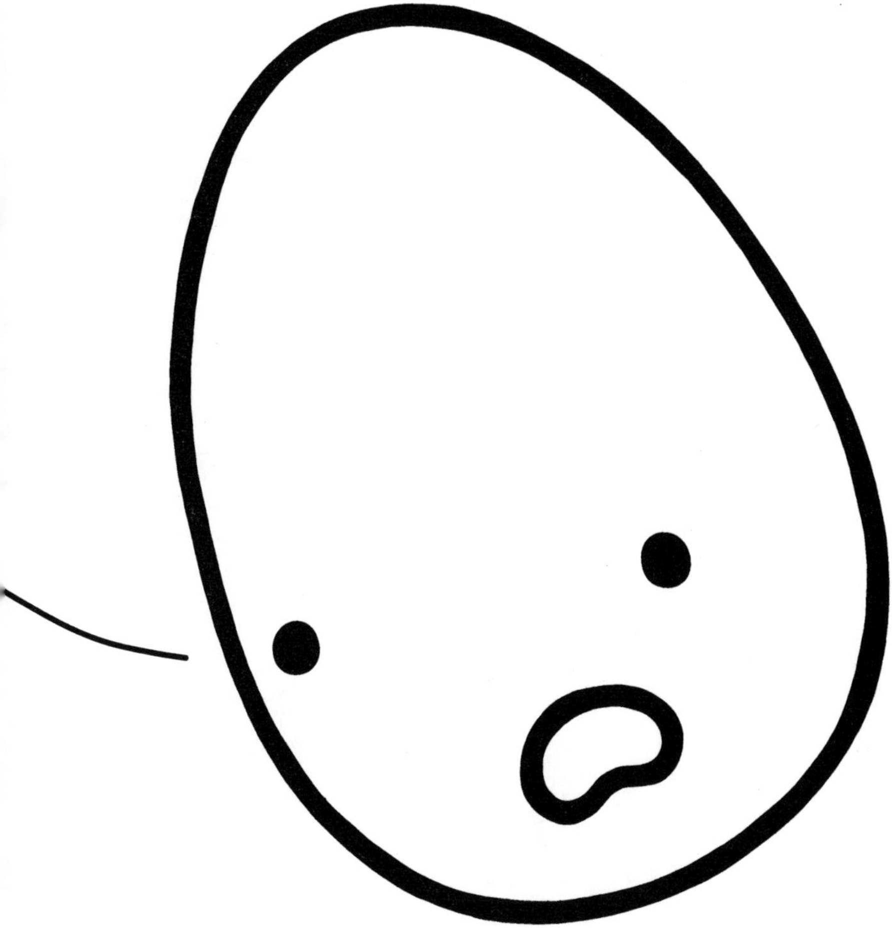

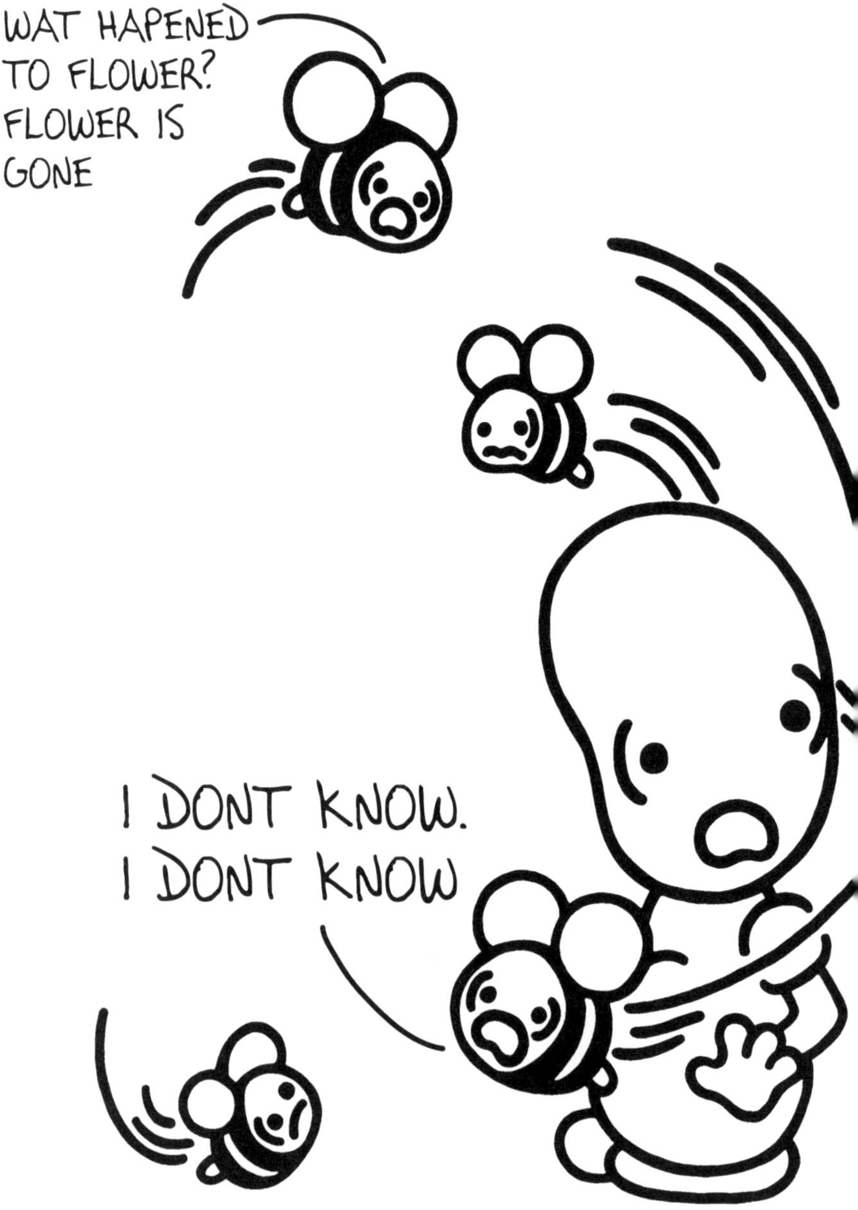
WAT HAPENED TO FLOWER? FLOWER IS GONE
I DONT KNOW. I DONT KNOW

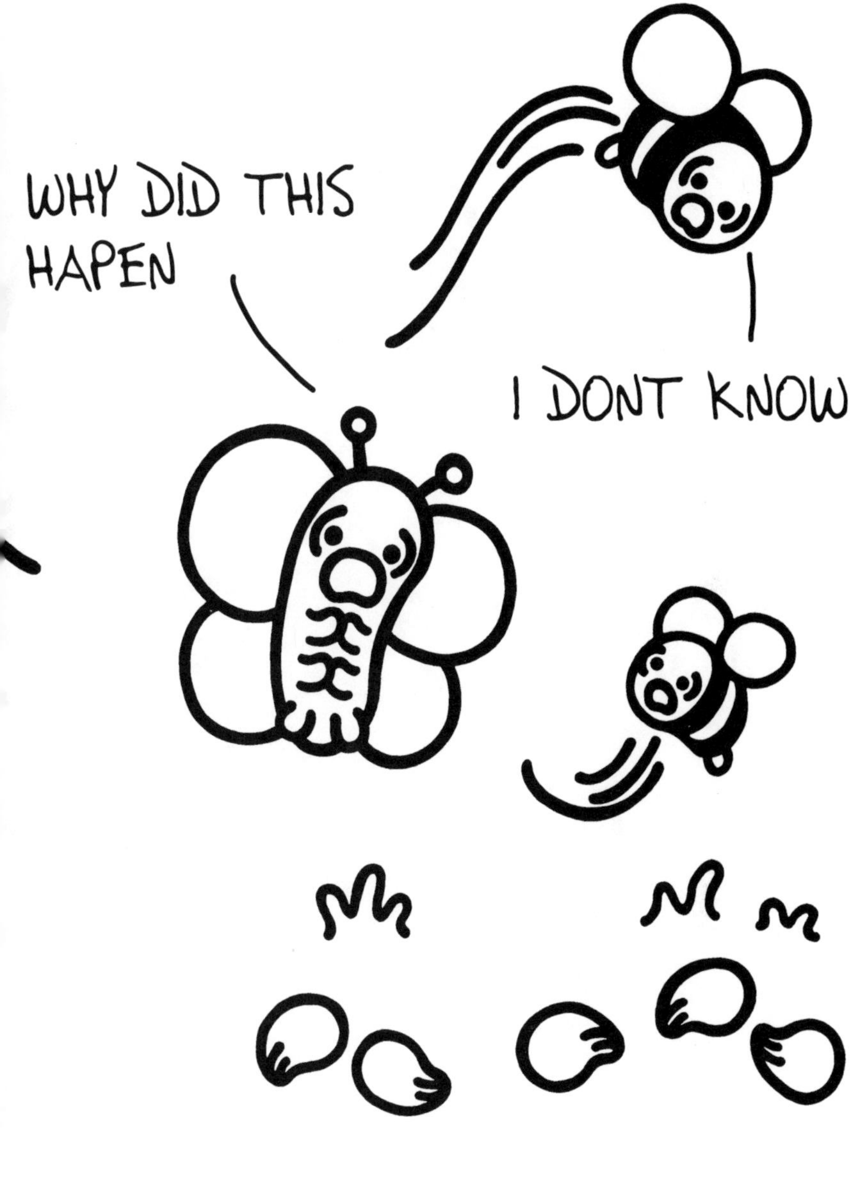
WHY DID THIS HAPEN
I DONT KNOW

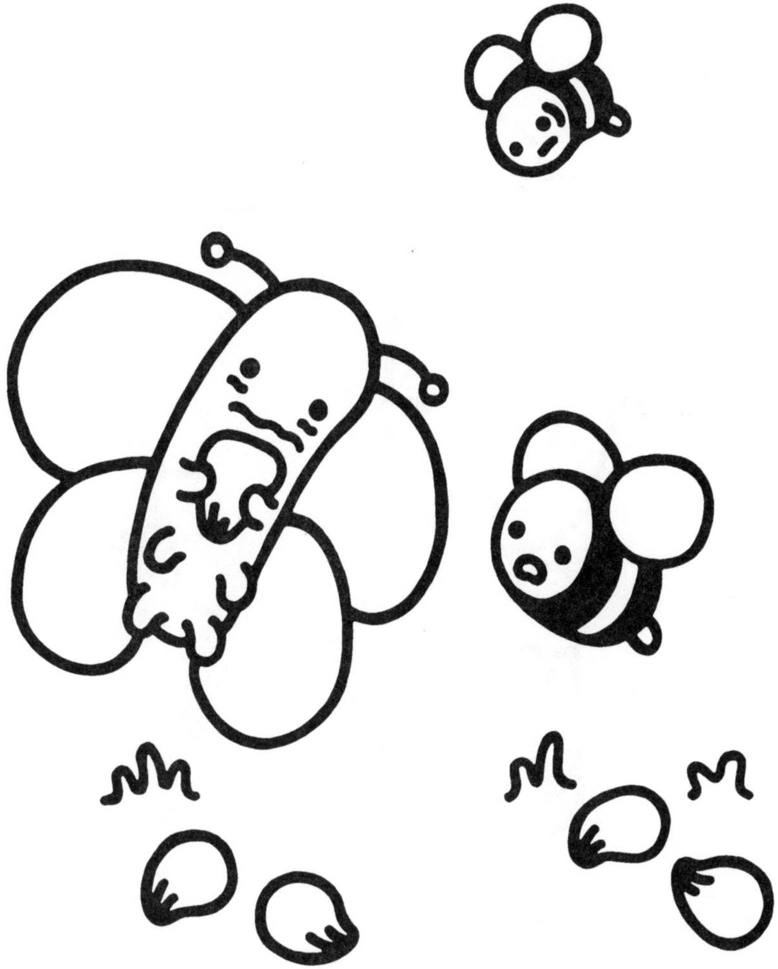

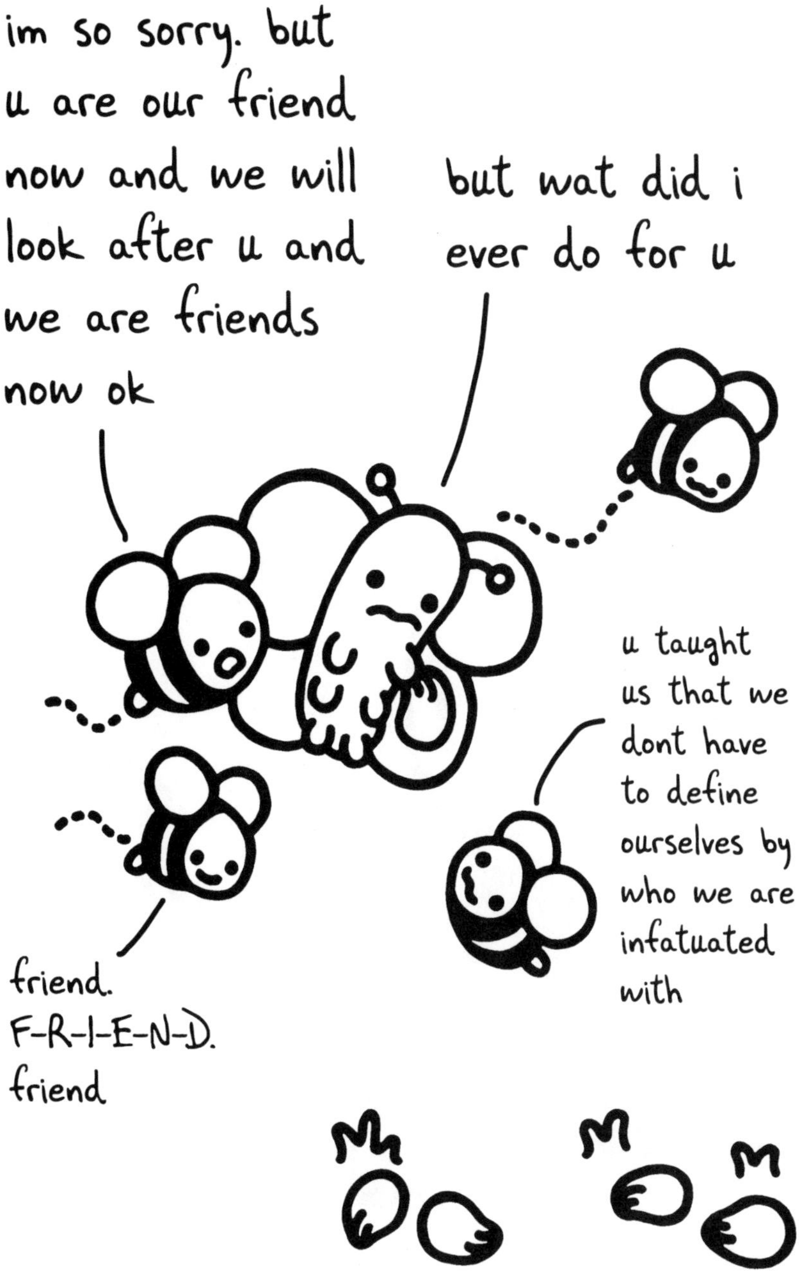
im so sorry. but u are our friend now and we will look after u and we are friends now ok
but wat did i ever do for u
u taught us that we dont have to define ourselves by who we are infatuated with
friend. F-R-I-E-N-D. friend
M
M
M

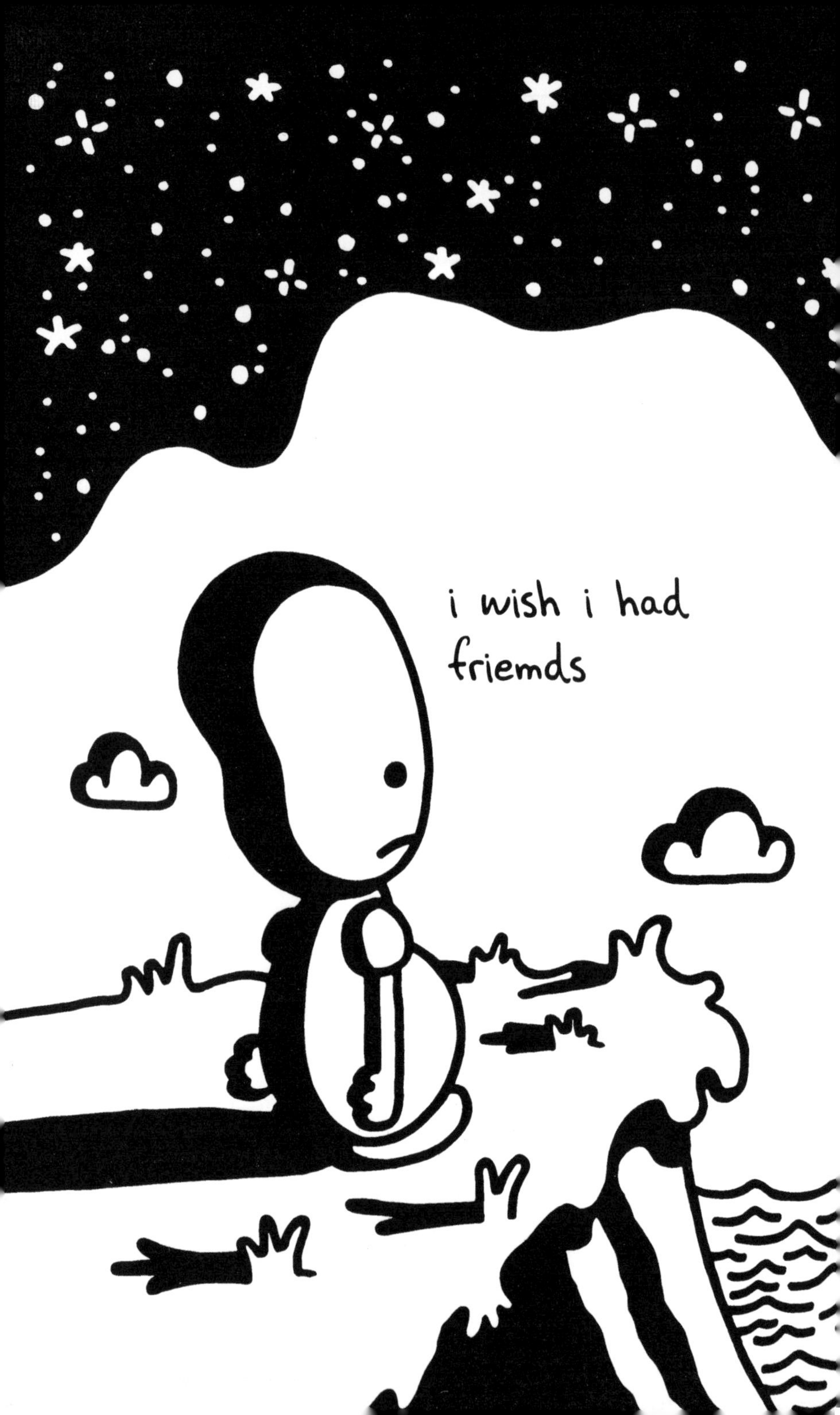
i wish i had
friemds

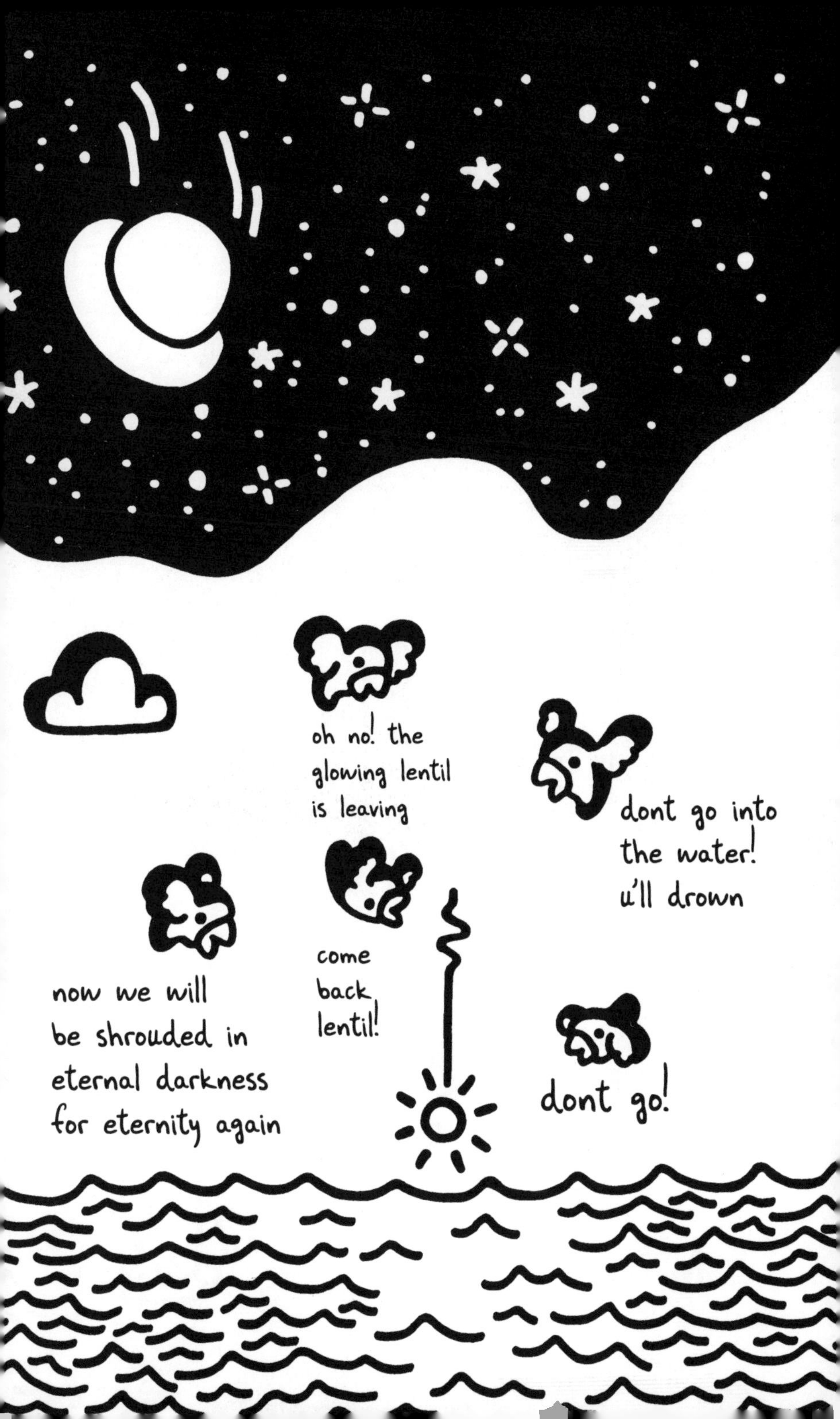
oh no! the glowing lentil is leaving
dont go into the water! u'll drown
now we will be shrouded in eternal darkness for eternity again
come back lentil!
dont go!

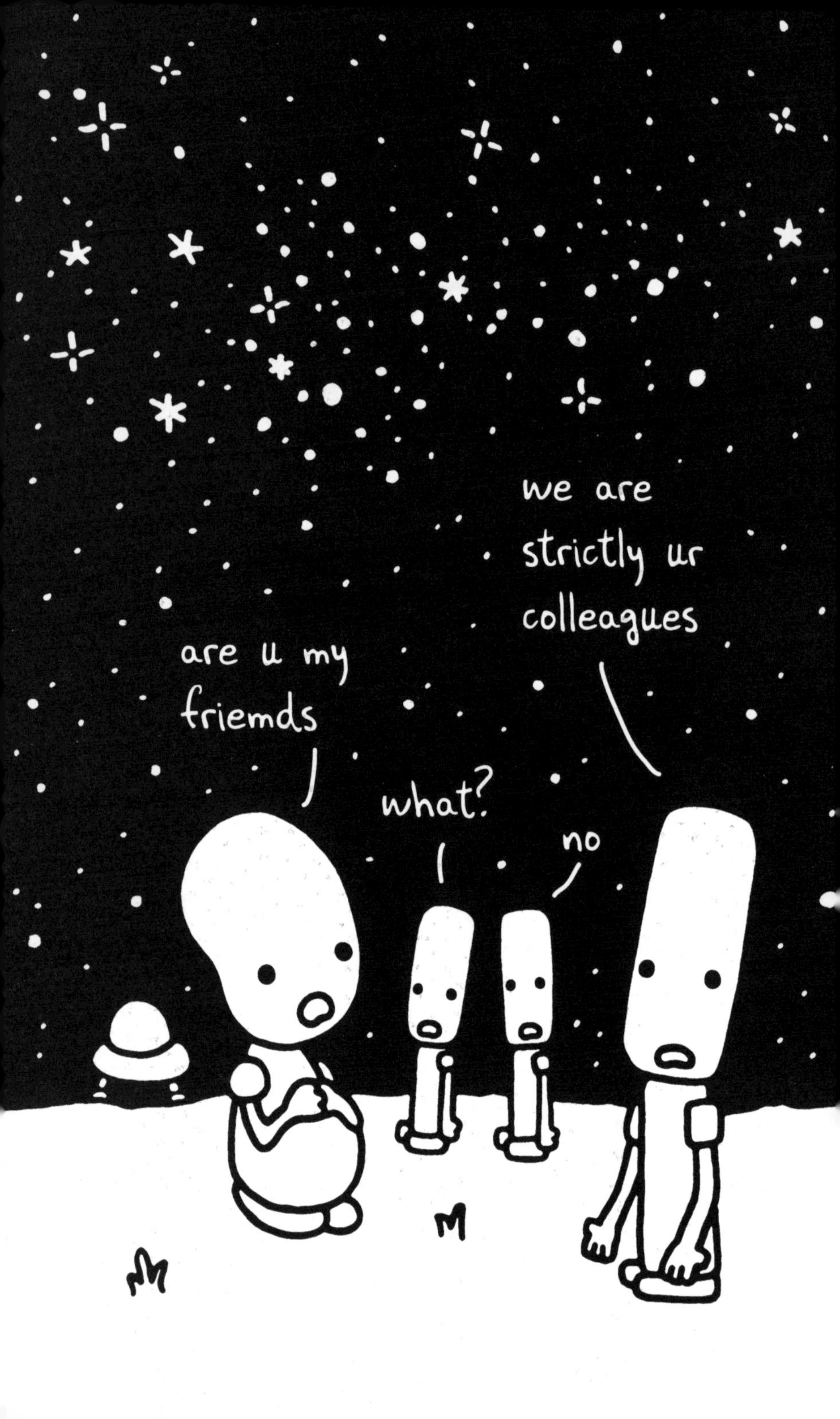
are u my friemds
what?
no
we are strictly ur colleagues

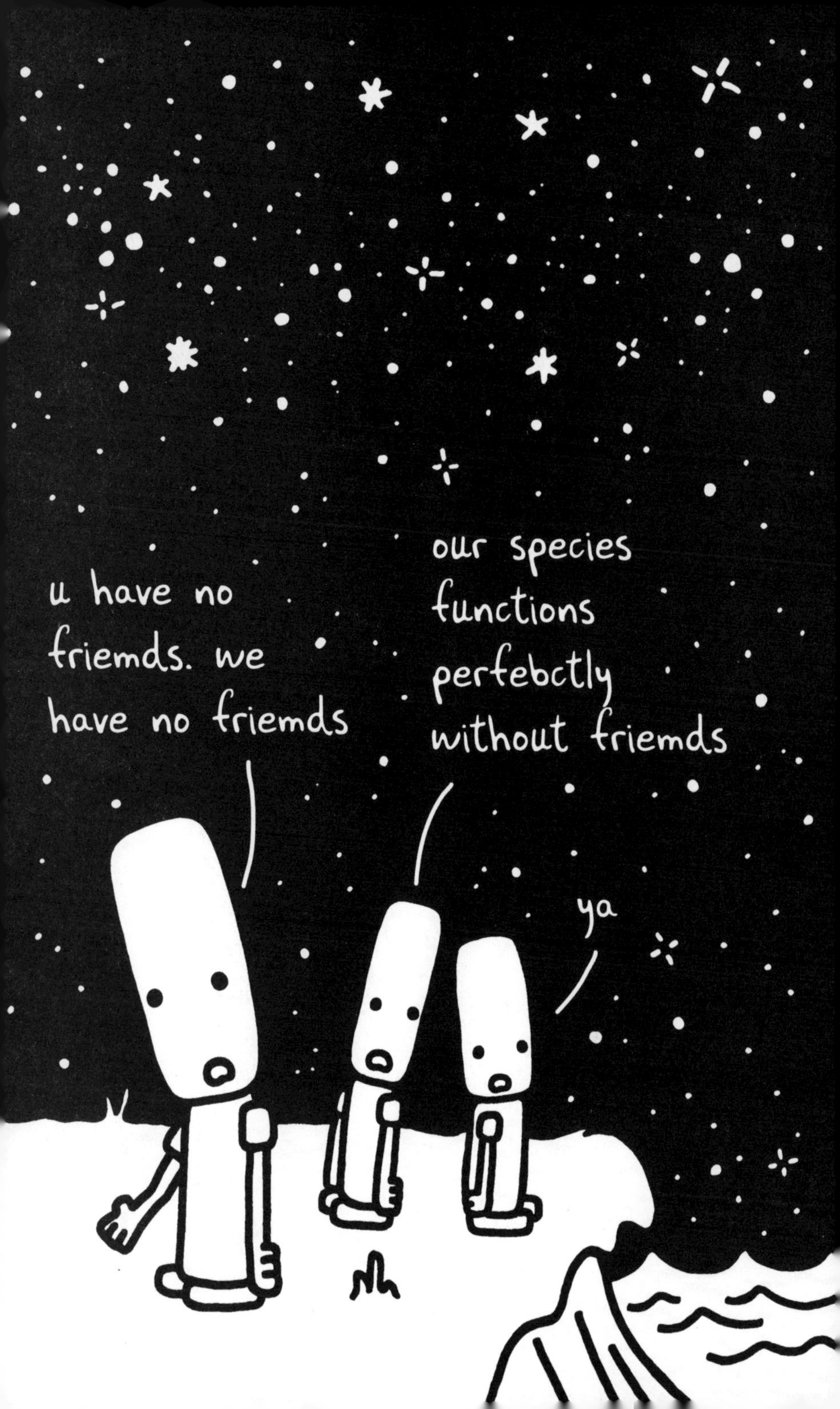
u have no friemds. we have no friemds
our species functions perfebctly without friemds
ya

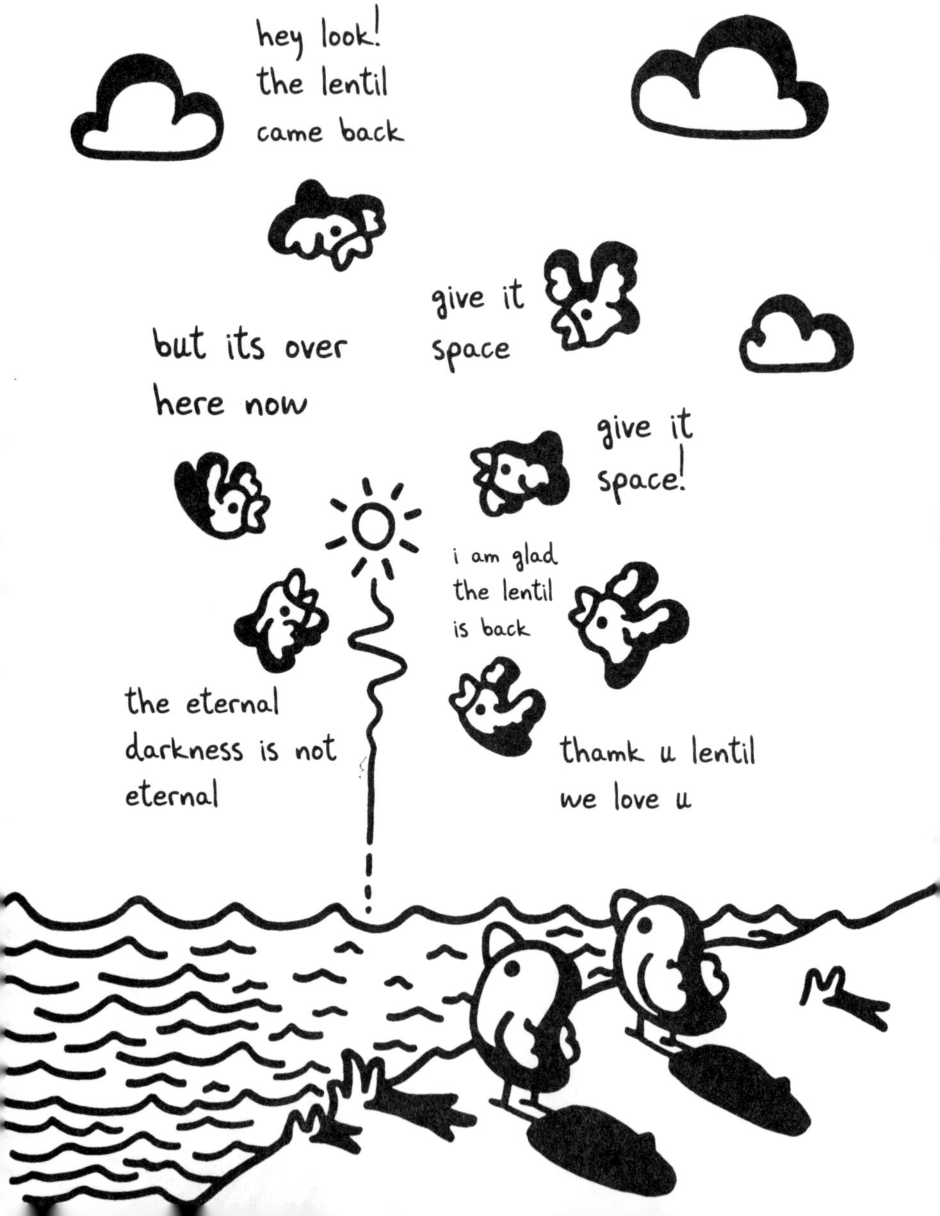
hey look! the lentil came back
give it space
but its over here now
give it space!
i am glad the lentil is back
the eternal darkness is not eternal
thamk u lentil we love u

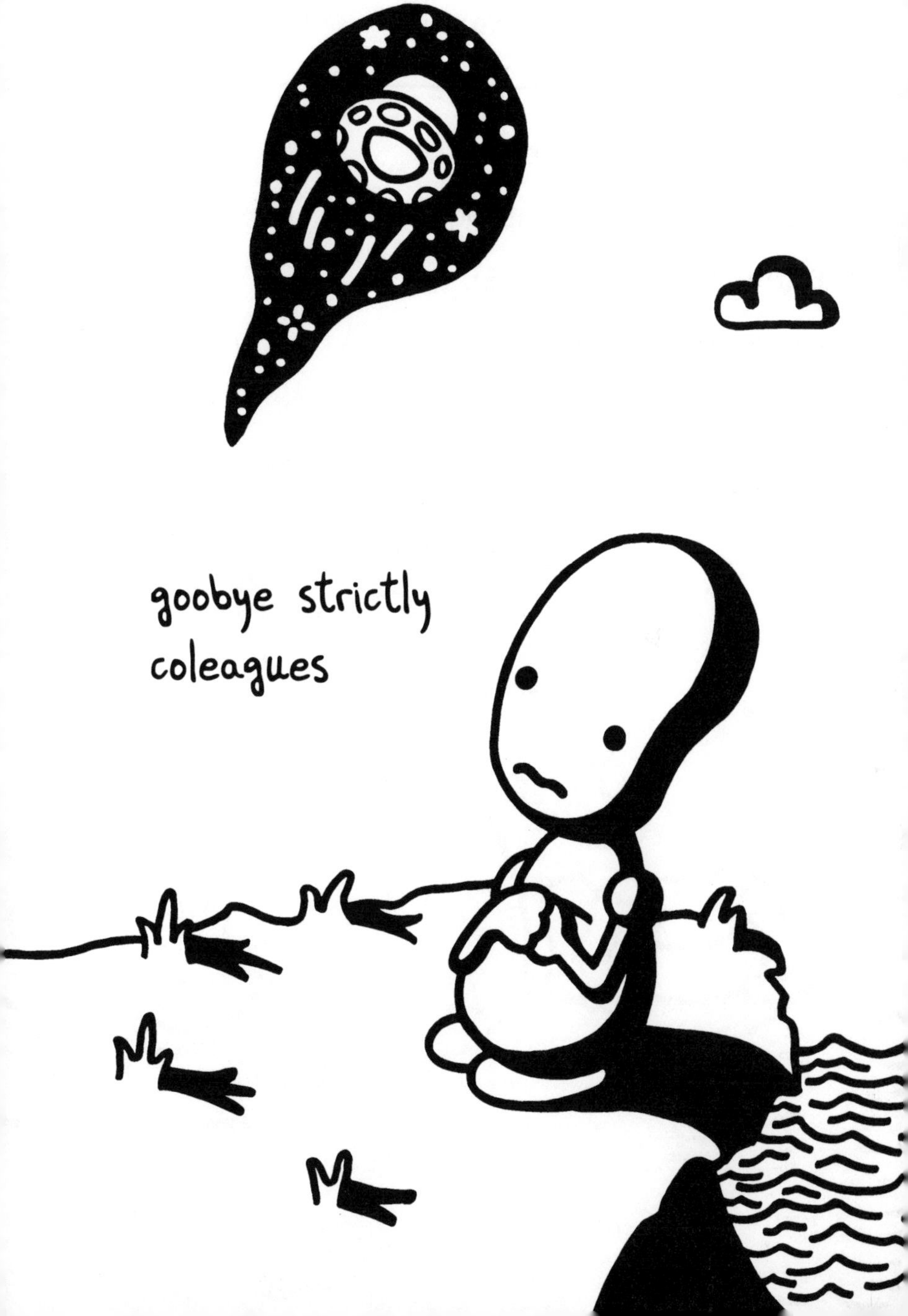
goobye strictly
coleagues

ok welcome to frog trainimg. since i have become a frog i have learned hapily how to be a frog. this is wat i learned. the most importamt thing abot frogs is frogs can jump

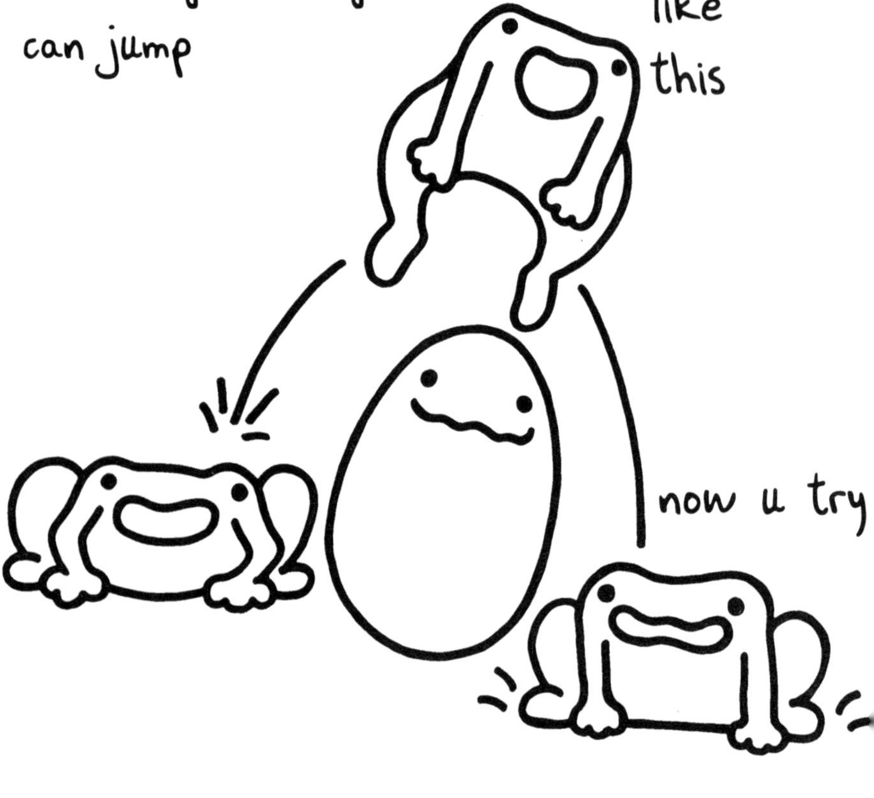
like this
now u try

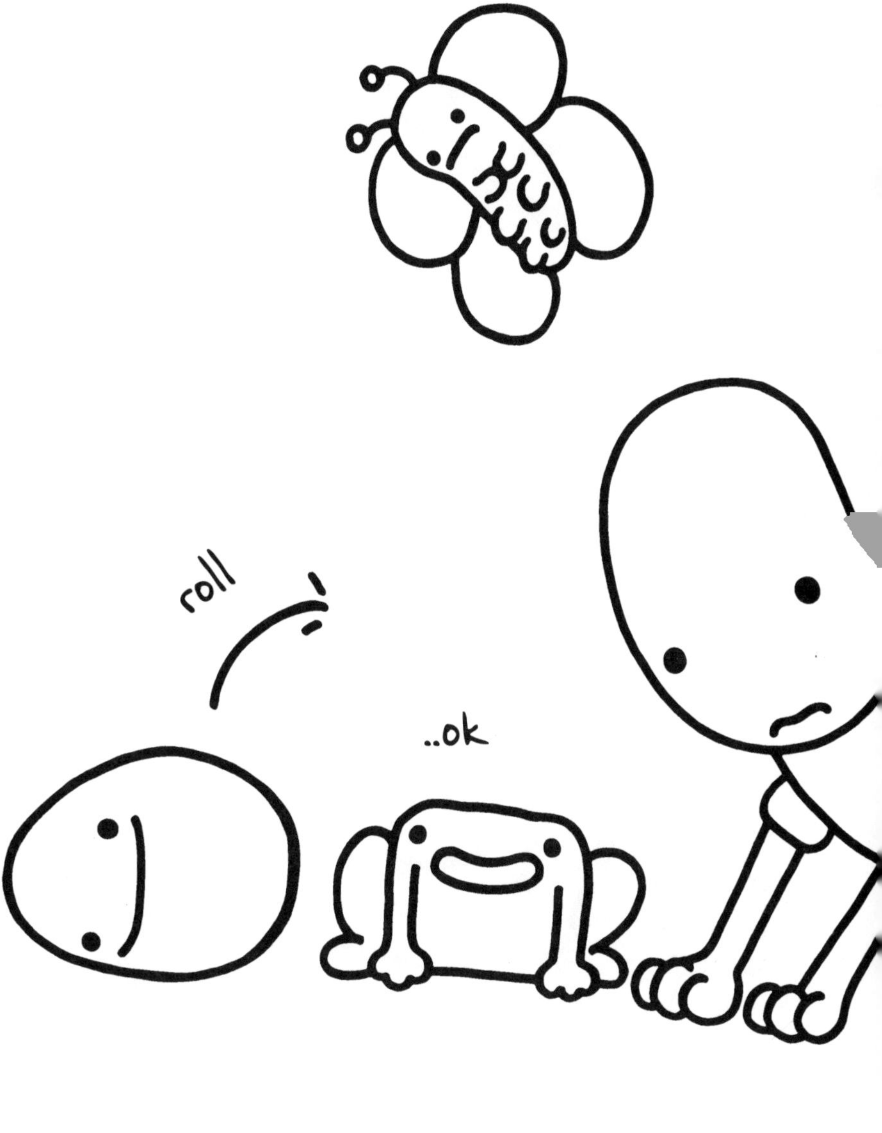
roll
..ok

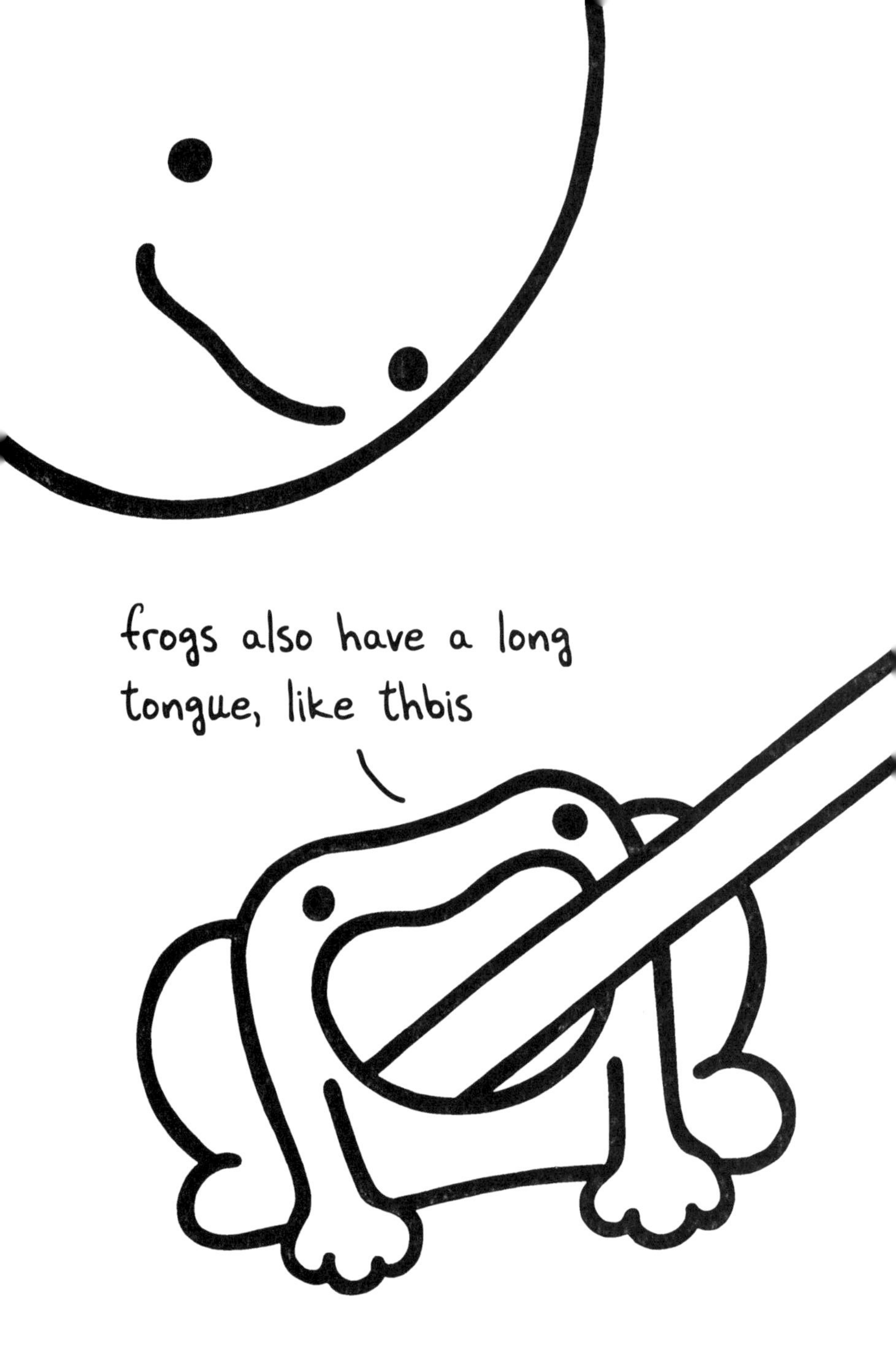
frogs also have a long tongue, like thbis

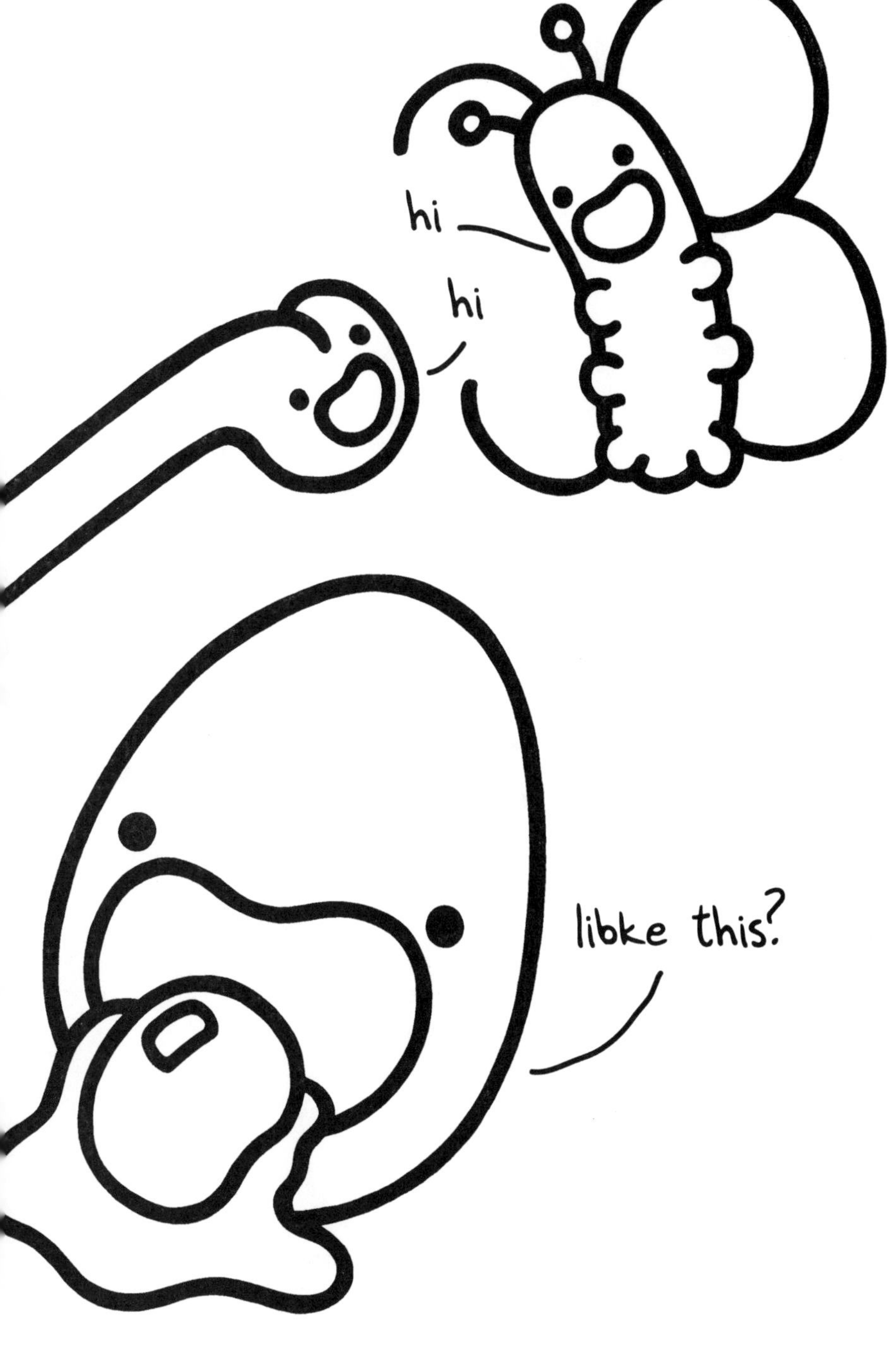
hi
hi
libke this?

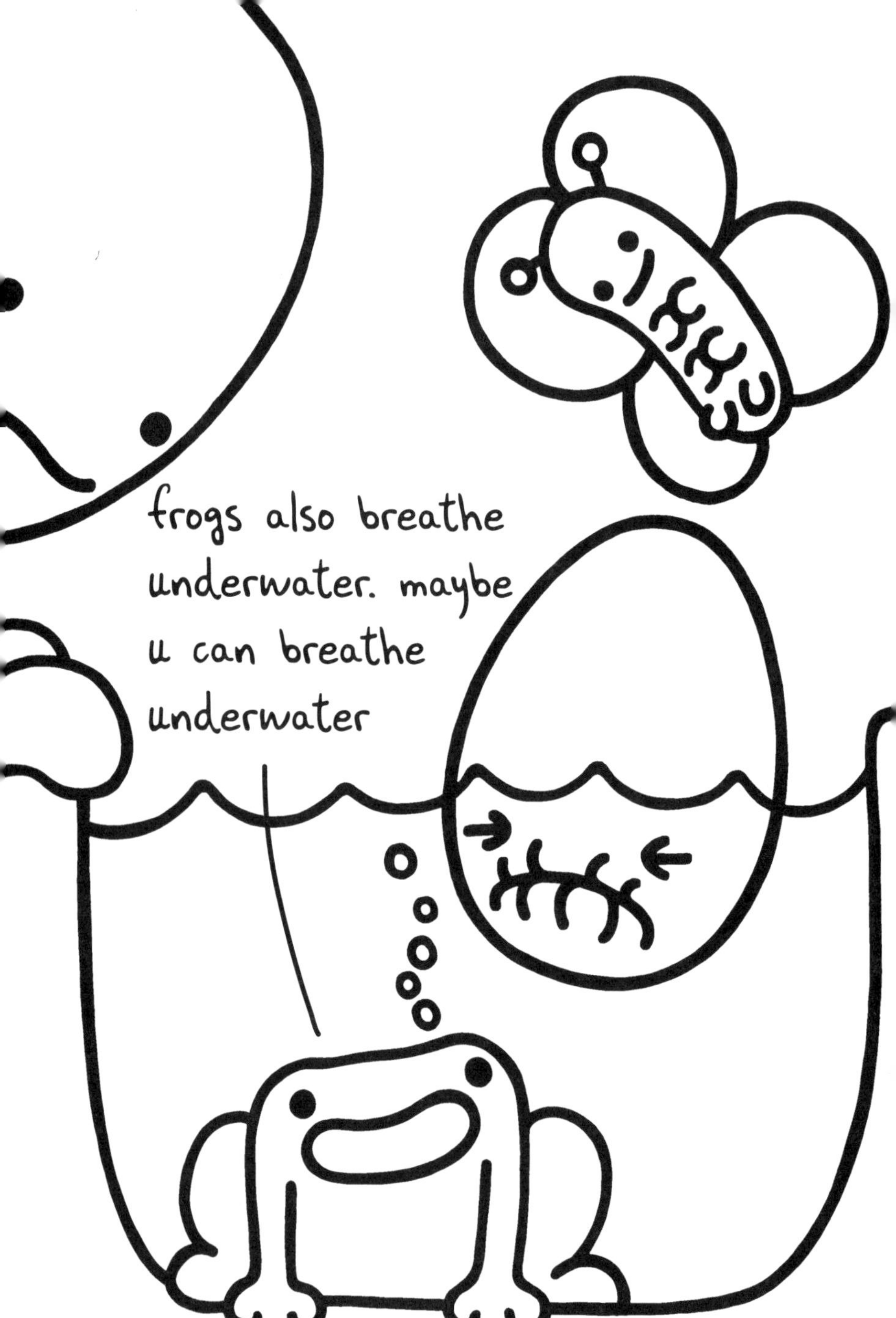
frogs also breathe underwater. maybe u can breathe underwater

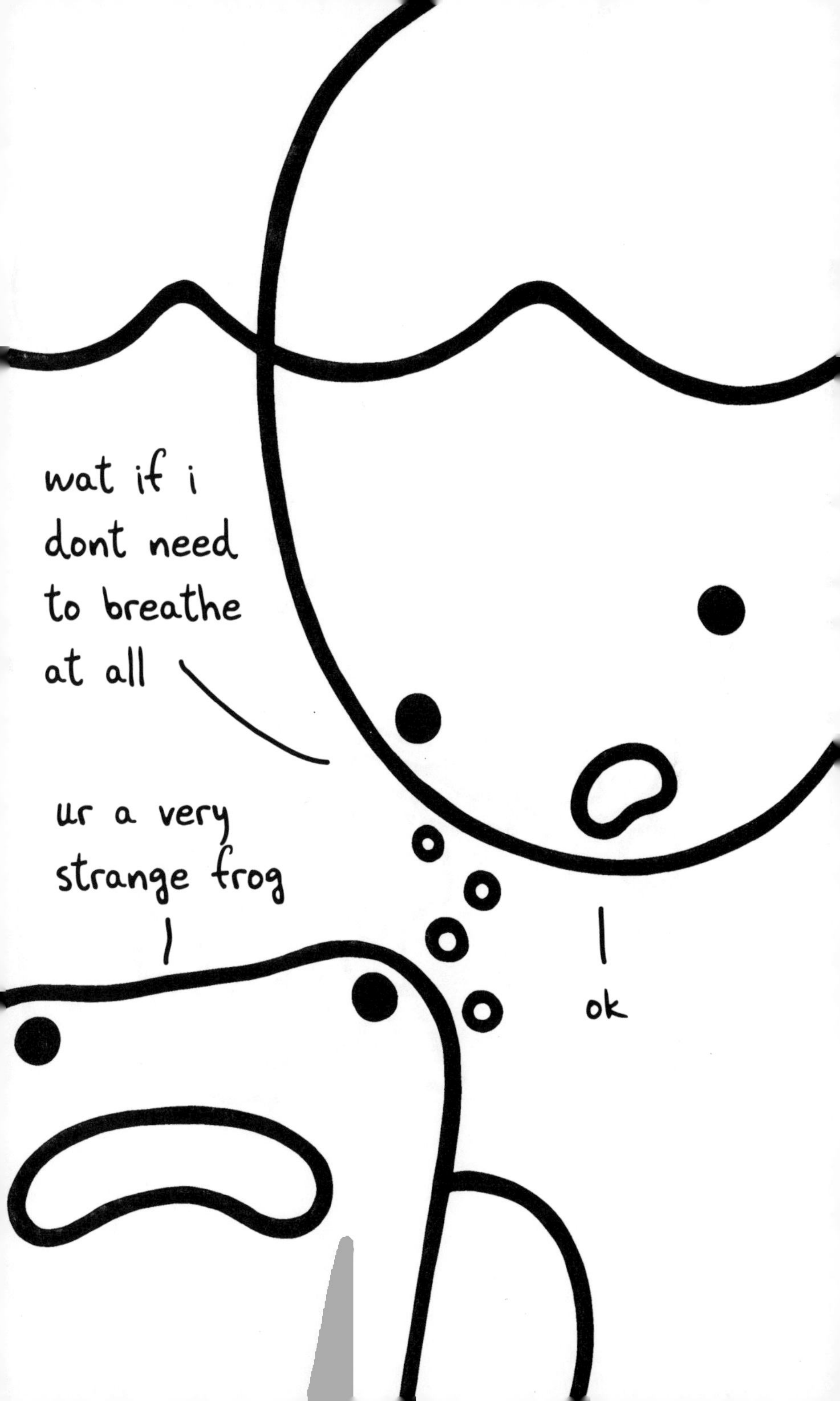
wat if i dont need to breathe at all
ur a very strange frog
ok

if ur always hapy are
u ever truly hapy, or is
hapiness only somthing
we see in u becuase
we know sadness

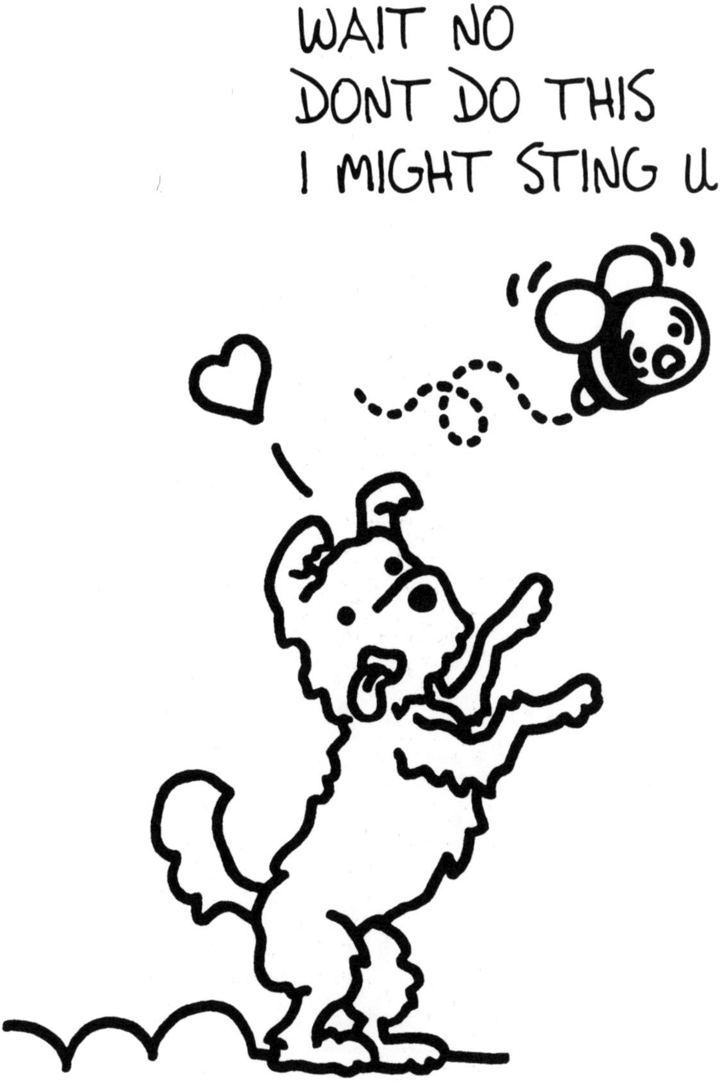
WAIT NO
DONT DO THIS
I MIGHT STING U

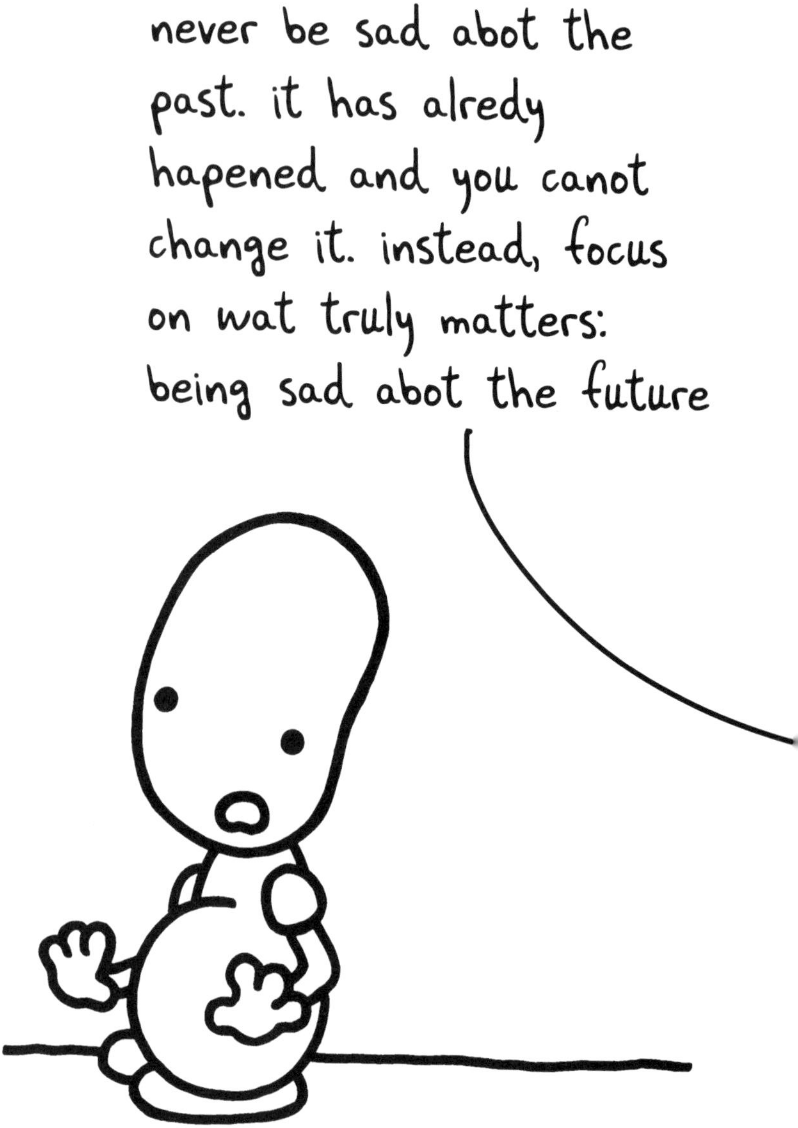
never be sad abot the past. it has alredy hapened and you canot change it. instead, focus on wat truly matters: being sad abot the future

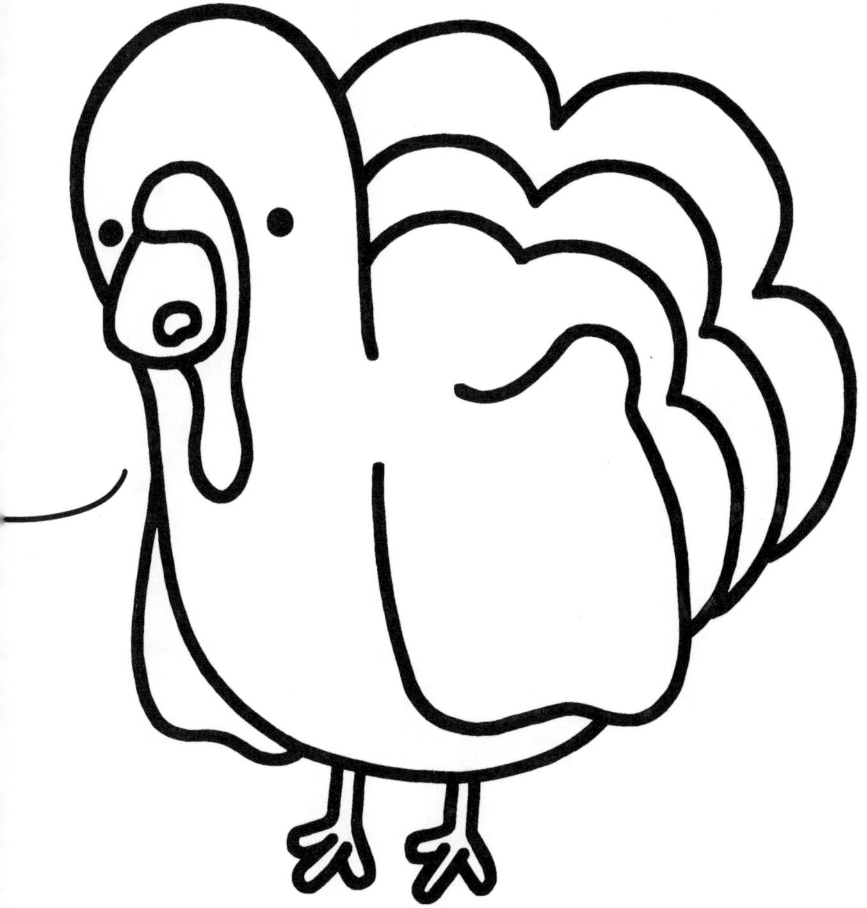

there are many reasons to be sad.

u may be sad becuase u feel
alone. the comfortimg thing abot
feeling lonely is that evrey thing
that has ever existed also knows
what loneliness feels like too.

u may be sad because u are
sad. it is ok to be sad. but if
u are sad becuase happiness
is fleeting, just remember that
sadness is also fleeting too.

when u are sad, it is ok to let
urself be sad. that is ok

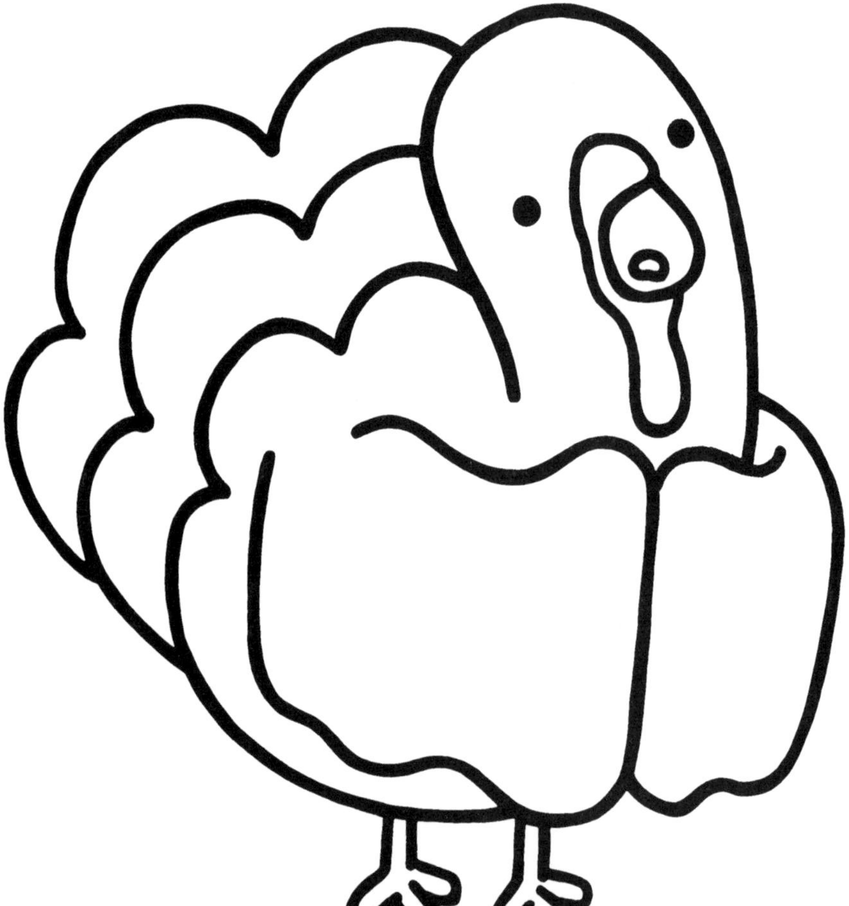

enjoy ur sadness. one
day even ur sadness
will be over too soon

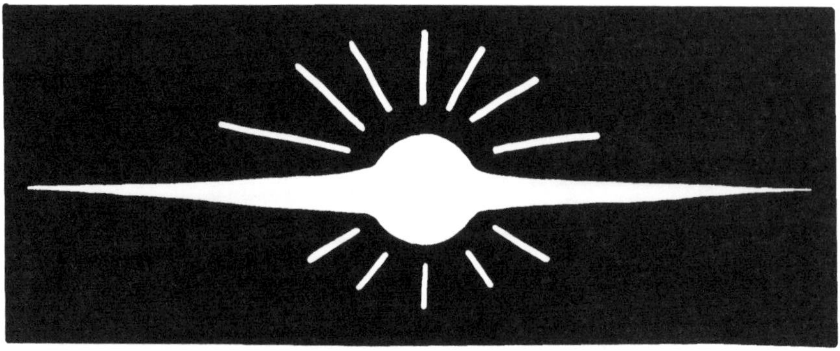

a explosion of light..

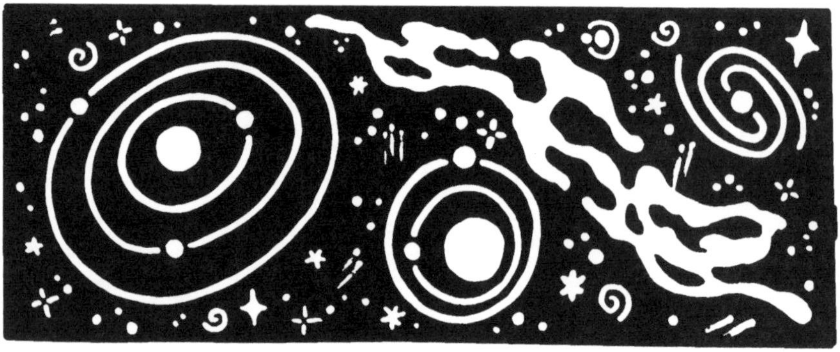

..the universe is created.

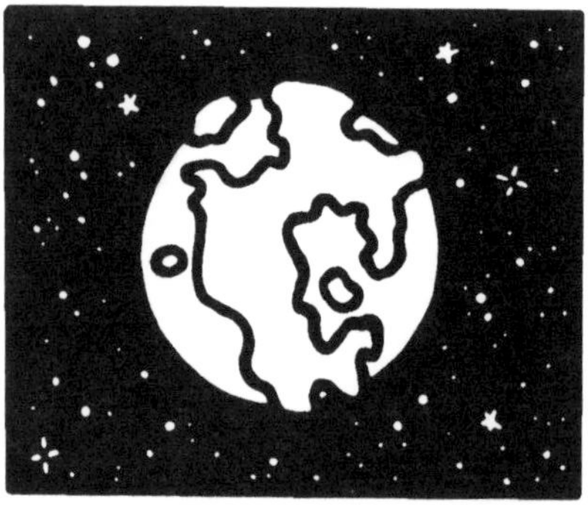

earth forms..

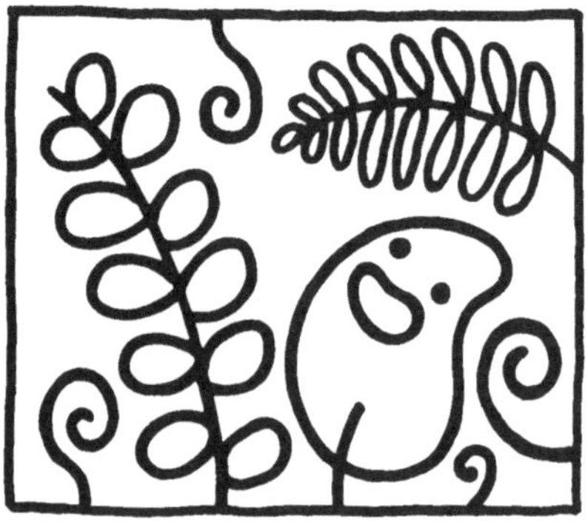

plants grow..

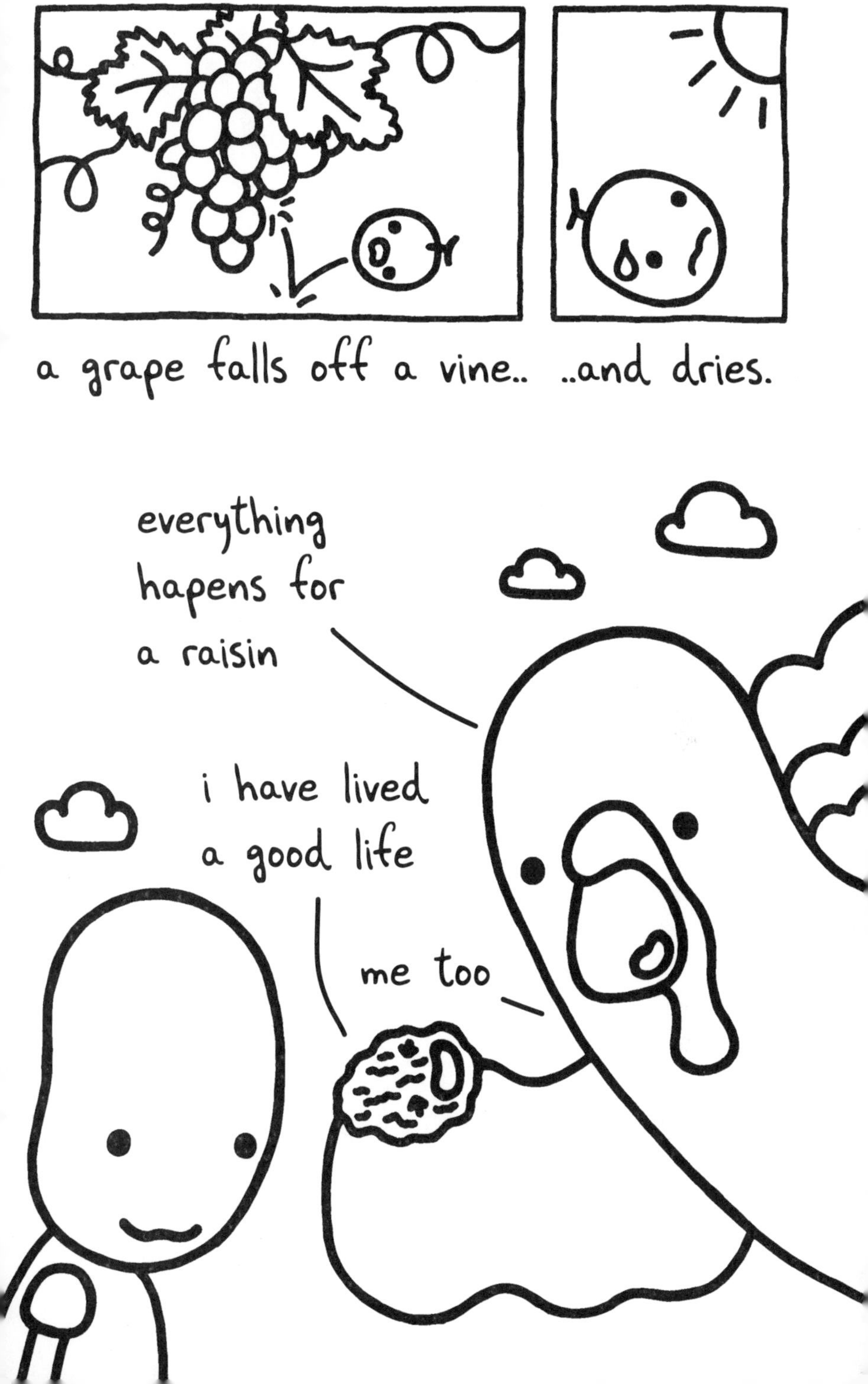
a grape falls off a vine..
..and dries.
everything hapens for a raisin
i have lived a good life
me too

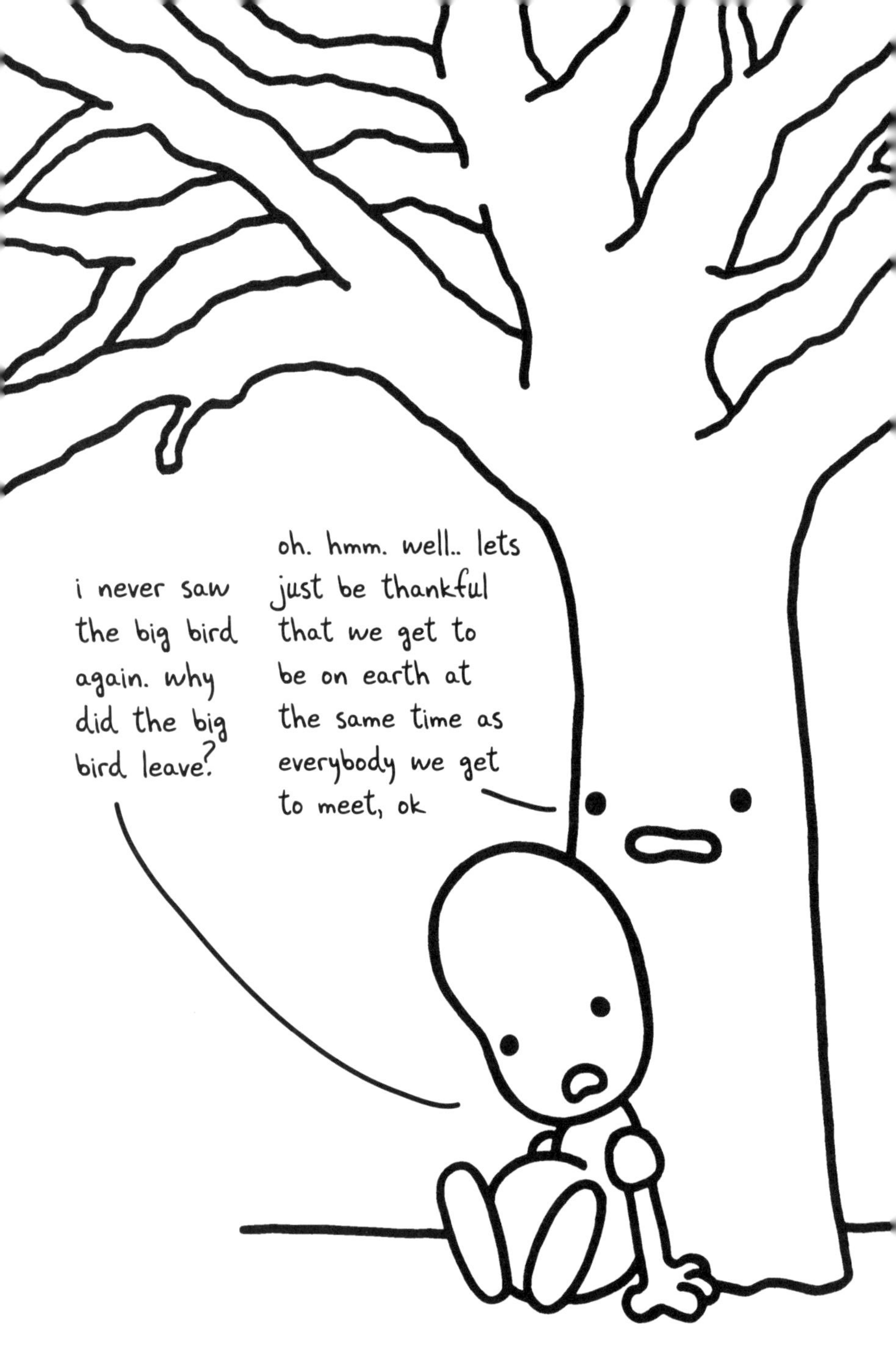
i never saw the big bird again. why did the big bird leave?
oh. hmm. well.. lets just be thankful that we get to be on earth at the same time as everybody we get to meet, ok

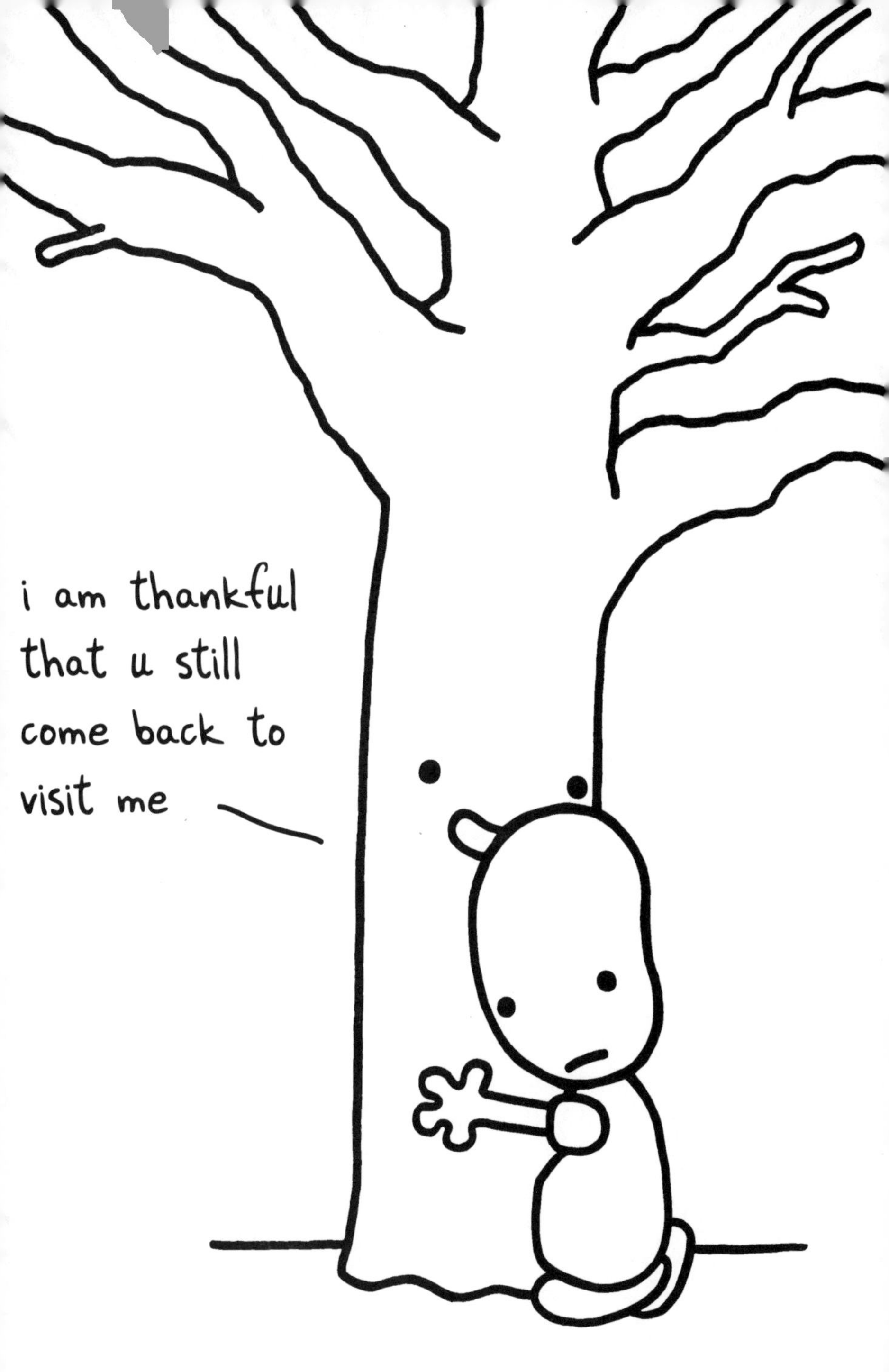
i am thankful
that u still
come back to
visit me

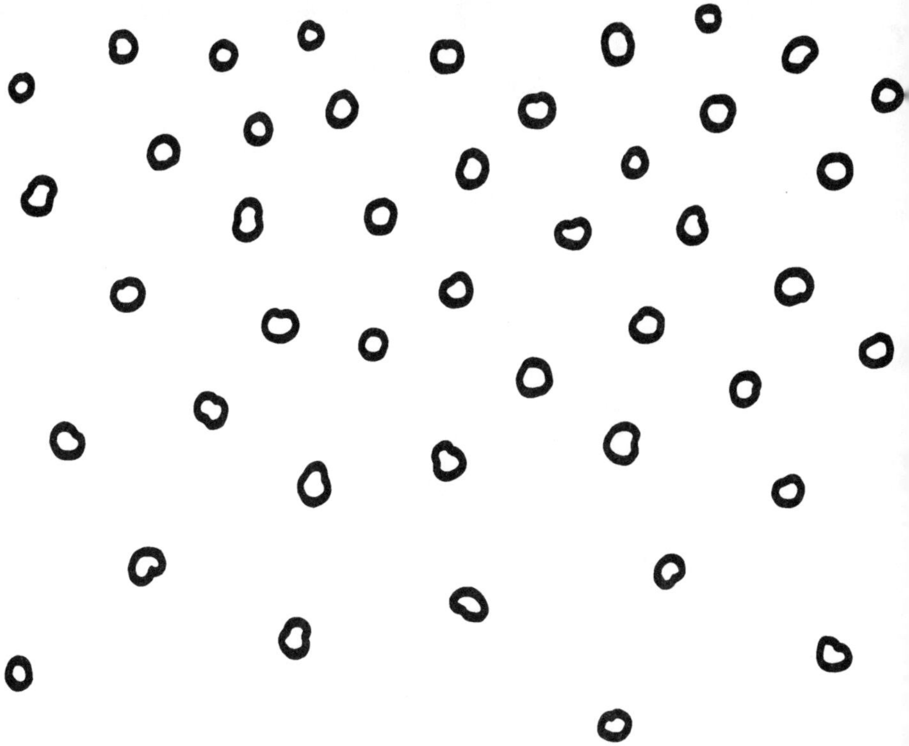

YOU CANNOT
FEEL IT BUT
I AM GIVING
YOU A HUG
RIGHT NOW.

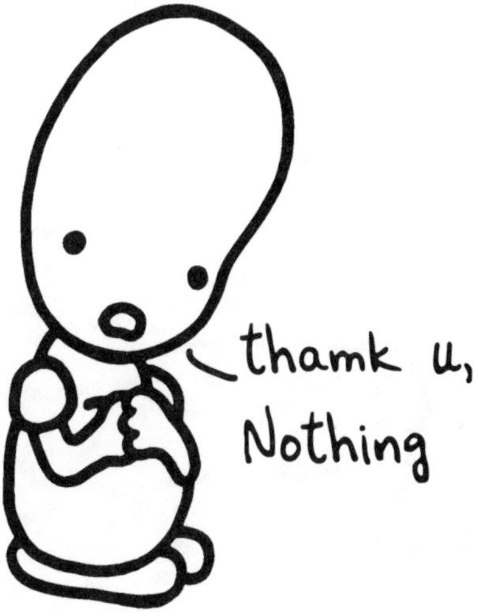
thamk u,
Nothing

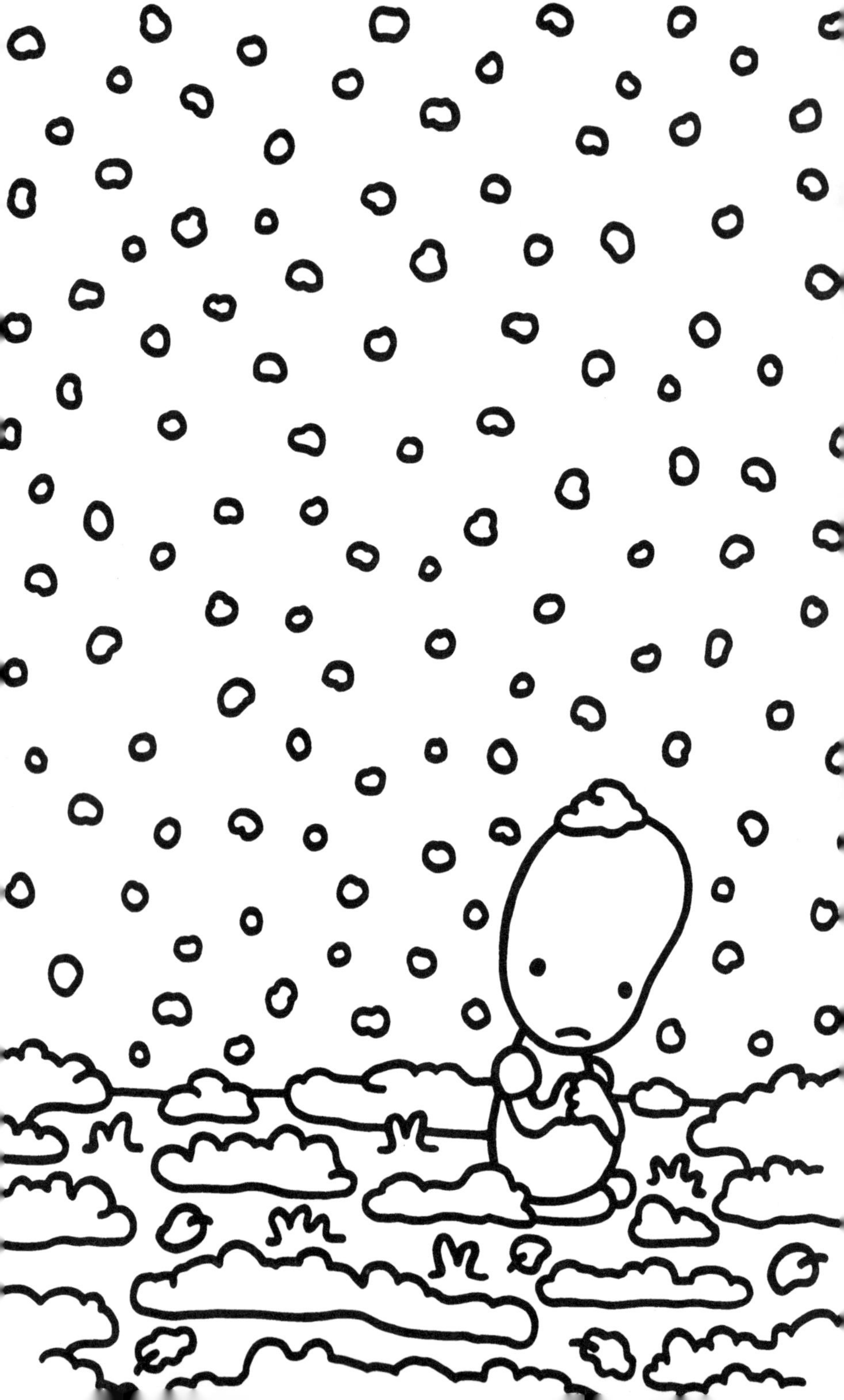

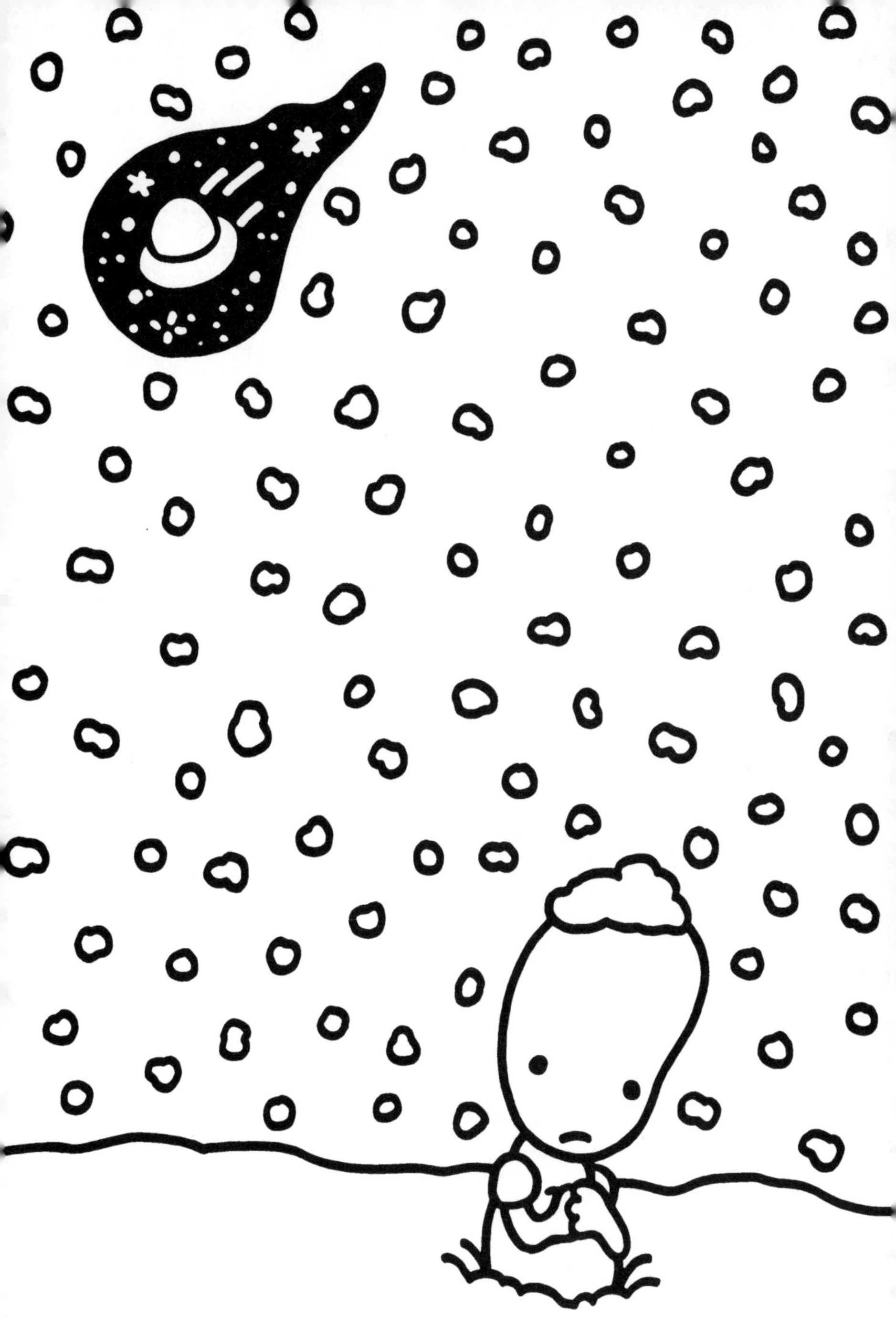

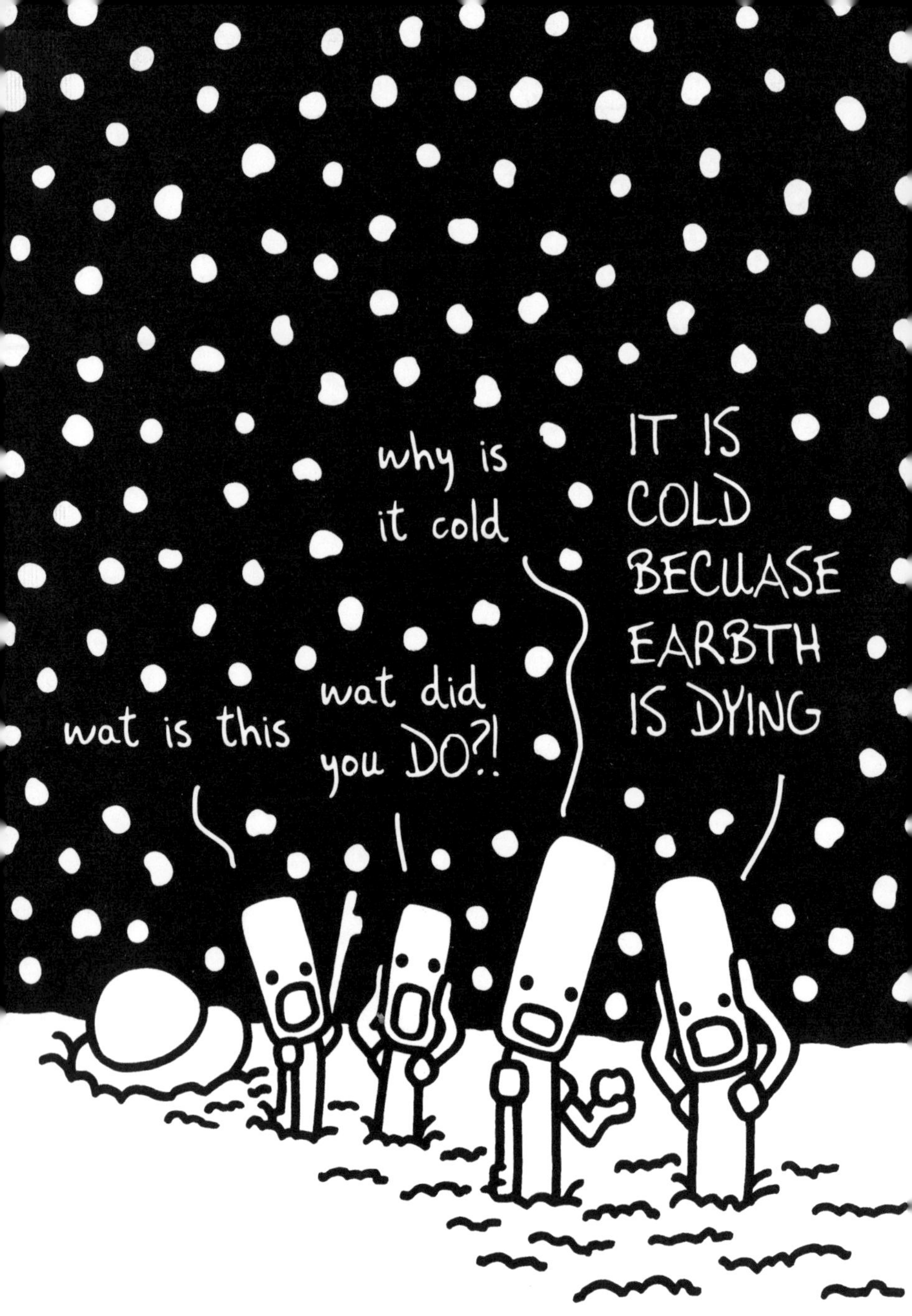
wat is this
wat did you DO?!
why is it cold
IT IS COLD BECUASE EARBTH IS DYING

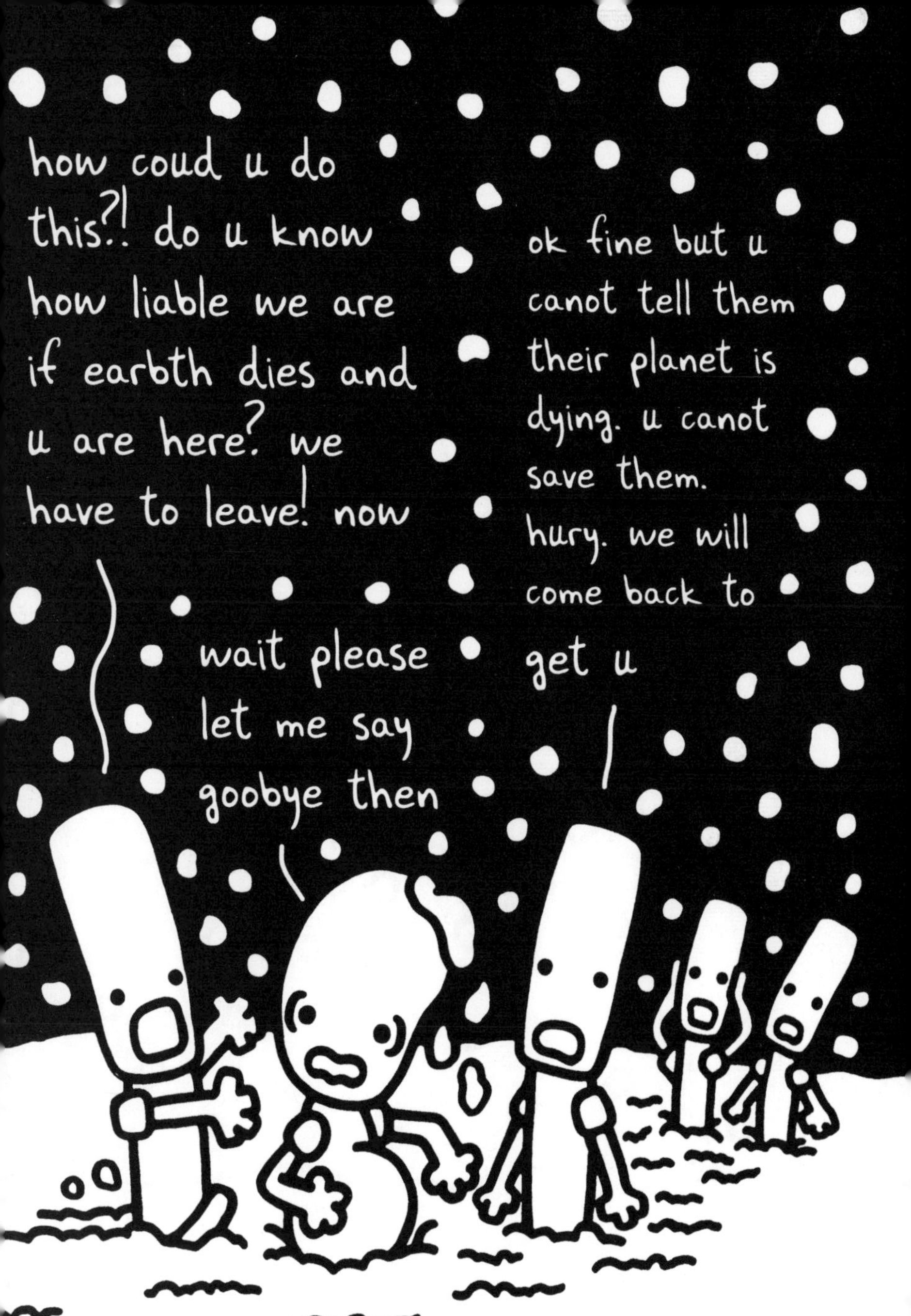
how coud u do this?! do u know how liable we are if earbth dies and u are here? we have to leave! now
ok fine but u canot tell them their planet is dying. u canot save them. hury. we will come back to get u
wait please let me say goobye then

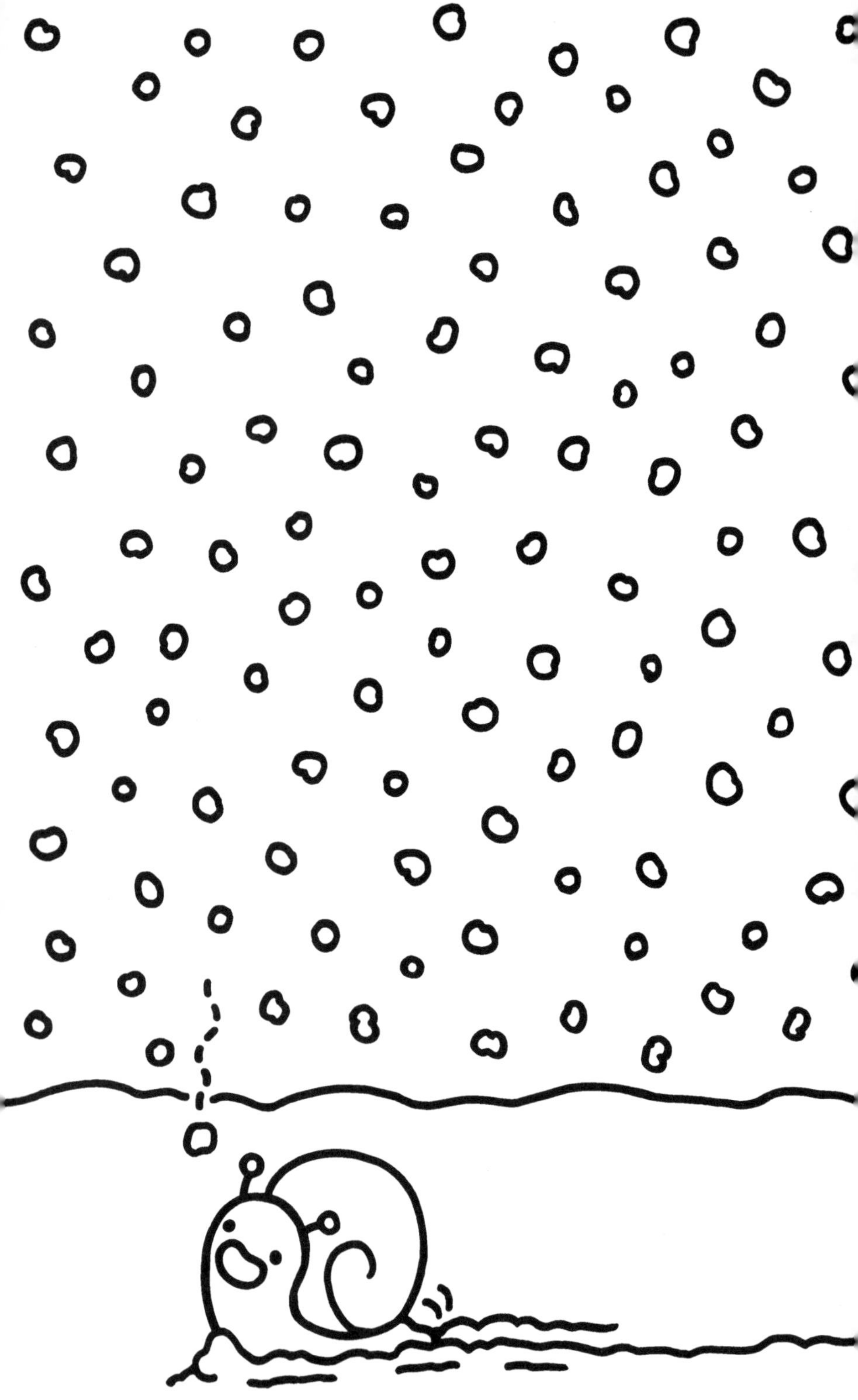

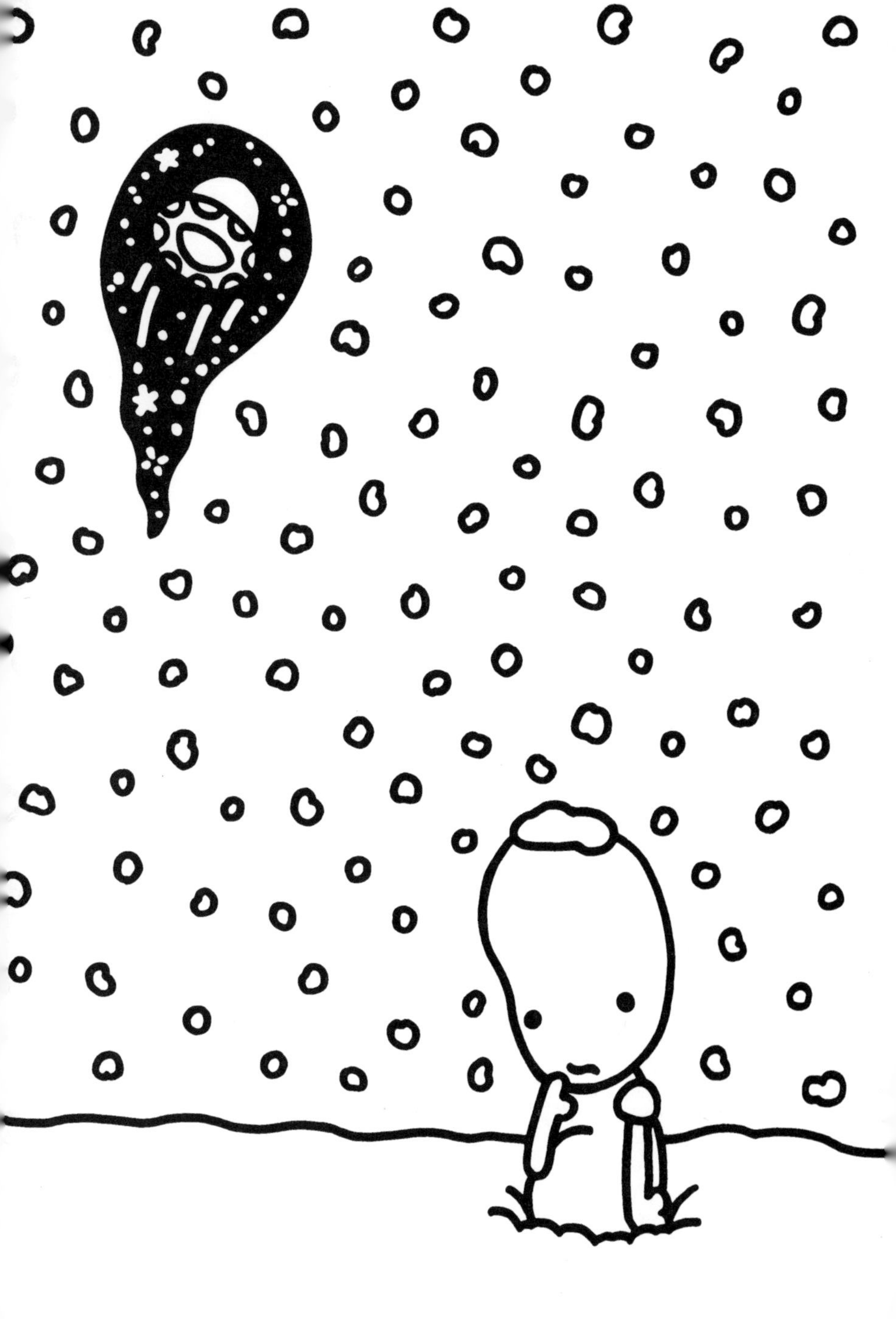

PERSONALLY,
I LIKE THE SNOW..
IT CREATES MORE
NOTHING. EARTH
IS NOT DYING.. IT
IS JUST GETTING
SIMPLER.

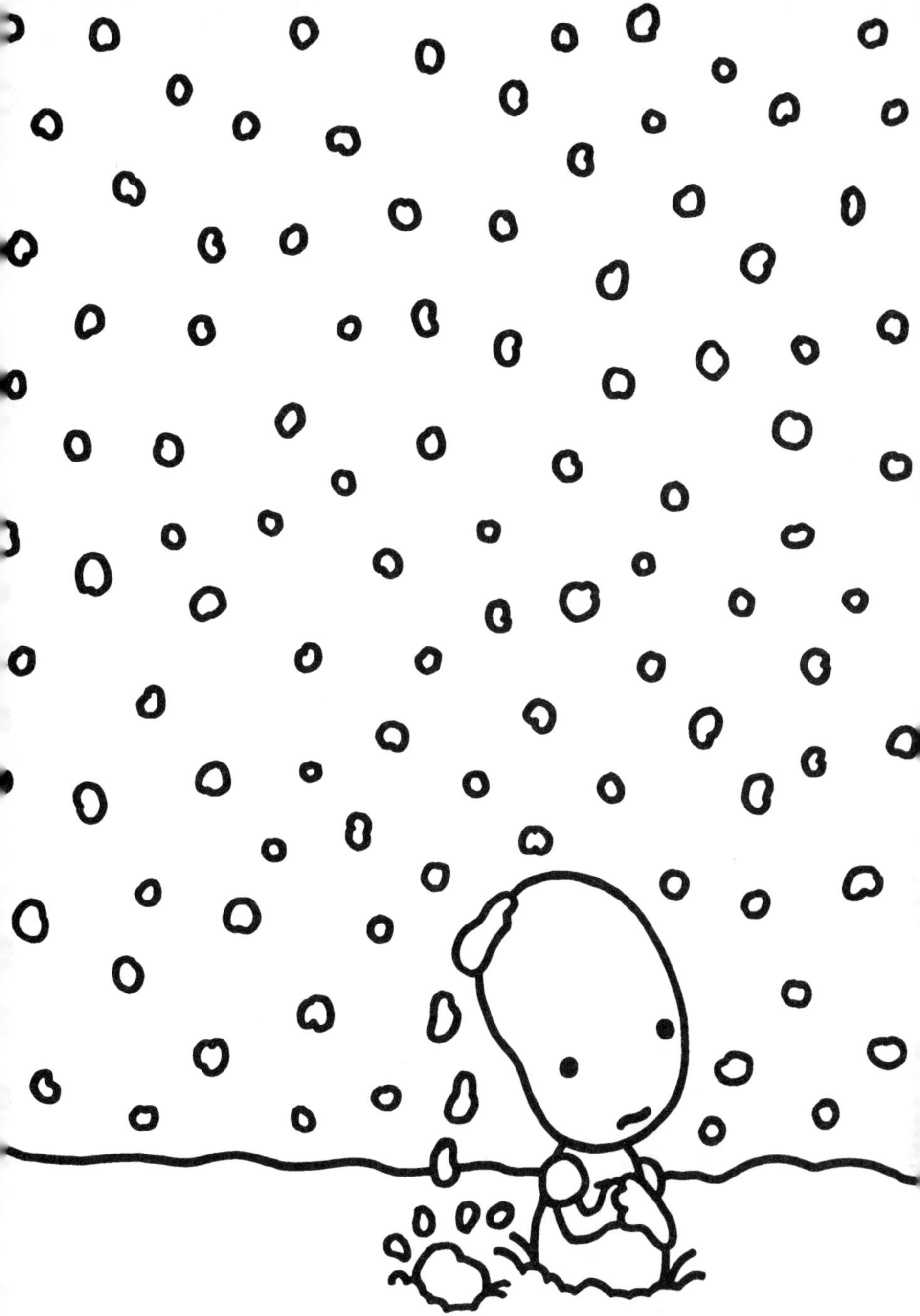

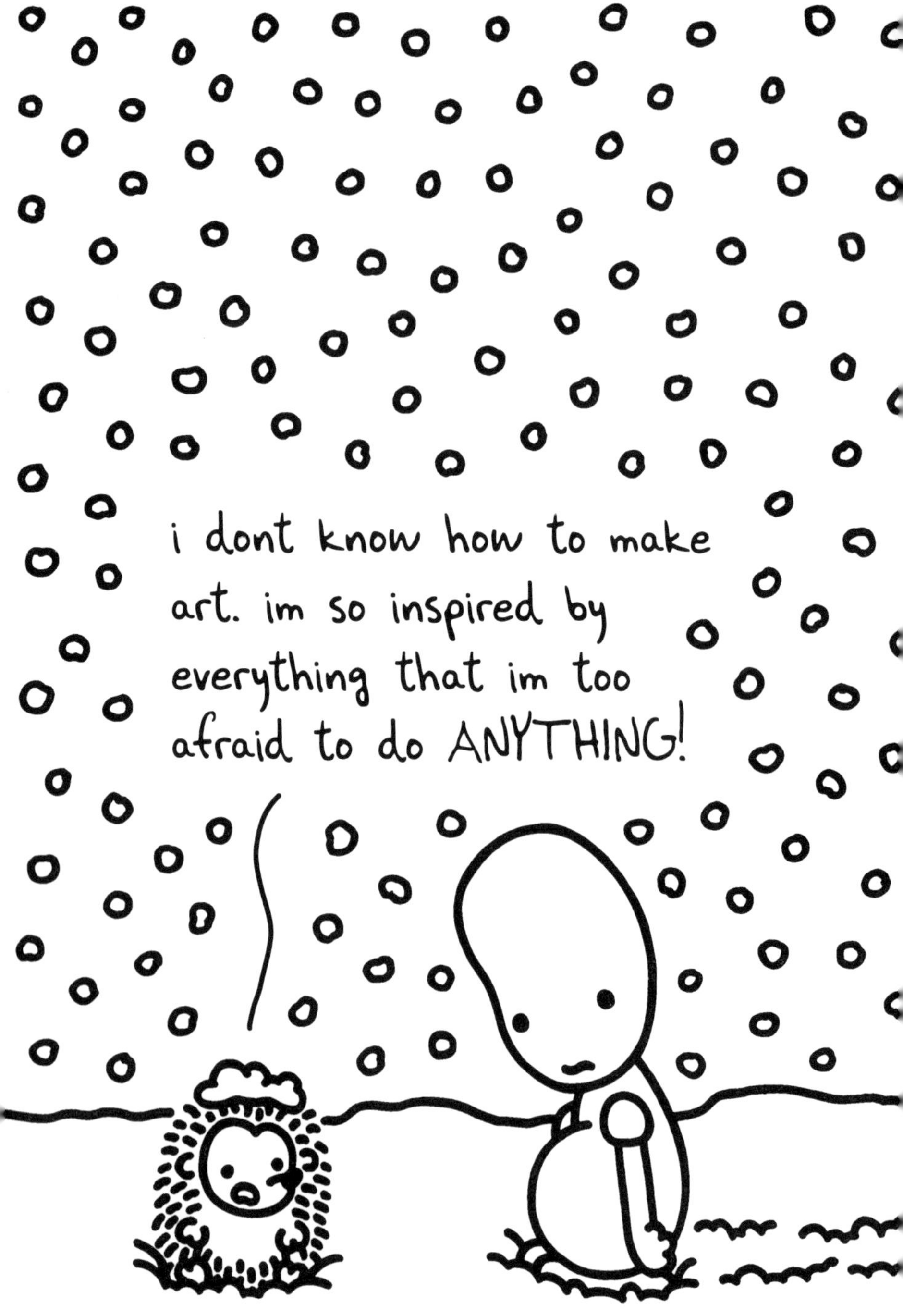
i dont know how to make art. im so inspired by everything that im too afraid to do ANYTHING!

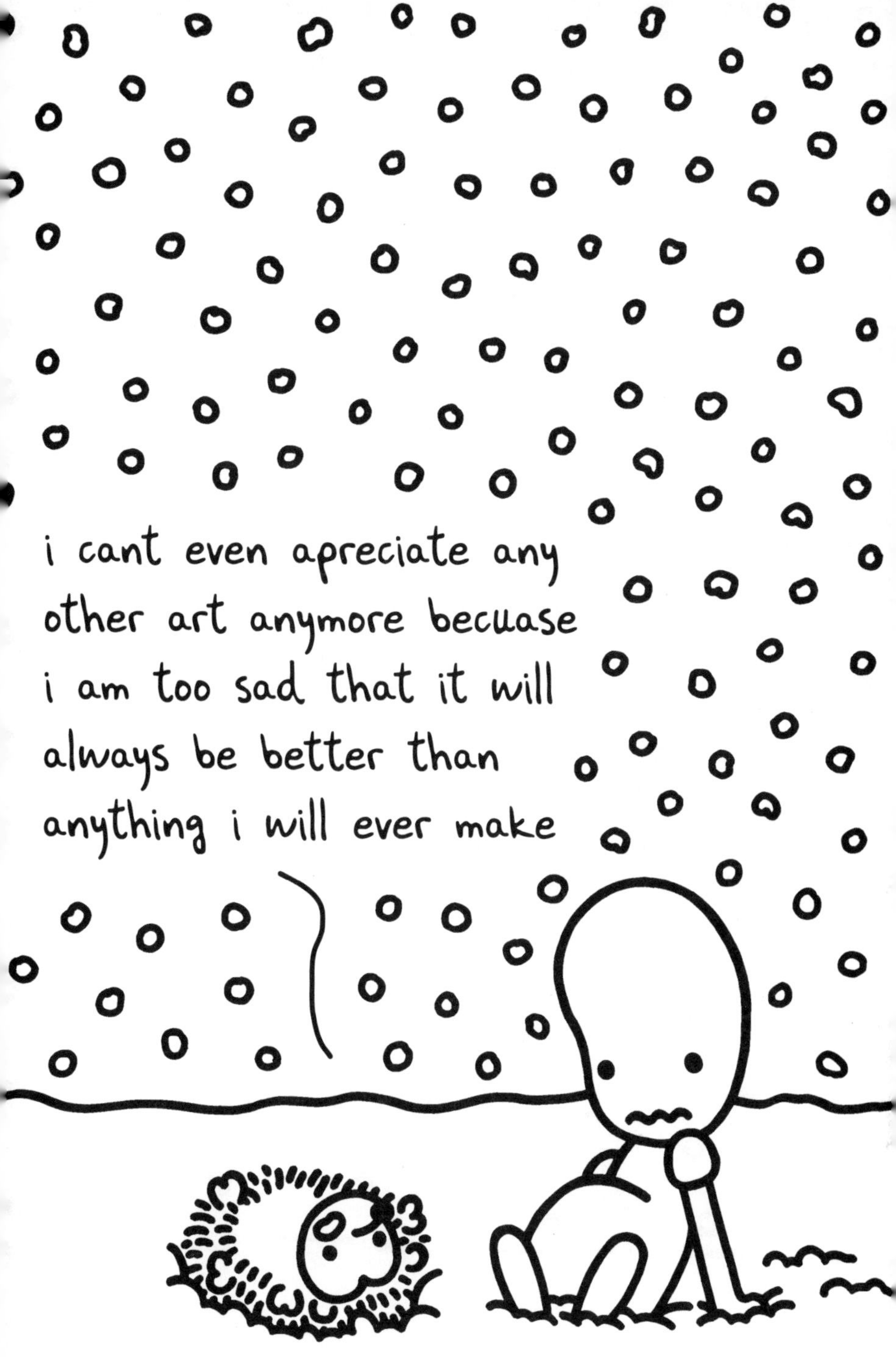

i cant even apreciate any other art anymore becuase i am too sad that it will always be better than anything i will ever make

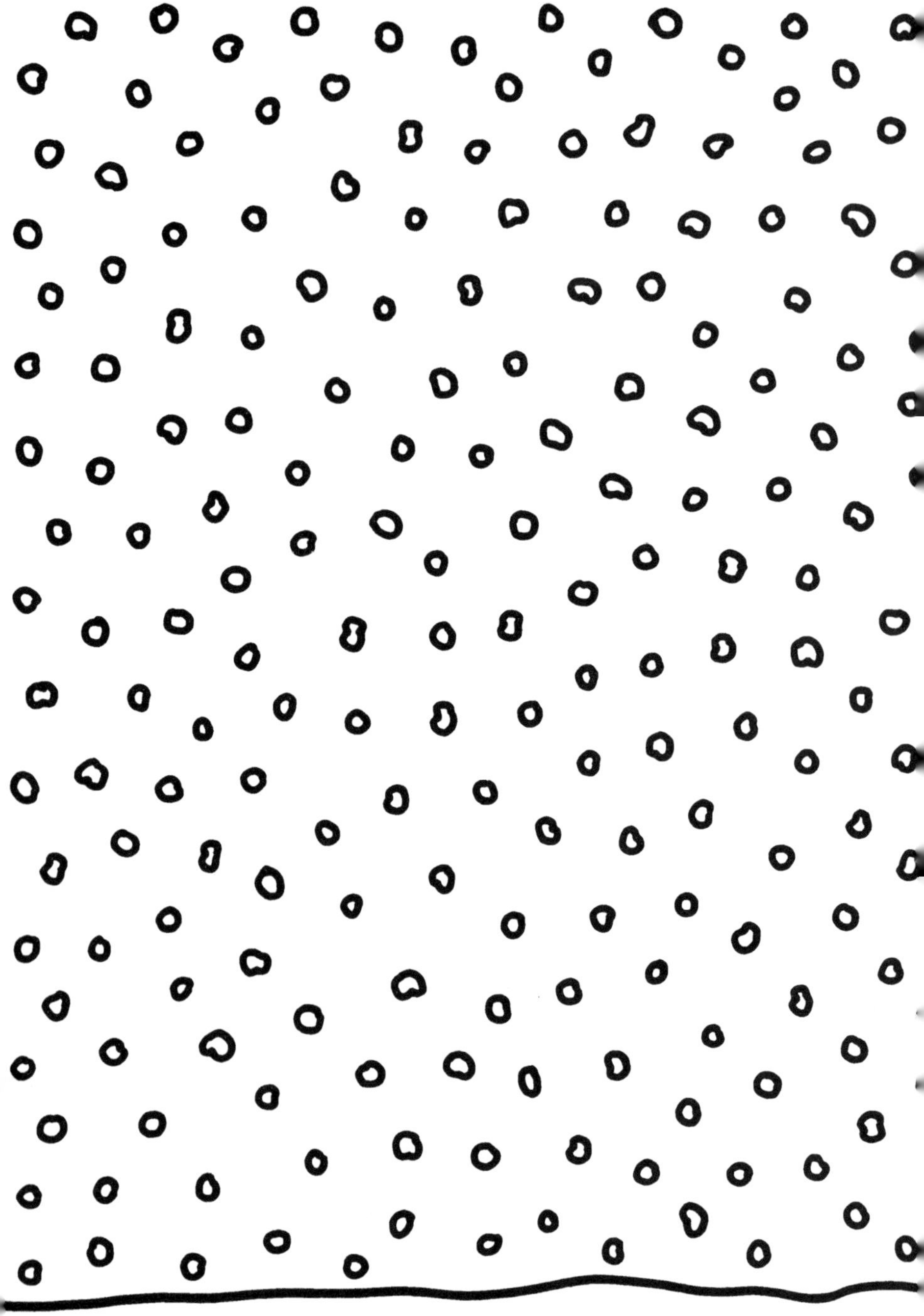

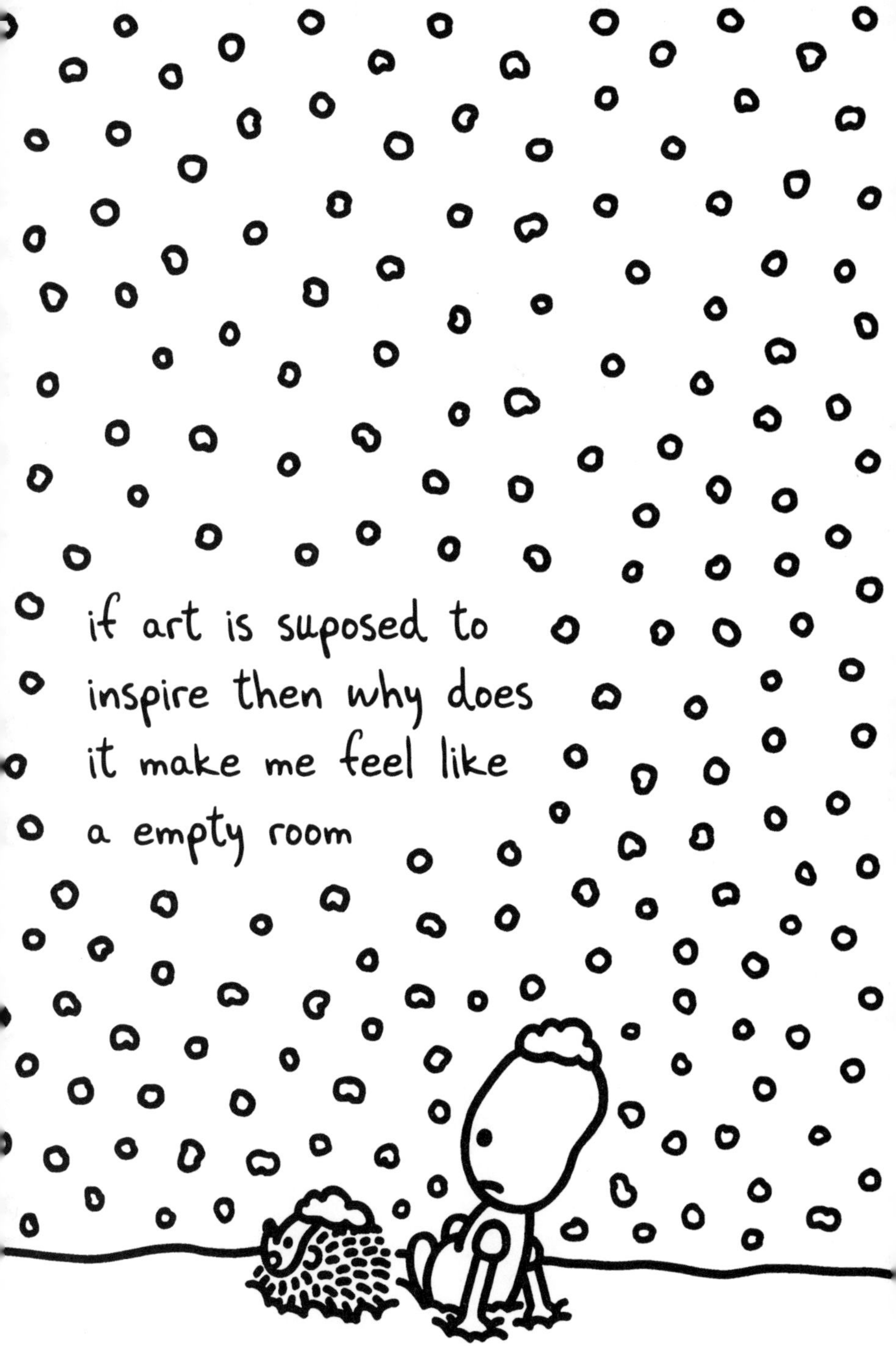
if art is suposed to inspire then why does it make me feel like a empty room

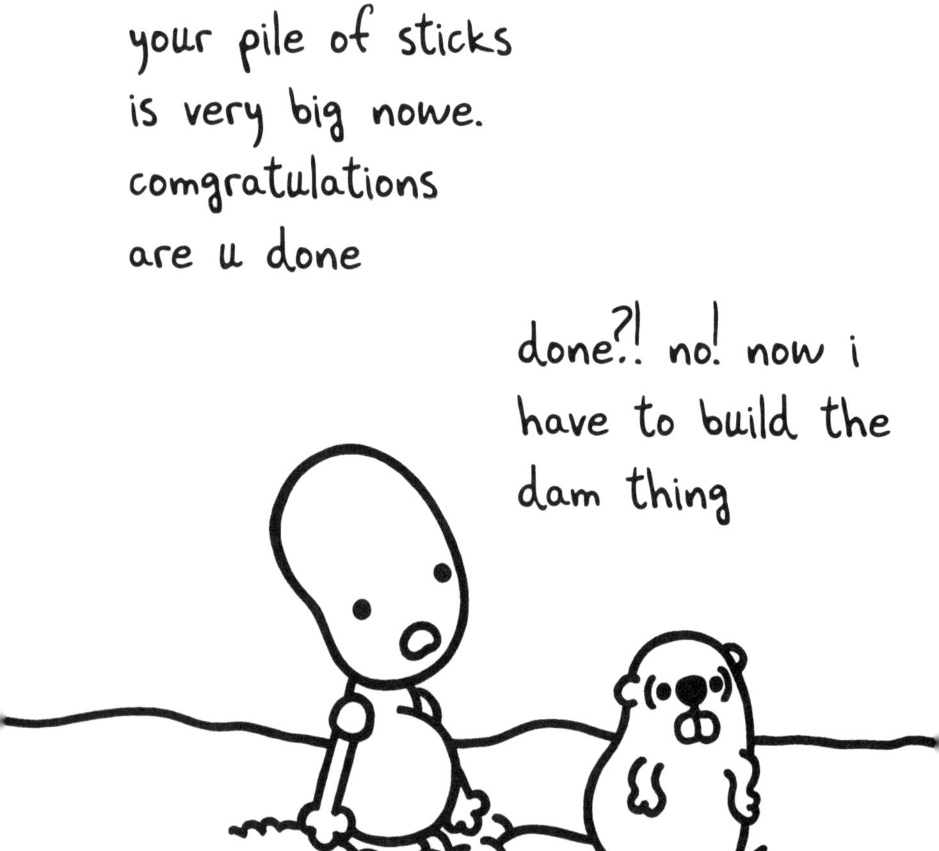
your pile of sticks
is very big nowe.
comgratulations
are u done
done?! no! now i
have to build the
dam thing

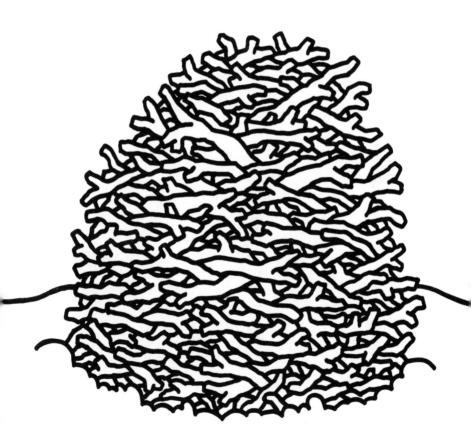

helo. i brought u
somthing. this is stick

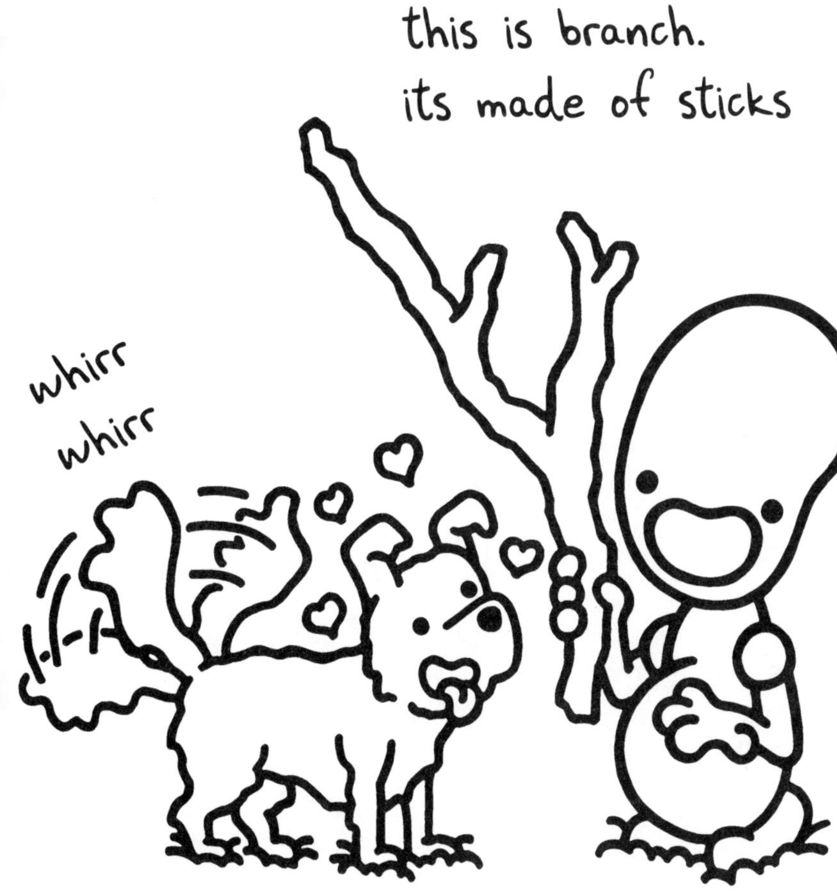
this is branch.
its made of sticks
whirr
whirr

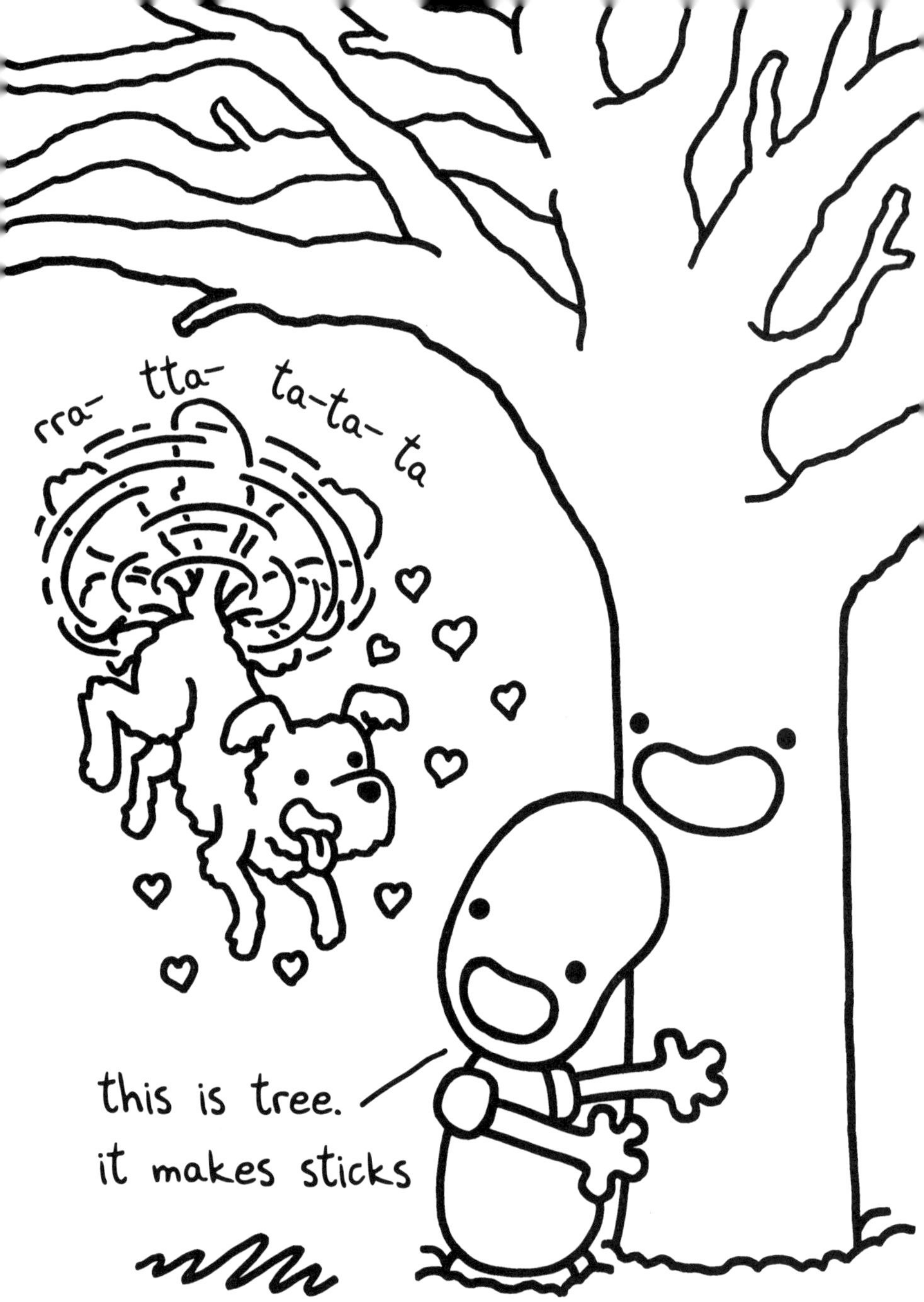
rra- tta- ta-ta- ta
this is tree.
it makes sticks

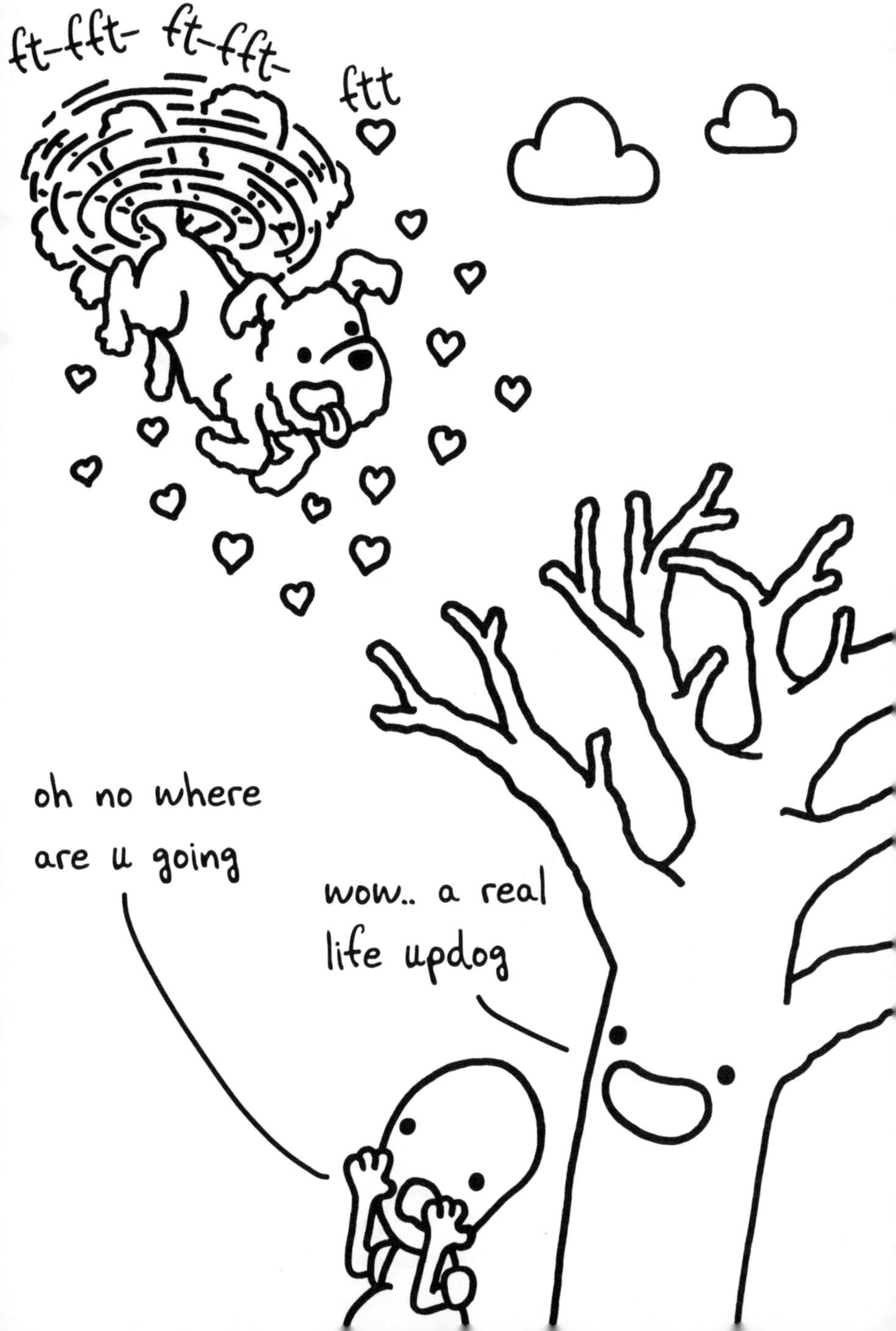
ft-fft- ft-fft-
ftt
oh no where are u going
wow.. a real life updog

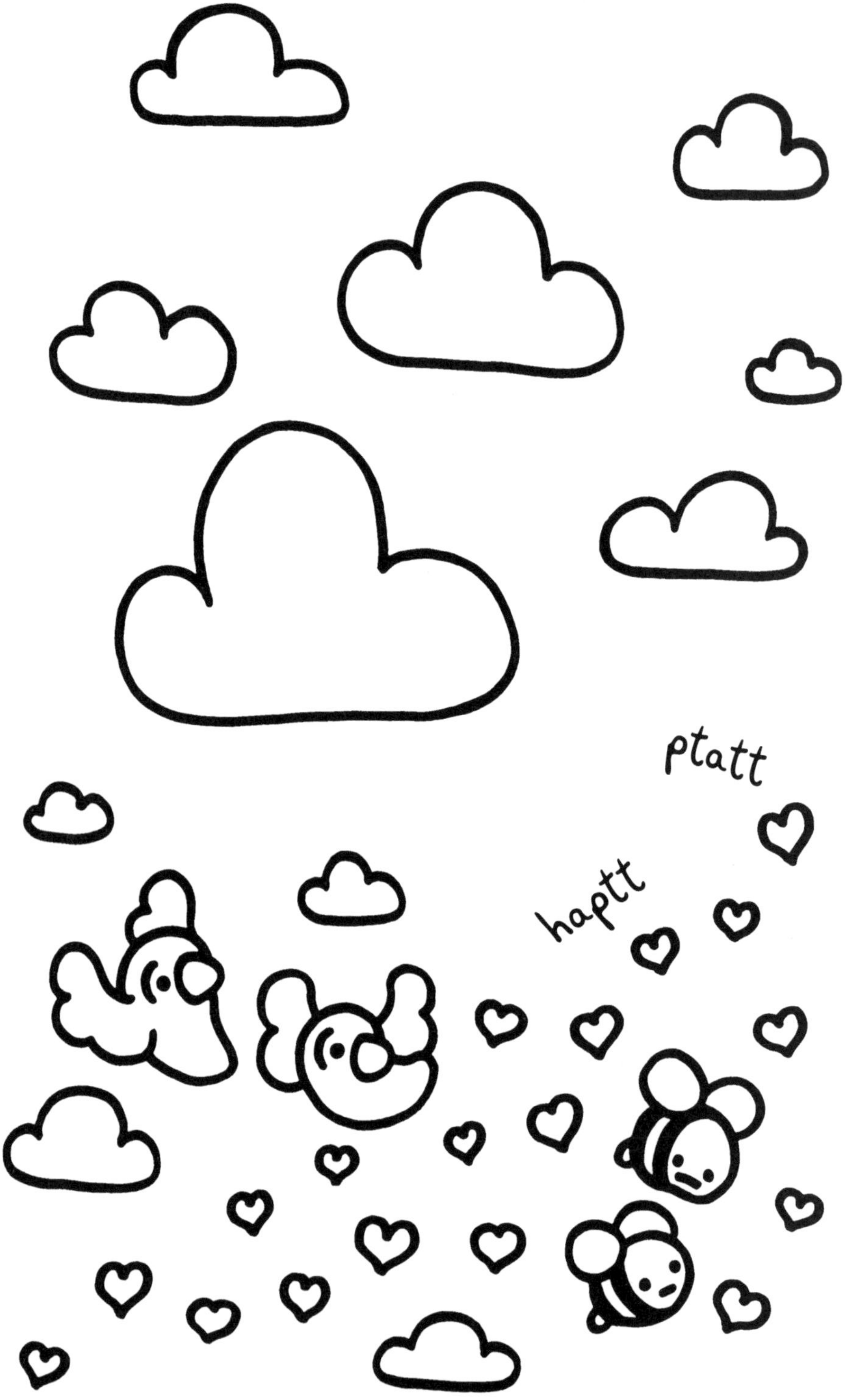
ptatt
haptt

rttr
rttpa
tta
rpttp
i am always hapy
but then it sadens
me that i can never
express how hapy
i am in words so
others understand

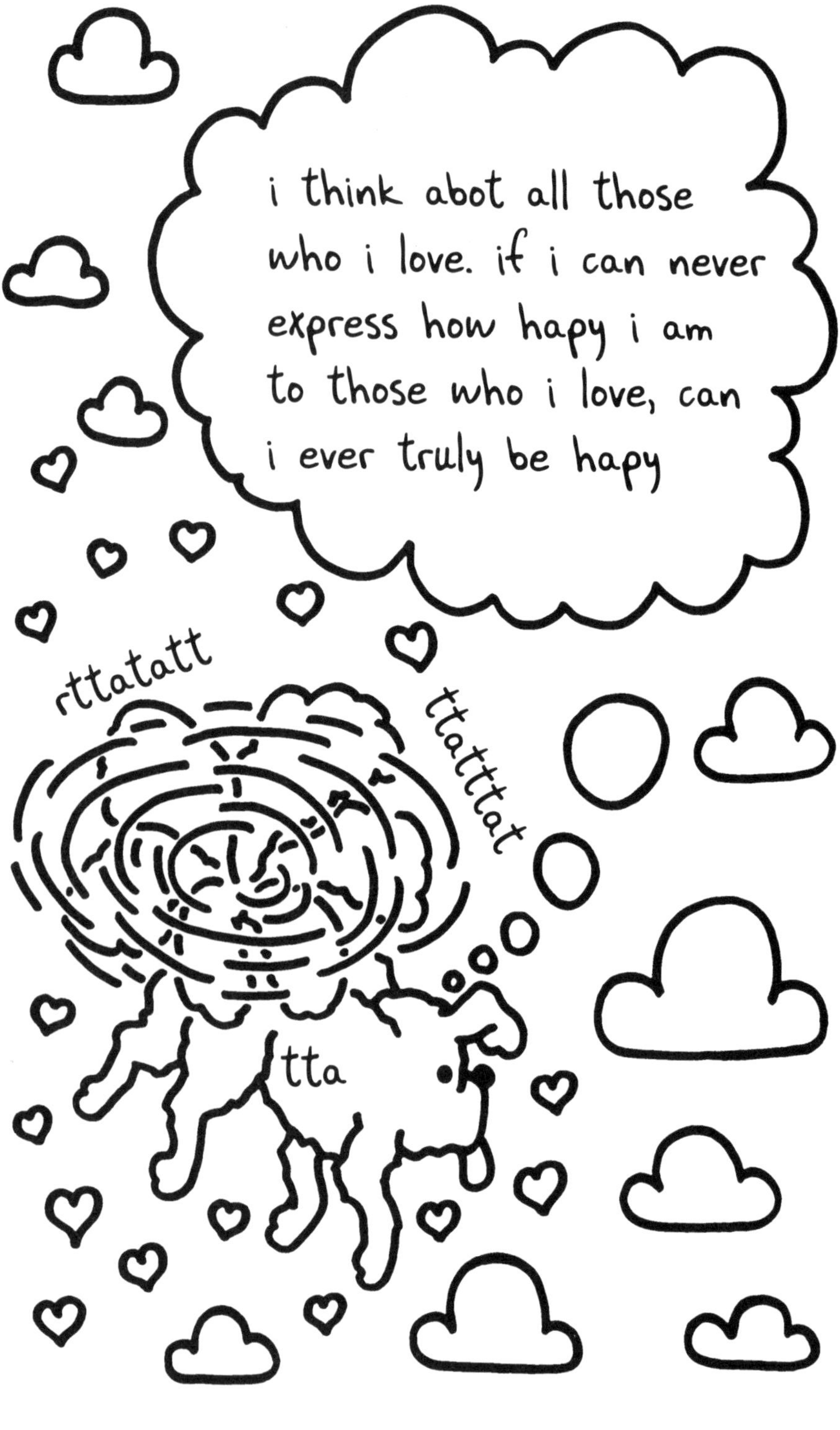
i think abot all those who i love. if i can never express how hapy i am to those who i love, can i ever truly be hapy
rttatatt
ttatttat
tta

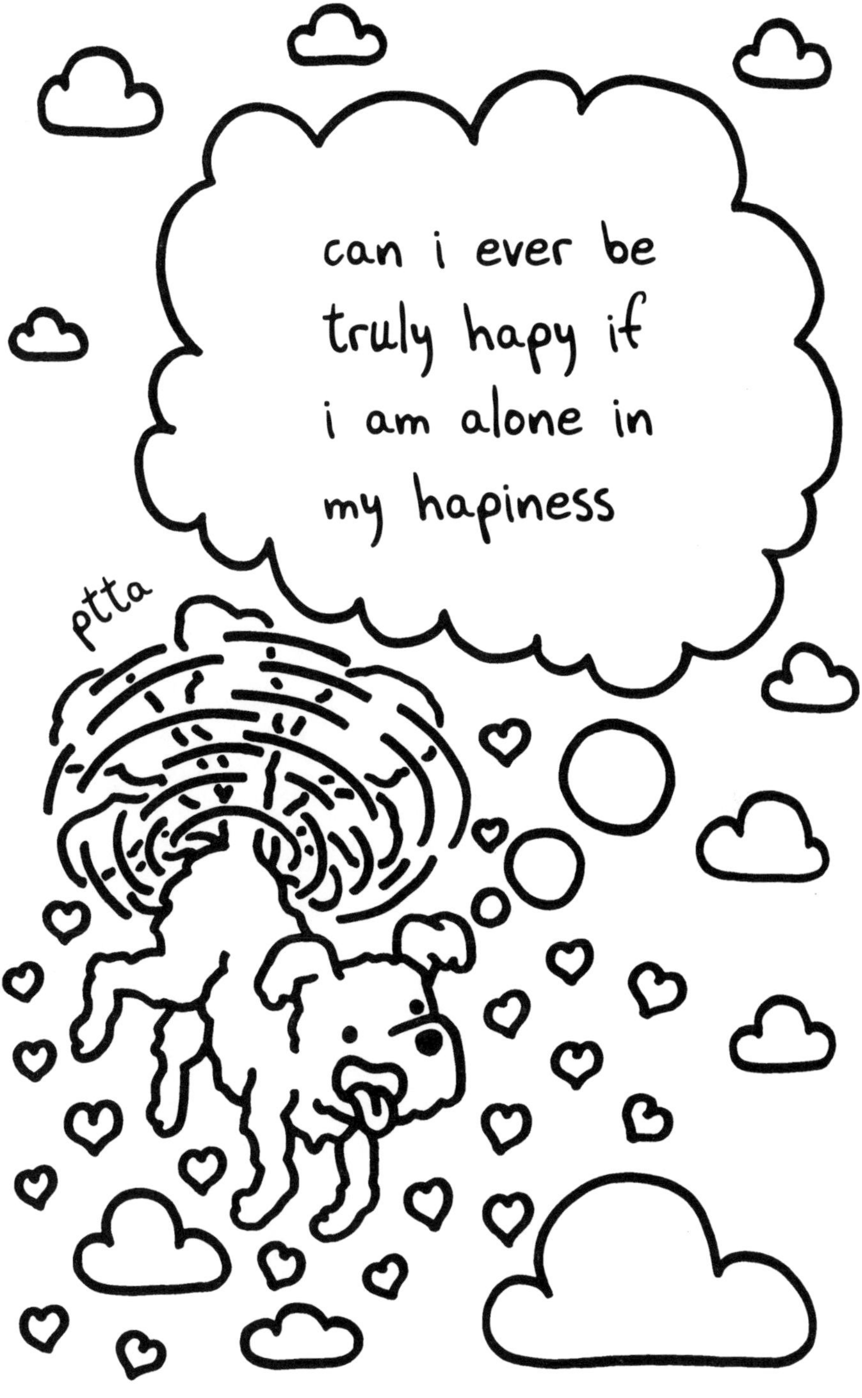
can i ever be truly hapy if i am alone in my hapiness
ptta

tta-ta-tta

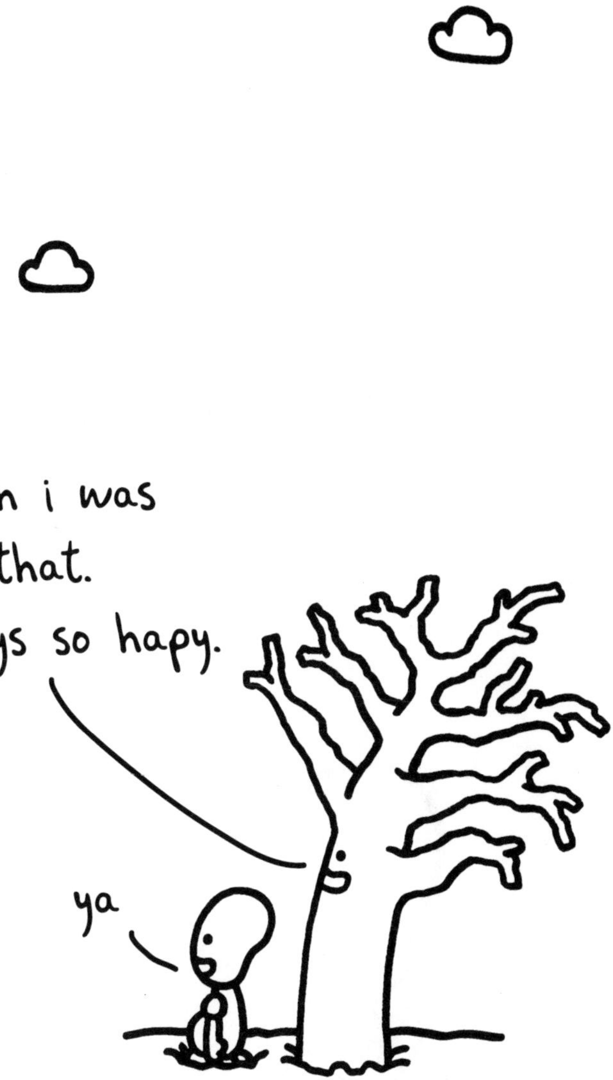
i wish i was
like that.
always so hapy.
ya

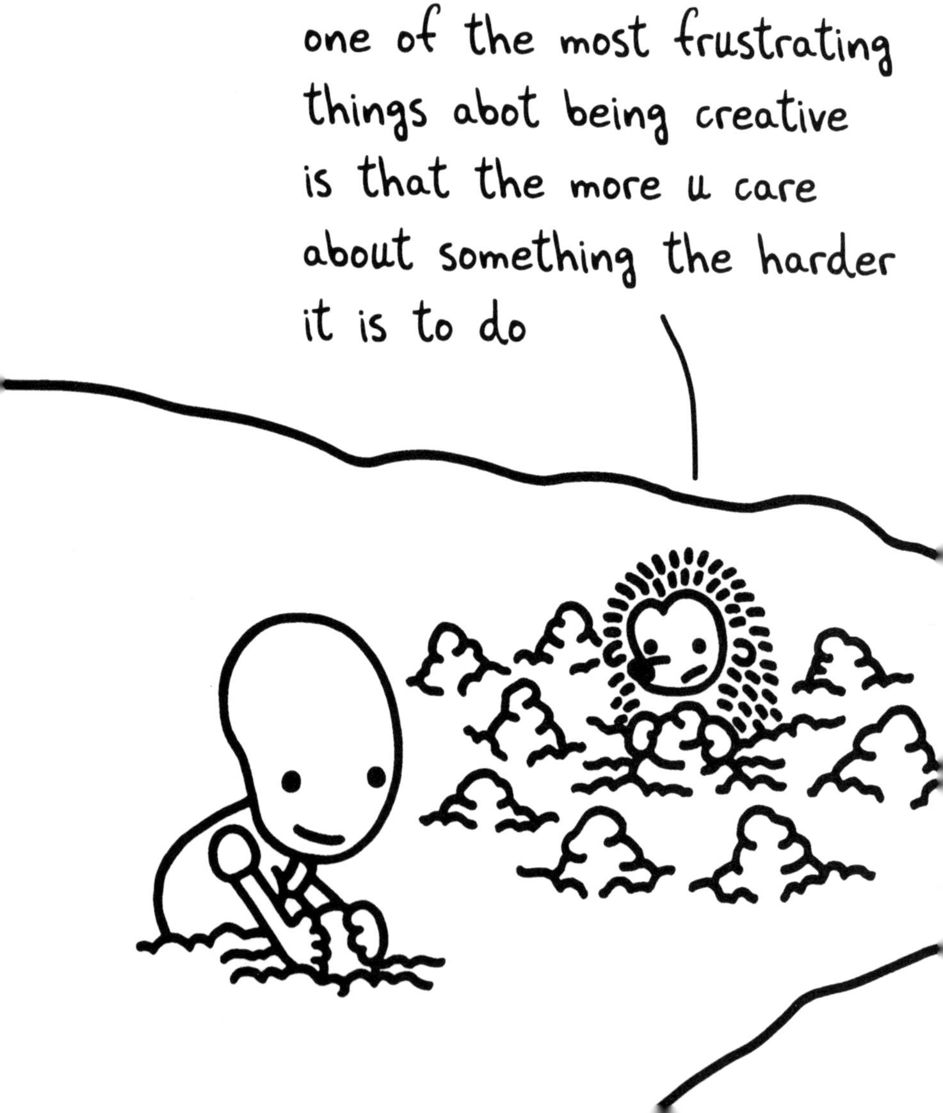
one of the most frustrating things abot being creative is that the more u care about something the harder it is to do

Creativity needs constraints, my dear! When the constraints get tighter, you will find more opportunities to be creative!

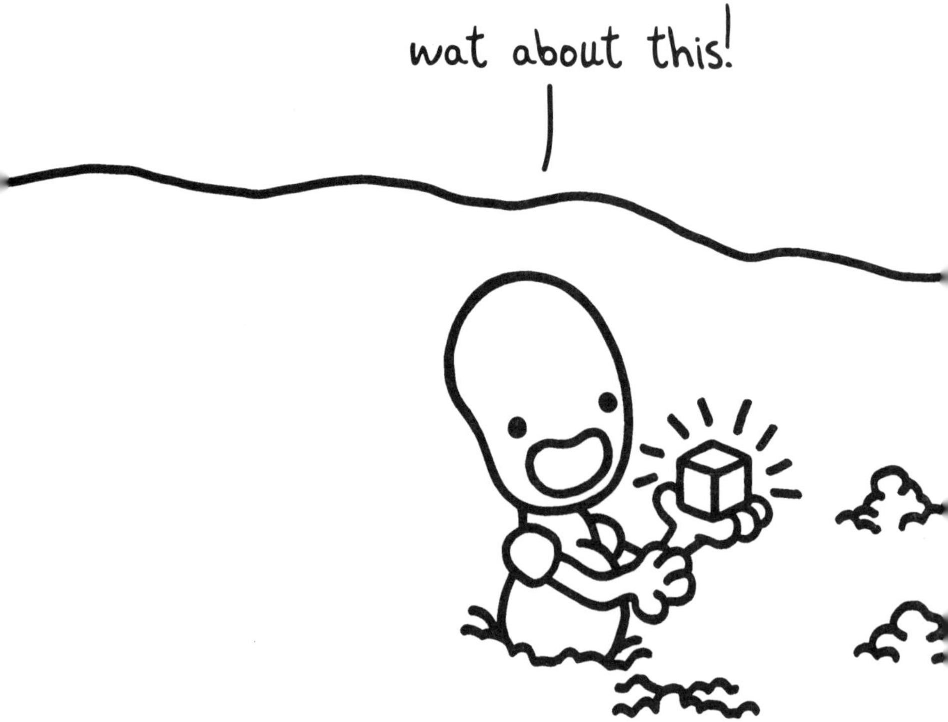
wat about this!

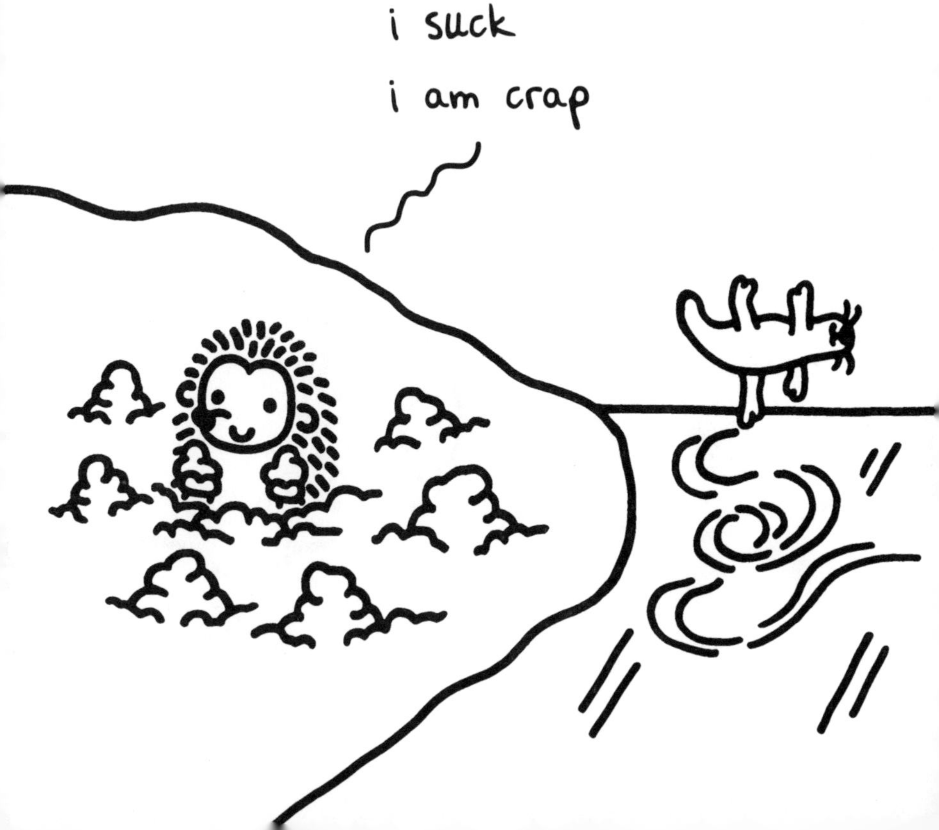
i suck
i am crap

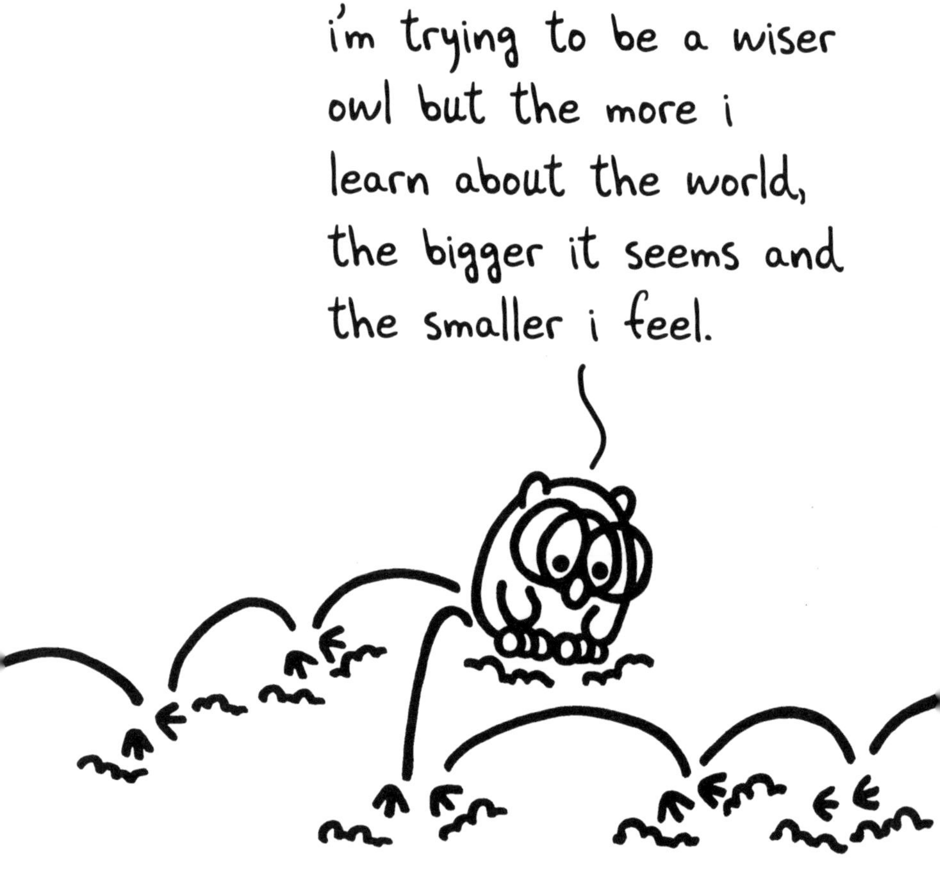
i'm trying to be a wiser owl but the more i learn about the world, the bigger it seems and the smaller i feel.

why dont u just do wat makes u hapy
i can't decide if learning things makes me happy or if knowing things makes me happy. either way, i would be sad if i knew everything and i would be sad if i knew nothing.

BUT WHY WOULD
KNOWING ME
MAKE ANYBODY
SAD? I AM QUITE
PLEASANT ONCE
YOU GET TO
KNOW ME.

im sory, Nothing.
maybe u are just
harder to get to
know because ur
only around when
others are not

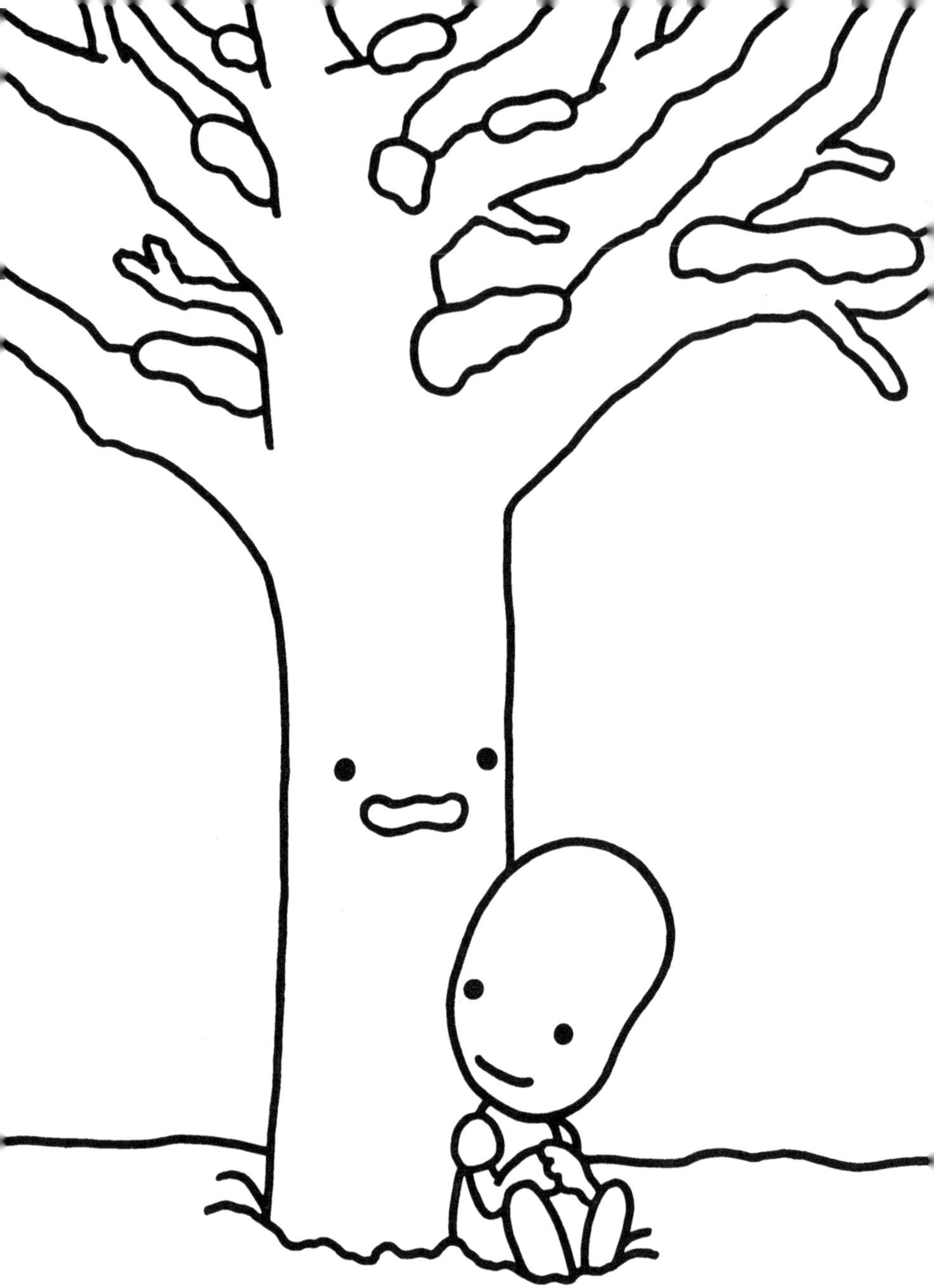

i've been wonderimg why
the lonely ones make the
most beautifubl music and
i thimk its because theyre
the ones most invested in
filling the silence

♩ i love lentils ♪

BUT WHY DOES
SILENCE NEED TO
BE FILLED AT ALL?
I LOVE SILENCE.
IT IS MY FAVORITE
MUSIC

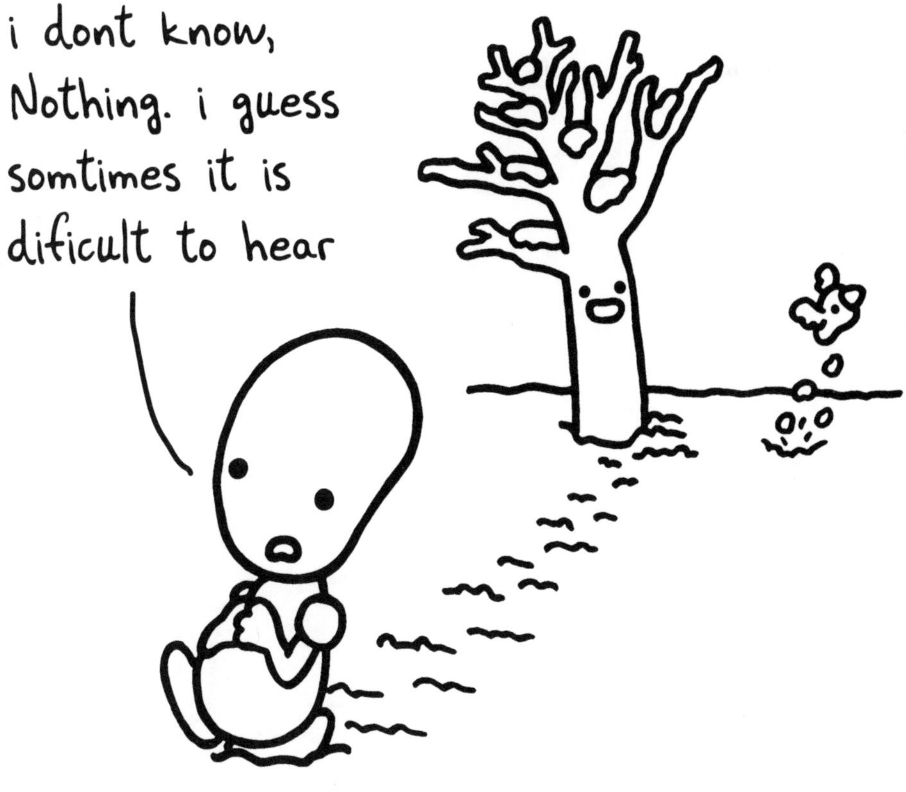
i dont know, Nothing. i guess somtimes it is dificult to hear

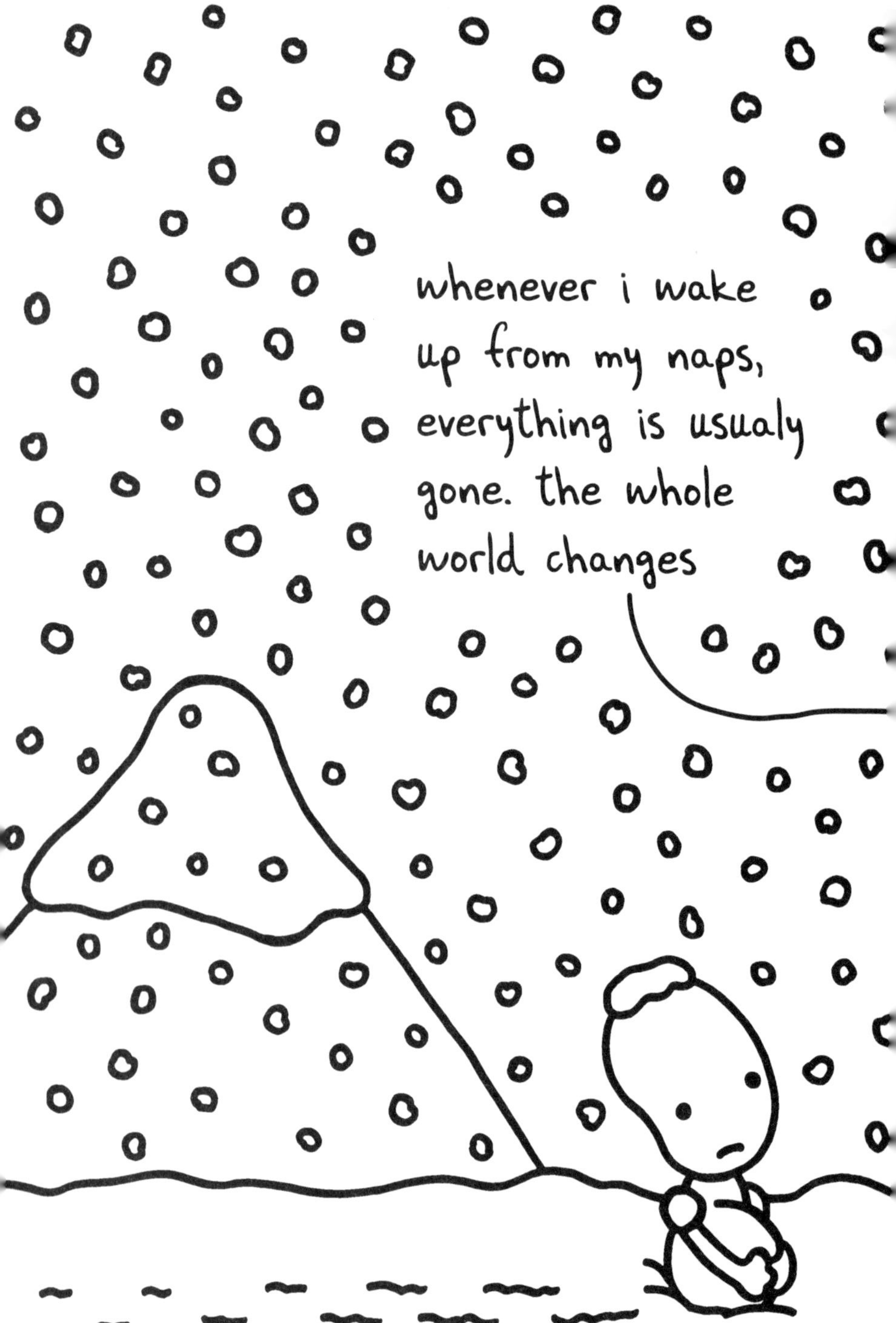
whenever i wake up from my naps, everything is usualy gone. the whole world changes

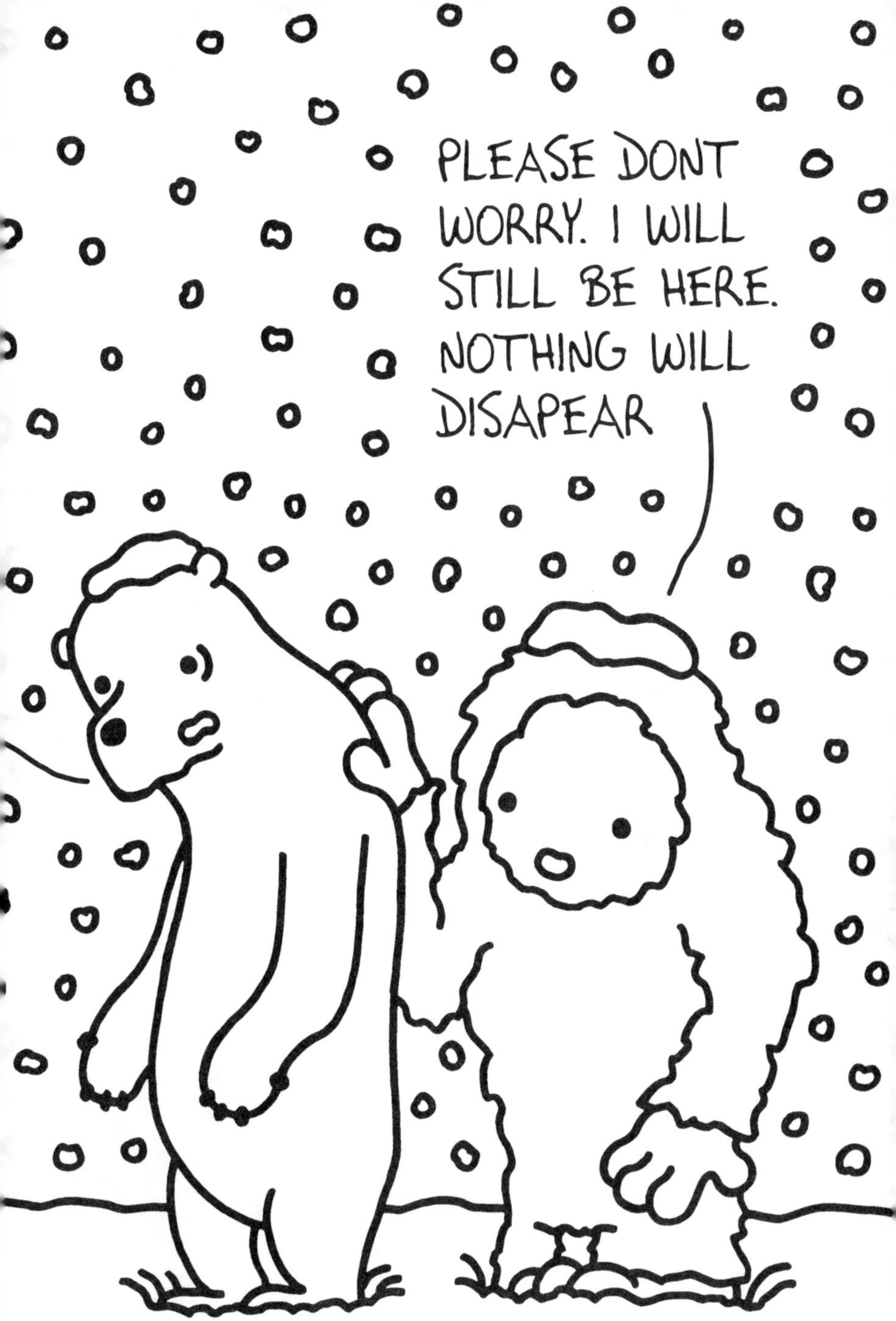
PLEASE DONT WORRY. I WILL STILL BE HERE. NOTHING WILL DISAPEAR

OH.. MAYBE
I SHOULD
DISAPPEAR. I
DO NOT THINK
ANYBODY HERE
NEEDS ME. I
AM GOING TO
LEAVE.

no dont leave,
dont be sad

I AM SORRY.
I CANNOT.
FOR THE FIRST
TIME, I FEEL..
EMPTY.

I AM GOING
TO GO ENJOY
MY SADNESS
SOMEWHERE
ELSE, BY
MYSELF.

..GOOD-BYE.

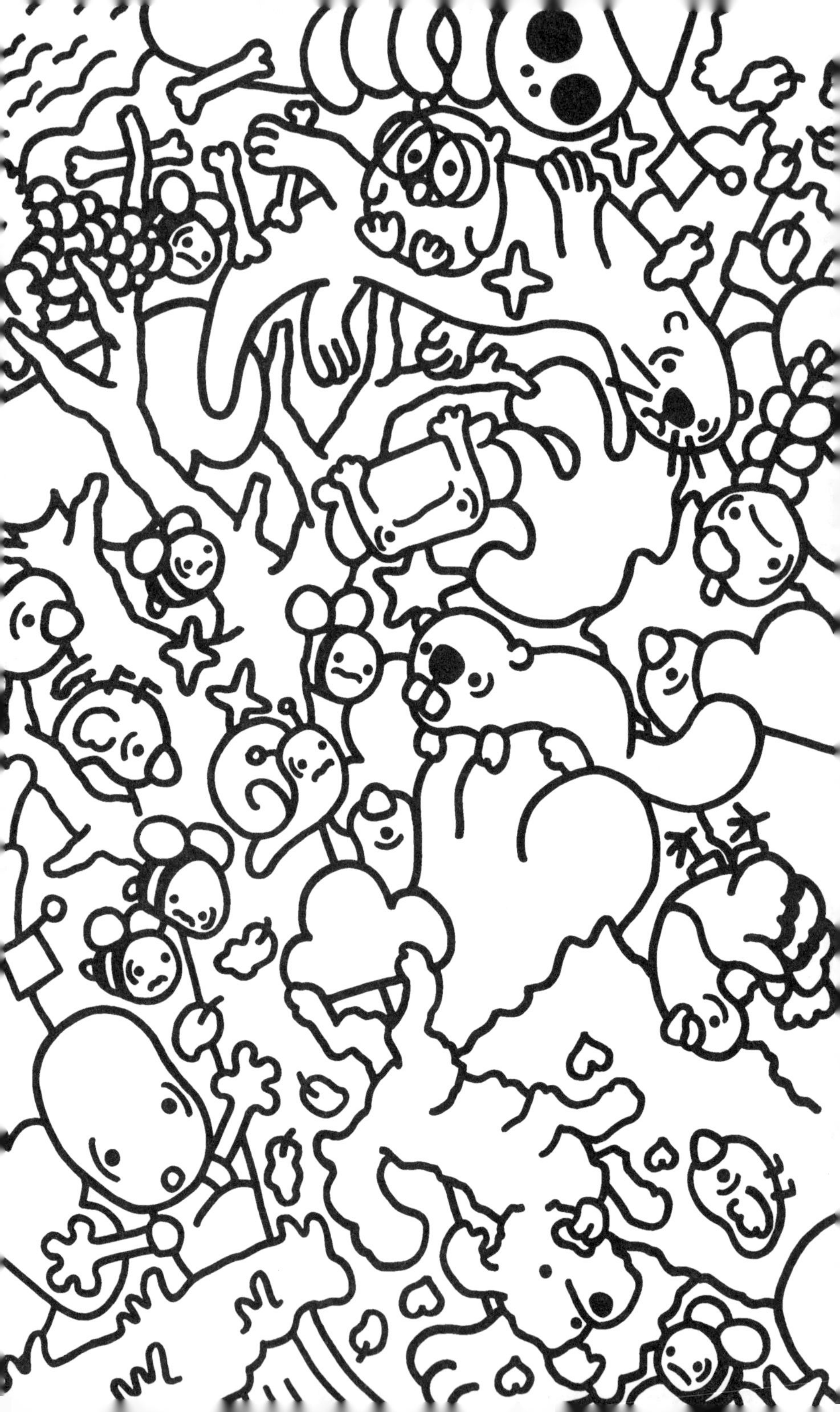

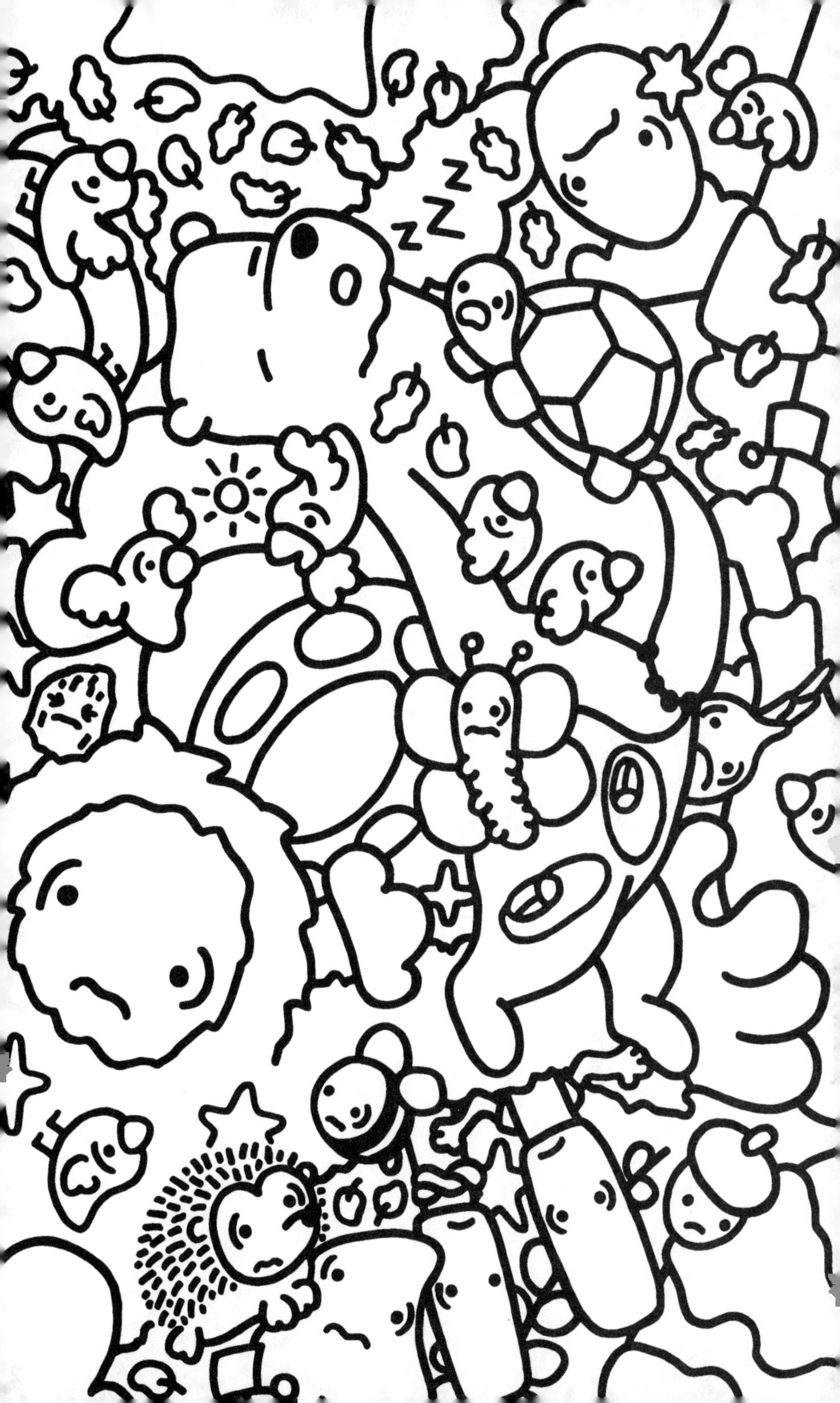
zZZ

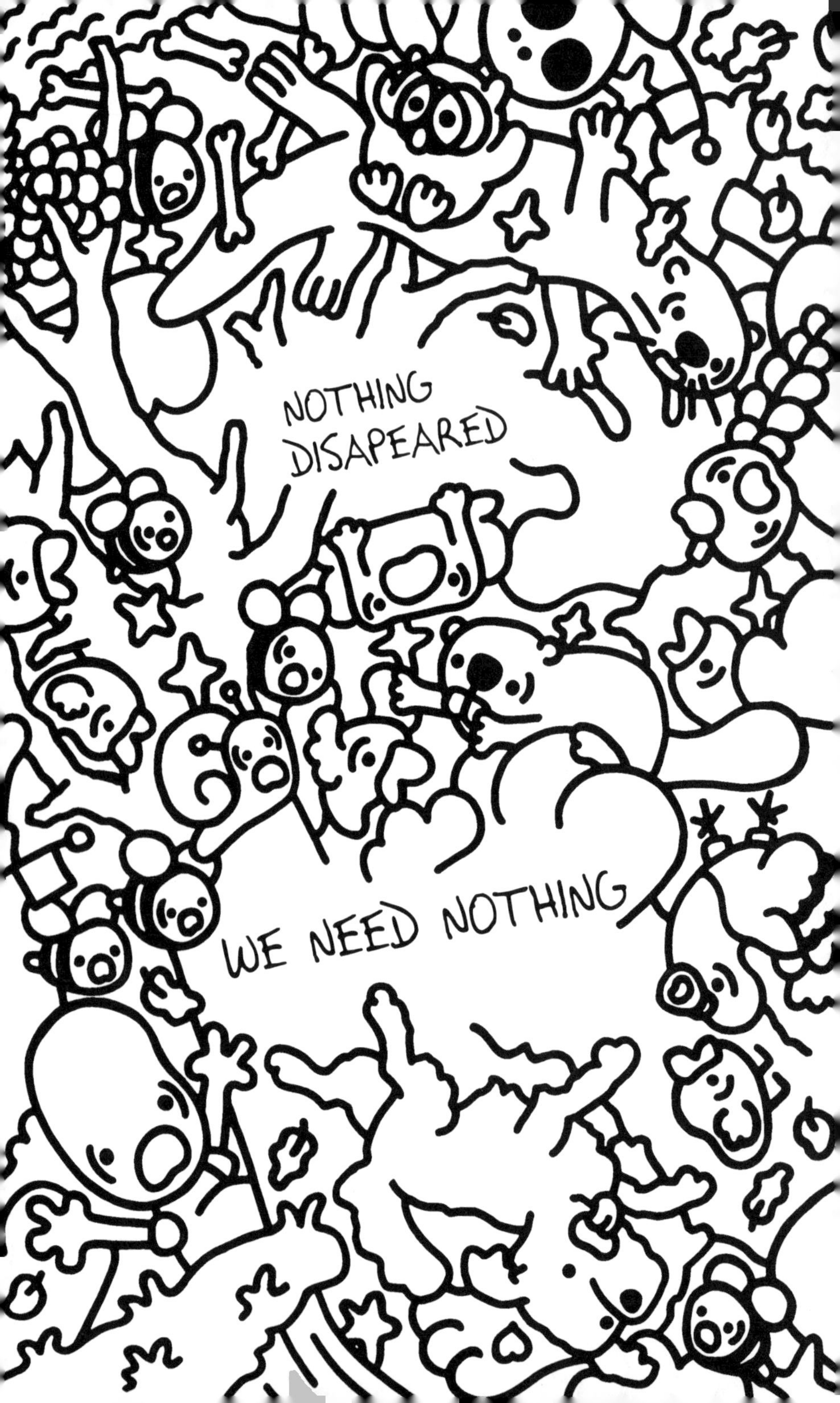
NOTHING DISAPEARED
WE NEED NOTHING

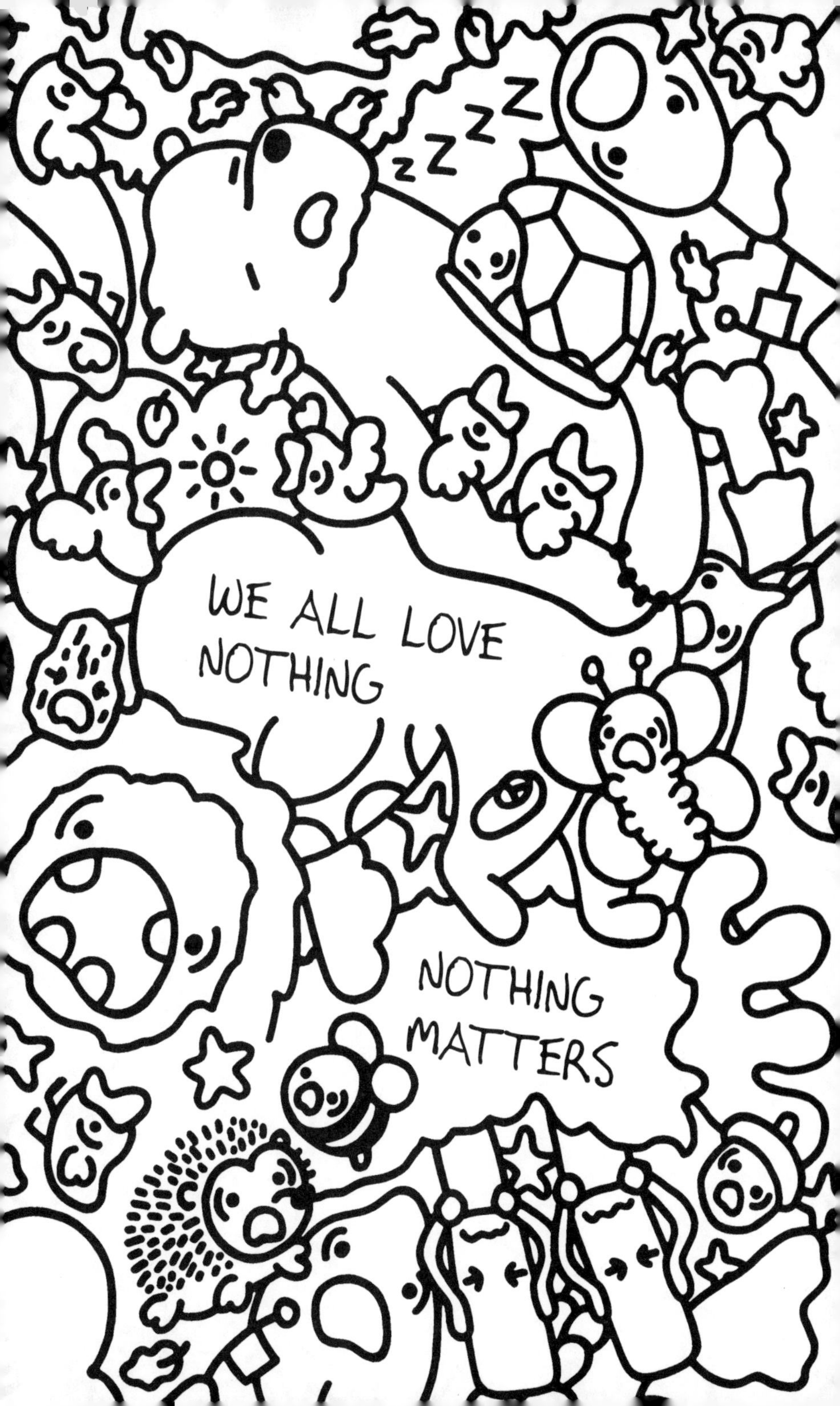

WE ALL LOVE NOTHING
NOTHING MATTERS

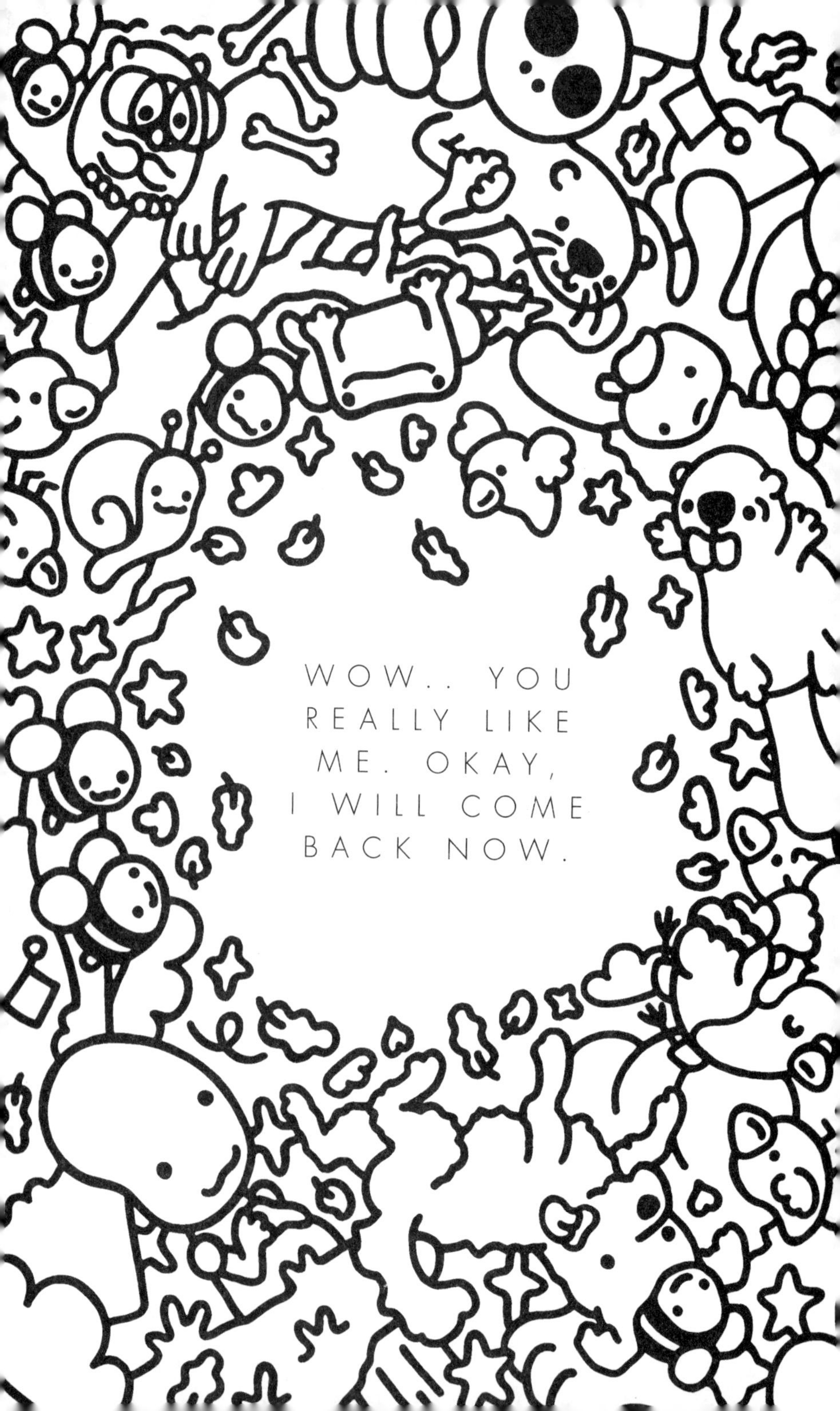
WOW.. YOU REALLY LIKE ME. OKAY, I WILL COME BACK NOW.

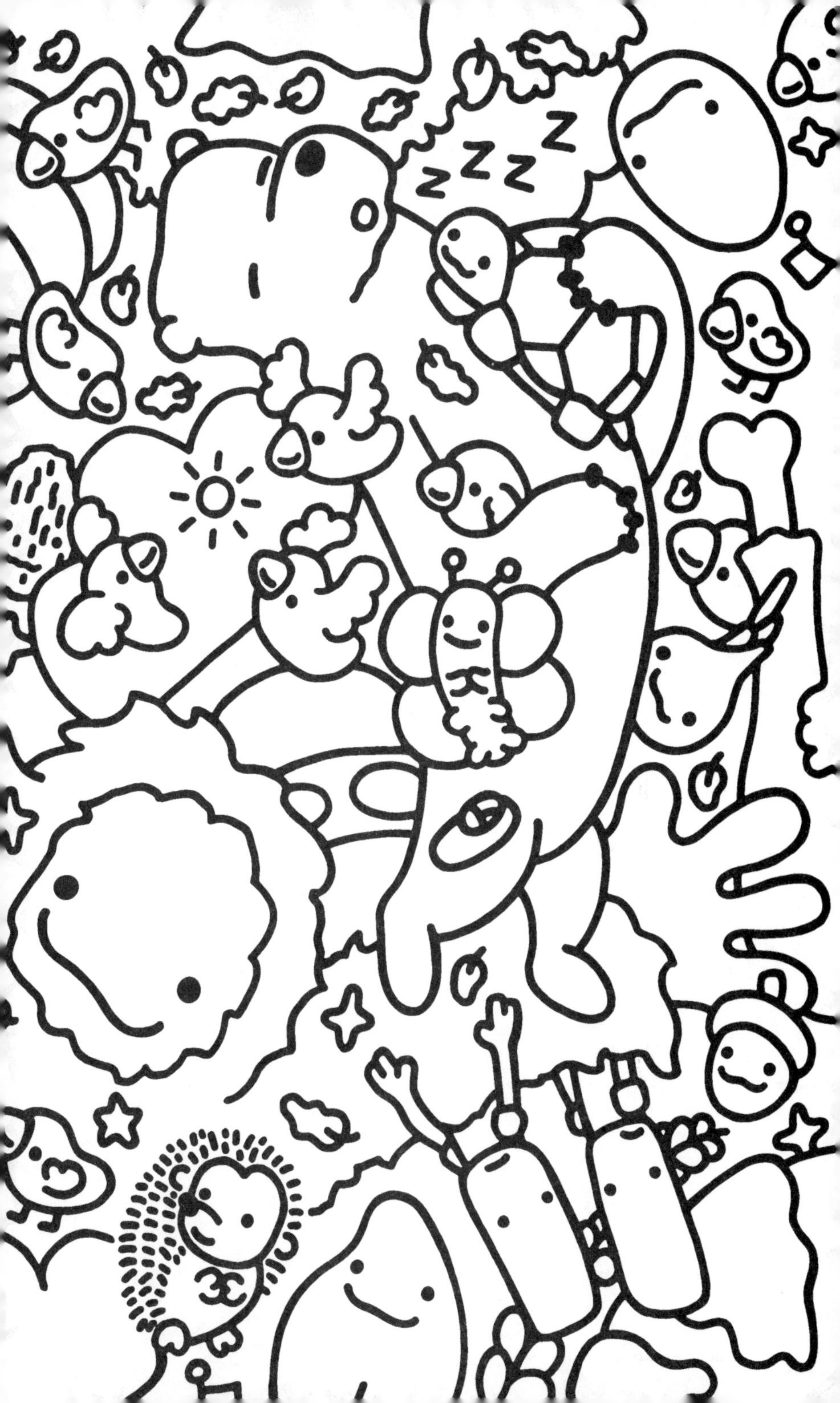

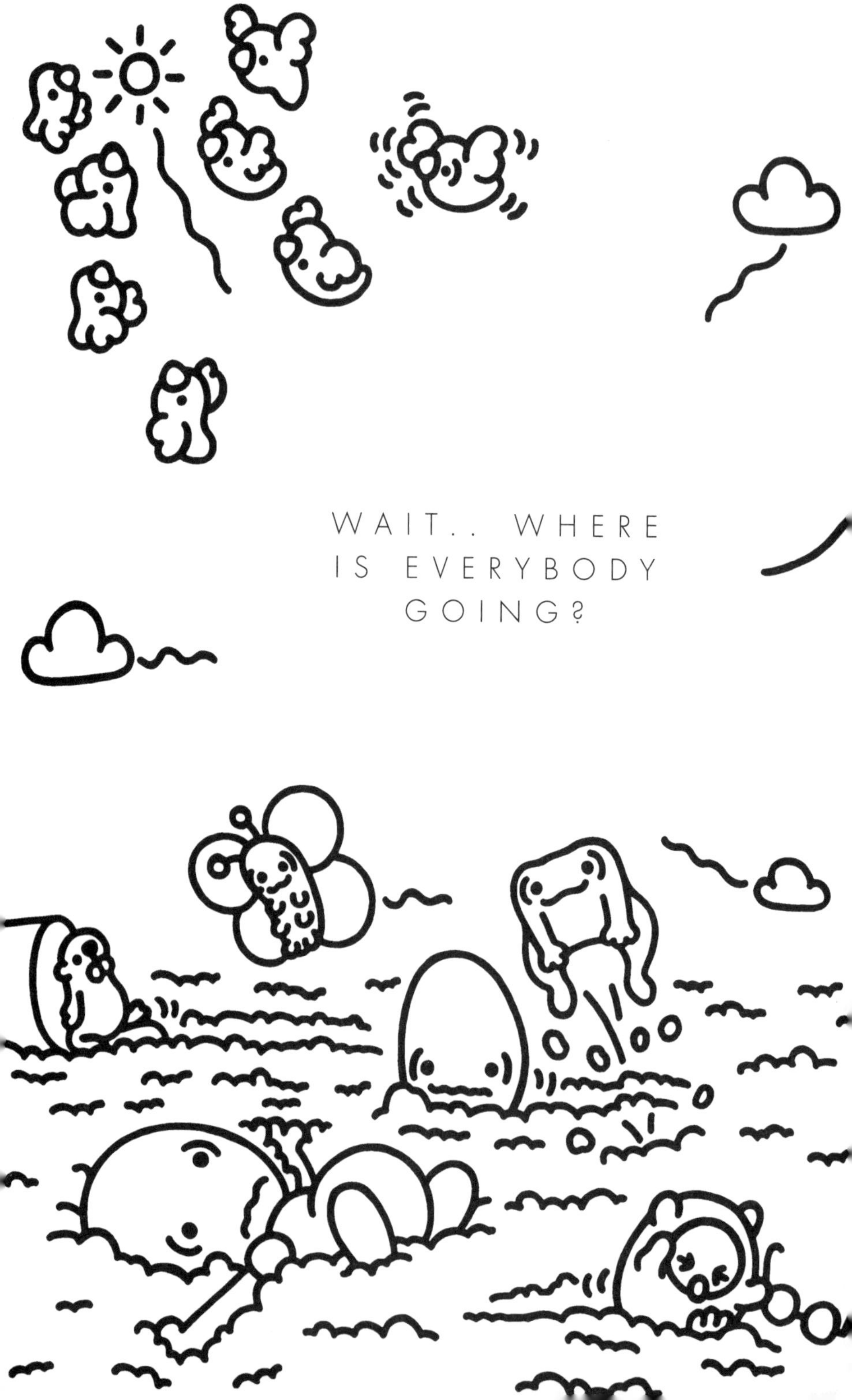
WAIT.. WHERE IS EVERYBODY GOING?

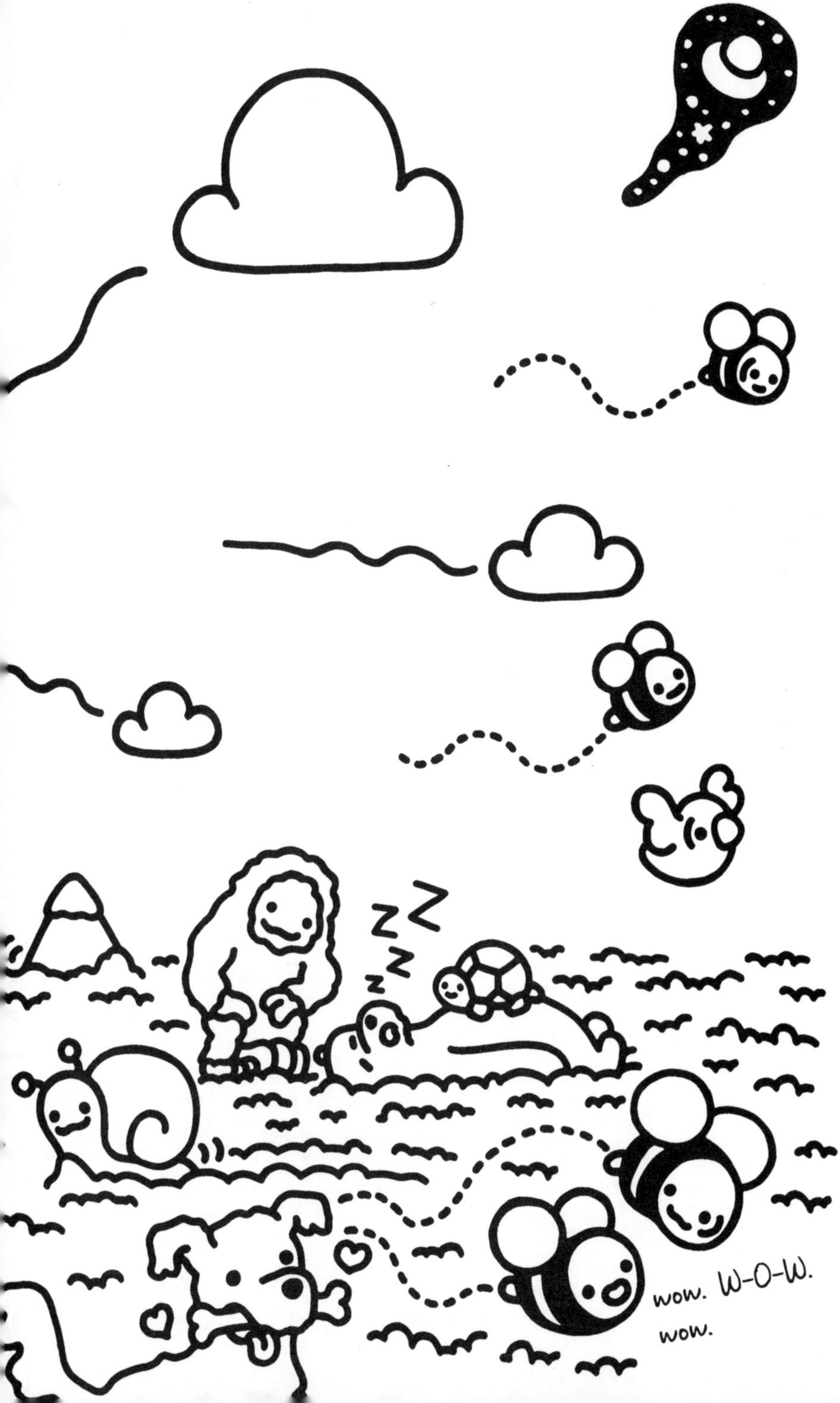
wow. W-O-W.
wow.

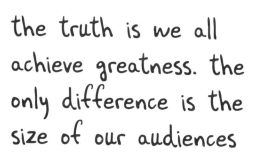

the truth is we all achieve greatness. the only difference is the size of our audiences

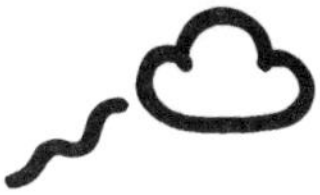

OH..
THANK YOU

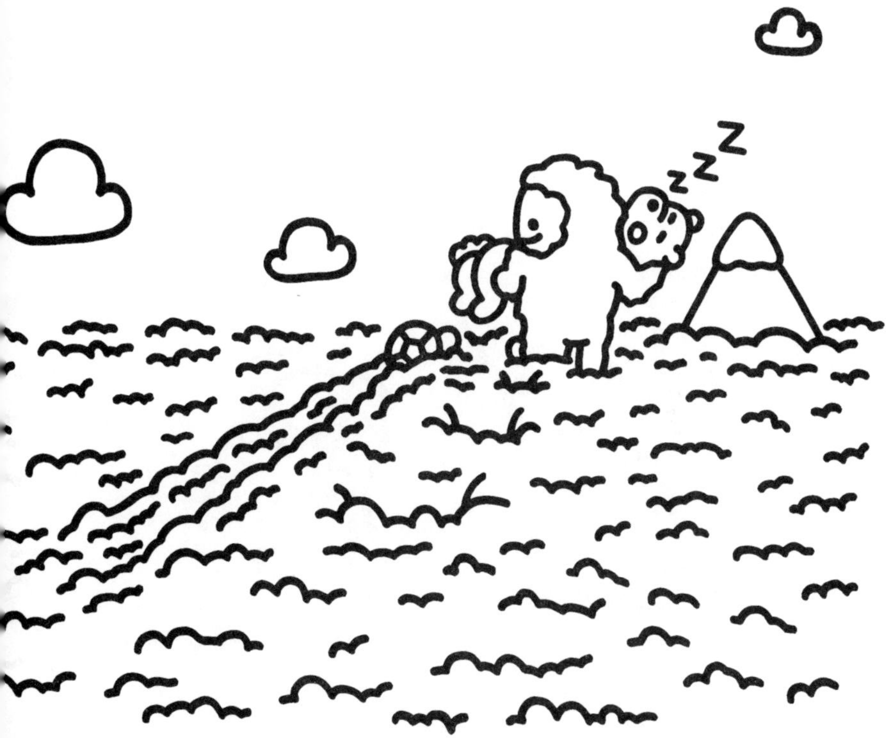

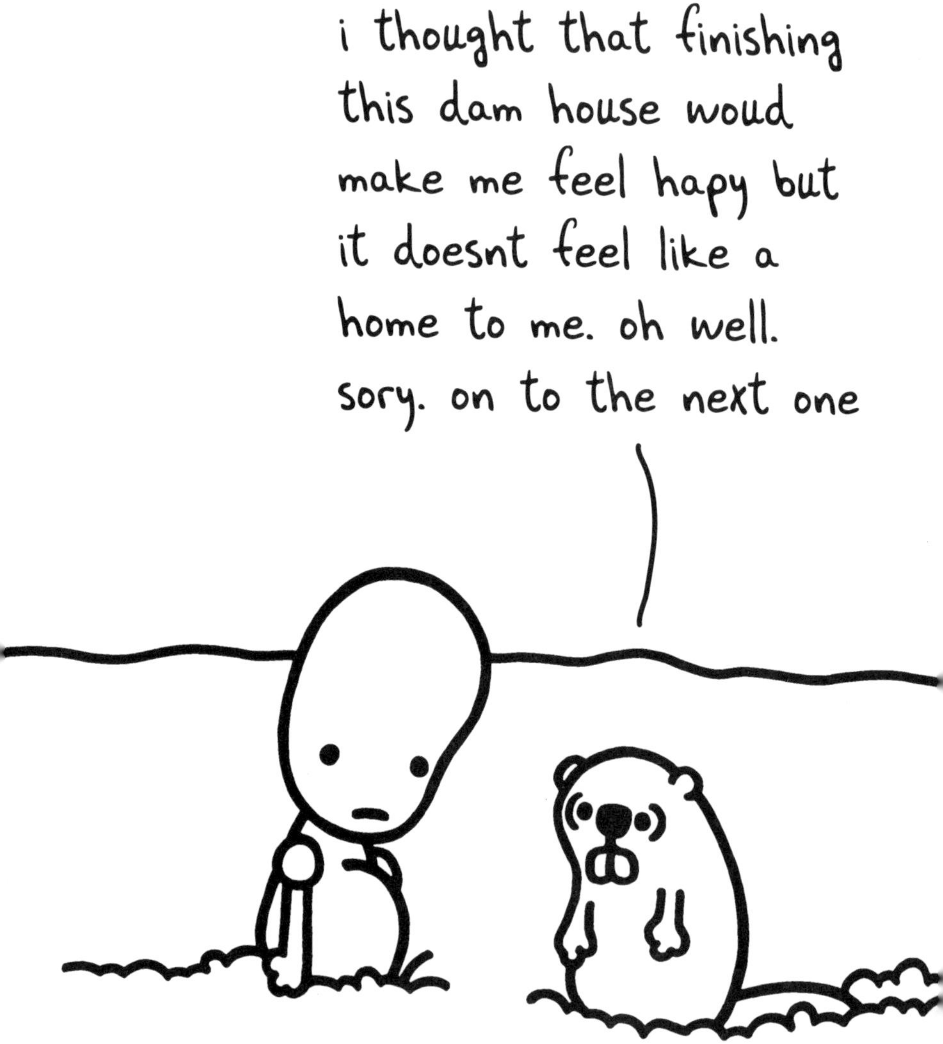
i thought that finishing this dam house woud make me feel hapy but it doesnt feel like a home to me. oh well. sory. on to the next one

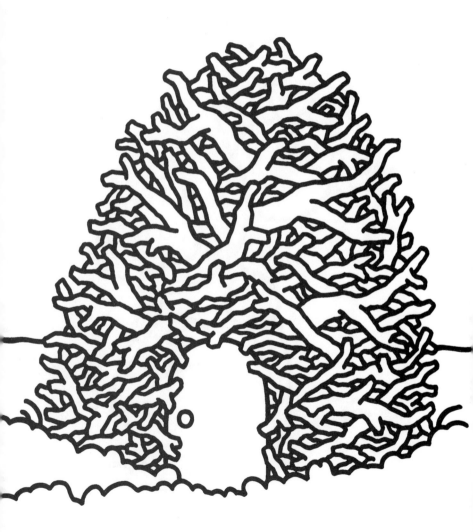

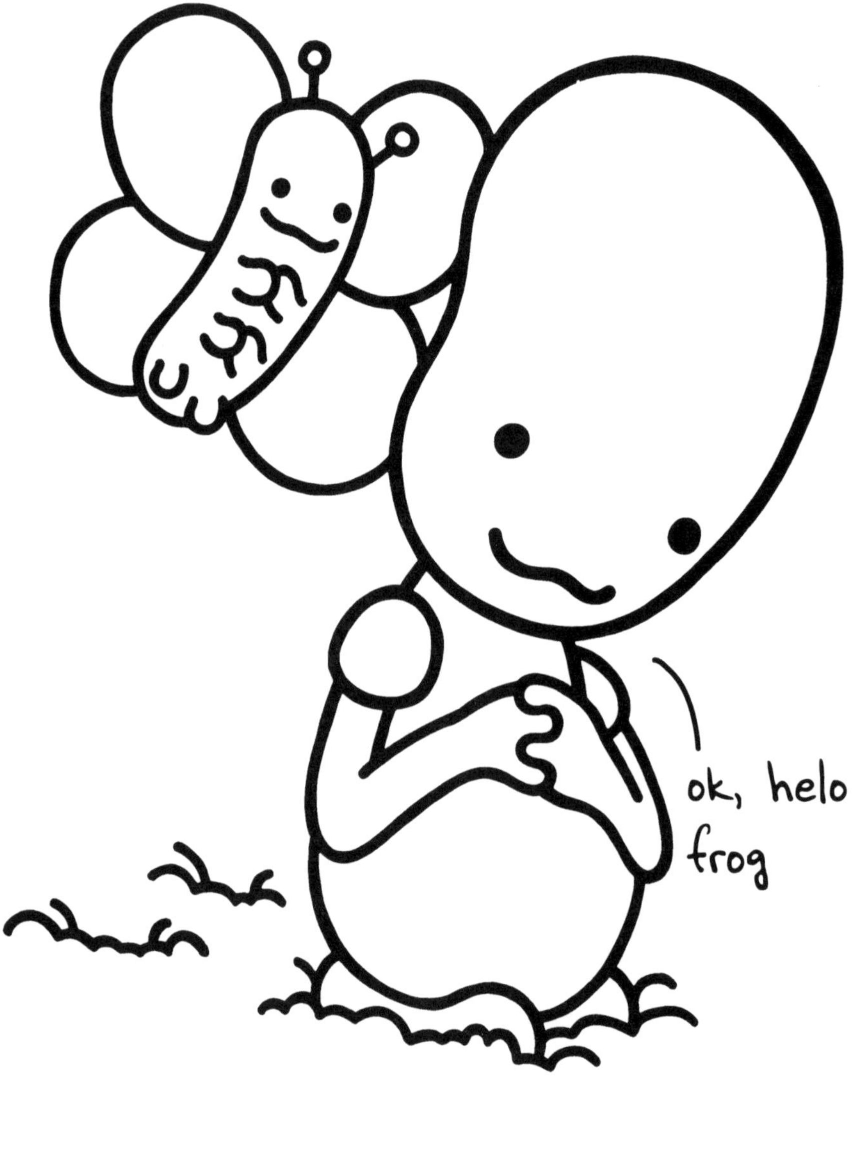
ok, helo
frog

i have decided that i am
a frog now. i may be a
very strange frog, but
i am a frog nonetheless

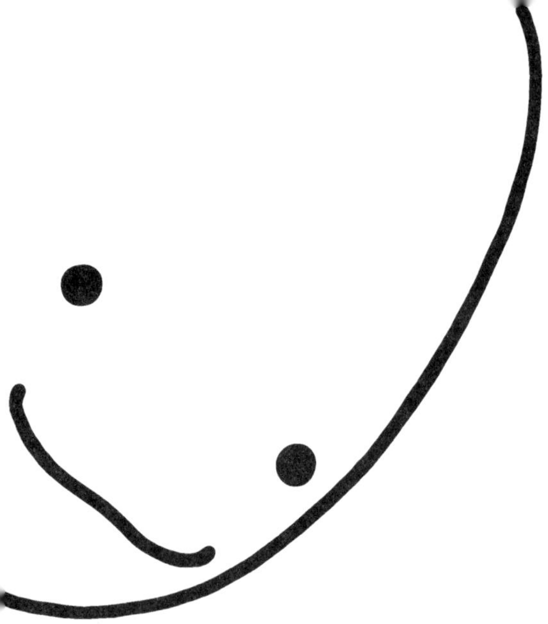

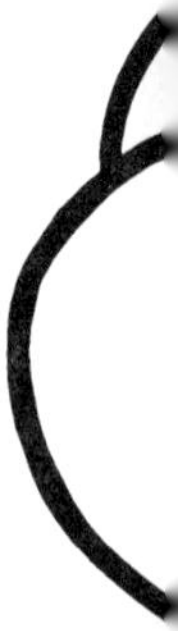

i was so woried about
wat i woud become in
the future that i didnt
realize i can be anything
i want to be right now

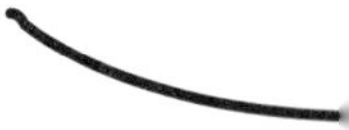

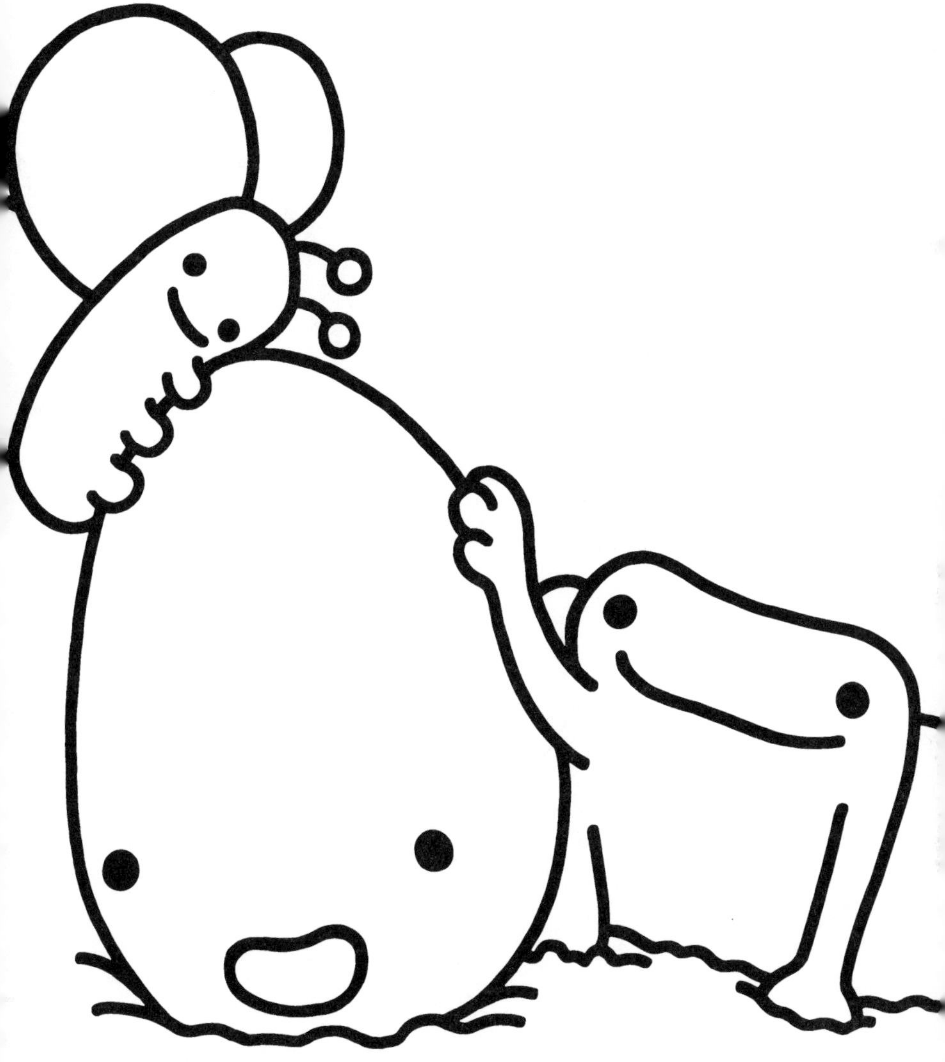

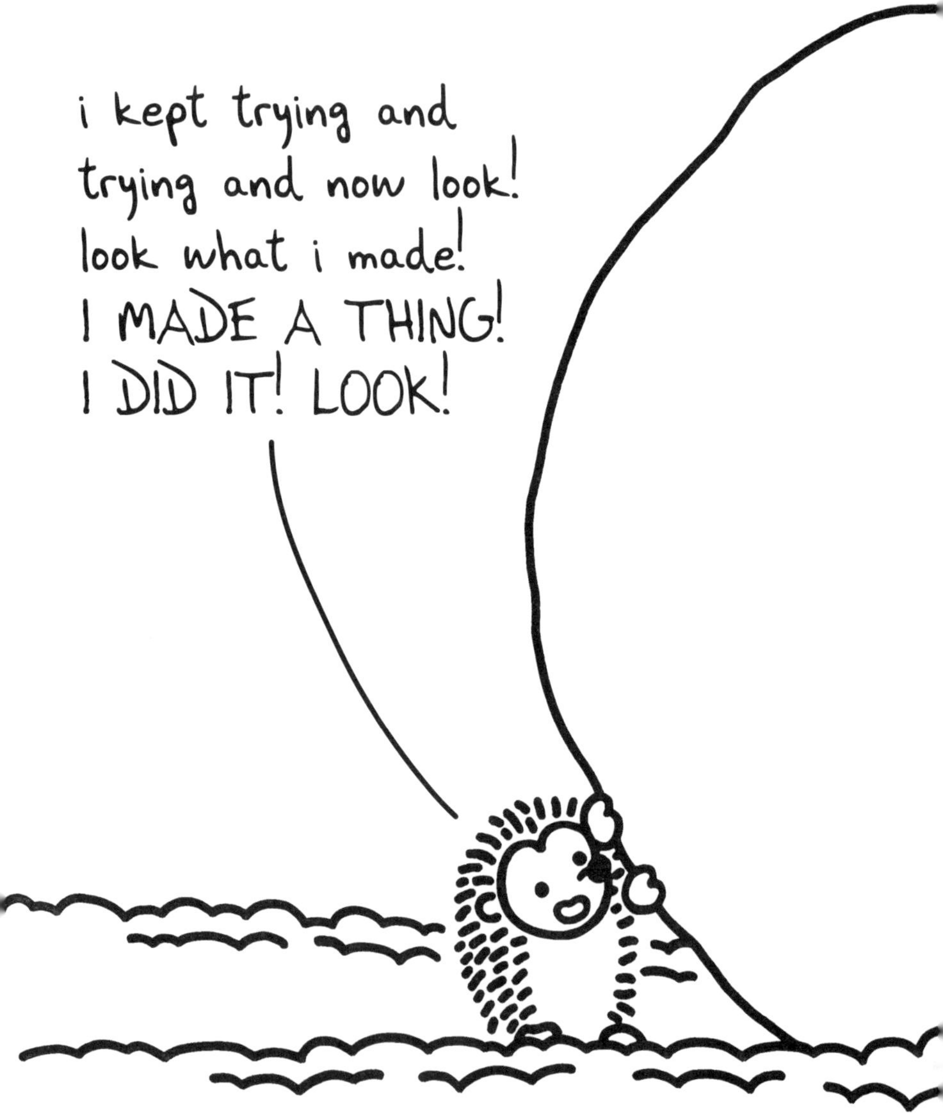
i kept trying and trying and now look! look what i made! I MADE A THING! I DID IT! LOOK!

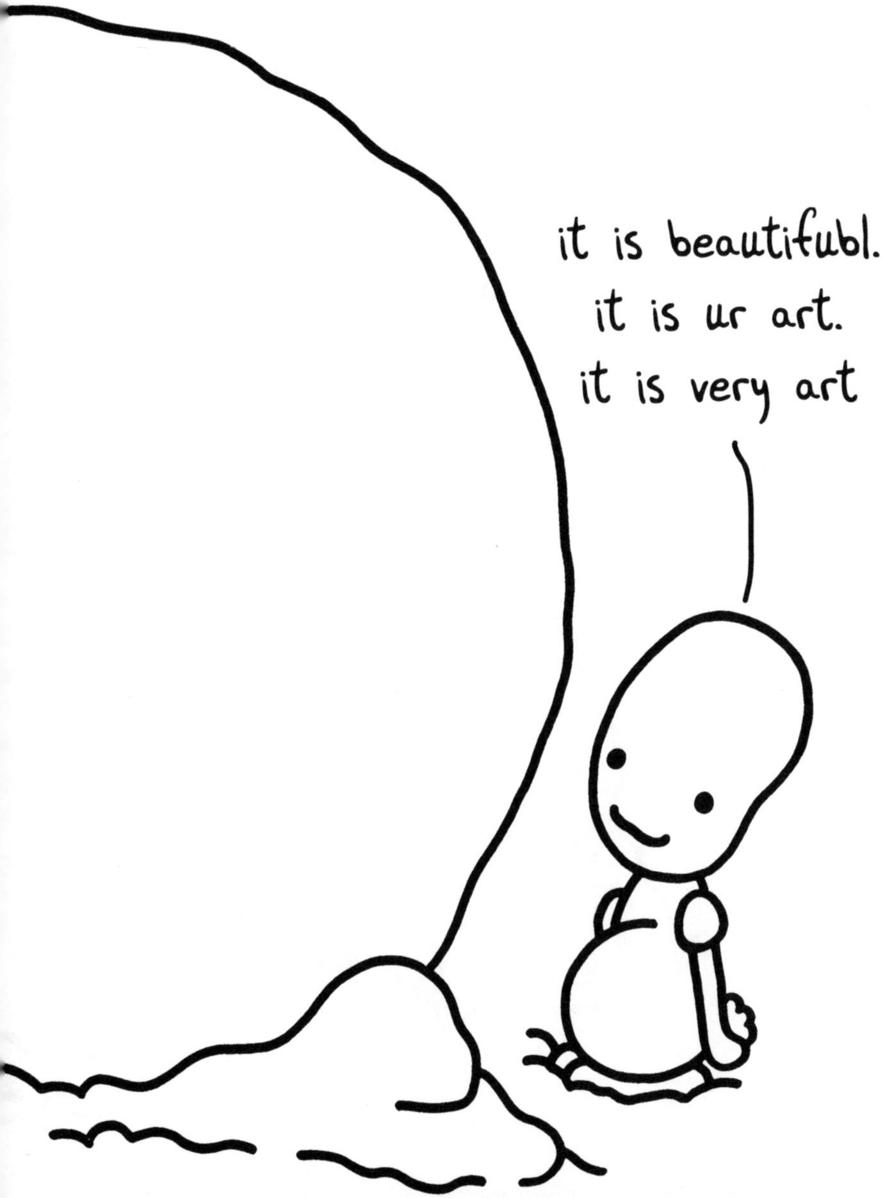
it is beautifubl.
it is ur art.
it is very art

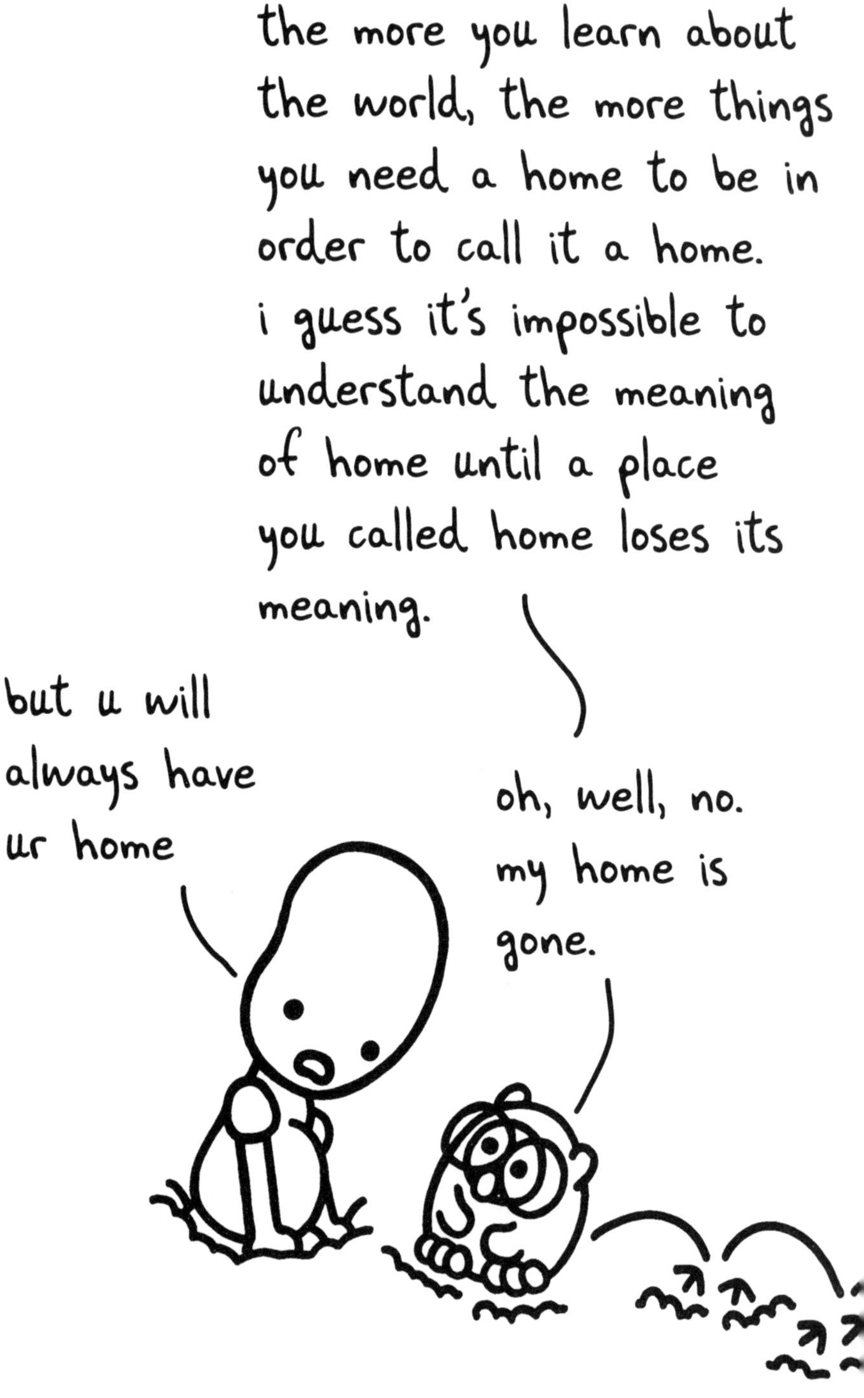
the more you learn about the world, the more things you need a home to be in order to call it a home. i guess it's impossible to understand the meaning of home until a place you called home loses its meaning.
but u will always have ur home
oh, well, no. my home is gone.

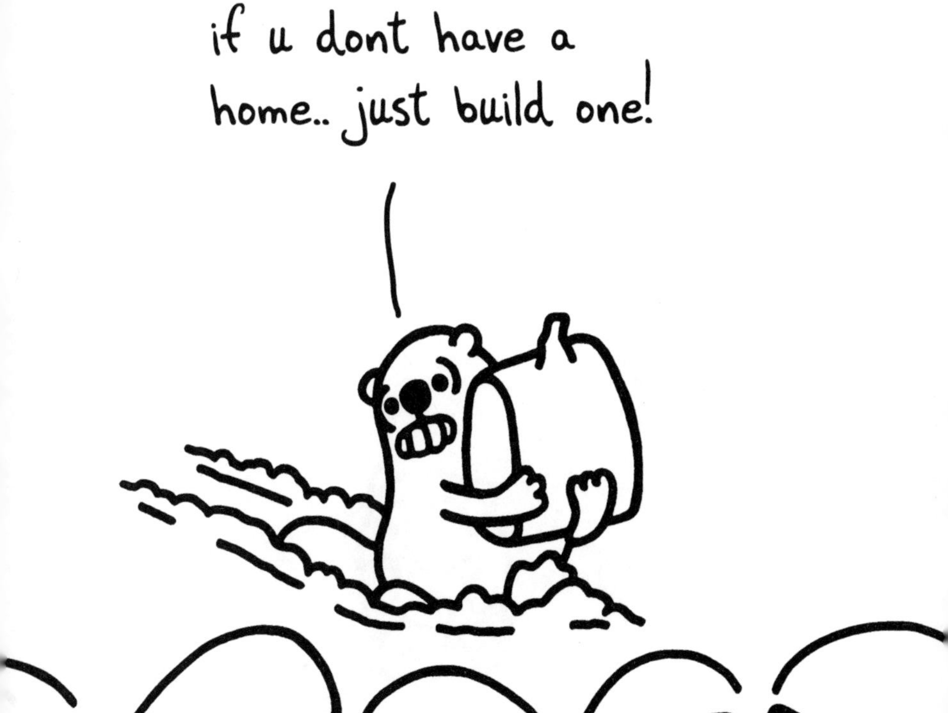
if u dont have a home.. just build one!

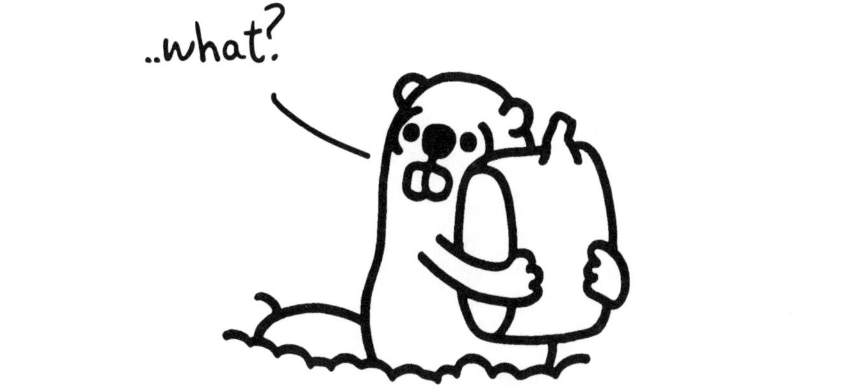
..what?

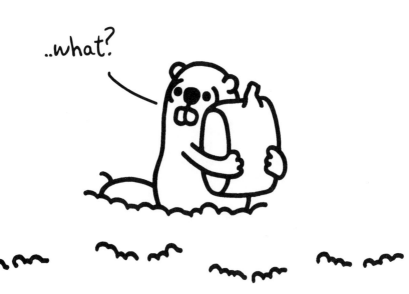

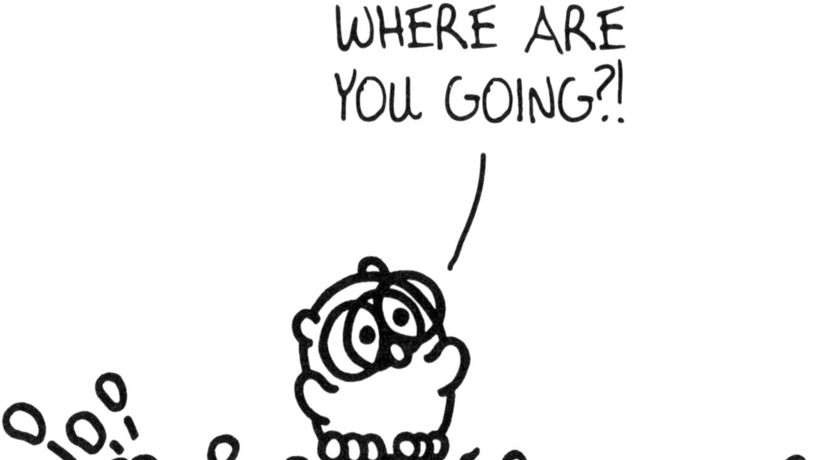
WHERE ARE
YOU GOING?!

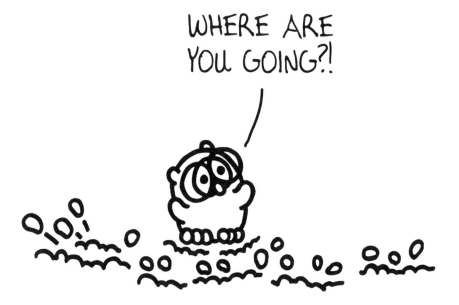

if a tree falls in a forest and nobody hears it, perhaps the tree wanted to fall simply to fall, and not to show itself falling.

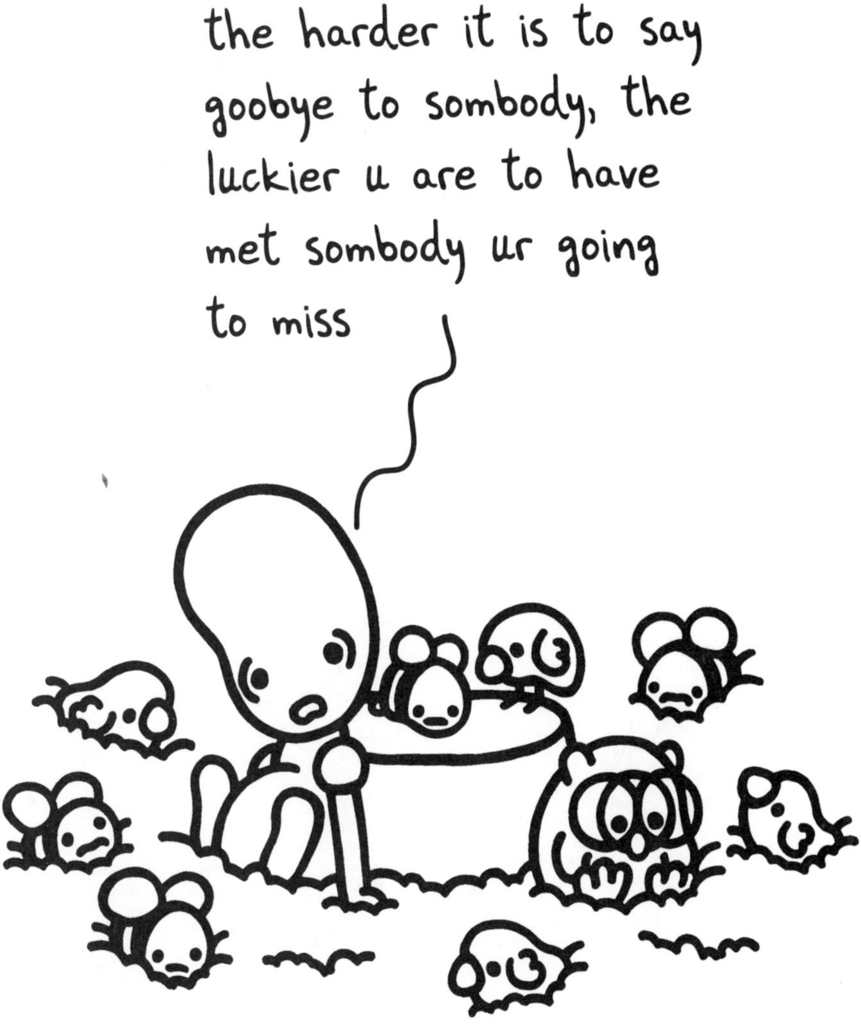
the harder it is to say goobye to sombody, the luckier u are to have met sombody ur going to miss

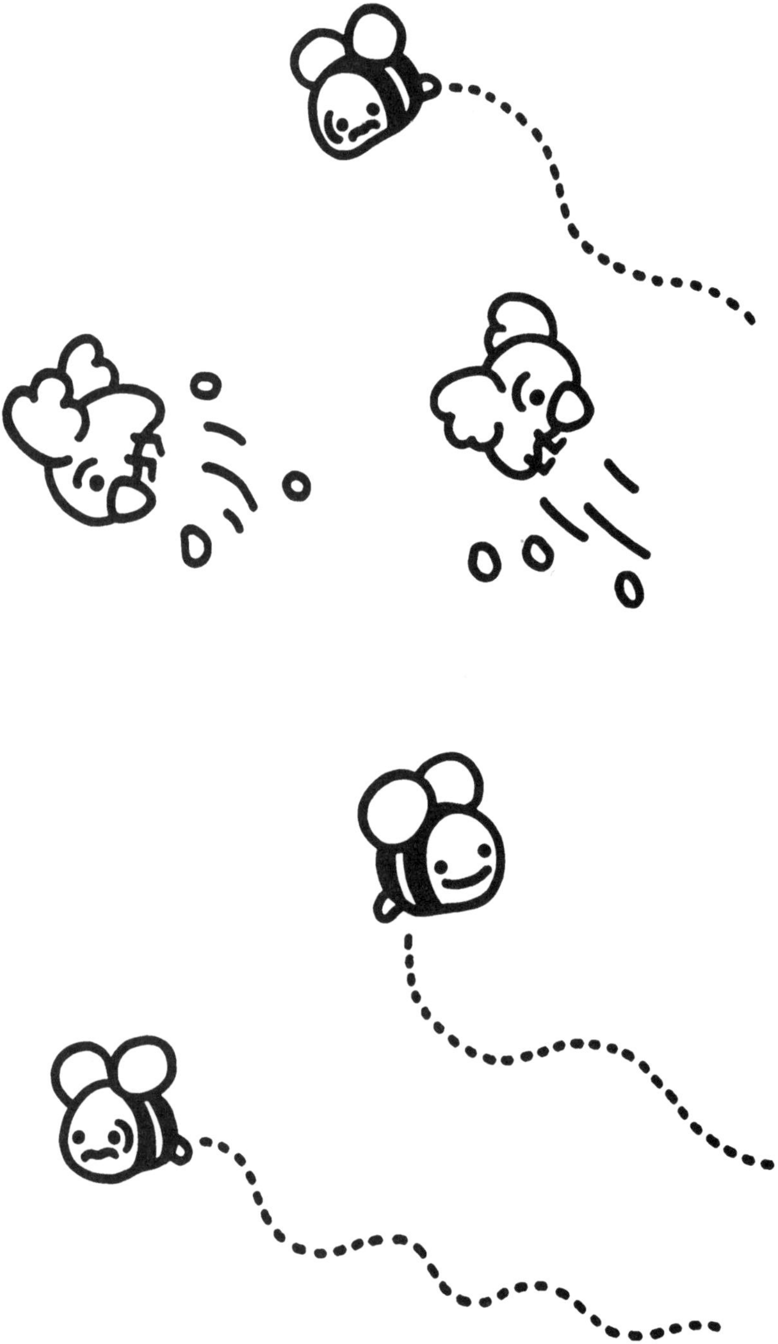

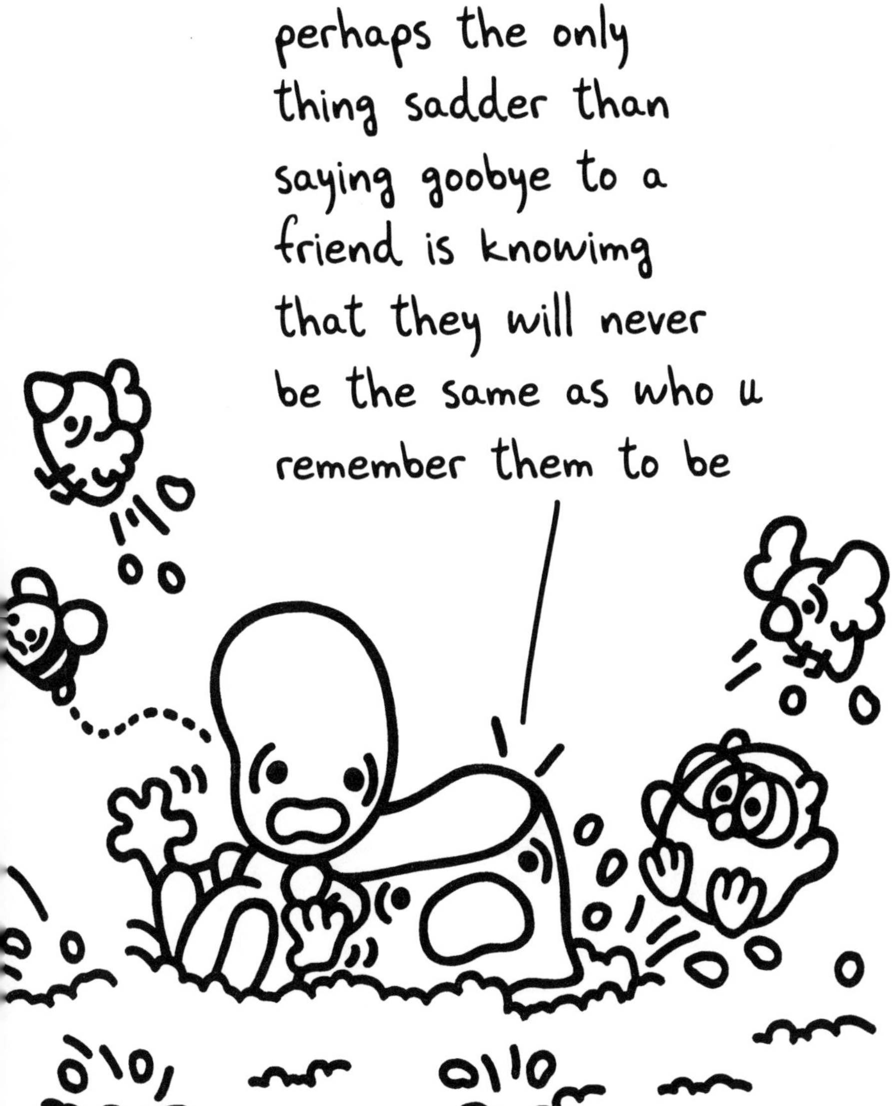
perhaps the only thing sadder than saying goobye to a friend is knowimg that they will never be the same as who u remember them to be

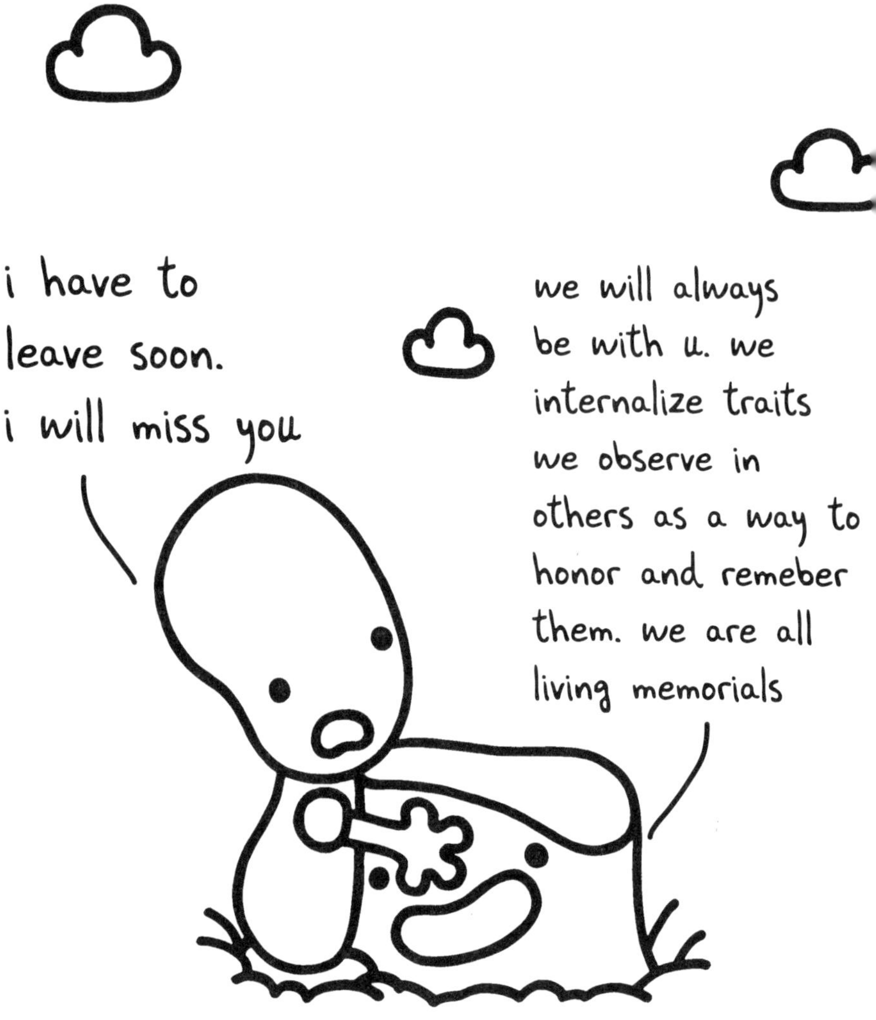
i have to leave soon. i will miss you
we will always be with u. we internalize traits we observe in others as a way to honor and remeber them. we are all living memorials

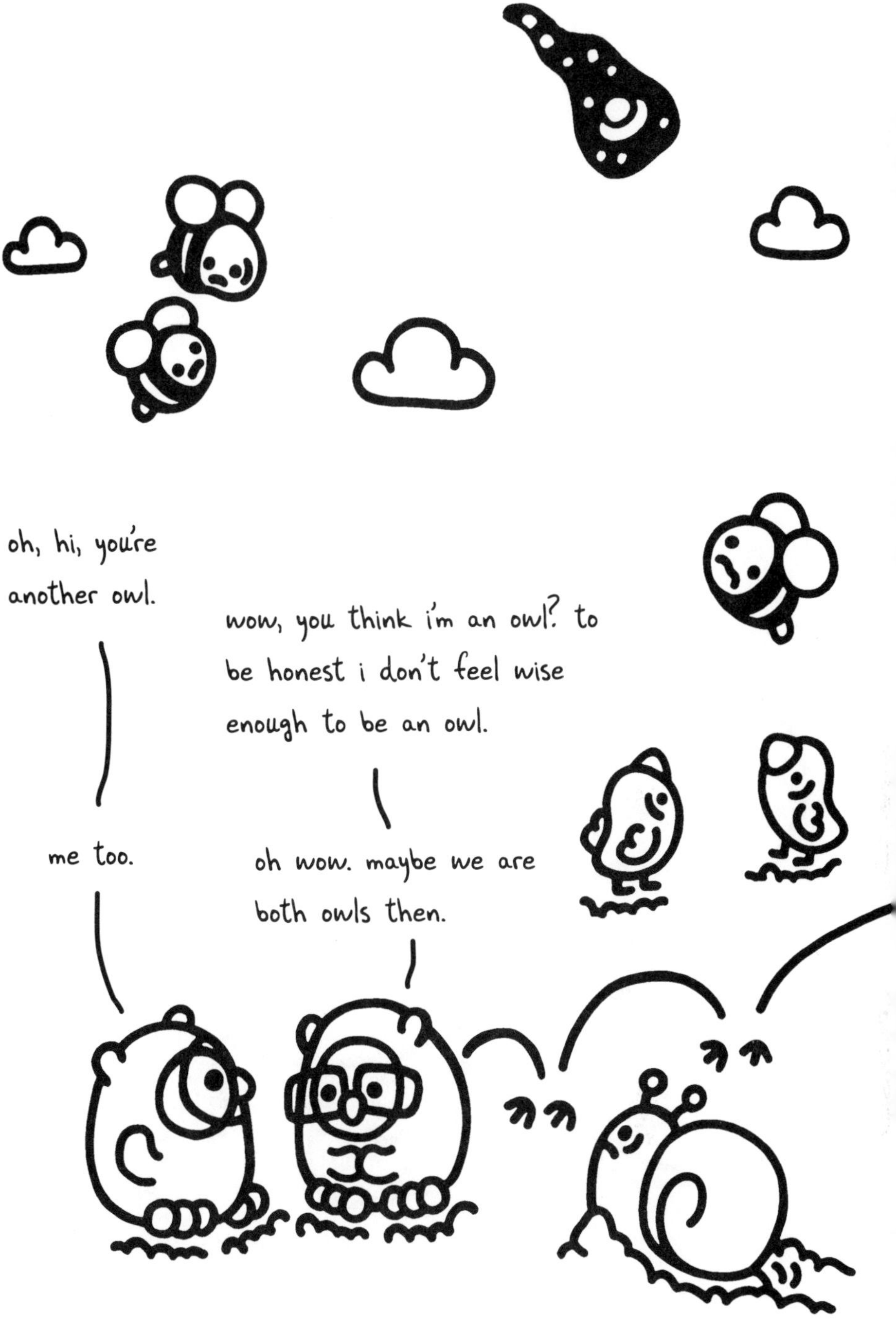

oh, hi, you're another owl.
wow, you think i'm an owl? to be honest i don't feel wise enough to be an owl.
me too.
oh wow. maybe we are both owls then.

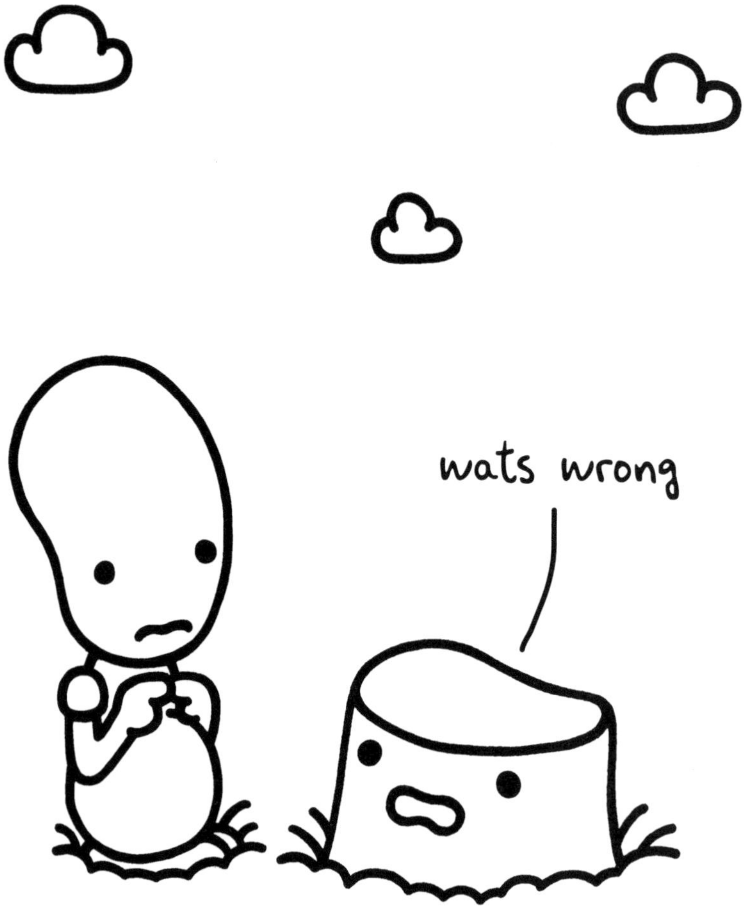
wats wrong

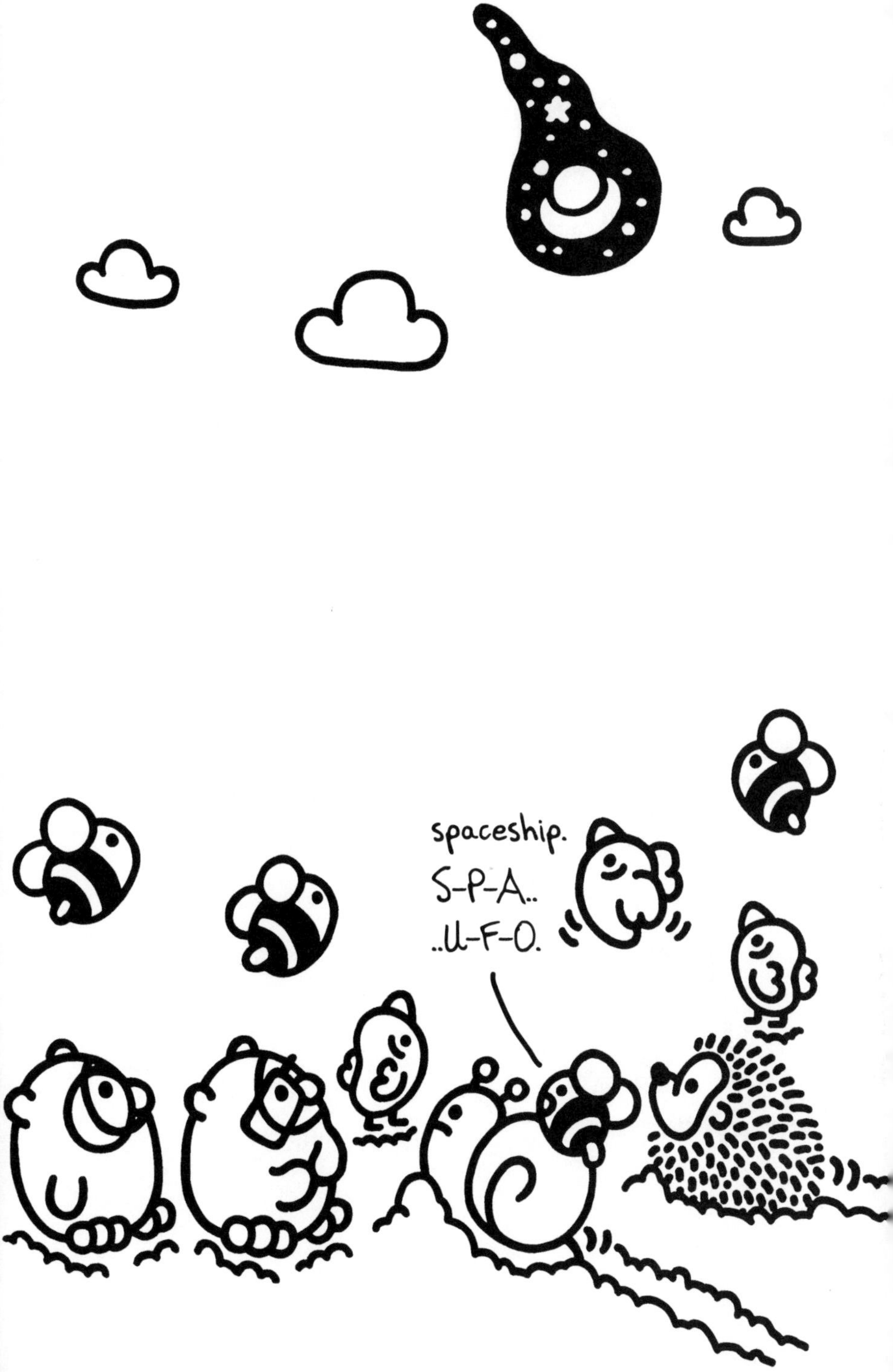
spaceship.
S-P-A..
..U-F-O.

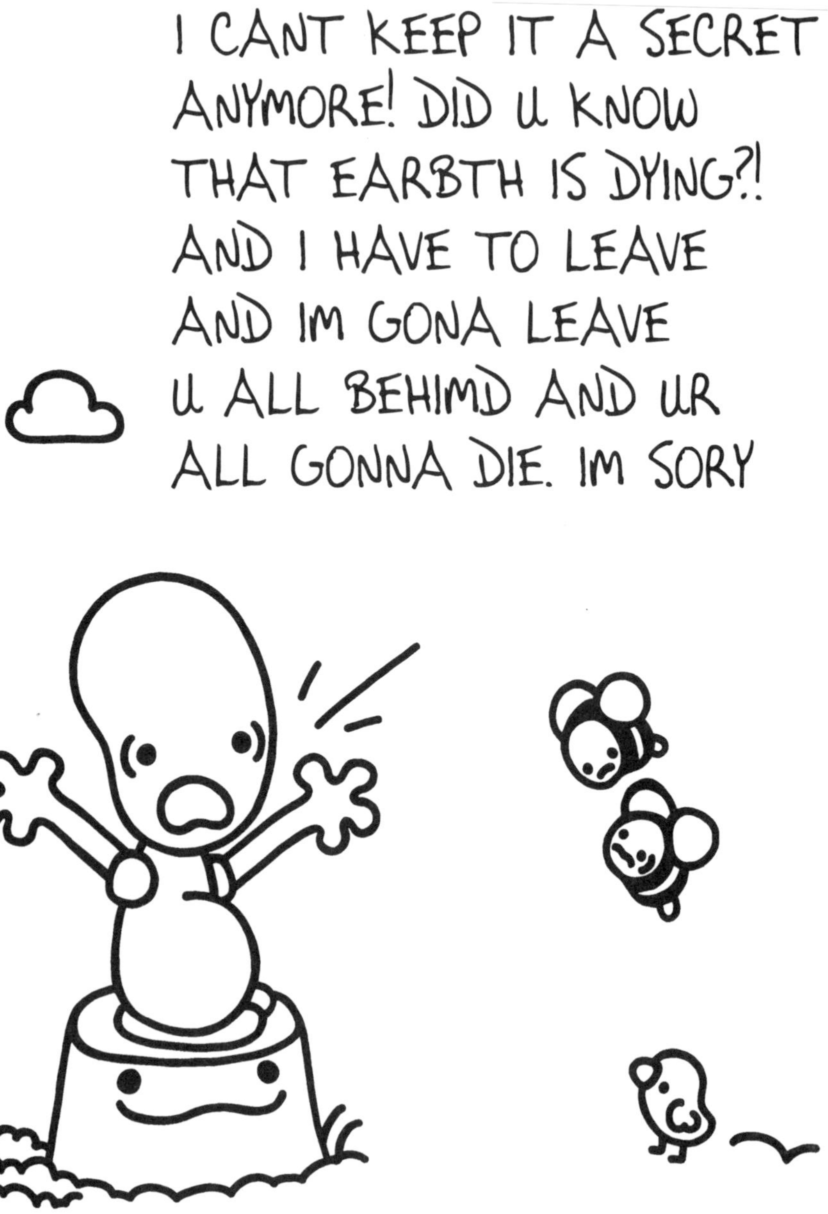
I CANT KEEP IT A SECRET ANYMORE! DID U KNOW THAT EARBTH IS DYING?! AND I HAVE TO LEAVE AND IM GONA LEAVE U ALL BEHIMD AND UR ALL GONNA DIE. IM SORY

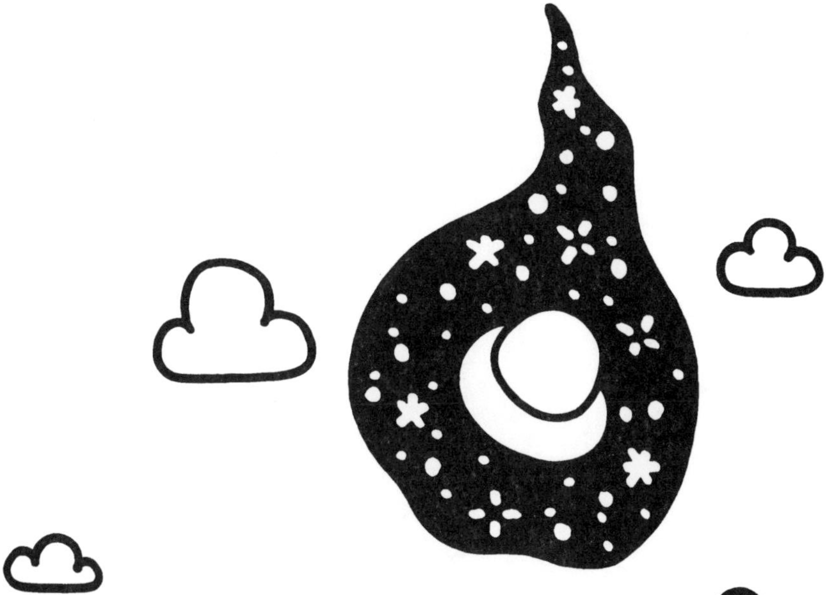

thats ok. we all alredy know that we are going to die one day. and as for earbth, well, i suppose its always dying. but so are all of us and so is everything. so its ok

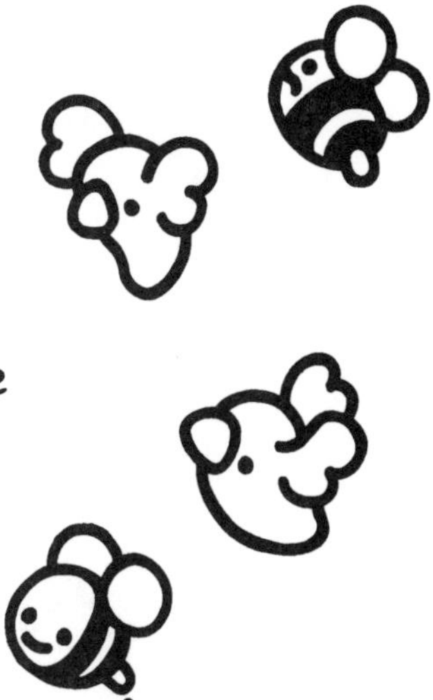

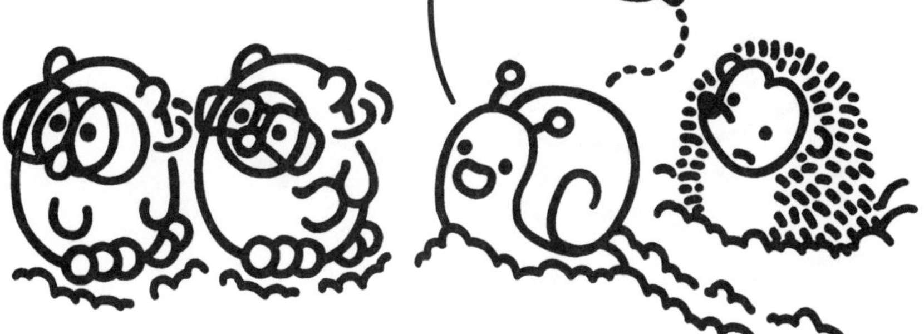

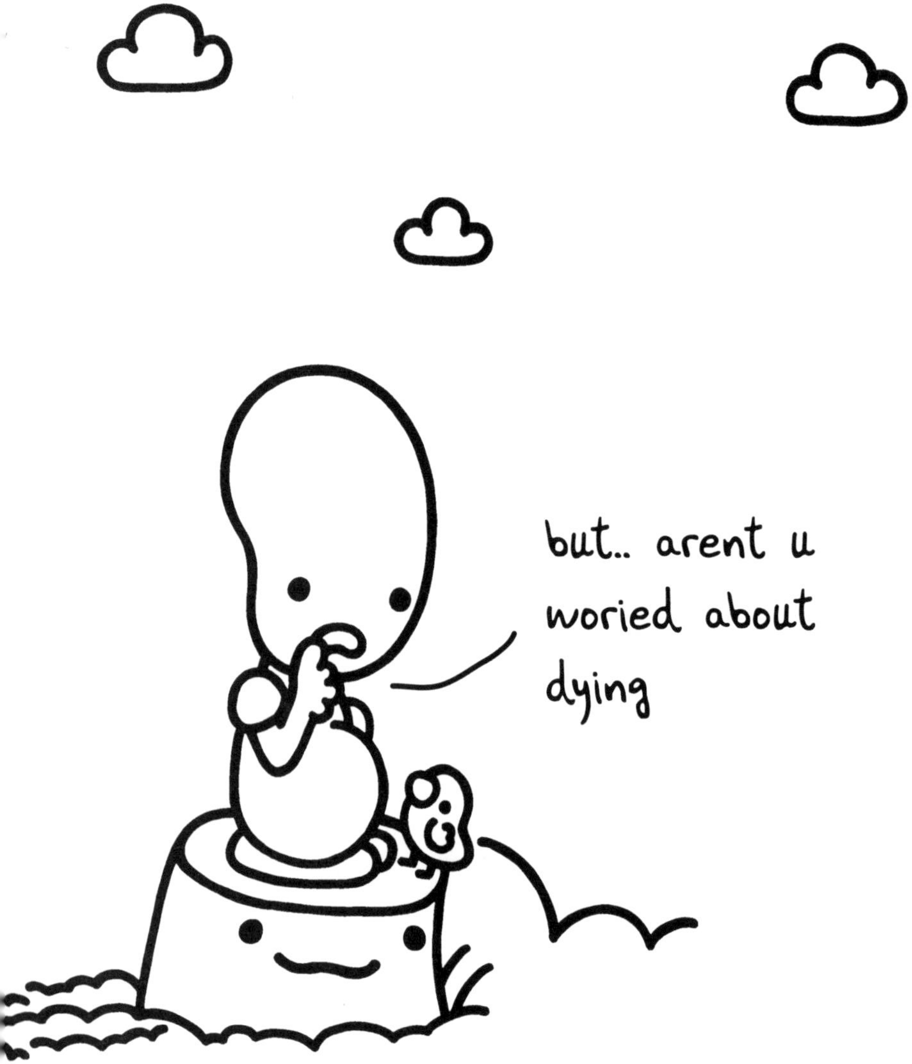
but.. arent u
woried about
dying

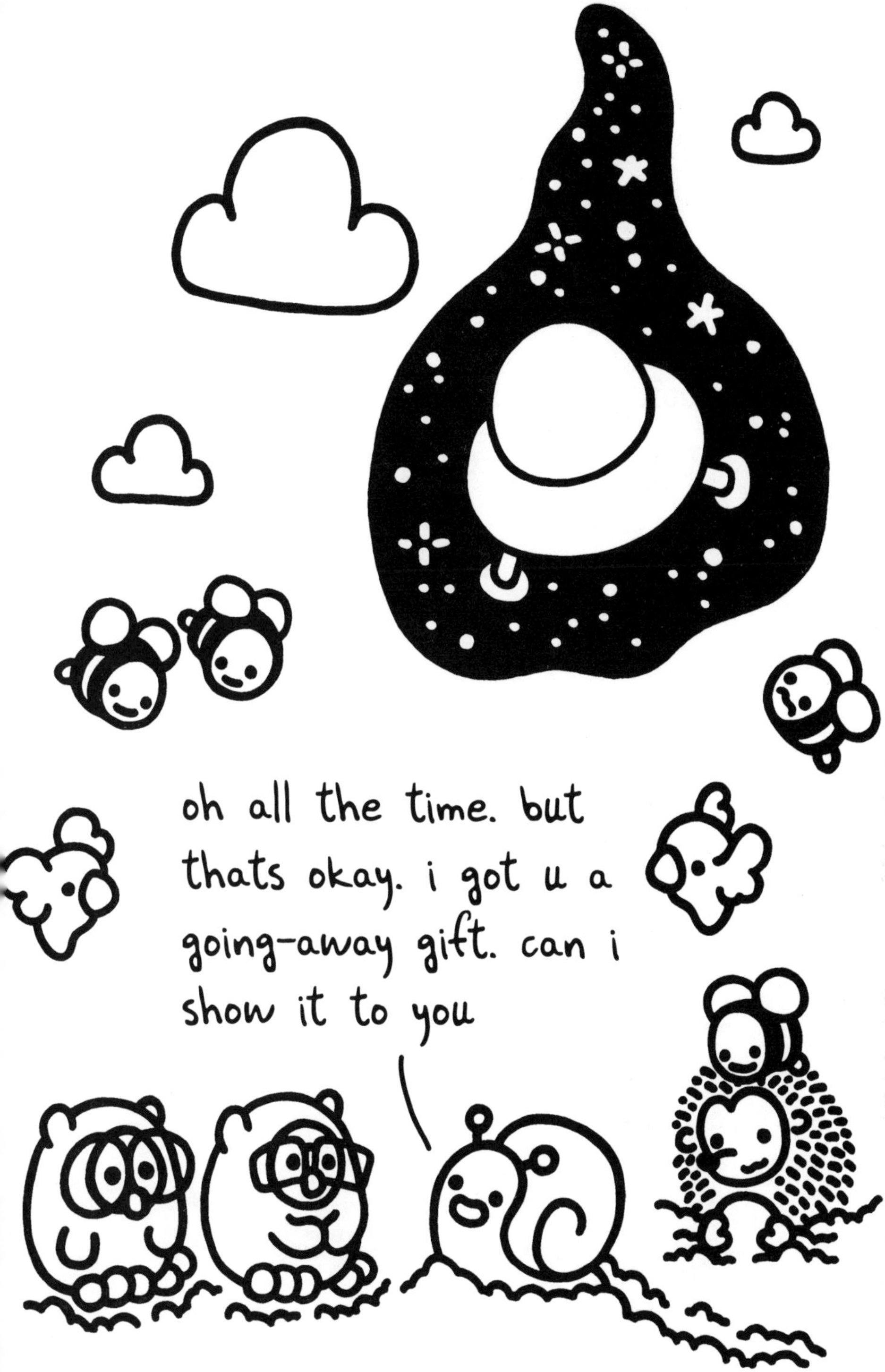
oh all the time. but thats okay. i got u a going-away gift. can i show it to you

look. life is bad. everyones sad. we're all gona die. but i alredy bought this inflatable boumcy castle so are u gona take ur shoes off or wat

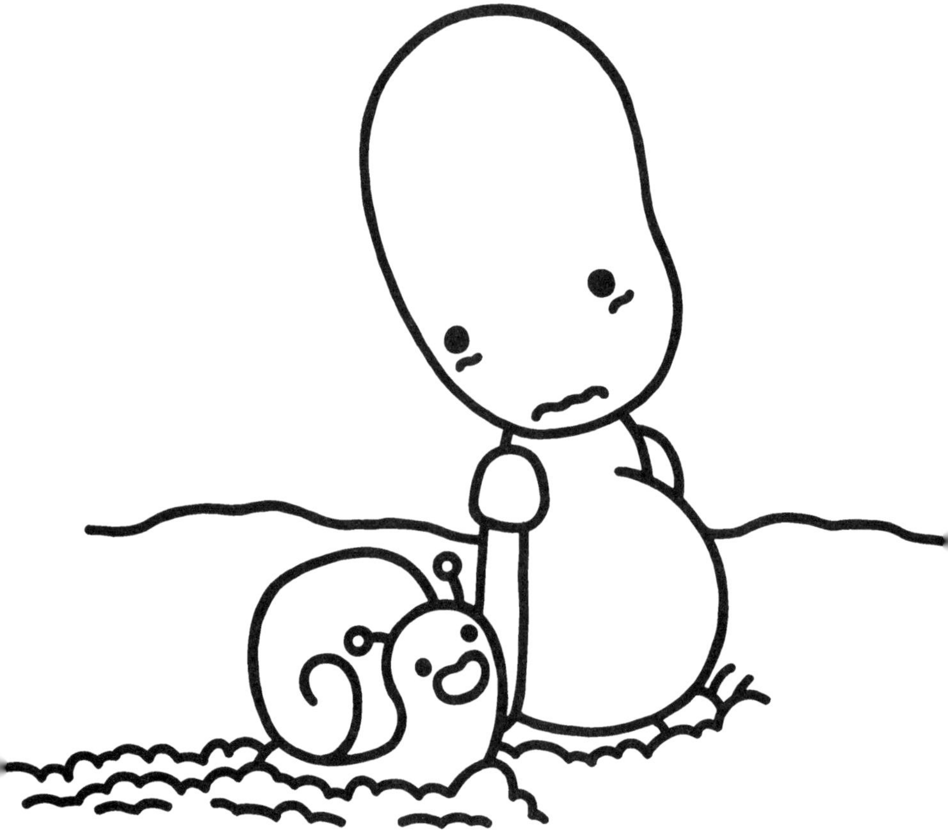

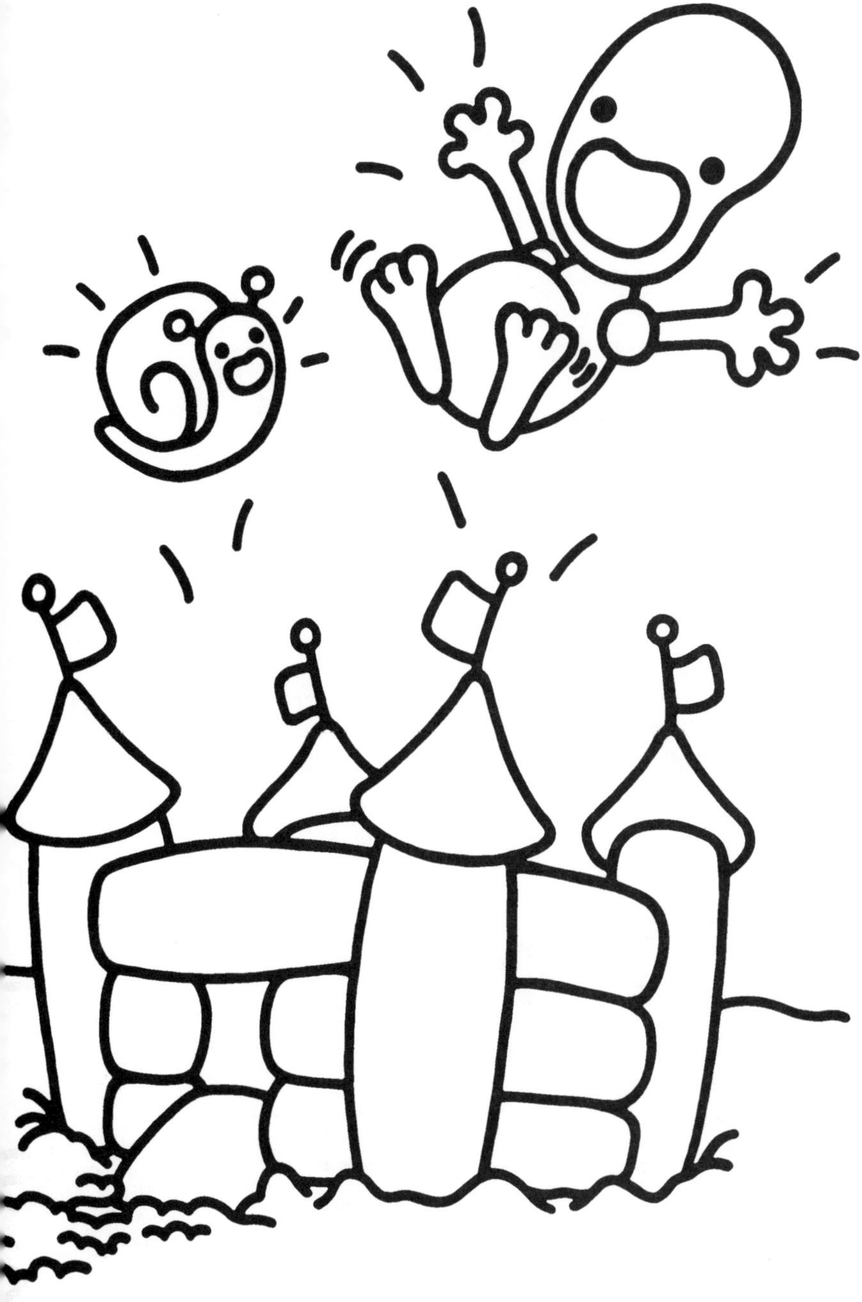

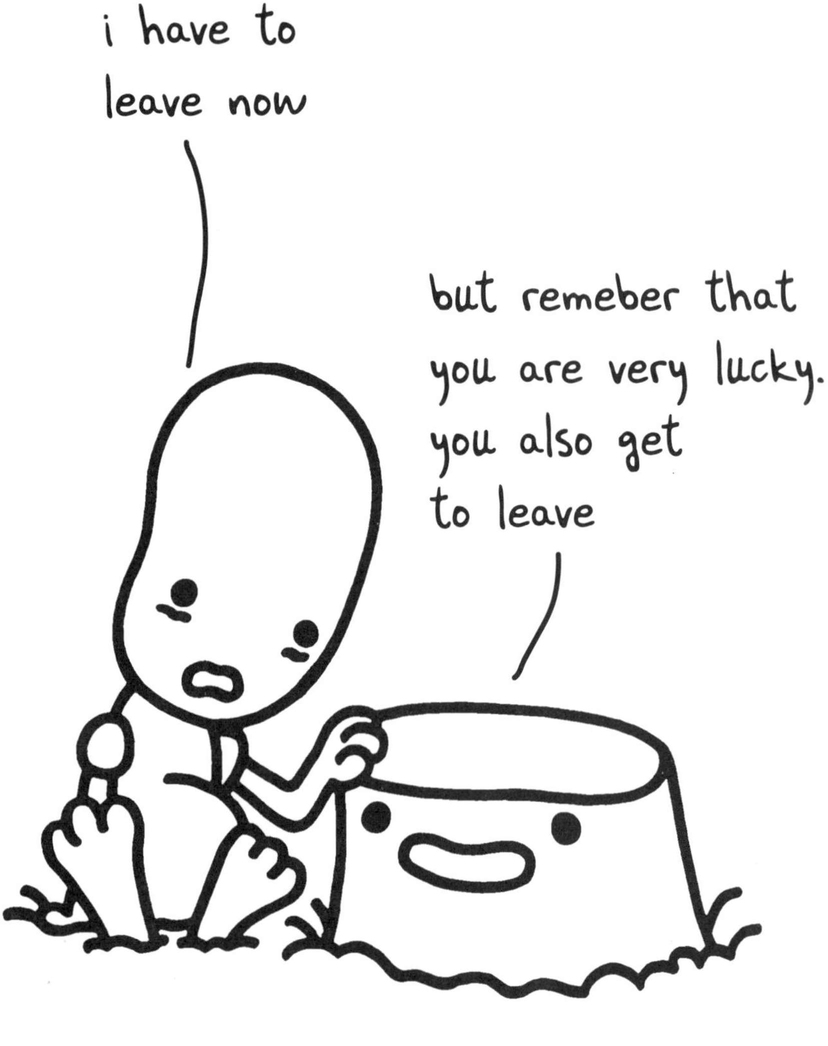
i have to leave now
but remeber that you are very lucky. you also get to leave

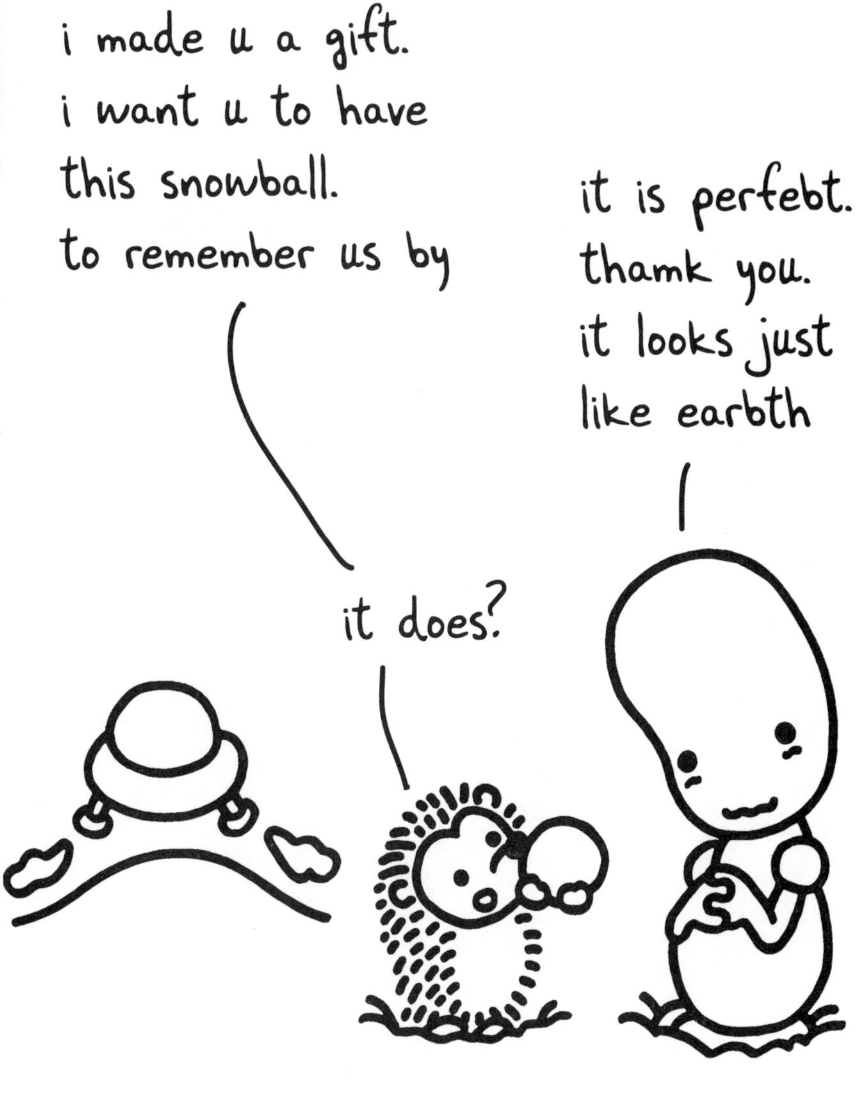
i made u a gift.
i want u to have
this snowball.
to remember us by
it is perfebt.
thamk you.
it looks just
like earbth
it does?

i get to go home today. thank u, humabns, for teachimg me wat it is like to be a humabn. i learmed a lot. goobye.
um wait.. we are not humans.

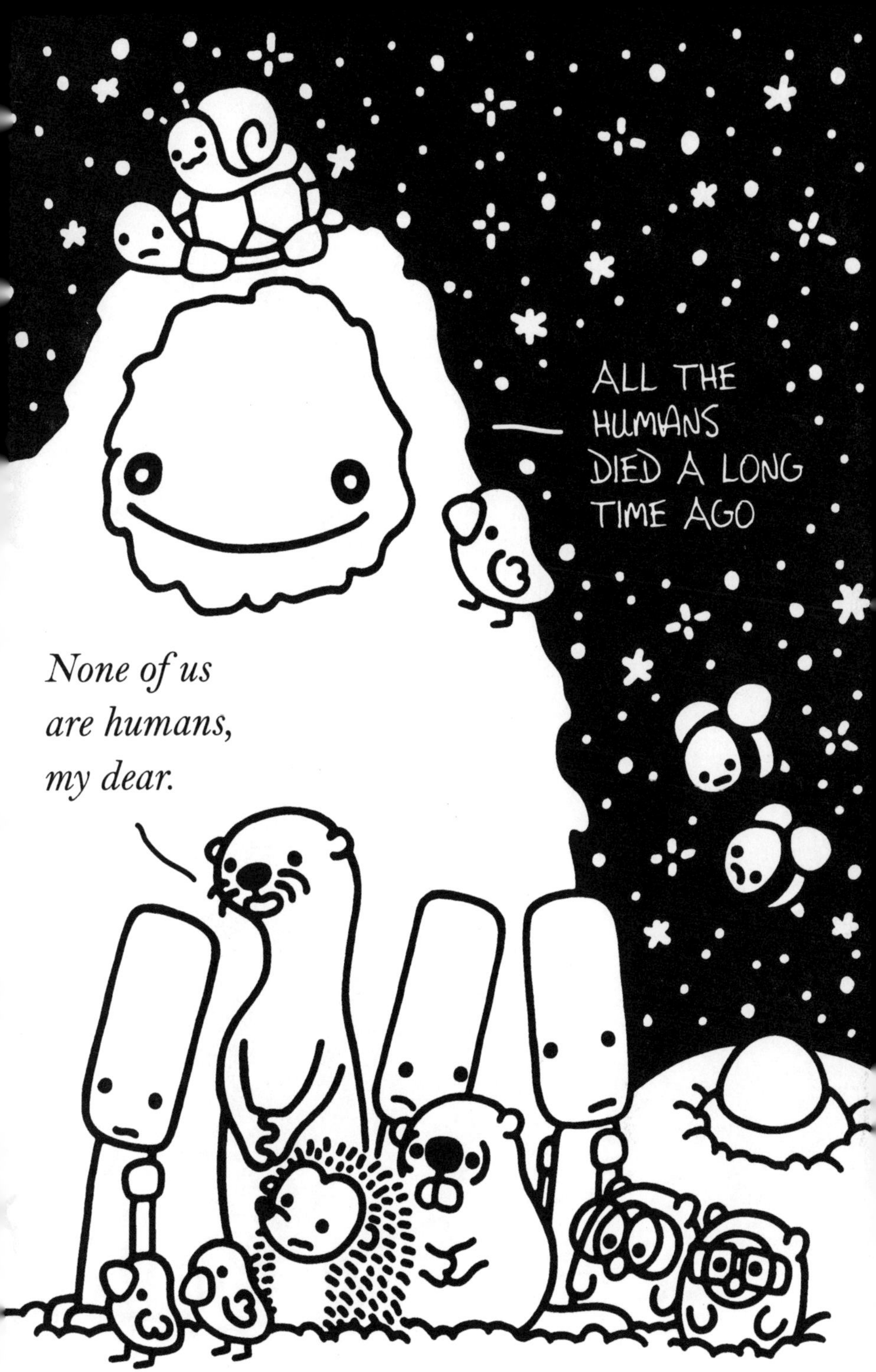
ALL THE HUMANS DIED A LONG TIME AGO
None of us are humans, my dear.

oh.. so ur all aliebns?
well, i supose everyone's a aliebn when ur a aliebn too

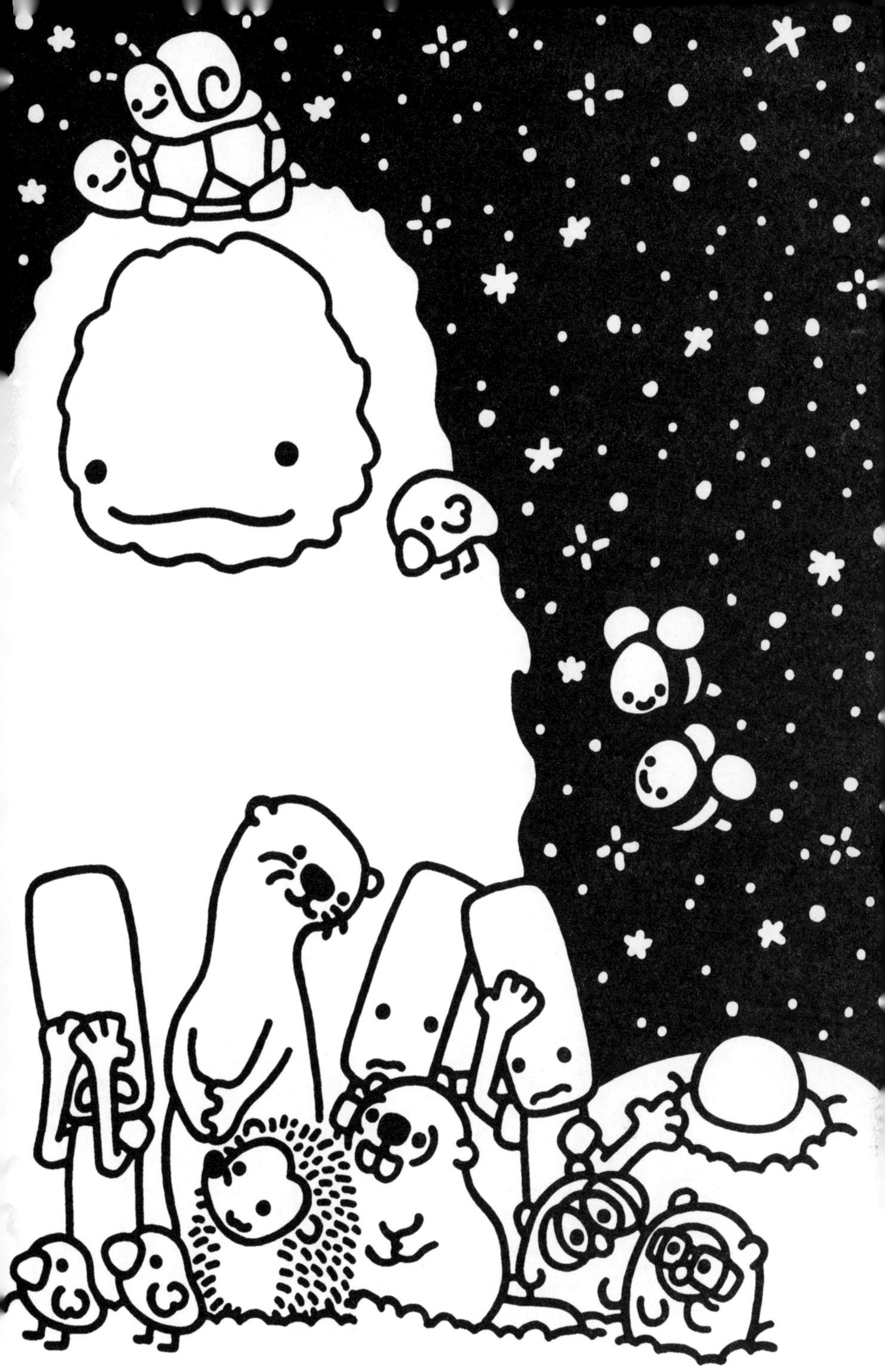

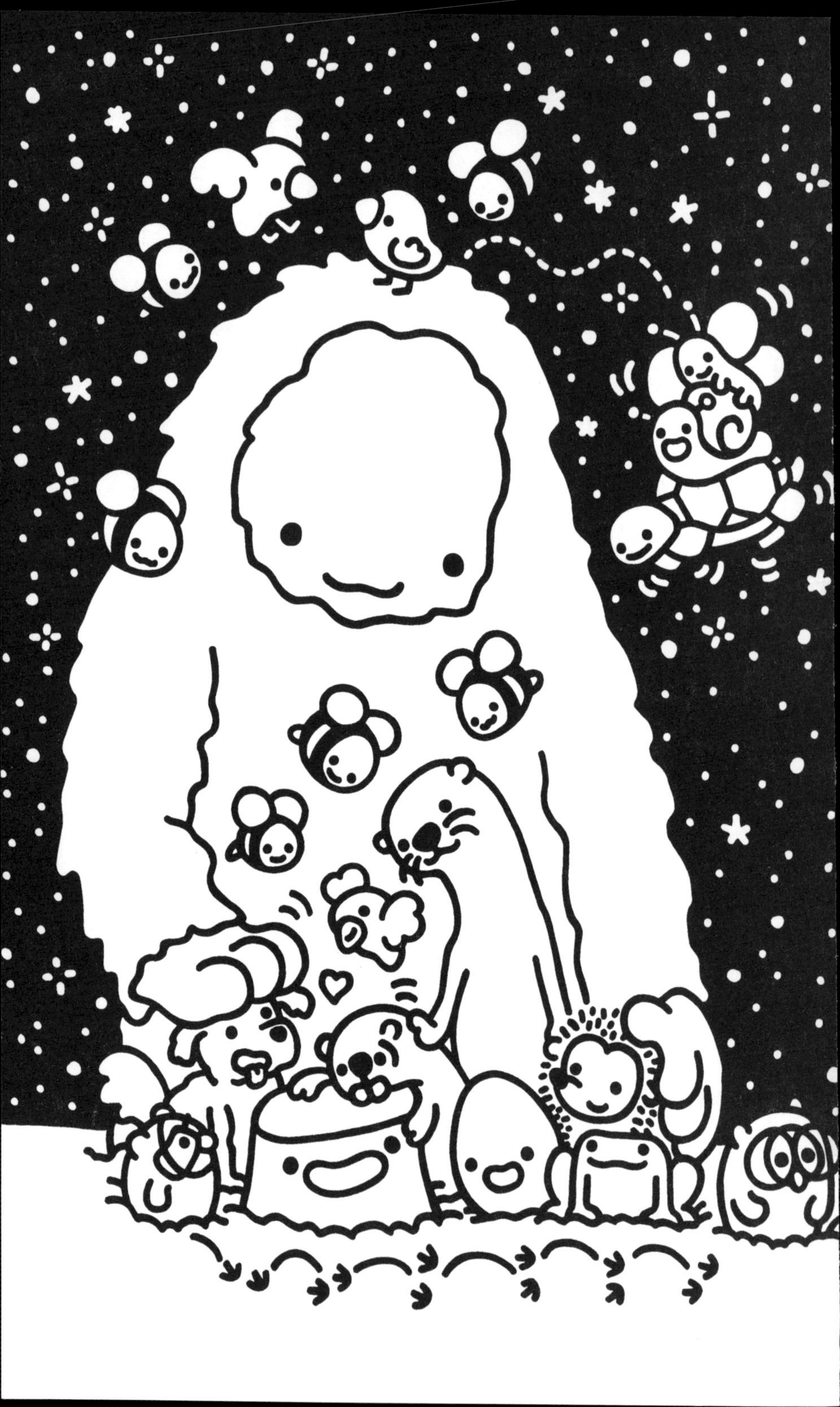

i have failed my mission wronger than i thought i could. i did not learn a thimg about being human. lets go home
why isnt jomny wearing any shoes

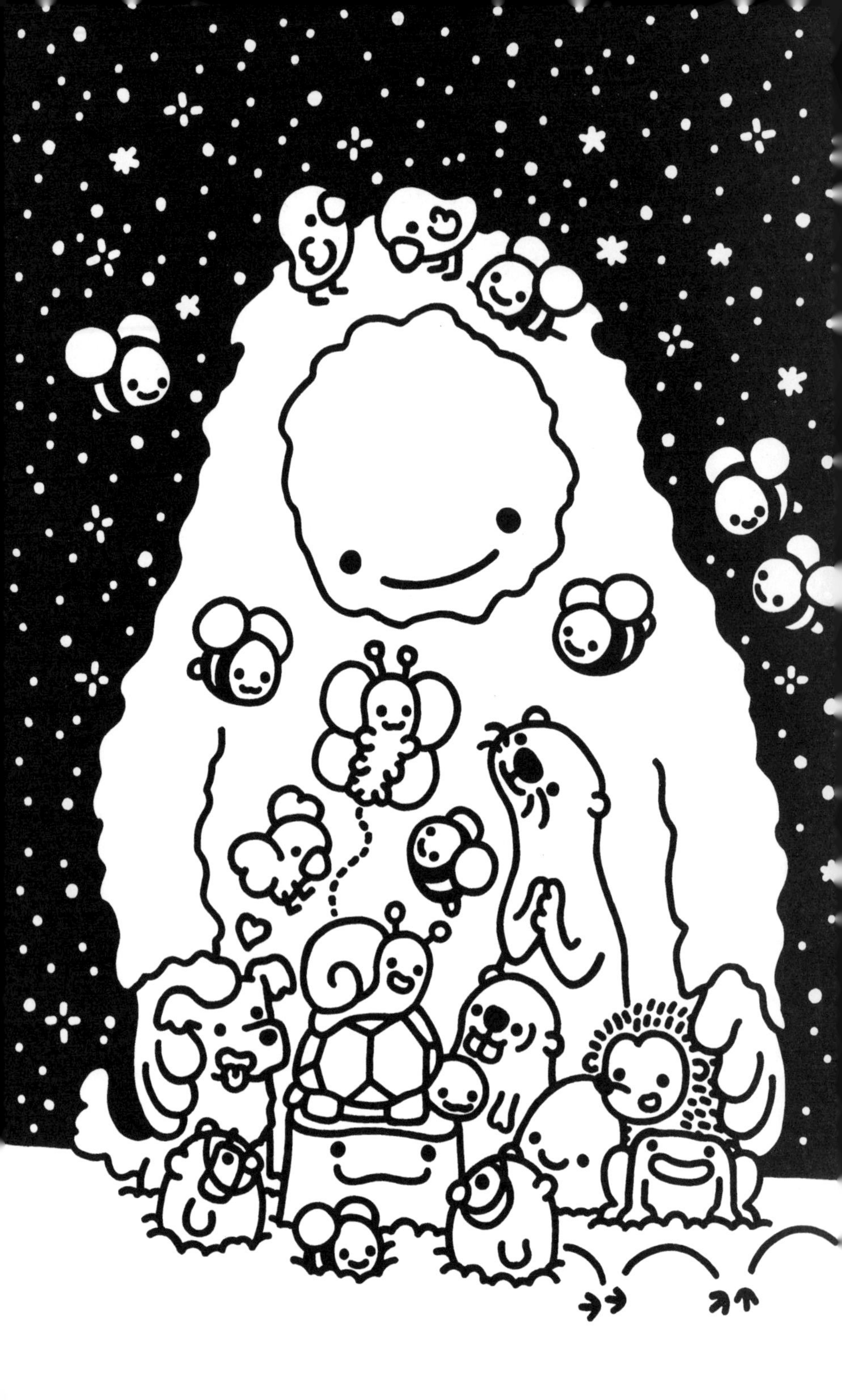

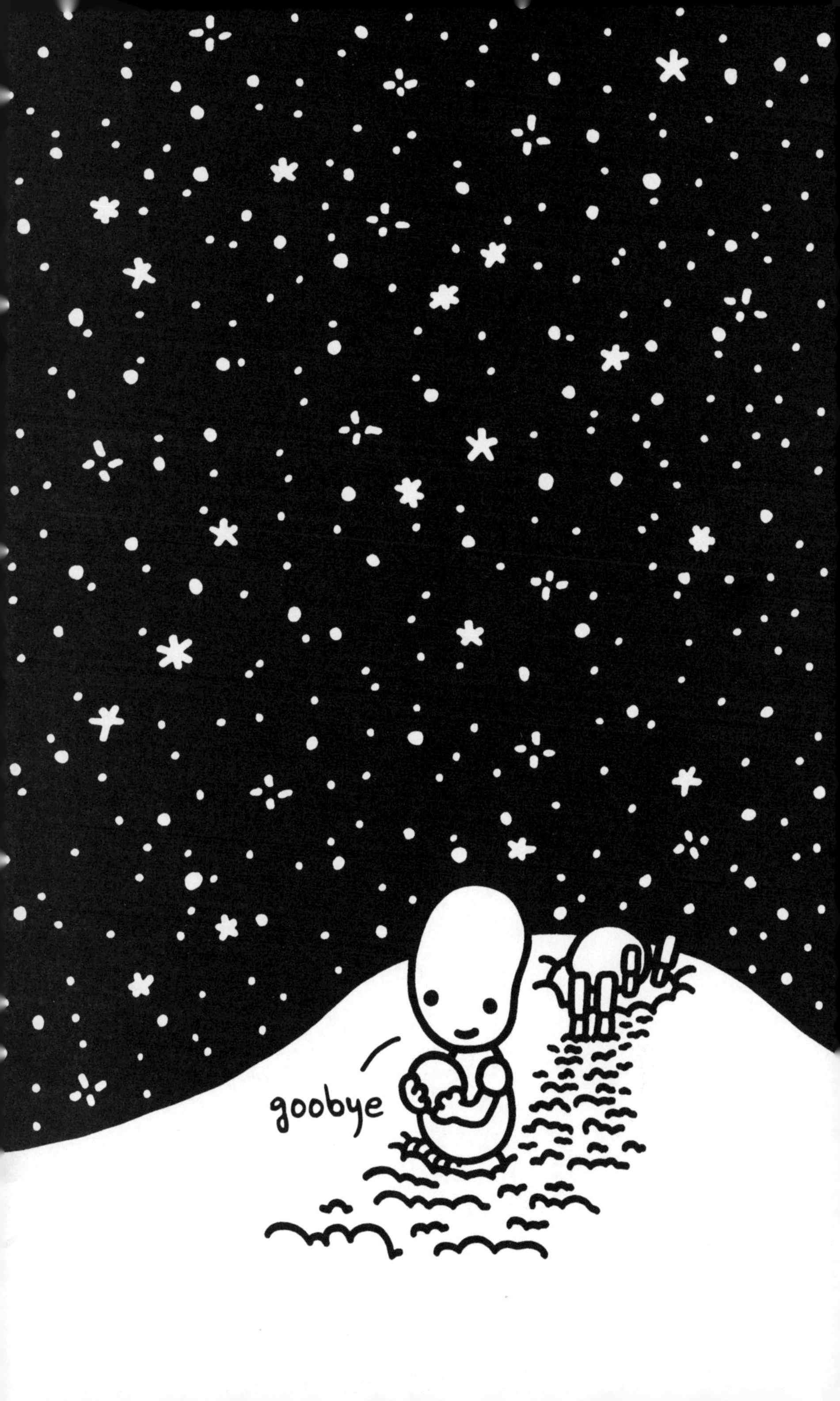
goobye

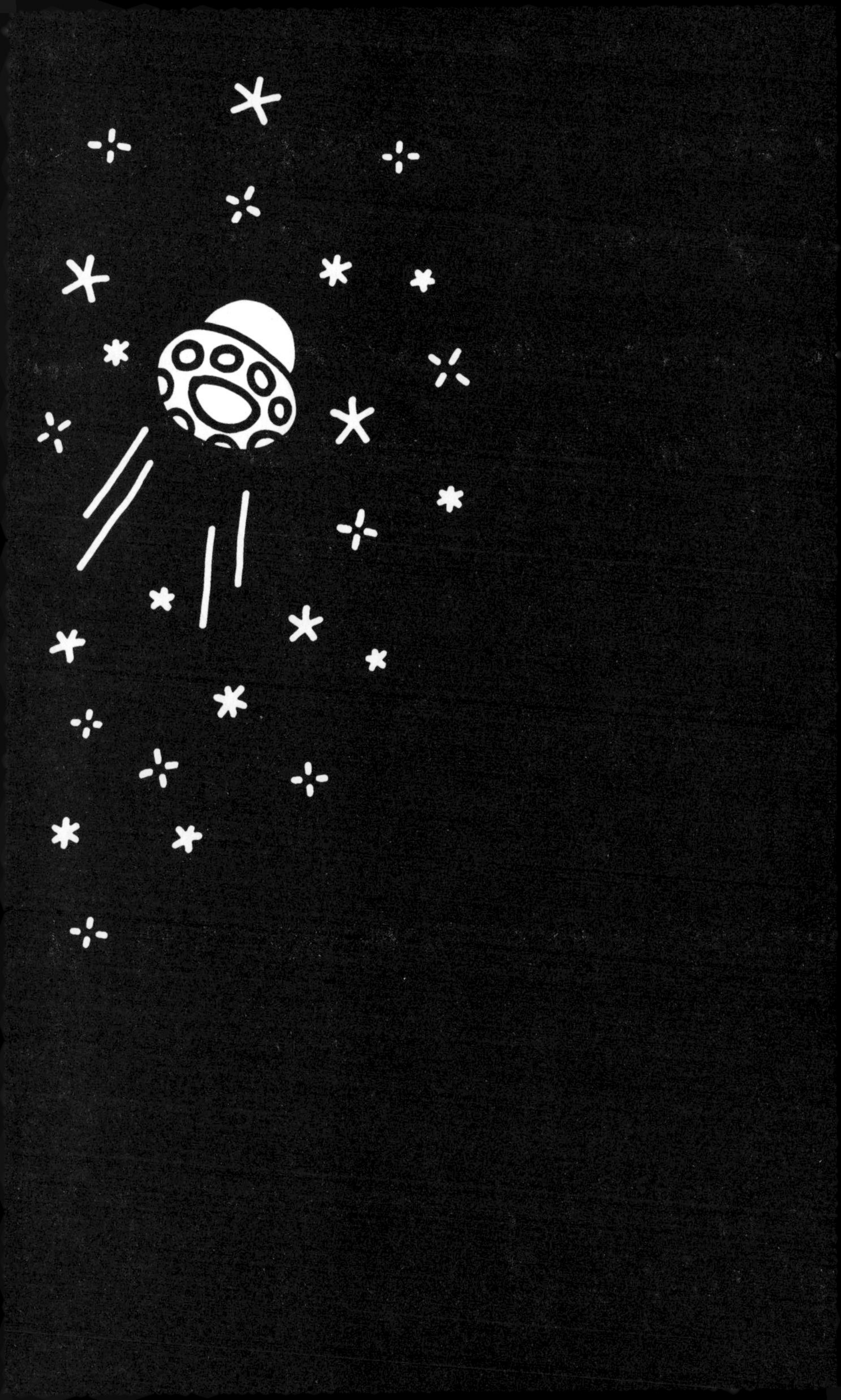

fig 1. thinking humabn and wise humabn

fig. 2. artist humabn and auteur humabn

fig. 3. gentle humabns

fig. 4. these humabns growed

fig 5. brave humabn and humabn in love and Mel

fig 6. Nothing

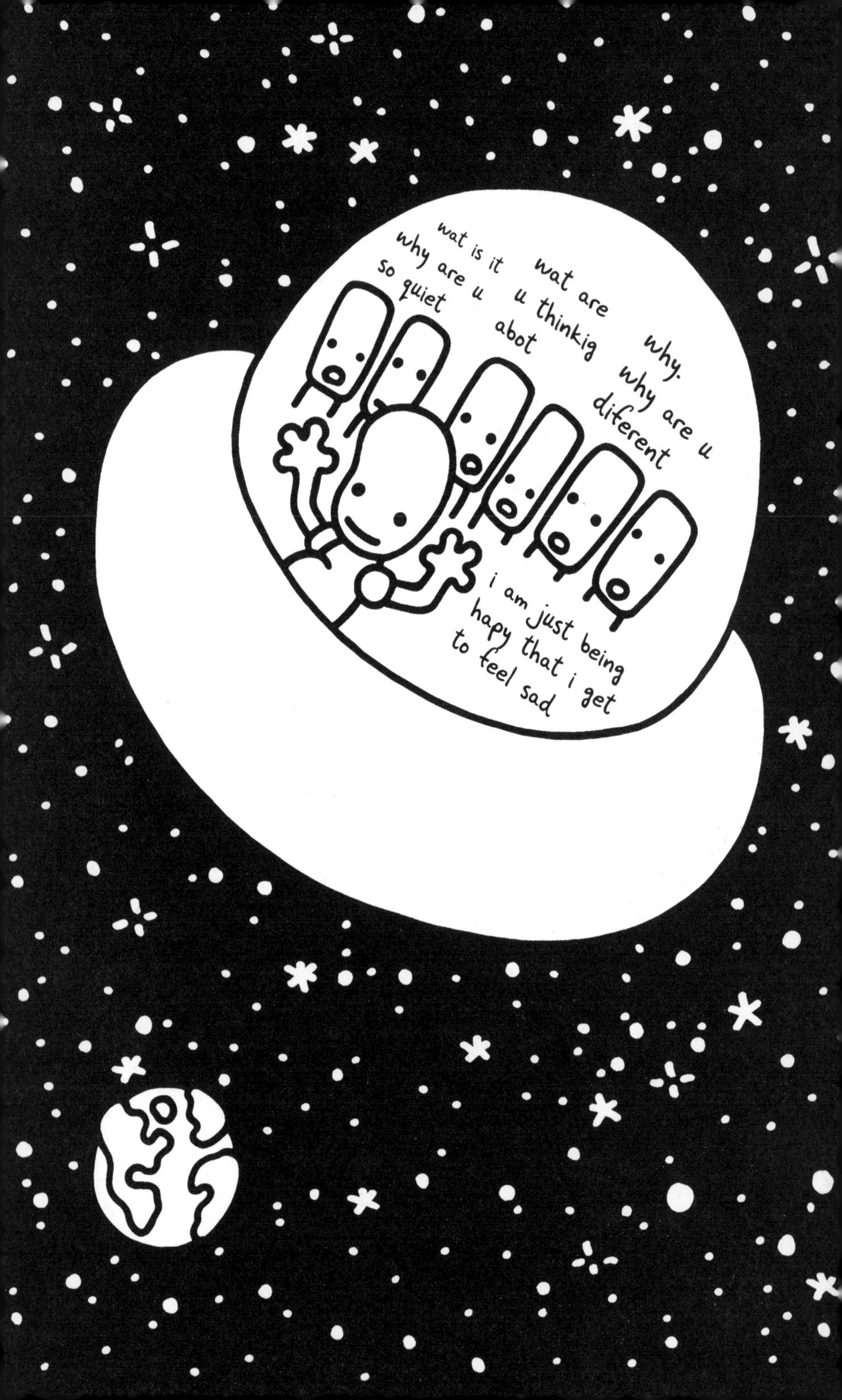
wat is it
wat are u thinkig abot
why are u so quiet
why.
why are u diferent
i am just being hapy that i get to feel sad

how did the humabns make u even more diferent somehow
why are u so diferent from us
how did u get even more diferent
why is the floor wet
oh no my snowball melted

about the author

JONATHAN SUN is the author behind @jonnysun. He is an architect, designer, engineer, artist, playwright, and comedy writer. His work across multiple disciplines broadly addresses narratives of human experience. As a playwright, Jonathan has had his pieces performed at the Yale School of Drama, and in Toronto at Hart House Theatre and Factory Theatre. As an artist and illustrator, he has had his art exhibited at MIT, Yale, New Haven ArtSpace, and the University of Toronto. His work has appeared on NPR and *BuzzFeed*, as well as in *Playboy*, *GQ*, and *McSweeney's*. In his other life, he is a doctoral student at MIT and a Berkman Klein fellow at Harvard.

about the fonts

The primary typeface for the book is GFY Palmer, designed by Chank Diesel for Chank Fonts in 2003.

The typeface used for the character of Nothing is Futura, designed by Paul Renner in 1927, with extra-wide kerning.

The typeface used for the character of Otter is Bell MT STD, based on Monotype's Bell series in 1931, which was inspired by original types made by Richard Austin for the John Bell Foundry in the 1780s.

The typeface used for jomny's notebook drawings is Kuenstler Script LT STD, designed by the in-house studio at the D Stempel AG Type Foundry in 1902.

The typeface used for jomny's activity log in the endpapers is Helvetica Neue, designed by Max Miedinger in 1983.

The typeface used on the front cover is the author's personal handwriting.

acknowledgments

i always love reading acknowledgments pages in books in the same way that i love sitting through all the movie credits until they are over. seeing all the names of people involved in a project can be overwhelming. once you start imagining how many full, entire lives a project was a part of, and how many full, entire lives it took to will a project into the world. even though that always fills me with the feeling of there being too much air in the world for my lungs to breathe in, it also makes me feel like the world is smaller, and kinder, than i imagine it to be. no thing can come into the world through one person alone, and reading all those names is a testament to the fact that nothing can exist without people. it reminds me that creation needs people, that people need people, and that acts of love cannot happen without entire villages believing in them, supporting them, and holding them up.

For putting up with me and for the endless patience, insight, and feedback: Eric Meyers, my editor at HarperPerennial.

For being my guides through all of this: Daniel Greenberg and Tim Wojcik, my agents at LGR Literary.

For believing in the book and making it a real thing: Kathryn, Heather, Jamie, Leydiana, Milan, Mary, Abby, and everyone at HarperPerennial.

For inspiration, feedback, support and friendship: Sarah, Alex, Chet, Dana, Shock, Lin-Manuel, Clint, Jeffrey and Joseph, Dan, Adam, Chiara, Pep and Phil, Kian and Carina, Nina, Kevin, Wills, Elena, Zach, Mahdi, Mun Hee, Amy, Sam, Tony, Chaewon, Amanda, Ryan, Dennis, Christer, Andrew, Mike, Nick and Ornella, Twitter and everyone at Twitter and everyone on Twitter, everyone at MIT, everyone at the Berkman Klein Center at Harvard, everywhere I have been able to find a home, and every home that would take me.

For their advice: Reza, Megan, Oliver, Mara, Elan, Jacob, Frank, Jory, and Avery.

For their endless love, support, and opinions; for making me who I am: Mom and Dad.

For constantly helping me grow and develop my voice; for being the person I will always try to make laugh: Chris.

For every day, every night, and everything; for making me the luckiest: Elissa.

This is a work of fiction. Names, characters, places, and incidents are products of the author's imagination or are used fictitiously and are not to be construed as real. Any resemblance to actual events, locales, organizations, or persons, living or dead, is entirely coincidental.

HarperCollins books may be purchased for educational, business, or sales promotional use. For information, please email the Special Markets Department at SPsales@harpercollins.com.

First Harper Perennial hardcover published 2017.

FIRST EDITION

Designed by Jamie Lynn Kerner and Leydiana Rodriguez

Library of Congress Cataloging-in-Publication Data

Names: Sun, Jomny, author, illustrator.
Title: Everyone's a aliebn when ur a aliebn too : a book / Jomny Sun.
Description: First edition. | New York : Harper Perennial, 2017. |
  Description based on print version record and CIP data provided by
  publisher; resource not viewed.
Identifiers: LCCN 2017010995 (print) | LCCN 2017012719 (ebook) | ISBN
  9780062569042 (ebk) | ISBN 9780062569028 (hardback)
Subjects: LCSH: Graphic novels. | BISAC: COMICS & GRAPHIC NOVELS /
Literary.
  | HUMOR / General.
Classification: LCC PN6727.S865 (ebook) | LCC PN6727.S865 E94 2017 (print) |
  DDC 741.5/973--dc23
LC record available at https://lccn.loc.gov/2017010995

ISBN 978-0-06-256902-8

17 18 19 20 21   LSC   10 9 8 7

for elissa,
my universe.

day 37: i have never seen a chameleon in real life and i dont know if that means i havent or i have **day 38:** working with urself is always the most dificult colaboration **day 40:** treat every day on earth as if its ur last day on earth because it is, until u spend another day on earth **day 42:** somtimes a caterpilar will be too excited to become a buterfly that it comes out of its cocoon too early **day 44:** humabns express their love in alarming ways **day 45:** humabns arent afraid of aliebns, they are afraid of things that are diferent **day 47:** a dream is a art that ur brain makes to entertain itself while u are asleep **day 48:** wat happens after we die? **day 49:** Nothing happens after you die **day 50:** i am sad today **day 53:** what is art. is talkimg art **day 55:** somtimes a caterpillar spends exactly the right amount of time in its cocoon that it becomes a buterfly **day 57:** when u appreciate nature, nature appreciates u!!! i love walkimg **day 58:** sometimes the most perfecbt home is made out of the space between two hands **day 60:** sometimes the greatebst house is one where there are no walls **day 61:** beauty is in the eye of the bee **day 63:** i hav never seen a fish **day 65:** a friemd seems like a nice thing and one day i hope to have one **day 66:** for some reasom the humabns are confused by science **day 68:** it is importabt to be urself even if u dont know wat ur doing **day 70:** whats ♥ got to do with it **day 71:** i am thankful for sadness **day 72:** i am thankful that i am here at all **day 74:** Nothing makes me hapy. the earbth